American Map Corporation

Road Atlas
United States • Canada • Mexico

Table of Contents

UNITED STATES....................2

STATE MAPS

Alabama 4
Alaska 6
Arizona 8
Arkansas 10
California – Northern.........12
California – Southern.........14
Colorado 20
Connecticut 22
Delaware 24
Florida – Northern............26
Florida – Southern 28
Georgia 30
Hawaii 32
Idaho 33
Illinois 34

Indiana...........................38
Iowa 40
Kansas 42
Kentucky 44
Louisiana 46
Maine.............................48
Maryland 50
Massachusetts 54
Michigan 56
Minnesota 60
Mississippi 62
Missouri 64
Montana 66
Nebraska 68
Nevada 70

New Hampshire...............71
New Jersey.....................72
New Mexico 74
New York - Northern.........76
New York - Southern.........78
North Carolina 82
North Dakota 85
Ohio - Northern................86
Ohio - Southern................88
Oklahoma 90
Oregon 92
Pennsylvania - Eastern.....96
Pennsylvania - Western.....94
Rhode Island 99
South Carolina 100

South Dakota 101
Tennessee.....................102
Texas - Eastern 106
Texas - Western 104
Utah 109
Vermont 110
Virginia 112
Washington 114
West Virginia 117
Wisconsin 118
Wyoming 120

CANADA............................121

PROVINCE MAPS

Alberta 123
British Columbia 122
Manitoba........................125
New Brunswick 130
Newfoundland.................131
Nova Scotia 130
Ontario 126
Prince Edward Island 130
Québec 128
Saskatchewan 124

MEXICO 132

PUERTO RICO 134

U.S. CITY MAPS

Akron, OH 86
Albany–Schenectady–
   Troy, NY.......................79
Albuquerque, NM 75
Allentown–Bethlehem, PA ...96
Amarillo, TX...................104
Anchorage, AK 6
Ann Arbor, MI 59
Annapolis, MD 50
Asheville, NC 83
Athens, GA 30
Atlanta, GA Area 29
Atlanta, GA Downtown 29
Atlantic City, NJ 72
Augusta, GA 30
Austin, TX......................105
Baltimore, MD Area 52
Baltimore, MD Downtown ...52
Baton Rogue, LA 47
Billings, MT 67
Biloxi–Gulfport, MS 62
Birmingham, AL.................5
Bismarck, ND 85
Boise, ID 33
Boston, MA Area 53
Boston, MA Downtown 53
Branson, MO 63
Bridgeport–New Haven, CT ...22
Buffalo–Niagara Falls, NY ...76
Burlington, VT 110
Canton–Massillon, OH 86
Carson City, NV 70
Casper, WY 120
Cedar Rapids, IA 41
Champaign–Urbana, IL 35
Charleston, SC 100
Charleston, WV 117
Charlotte, NC 84
Charlottesville, VA 111
Chattanooga, TN 103
Cheyenne, WY 120
Chicago, IL Area 36
Chicago, IL Downtown 37
Cincinnati, OH 88
Cleveland, OH 86
Colorado Springs, CO 20
Columbia, MO 65
Columbia, SC 100
Columbus, GA 31
Columbus, OH 89
Corpus Christi, TX...........106

Dallas–Fort Worth, TX........108
Dallas, TX Downtown 108
Davenport, IA–
   Rock Island, IL 35
Dayton, OH.....................88
Daytona Beach, FL 27
Denver, CO.....................19
Des Moines, IA 41
Detroit, MI.......................58
Dover, DE 24
Duluth, MN–Superior, WI ...60
Eau Claire, WI 118
El Paso, TX....................104
Erie, PA 94
Eugene, OR 93
Evansville, IN..................39
Fargo, ND 85
Flagstaff, AZ 7
Flint, MI 59
Fort Myers–
   Cape Coral, FL 28
Fort Smith, AR 11
Fort Wayne, IN 38
Frankfort, KY 45
Fresno, CA 13
Grand Rapids, MI 59
Green Bay, WI 118
Greenville–
   Spartanburg, SC 100
Harrisburg, PA 97
Hartford, CT 23
Helena, MT 67
Honolulu, HI 32
Hot Springs, AR 11
Houston–Galveston, TX ...108
Houston, TX Downtown 108
Idaho Falls, ID 33
Indianapolis, IN 37
Jackson, MS 62
Jacksonville, FL 26
Jefferson City, MO 65
Joplin, MO 63
Kansas City, KS/MO 63
Knoxville, TN 103
Lancaster, PA 95
Laredo, TX.....................107
Las Vegas, NV–The Strip ...70
Las Vegas, NV 70
Lexington, KY 45
Lincoln, NE 69
Little Rock, AR 11

Los Angeles, CA Area...........16
Los Angeles, CA Downtown...16
Louisville, KY 44
Lubbock, TX 104
Macon, GA 31
Madison, WI 119
Manchester, NH 71
Memphis, TN 102
Miami, FL 25
Milwaukee, WI Area 119
Milwaukee, WI Downtown ...119
Minneapolis–St. Paul, MN ...59
Mobile, AL 5
Montgomery, AL.................4
Muncie, IN 38
Nashua, NH 71
Nashville, TN 102
New Bedford–Fall River, MA ...54
New London, CT 23
New Orleans, LA 47
New Orleans, LA–
   French Quarter............47
New York, NY Area...........80
New York, NY Downtown ...80
Norfolk–Virginia Beach–
   Newport News, VA 111
Odessa–Midland, TX........104
Ogden, UT 109
Oklahoma City–
   Norman, OK 90
Olympia, WA..................114
Omaha, NE–
   Council Bluffs, IA 69
Orlando, FL 26
Palm Springs, CA 15
Peoria, IL 37
Petersburg, VA 111
Philadelphia, PA Area...........98
Philadelphia, PA Downtown ...98
Phoenix, AZ 7
Pittsburgh, PA Area...........98
Pittsburgh, PA Downtown ...98
Pocatello, ID 33
Portland, ME 48
Portland, OR 93
Providence, RI 99
Pueblo, CO 20
Raleigh–Durham, NC 84
Rapid City, SD 101
Reading, PA 97
Reno, NV 70

Richmond, VA 113
Roanoke, VA 112
Rochester, MN 61
Rochester, NY 76
Rockford, IL 34
Sacramento, CA 12
St. Louis, MO Area 65
St. Louis, MO Downtown ...65
Salem, OR 93
Salt Lake City, UT 109
San Antonio, TX 107
San Diego, CA 14
San Francisco, CA
   Bay Area......................18
San Francisco, CA
   Downtown 19
Santa Fe, NM 75
Savannah, GA 31
Scranton–Wilkes-Barre, PA ...96
Seattle–Tacoma, WA 114
Seattle, WA Downtown 114
Sioux City, IA 40
Sioux Falls, SD 101
South Bend, IN 37
Spokane, WA 115
Springfield, IL 35
Springfield, MA 54
Springfield, MO 63
Springfield, OH 88
Stamford, CT 22
Stockton, CA 12
Syracuse, NY 76
Tallahassee, FL 26
Tampa–St. Petersburg, FL ...25
Toledo, OH 86
Topeka, KS 42
Tucson, AZ 7
Tulsa, OK 90
Washington, DC Area 116
Washington, DC Downtown ...116
Washington, DC
   suburban Maryland 50
Washington, DC
   suburban Virginia 111
Waterbury, CT 22
Wichita, KS 43
Wilmington, DE 24
Winston-Salem–
   Greensboro, NC 84
Worcester, MA 54
Youngstown–Warren, OH ...89

CANADIAN CITY MAPS

Calgary, AB 123
Edmonton, AB 123
Halifax, NS 131
Hamilton, ON 126
London, ON 126
Montréal, PQ 128
Ottawa, ON....................128
Québec, PQ 128
Sherbrooke, PQ 129
Toronto, ON Area 127
Toronto, ON Downtown 127
Vancouver, BC 122
Winnipeg, MB 125

MEXICAN CITY MAPS

Mexico City....................133

PARK MAPS

Acadia N.P., ME 49
Black Hills Area, SD 101
Crater Lake N.P., OR.........93
Everglades N.P., FL 25
Glacier N.P., MT–Waterton
   Lakes N.P., AB..............66
Grand Canyon N.P., AZ......9
Grand Teton N.P., WY 120
Great Smoky Mts.
   N.P., NC/TN.................84
Isle Royale N.P., MI 56
Kings Canyon N.P–
   Sequoia N.P., CA 13
Lake Tahoe, CA/NV 13
Land Between
   the Lakes, KY/TN 45
Lassen Volcanic N.P., CA ...13
Mt. Rainier N.P., WA 114
Rocky Mtn. N.P., CO..........19
Santa Catalina Island, CA ...16
Yellowstone N.P., WY 120
Yosemite N.P., CA 13

INDEX................................134

U.S. MILEAGE CHART......143

MILEAGE AND
DRIVING TIME MAP 144

Legend

TRANSPORTATION

Controlled Access Highways

——— Free

——— Toll

▪▪▪▪▪▪▪ Under Construction

Other Highways

——— Divided Highway

——— Primary Highway

——— Secondary Highway

——— Other Paved Road

– – – Unpaved Road

··········· Scenic Route

Highway Markers

🔵95 Interstate Route

🛡12 US Route

⬭12 State or
Provincial Route

▭12 County or Other Route

⬠2 Mexican
Federal Route

⬡00 Canadian Autoroute

🍁 Trans-Canada Highway

Interchanges,
Exit Numbers &
Distances Between Points
(Miles in U.S.; kilometers in Canada and Mexico)

Ⓢ Service Area, Wayside
Ⓡ & Rest Area
(Yellow with facilities)

BOUNDARIES

—··— State Boundary

—·—·— International Boundary

▭ POLK County Boundary
and Name

············· Time Zone

··············· Continental Divide

AREAS

▨ National Park

▨ National Forest or
other recreational area

▨ Military Lands

▨ Indian Reservation

▨ Built-up area

CITIES AND TOWNS

Type size indicates
relative importance

• Phoenix

• Glendale

• Sun City

• Buckeye

• Benson

• Heber

SYMBOLS

Ⓢ State Capital

Ⓝ National Capital

⊙ County Seat

+ Mountain peak

= Pass

▢ Point of interest

i Visitor Information
Center

H Hospital (City maps)

Published by American Map Corporation
46-35 54th Road, Maspeth, NY 11378
© 1998 GeoSystems Global Corporation
All rights reserved. Printed in Canada.

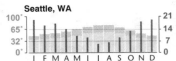

1 Segment Represents 100 Miles

1 Segment Represents 100 Kilometers

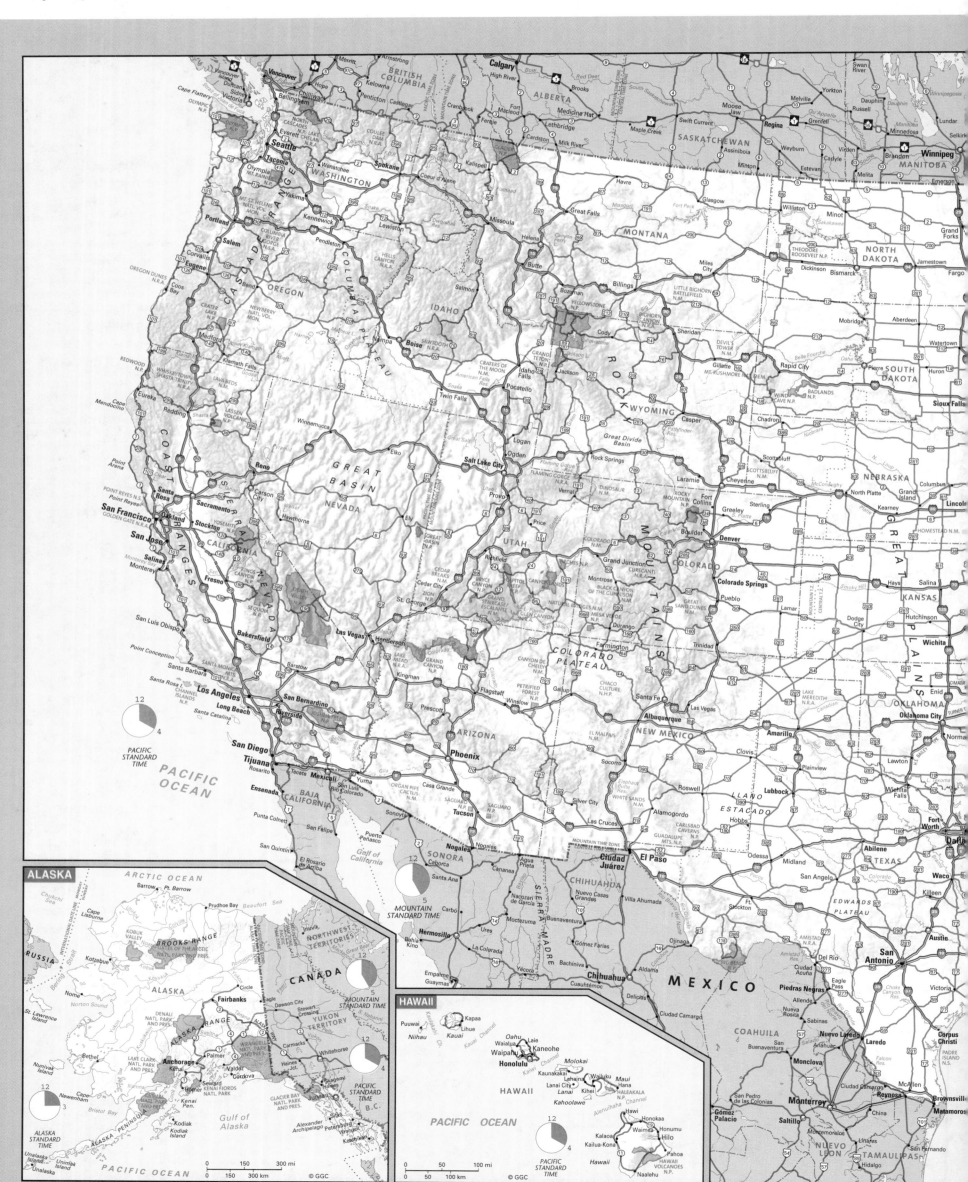

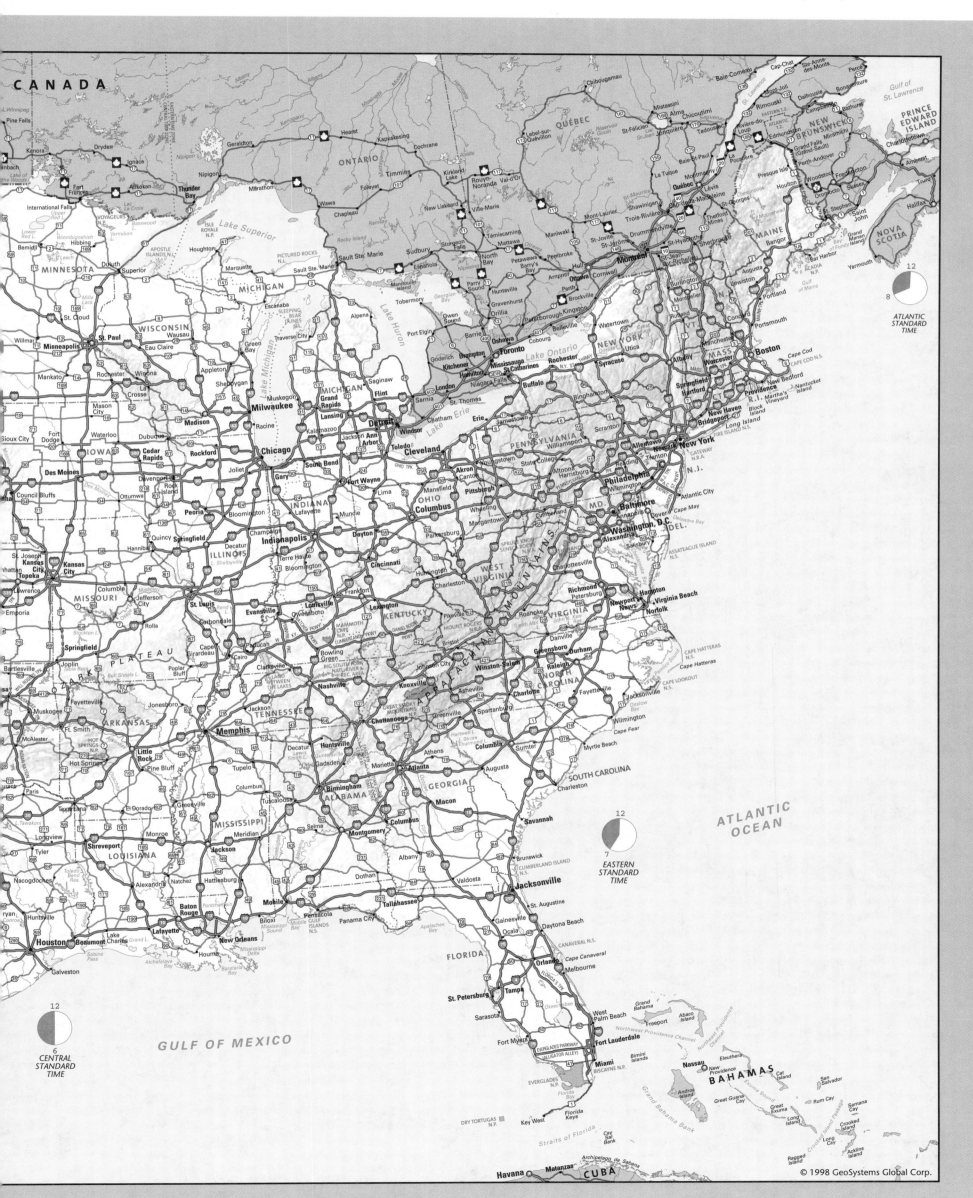

Kansas City, MO

Miami, FL

1 Segment Represents 100 Miles

1 Segment Represents 100 Kilometers

ATLANTIC STANDARD TIME

EASTERN STANDARD TIME

CENTRAL STANDARD TIME

© 1998 GeoSystems Global Corp.

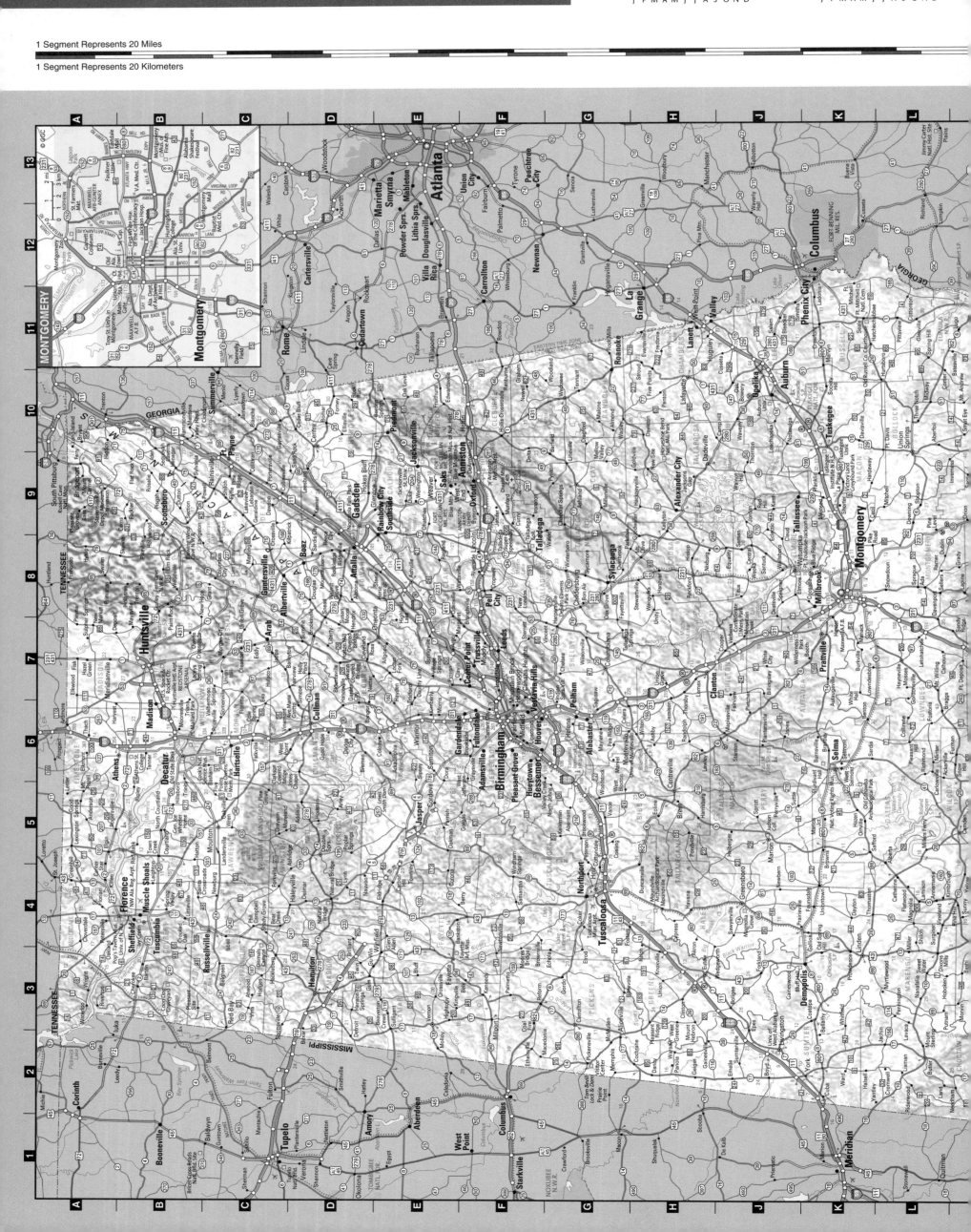

Weather - Legend
Average daily high temperature, F°
Average daily low temperature, F°
Average no. of days w/precipitation

Huntsville

1 Segment Represents 20 Miles

1 Segment Represents 20 Kilometers

MONTGOMERY

Montgomery

Montgomery

Mobile

1 Segment Represents 20 Miles

1 Segment Represents 20 Kilometers

Quick Reference Index

For index to counties and places see page 134.

Abbeville	N-11	Huntsville	B-7
Adamsville	F-6	Irondale	F-7
Alabaster	G-6	Jackson	N-3
Albertville	C-8	Jacksonville	E-9
Alexander City	H-9	Jasper	E-5
Aliceville	G-2	Ladonia	K-11
Andalusia	P-7	Lafayette	H-10
Anniston	F-9	Lanett	H-11
Arab	C-7	Leeds	F-7
Athens	A-6	Lincoln	F-8
Atmore	Q-4	Linden	K-3
Attalla	D-8	Lipscomb	F-6
Auburn	J-10	Livingston	J-2
Bay Minette	Q-3	Luverne	N-8
Bayou La Batre	S-2	Madison	B-7
Bessemer	F-6	Marion	J-5
Birmingham	F-6	Meridianville	A-7
Boaz	D-8	Midfield	F-6
Brent	H-5	Millbrook	K-8
Brewton	Q-6	Mobile	R-3
Bridgeport	C-9	Monroeville	N-5
Brundidge	M-9	Montevallo	G-6
Cahaba Heights	F-7	Montgomery	K-8
Camden	M-5	Moody	F-7
Center Point	F-7	Moulton	C-5
Centre	D-10	Mountain Brook	F-6
Centreville	H-5	Muscle Shoals	B-4
Chickasaw	R-3	Northport	G-4
Childersburg	G-8	Oneonta	E-7
Citronelle	Q-2	Opelika	J-10
Clanton	H-7	Opp	P-8
Columbiana	G-7	Oxford	F-9
Cordova	E-5	Ozark	N-10
Cullman	D-6	Pelham	G-6
Dadeville	H-9	Pell City	F-8
Daleville	P-10	Phenix City	K-12
Daphne	R-3	Piedmont	E-10
Decatur	B-6	Pleasant Grove	F-6
Demopolis	K-3	Prattville	K-7
Dothan	P-10	Prichard	R-3
East Brewton	Q-6	Rainbow City	E-9
Elba	P-9	Rainsville	C-9
Enterprise	P-9	Red Bay	C-3
Eufaula	M-11	Roanoke	G-10
Evergreen	N-6	Russellville	C-4
Fairfield	F-6	Saks	E-9
Fairhope	S-3	Saraland	R-3
Fayette	E-3	Satsuma	R-3
Florence	A-4	Scottsboro	B-8
Foley	S-4	Selma	K-6
Fort Payne	C-9	Sheffield	B-4
Fultondale	F-6	Smiths	J-11
Gadsden	D-9	Southside	E-9
Gardendale	F-6	Spanish Fort	R-3
Geneva	Q-9	Sumiton	E-6
Glencoe	D-9	Sylacauga	G-8
Grand Bay	S-2	Talladega	F-8
Greensboro	J-4	Tallassee	J-9
Greenville	M-7	Tarrant City	F-6
Guin	D-3	Theodore	S-2
Gulf Shores	T-4	Thomasville	M-4
Guntersville	C-8	Tillmans Corner	R-2
Haleyville	C-4	Troy	M-9
Hamilton	D-3	Trussville	F-7
Hartford	Q-10	Tuscaloosa	G-4
Hartselle	C-6	Tuscumbia	B-4
Headland	P-11	Tuskegee	K-10
Heflin	F-10	Union Springs	L-9
Helena	G-6	Valley	H-11
Hokes Bluff	D-9	Vestavia Hills	F-6
Holt	G-4	Warrior	E-6
Homewood	F-6	Weaver	E-9
Hoover	F-6	Wetumpka	J-8
Hueytown	F-6	Winfield	E-3
Huguley	H-11	York	K-2

Selected Attractions

Bellingrath Gardens & Home	S-2
DeSoto Caverns Park	G-8
Fort Morgan Historic Site	T-3
Horseshoe Bend National Military Park	H-9
National Voting Rights Museum	K-6
Natural Bridge	D-4
Russell Cave National Monument	A-9
Talladega Super-speedway	F-8
Tuskegee Institute National Historic Site	K-9
U.S. Space & Rocket Center	B-7

Adjacent States

Florida	26 & 28
Georgia	30
Mississippi	62
Tennessee	102

© 1998 GeoSystems Global Corp.

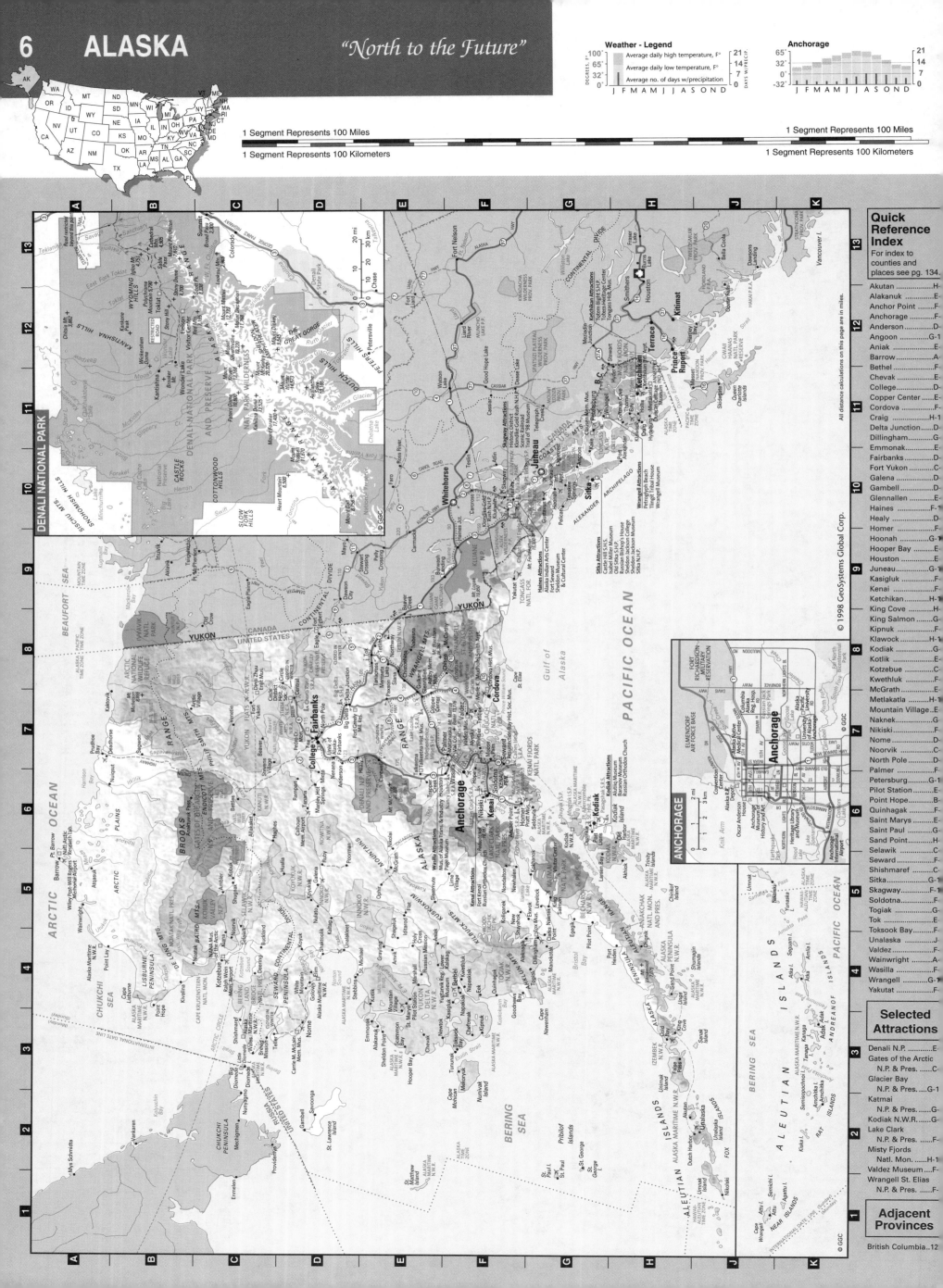

Weather - Legend

Average daily high temperature, F°
Average daily low temperature, F°
Average no. of days w/precipitation

Anchorage

1 Segment Represents 100 Miles
1 Segment Represents 100 Kilometers

© 1998 GeoSystems Global Corp.

Quick Reference Index

For index to counties and places see pg. 134.

All distance calculations on this page are in miles.

Akutan	H-
Alakanuk	F-
Anchor Point	F-
Anchorage	F-
Anderson	D-
Angoon	G-1
Aniak	E-
Barrow	A-
Bethel	E-
Chevak	E-
College	E-
Copper Center	E-
Cordova	F-
Craig	H-1
Delta Junction	D-
Dillingham	G-1
Emmonak	E-
Fairbanks	D-
Fort Yukon	C-
Galena	D-
Gambell	E-
Glennallen	E-
Haines	F-1
Healy	D-
Homer	F-
Hoonah	G-1
Hooper Bay	E-
Houston	E-
Juneau	G-1
Kasigluk	E-
Kenai	F-
Ketchikan	H-1
King Cove	H-
King Salmon	G-1
Kipnuk	E-
Klawock	H-1
Kodiak	G-
Kotlik	E-
Kotzebue	C-
Kwethluk	E-
McGrath	E-
Metlakatla	H-1
Mountain Village	E-
Naknek	G-
Nikiski	F-
Nome	D-
Noorvik	C-
North Pole	D-
Palmer	F-
Petersburg	G-1
Pilot Station	E-
Point Hope	B-
Quinhagak	E-
Saint Marys	E-
Saint Paul	H-
Sand Point	H-
Selawik	C-
Seward	F-
Shishmaref	C-
Sitka	G-1
Skagway	F-1
Soldotna	F-
Togiak	G-
Tok	D-
Toksook Bay	J-
Unalaska	F-
Valdez	F-
Wainwright	A-
Wasilla	F-
Wrangell	G-1
Yakutat	F-

Selected Attractions

Denali N.P.	E-
Gates of the Arctic N.P. & Pres.	C-
Glacier Bay N.P. & Pres.	G-1
Katmai N.P. & Pres.	G-
Kodiak N.W.R.	G-
Lake Clark N.P. & Pres.	F-
Misty Fjords Natl. Mon.	H-1
Valdez Museum	F-
Wrangell St. Elias N.P. & Pres.	F-

Adjacent Provinces

British Columbia..12

1 Segment Represents 4 Miles (Phoenix map)

1 Segment Represents 4 Kilometers (Phoenix map)

1 Segment Represents 4 Miles (Phoenix map)

1 Segment Represents 4 Kilometers (Phoenix map)

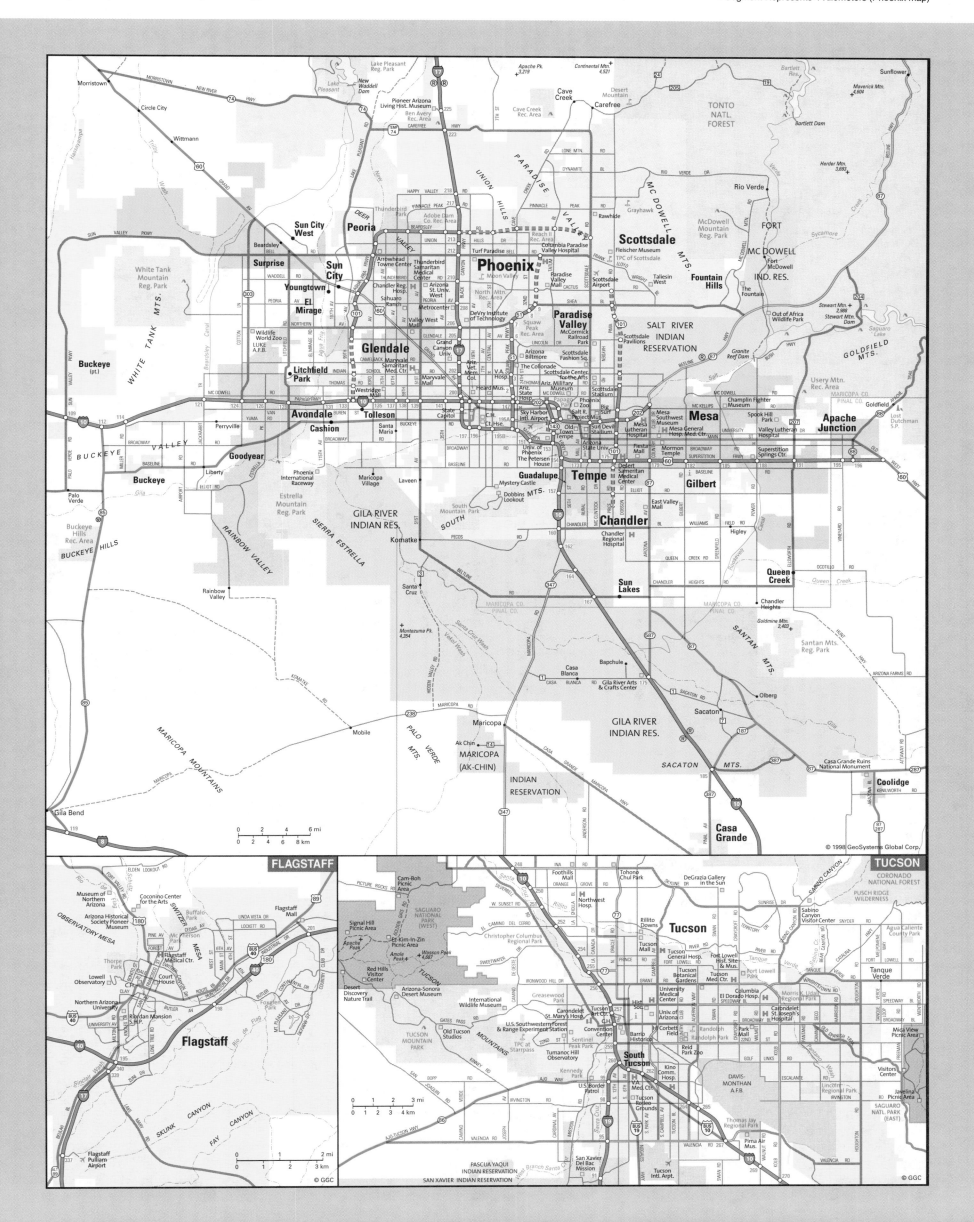

© 1998 GeoSystems Global Corp.

© GGC

© GGC

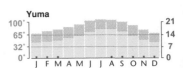

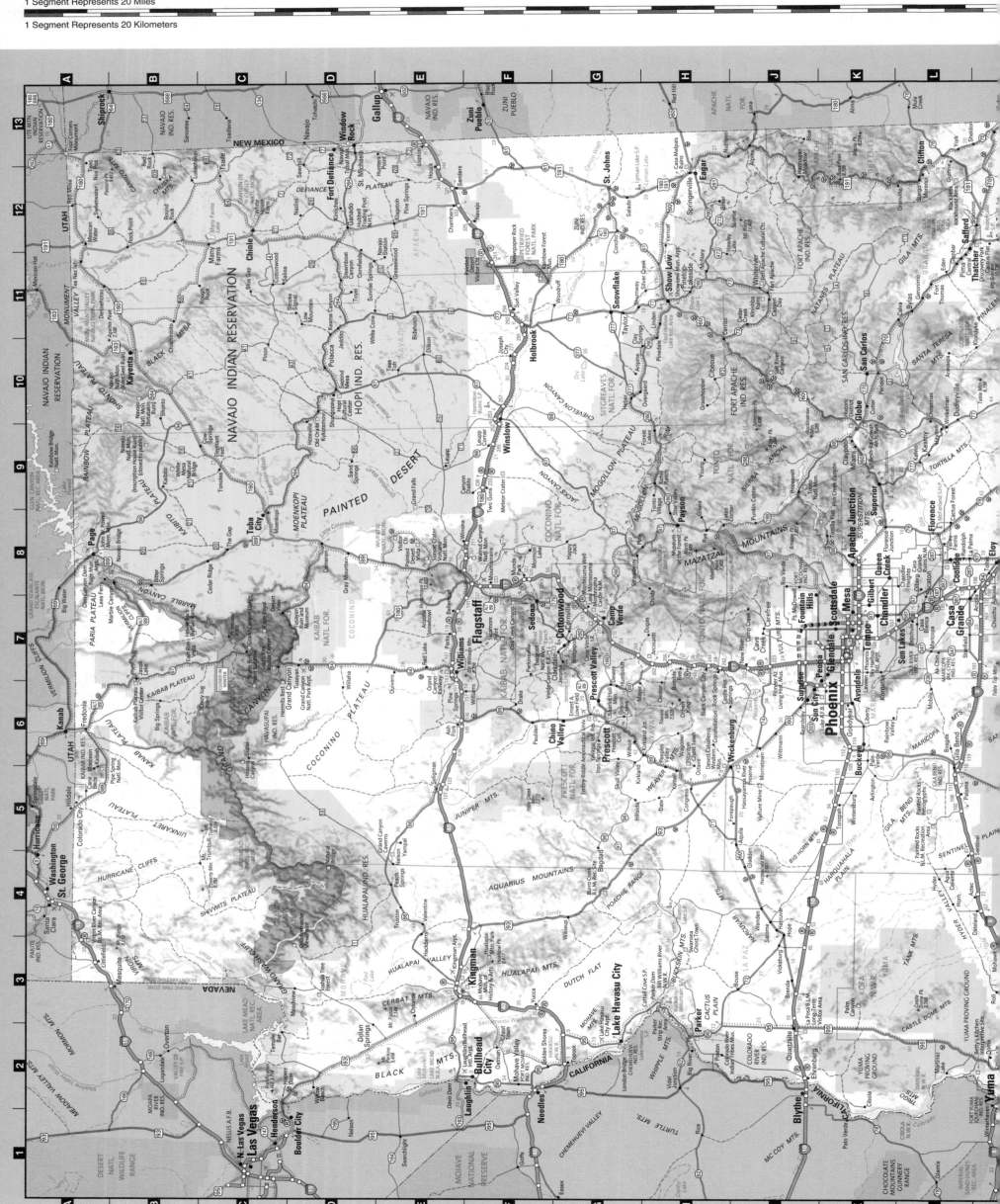

1 Segment Represents 20 Miles

1 Segment Represents 20 Kilometers

Flagstaff

Phoenix

1 Segment Represents 20 Miles

1 Segment Represents 20 Kilometers

GRAND CANYON N.P.

© 1998 GeoSystems Global Corp.

Quick Reference Index

For index to counties and places see page 134.

Ajo	N-5	Maricopa	L-7
Apache Junction	K-8	Mayer	G-6
Arizola	M-8	Mesa	K-7
Arizona City	M-8	Miami	K-9
Avondale	K-6	Moenkopi	C-8
Bagdad	G-5	Mohave Valley	F-2
Benson	P-10	Morenci	L-12
Bisbee	Q-11	Mountainaire	F-8
Black Canyon City	H-7	Naco	Q-11
Bowie	N-12	Nogales	Q-9
Buckeye	K-6	Oracle	M-10
Bullhead City	F-2	Oro Valley	N-9
Bylas	L-11	Page	A-8
Cactus Flat	M-12	Parker	H-2
Camp Verde	G-7	Patagonia	Q-10
Canyon Day	J-11	Payson	H-8
Carefree	J-7	Peach Springs	E-4
Casa Grande	L-7	Peoria	K-7
Catalina	M-9	Peridot	K-10
Cave Creek	J-7	Phoenix	K-7
Chandler	K-7	Pima	L-11
Chandler Heights	L-8	Pinetop-Lakeside	H-11
Chinle	C-12	Pirtleville	Q-12
Chino Valley	G-6	Polacca	D-10
Cibecue	H-10	Prescott	G-6
Clarkdale	G-7	Prescott Valley	G-6
Claypool	K-9	Quartzsite	J-2
Clifton	L-12	Queen Creek	K-8
Colorado City	A-5	Sacaton	L-7
Coolidge	L-8	Safford	L-12
Cornville	G-7	Sahuarita	P-9
Cortaro	N-9	Saint David	P-11
Cottonwood	G-7	Saint Johns	G-12
Dennehotso	A-11	Saint Michaels	D-13
Dewey	G-6	San Carlos	K-10
Dilkon	E-10	San Luis	M-1
Dolan Springs	D-2	San Manuel	M-10
Douglas	Q-12	Scottsdale	K-7
Dudleyville	L-10	Second Mesa	D-10
Duncan	M-13	Sedona	F-7
Eagar	H-12	Sells	P-7
Ehrenberg	J-2	Shonto	B-10
Eloy	M-8	Show Low	H-11
Flagstaff	F-8	Shungopavi	D-10
Florence	L-8	Sierra Vista	Q-10
Fort Defiance	D-13	Snowflake	G-11
Fort Grant	M-11	Somerton	M-1
Fountain Hills	J-7	South Tucson	N-9
Fredonia	A-6	Springerville	H-12
Ganado	D-12	Stanfield	L-7
Gila Bend	L-5	Steamboat Canyon	D-11
Gilbert	K-7	Sun City	J-6
Glendale	K-6	Sun Lakes	L-7
Globe	K-9	Superior	K-9
Goodyear	K-6	Surprise	J-6
Grand Canyon	C-7	Swift Trail Jct.	M-12
Green Valley	P-9	Tanque Verde	N-10
Hayden	L-9	Taylor	G-11
Holbrook	F-11	Tempe	K-7
Hotevilla	D-10	Thatcher	M-12
Huachuca City	P-10	Three Points	N-8
Joseph City	F-10	Tombstone	P-11
Kaibito	B-9	Tsaile	C-12
Kayenta	B-10	Tuba City	C-8
Kearny	L-9	Tucson	N-9
Kingman	E-3	Vail	N-10
Komatke	K-7	Wellton	M-3
Kykotsmovi	D-10	Whiteriver	J-11
Lake Havasu City	G-2	Wickenburg	J-6
Lake Montezuma	G-7	Willcox	N-11
Laveen	K-7	Williams	E-7
Leupp	E-9	Window Rock	D-13
Mammoth	M-10	Winkelman	L-9
Many Farms	C-12	Winslow	F-10
Marana	N-8	Yuma	M-2

Selected Attractions

Fort Bowie National Historic Site	N-12
Four Corners Monument	A-13
Grand Canyon National Park	C-6
Hermits Rest	C-6
Lake Mead National Recreation Area	E-2
Montezuma Castle National Monument	G-7
Monument Valley Navajo Tribal Park	A-11
Petrified Forest National Park	F-11
Sunset Crater Volcano National Monument	E-8
Titan Missile Museum	P-9

Adjacent States

California	12 & 14
Colorado	20
Mexico	132
Nevada	70
New Mexico	74
Utah	109

"The People Rule"

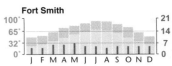

Weather - Legend
Average daily high temperature, F
Average daily low temperature, F
Average no. of days w/precipitation

Fort Smith

1 Segment Represents 20 Miles

1 Segment Represents 20 Kilometers

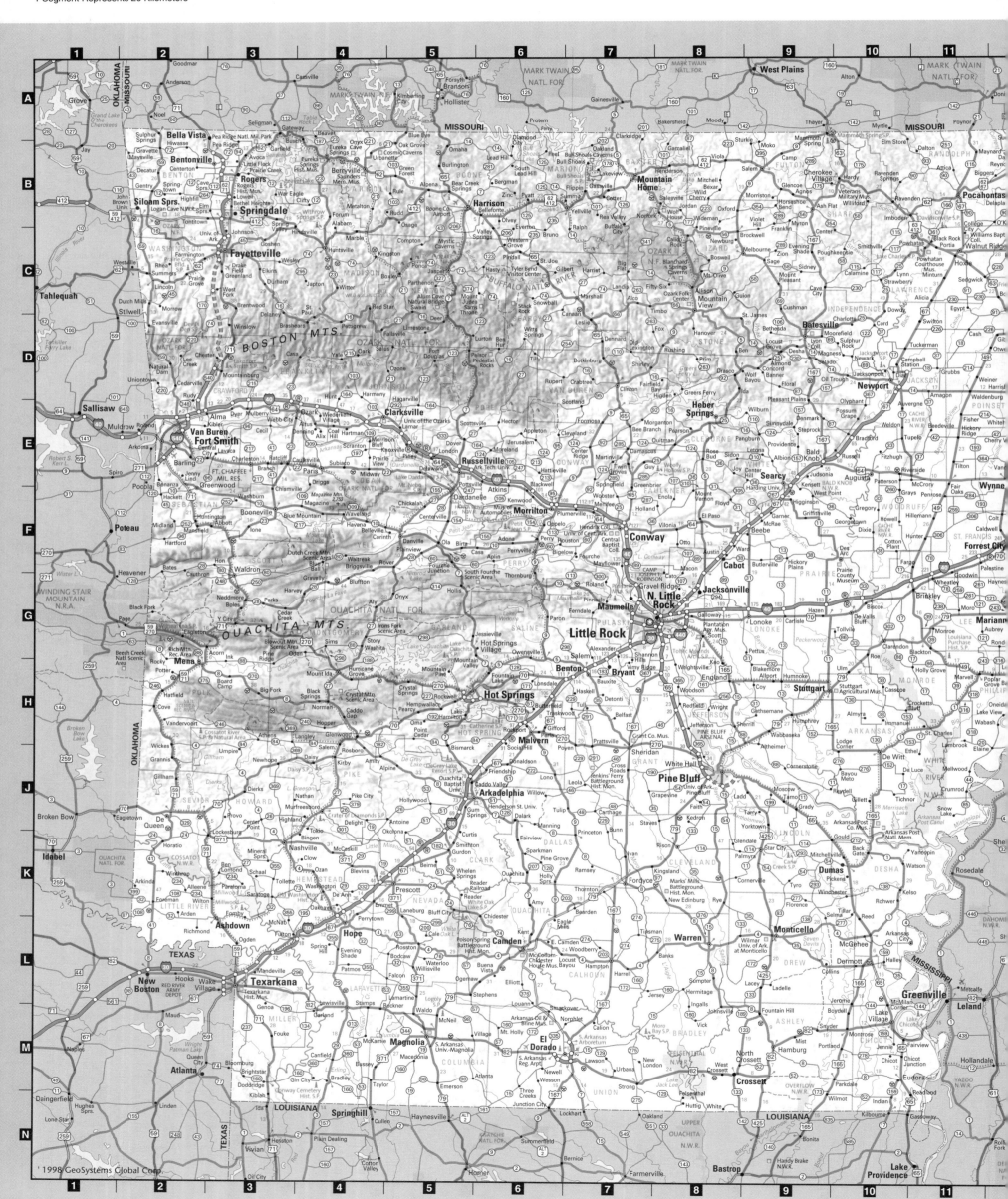

'1998 GeoSystems Global Corp.

"The People Rule"

1 Segment Represents 20 Miles

1 Segment Represents 20 Kilometers

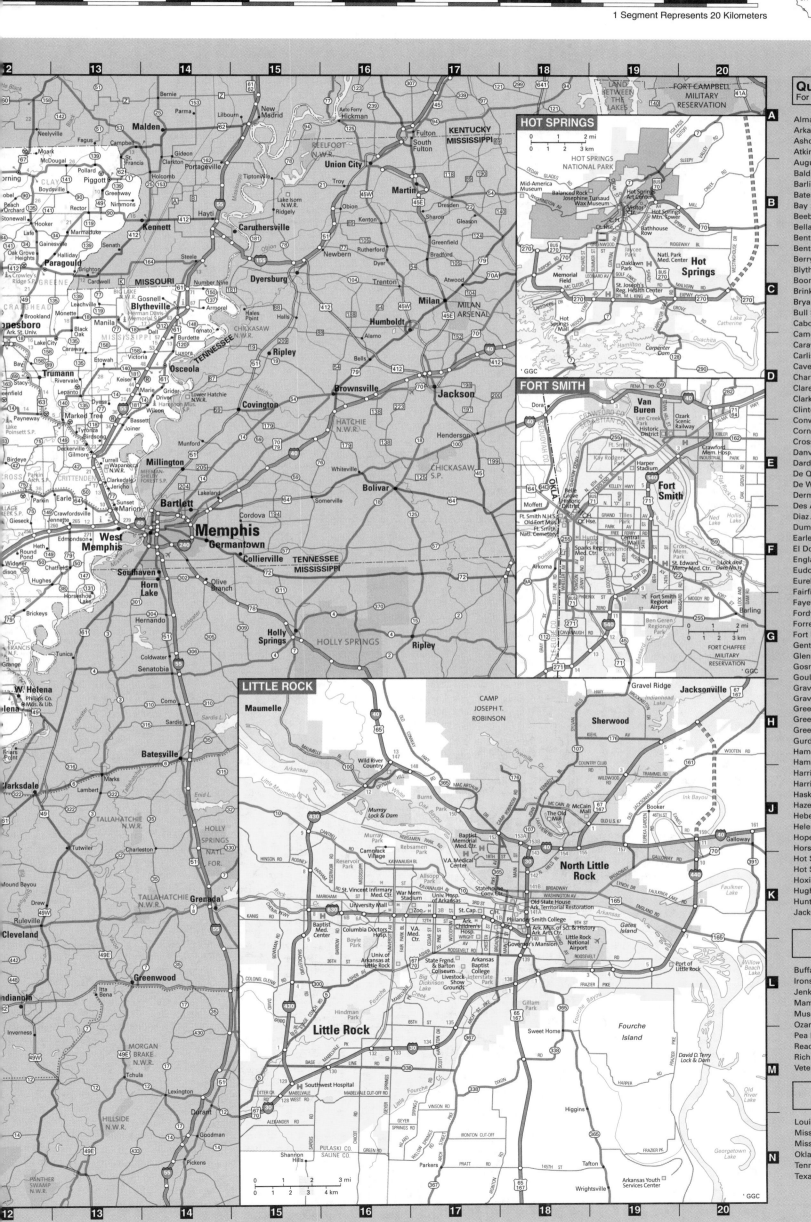

Quick Reference Index

For index to counties and places see page 134.

Alma	E-2	Jonesboro	D-12
Arkadelphia	J-5	Judsonia	E-9
Ashdown	L-3	Kensett	F-9
Atkins	E-6	Lake City	D-13
Augusta	E-10	Lake Village	M-10
Bald Knob	E-10	Leachville	C-13
Barling	E-2	Lepanto	D-13
Batesville	D-9	Lewisville	M-4
Bay	D-12	Lincoln	C-2
Beebe	F-9	Little Rock	G-7
Bella Vista	A-3	Lonoke	G-9
Benton	H-7	Magnolia	M-5
Bentonville	B-3	Malvern	H-6
Berryville	B-4	Manila	C-13
Blytheville	C-14	Marianna	G-12
Booneville	F-3	Marion	F-13
Brinkley	G-11	Marked Tree	D-13
Bryant	H-7	Marvell	H-11
Bull Shoals	B-7	Maumelle	G-7
Cabot	F-8	Mayflower	F-7
Camden	L-6	McCrory	E-11
Caraway	D-13	McGehee	L-10
Carlisle	G-9	Melbourne	C-9
Cave City	C-10	Mena	H-2
Charleston	E-3	Monticello	L-9
Clarendon	G-10	Morrilton	F-6
Clarksville	E-4	Mountain Home	B-7
Clinton	D-7	Mountain View	C-8
Conway	F-7	Mulberry	E-3
Corning	B-12	Murfreesboro	J-4
Crossett	M-9	Nashville	K-3
Danville	F-5	Newport	D-10
Dardanelle	F-5	North Crossett	M-9
De Queen	J-2	North Little Rock	G-8
De Witt	J-10	Osceola	D-14
Dermott	L-10	Ozark	E-3
Des Arc	F-10	Paragould	C-12
Diaz	D-10	Paris	E-4
Dumas	K-10	Parkin	E-12
Earle	E-13	Pea Ridge	B-3
El Dorado	M-7	Piggott	B-13
England	H-8	Pine Bluff	J-8
Eudora	M-11	Pocahontas	B-11
Eureka Springs	B-4	Prairie Grove	C-2
Fairfield Bay	D-8	Prescott	K-5
Fayetteville	C-3	Rector	B-13
Fordyce	K-7	Rockwell	H-5
Forrest City	F-12	Rogers	B-3
Fort Smith	E-2	Russellville	E-5
Gentry	B-2	Salem	G-7
Glenwood	H-4	Salem	B-9
Gosnell	C-14	Searcy	E-9
Gould	K-10	Shannon Hills	G-7
Gravel Ridge	G-8	Sheridan	J-7
Gravette	B-2	Siloam Springs	B-2
Green Forest	B-5	Smackover	M-6
Greenbrier	F-7	Springdale	B-3
Greenwood	F-2	Stamps	M-4
Gurdon	K-5	Star City	K-9
Hamburg	M-9	Stuttgart	H-10
Hampton	L-7	Texarkana	L-3
Harrisburg	D-12	Trumann	D-12
Harrison	B-5	Tuckerman	D-11
Haskell	H-7	Tyronza	E-13
Hazen	G-10	Van Buren	E-2
Heber Springs	E-8	Waldo	M-5
Helena	H-12	Waldron	G-3
Hope	L-4	Walnut Ridge	C-11
Horseshoe Bend	B-9	Warren	L-8
Hot Springs	H-5	West Crossett	M-8
Hot Springs Village	G-6	West Fork	C-3
Hoxie	C-11	West Helena	H-12
Hughes	G-13	West Memphis	F-13
Huntsville	C-4	White Hall	J-8
Jacksonville	G-8	Wynne	F-12

Selected Attractions

Buffalo National River	C-8
Irons Fork Scenic Area	G-6
Jenkins' Ferry Battleground Historic Monument	J-9
Mammoth Springs State Park	A-12
Museum of Automobiles	F-8
Ozark Folk Center	C-10
Pea Ridge National Military Park	B-5
Reader Railroad	K-7
Rich Mountain Recreation Area	G-4
Veterans Military Museum	B-12

Adjacent States

Louisiana	46
Mississippi	62
Missouri	64
Oklahoma	90
Tennessee	102
Texas	104 & 106

"Eureka (I Have Found It)"

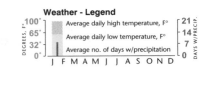

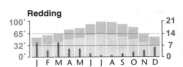

1 Segment Represents 20 Miles

1 Segment Represents 20 Kilometers

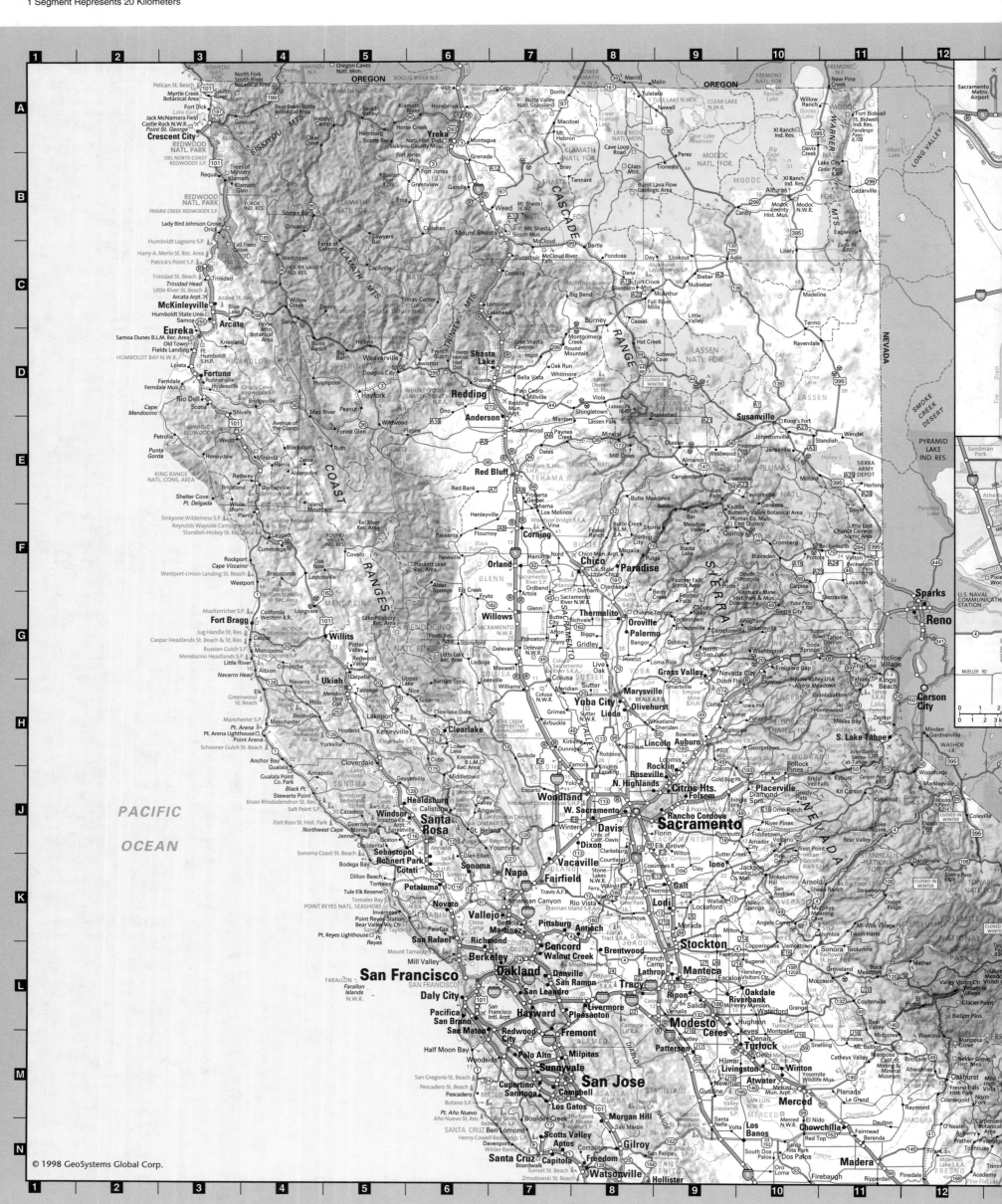

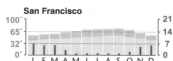

Sacramento | San Francisco

1 Segment Represents 20 Miles

1 Segment Represents 20 Kilometers

Quick Reference Index

For index to counties and places see page 134.

American Canyon K-7	Morada K-9
Anderson E-7	Morgan Hill M-8
Angwin J-6	Mount Shasta B-7
Antioch K-8	Napa K-7
Arcata C-3	Newman M-9
Arnold K-11	North Highlands J-9
Atwater M-10	Novato K-6
Auburn H-9	Oakdale L-10
Benicia K-7	Oakland L-7
Berkeley L-7	Olivehurst H-8
Bishop M-15	Orland F-7
Boulder Creek M-7	Oroville G-8
Brentwood L-8	Pacifica L-6
Burney C-8	Palermo G-8
Calistoga J-6	Palo Alto M-7
Campbell M-7	Paradise F-8
Ceres L-9	Patterson M-9
Chico F-8	Petaluma K-6
Citrus Heights J-9	Pittsburg K-7
Clearlake H-6	Placerville J-10
Cloverdale H-5	Planada M-11
Colusa H-7	Pleasanton L-7
Concord L-7	Pollock Pines H-10
Corning F-7	Rancho Cordova J-9
Cotati K-6	Red Bluff E-7
Crescent City A-3	Redding D-6
Cupertino M-7	Redwood City M-7
Daly City L-6	Richmond L-6
Danville L-7	Ripon L-9
Davis J-8	Riverbank L-9
Denair M-10	Rocklin J-9
Dixon J-8	Rohnert Park K-6
Durham F-8	Roseville J-9
Elk Grove J-8	Sacramento J-8
Escalon L-9	Saint Helena J-6
Eureka D-3	Salida L-9
Fairfax K-6	San Bruno L-6
Fairfield K-7	San Carlos M-7
Florin J-8	San Francisco L-6
Folsom J-9	San Jose M-7
Fort Bragg G-4	San Leandro L-7
Fortuna D-3	San Mateo L-6
Fremont L-7	San Rafael K-6
Galt K-9	San Ramon L-7
Grass Valley G-9	Santa Rosa J-6
Gridley G-8	Saratoga M-7
Gustine M-9	Sebastopol J-5
Half Moon Bay M-6	Shasta Lake D-7
Hayward L-7	Sonoma K-7
Healdsburg J-6	Sonora K-11
Hilmar M-10	South Lake Tahoe ..H-11
Ione K-9	Stockton L-9
Jackson K-10	Sunnyvale M-7
Lakeport H-5	Susanville E-10
Lathrop L-9	Thermalito G-8
Lincoln H-9	Tracy L-9
Linda H-8	Truckee G-11
Live Oak G-8	Turlock M-10
Livermore L-8	Ukiah H-5
Livingston M-10	Union City L-7
Lodi K-9	Vacaville K-7
Loomis H-9	Vallejo K-7
Los Altos M-7	Walnut Creek L-7
Los Gatos M-7	Waterford L-10
Magalia F-8	West Sacramento J-8
Mammoth Lakes L-13	Willits G-5
Manteca L-9	Willows G-7
Martinez K-7	Wilton J-9
Marysville H-8	Windsor J-6
McKinleyville C-3	Winters J-8
Merced M-10	Winton M-10
Mill Valley L-6	Woodland J-8
Millbrae L-6	Woodside M-7
Milpitas M-7	Yreka A-6
Modesto L-9	Yuba City H-8

Selected Attractions

Bridal Veil Falls.........................	J-10
Death Valley National Park...........	N-16
Kings Canyon National Park.........	N-14
Lake Tahoe................................	H-11
Lassen Volcanic National Park	D-9
Lava Beds National Monument	A-8
Point Arean Lighthouse................	H-4
Point Reyes National Seashore	K-5
Redwood National Park	C-3
Yosemite National Park	K-12

Adjacent States

Arizona	8
California - Southern	14
Nevada	70
Mexico	132
Oregon	92

"*Eureka*
(I Have Found It)"

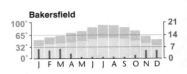

1 Segment Represents 20 Miles

1 Segment Represents 20 Kilometers

© 1998 GeoSystems Global Corp.

"Eureka (I Have Found It)"

Los Angeles

San Diego

J F M A M J J A S O N D

PALM SPRINGS

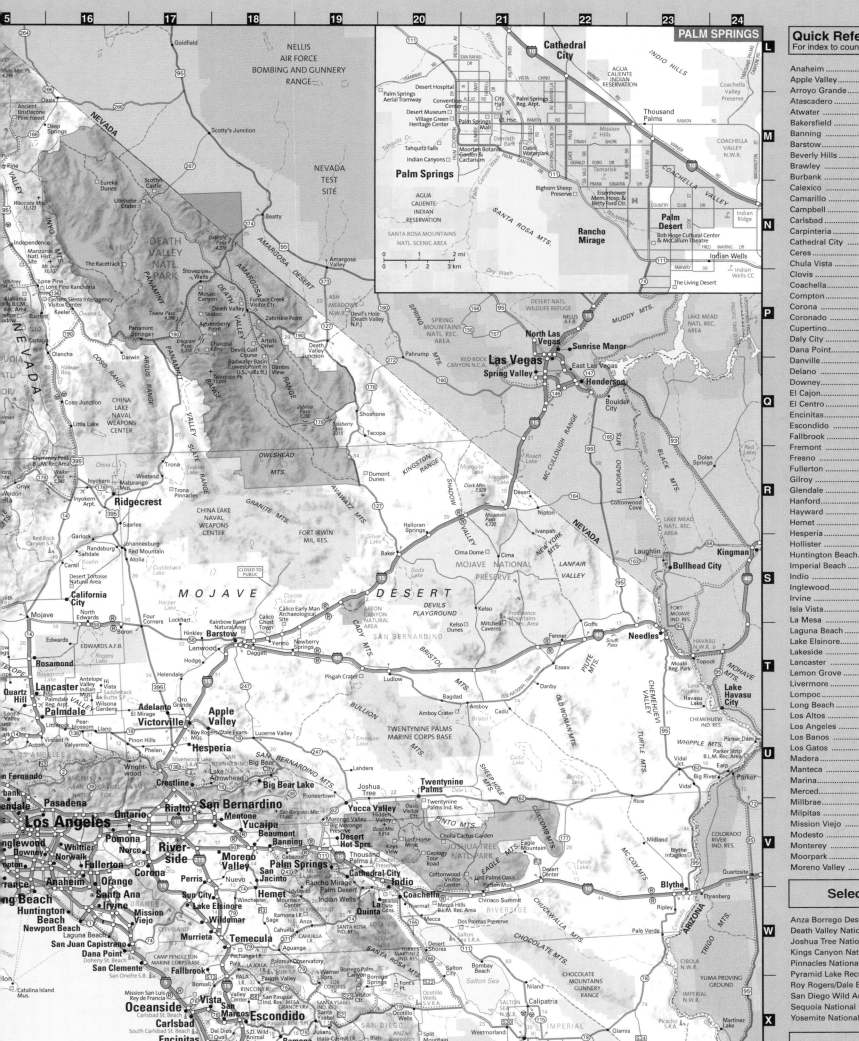

1 Segment Represents 20 Miles

1 Segment Represents 20 Kilometers

Quick Reference Index

For index to counties and places see page 134.

Anaheim	V-16	Morgan Hill	M-8
Apple Valley	U-17	Murrieta	V-21
Arroyo Grande	S-10	Newport Beach	W-16
Atascadero	R-10	Norco	V-17
Atwater	M-10	Norwalk	V-15
Bakersfield	S-13	Oakland	L-7
Banning	V-18	Oceanside	X-17
Barstow	T-18	Oildale	S-13
Beverly Hills	V-15	Ontario	V-17
Brawley	X-21	Orange	V-16
Burbank	U-15	Oxnard	V-13
Calexico	Y-21	Pacific Grove	P-7
Camarillo	U-14	Pacifica	L-6
Campbell	M-7	Palm Desert	V-19
Carlsbad	X-17	Palm Springs	V-18
Carpinteria	U-12	Palmdale	U-15
Cathedral City	V-19	Palo Alto	M-7
Ceres	L-9	Pasadena	V-15
Chula Vista	Y-18	Paso Robles	R-10
Clovis	N-12	Perris	V-17
Coachella	W-20	Pomona	V-15
Compton	V-15	Port Hueneme	V-13
Corona	V-17	Porterville	Q-13
Coronado	Y-18	Poway	X-18
Cupertino	M-7	Redlands	V-18
Daly City	L-6	Redwood City	M-7
Dana Point	W-16	Reedley	P-13
Danville	L-7	Rialto	V-17
Delano	R-13	Ridgecrest	R-16
Downey	V-15	Riverside	V-17
El Cajon	Y-18	Salinas	P-8
El Centro	Y-21	San Bernardino	V-17
Encinitas	X-17	San Carlos	M-7
Escondido	X-18	San Clemente	W-16
Fallbrook	W-17	San Diego	Y-18
Fremont	L-7	San Fernando	U-15
Fresno	N-12	San Francisco	L-6
Fullerton	V-16	San Jacinto	V-18
Gilroy	N-8	San Jose	M-7
Glendale	V-15	San Juan
Hanford	P-12	Capistrano	W-16
Hayward	L-7	San Leandro	L-7
Hemet	V-18	San Luis Obispo	S-10
Hesperia	U-17	San Marcos	X-18
Hollister	N-8	San Mateo	L-6
Huntington Beach	W-16	Santa Ana	W-16
Imperial Beach	Y-18	Santa Barbara	U-12
Indio	V-20	Santa Clarita	U-15
Inglewood	V-15	Santa Cruz	N-7
Irvine	W-16	Santa Maria	T-10
Isla Vista	U-12	Santa Monica	V-15
La Mesa	Y-18	Santa Paula	U-13
Laguna Beach	W-16	Santee	Y-18
Lake Elsinore	V-17	Saratoga	M-7
Lakeside	Y-18	Seaside	P-8
Lancaster	T-15	Selma	T-12
Lemon Grove	Y-18	Simi Valley	U-14
Livermore	L-8	Spring Valley	Y-18
Lompoc	T-10	Sun City	W-18
Long Beach	W-15	Sunnyvale	M-7
Los Altos	M-7	Temecula	V-18
Los Angeles	V-15	Thousand Oaks	V-14
Los Banos	N-10	Torrance	V-15
Los Gatos	M-7	Tracy	L-8
Madera	N-11	Tulare	Q-13
Manteca	L-9	Turlock	M-10
Marina	P-8	Union City	L-7
Merced	M-10	Ventura	U-13
Millbrae	L-6	Victorville	U-17
Milpitas	M-7	Visalia	P-13
Mission Viejo	W-17	Vista	X-17
Modesto	L-9	Watsonville	N-8
Monterey	P-7	Whittier	V-16
Moorpark	U-14	Yucaipa	V-18
Moreno Valley	V-18	Yucca Valley	V-19

Selected Attractions

Anza Borrego Desert State Park	X-20
Death Valley National Park	N-17
Joshua Tree National Park	V-21
Kings Canyon National Park	N-14
Pinnacles National Monument	P-9
Pyramid Lake Recreation Area	T-14
Roy Rogers/Dale Evans Museum	U-17
San Diego Wild Animal Park	X-18
Sequoia National Park	P-14
Yosemite National Park	L-12

Adjacent States

Arizona	8
California - Northern	14
Nevada	70
Mexico	132
Oregon	92

1 Segment Represents 5 Miles (area map)

1 Segment Represents 5 Kilometers (area map)

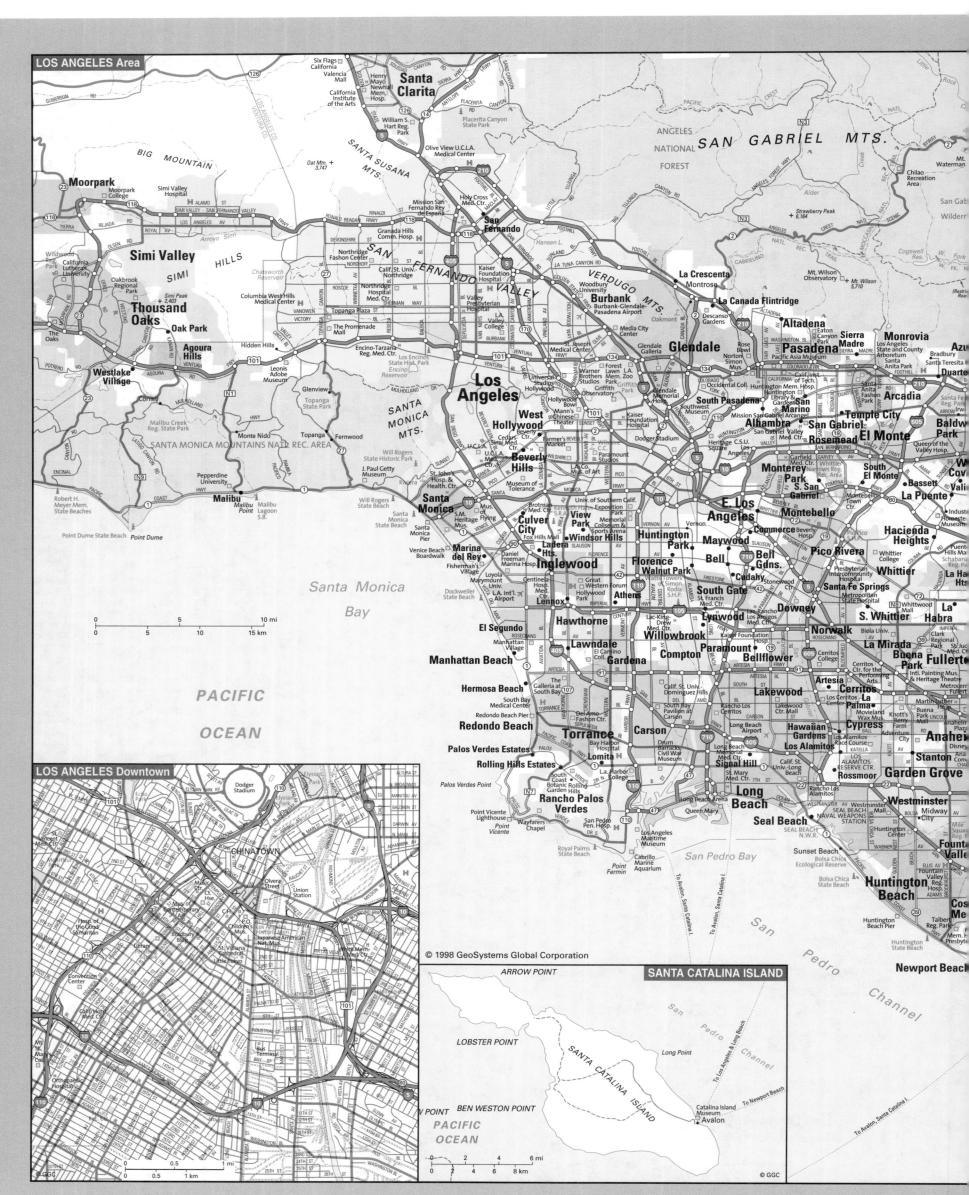

© 1998 GeoSystems Global Corporation

1 Segment Represents 5 Miles (area map)

1 Segment Represents 5 Kilometers (area map)

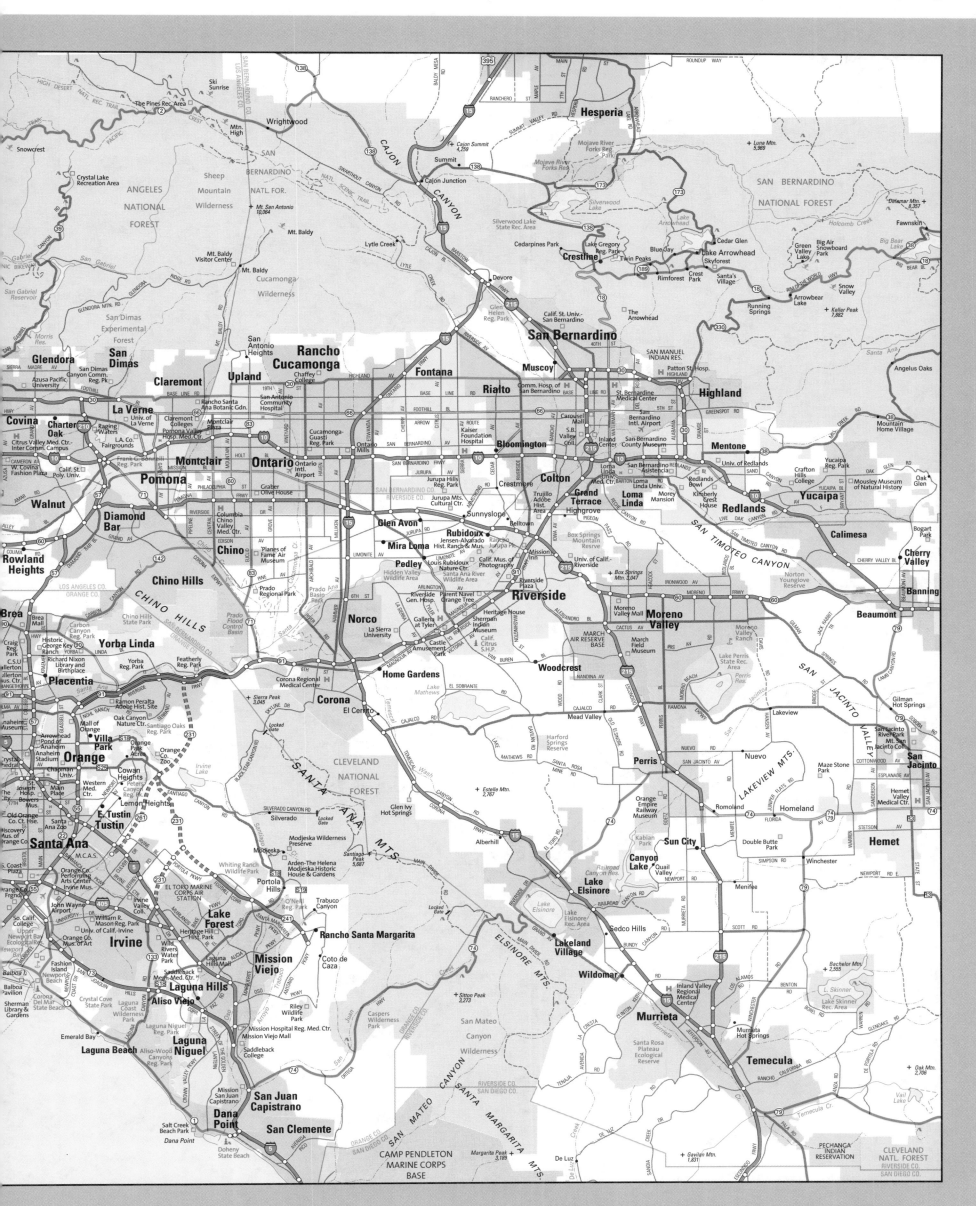

1 Segment Represents 4 Miles

1 Segment Represents 4 Kilometers

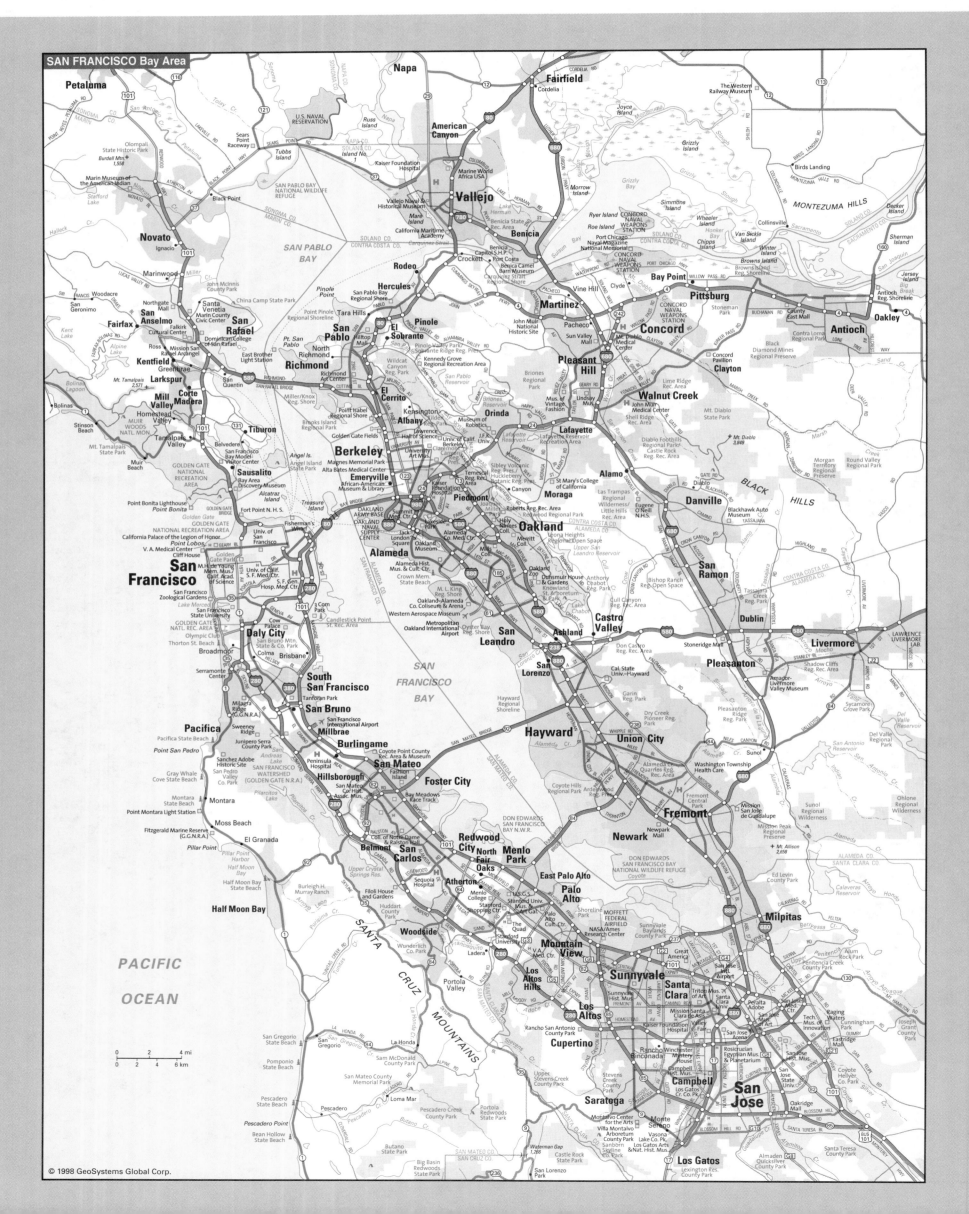

SAN FRANCISCO Bay Area

PACIFIC

OCEAN

San Francisco, CA Downtown
Rocky Mountain Natl. Park, CO
Denver, CO Area

CITY MAPS: San Francisco, CA – Denver, CO **19**

1 Segment Represents 4 Miles (Denver map)

1 Segment Represents 4 Kilometers (Denver map)

1 Segment Represents 4 Miles (Denver map)

1 Segment Represents 4 Kilometers (Denver map)

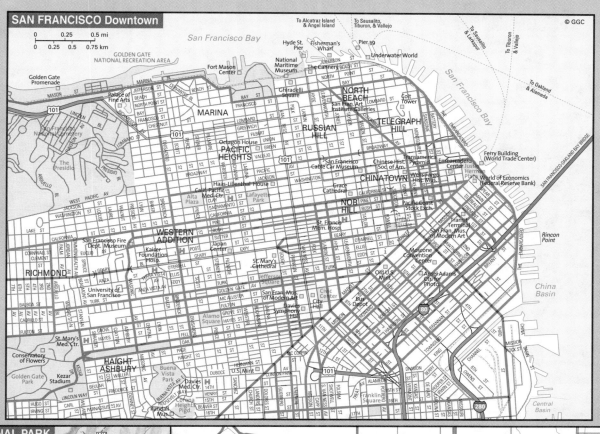

SAN FRANCISCO Downtown

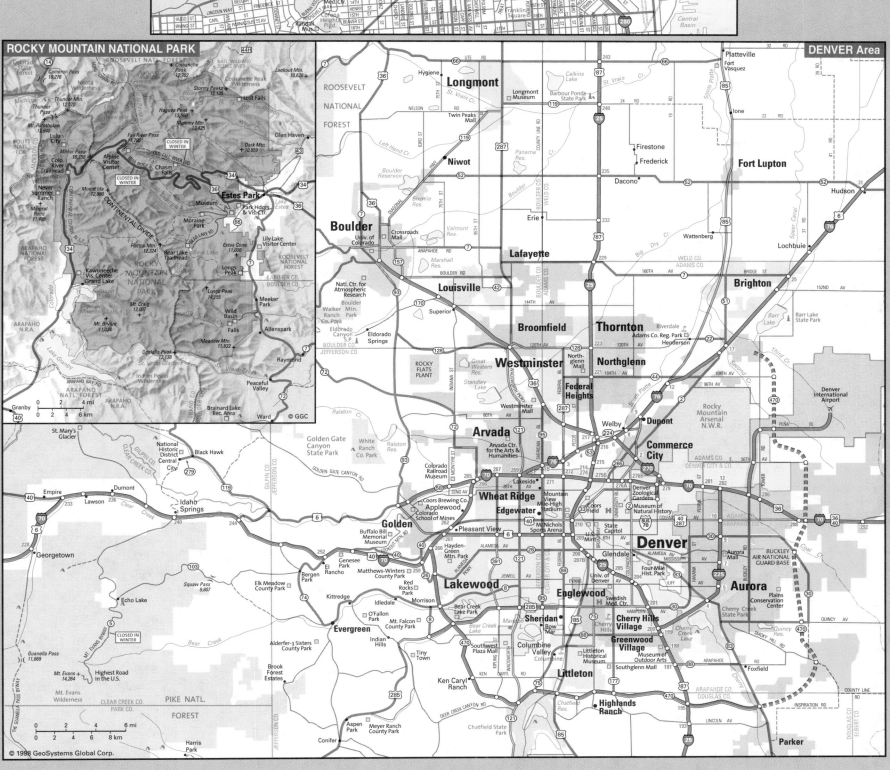

ROCKY MOUNTAIN NATIONAL PARK

DENVER Area

© 1998 GeoSystems Global Corp.

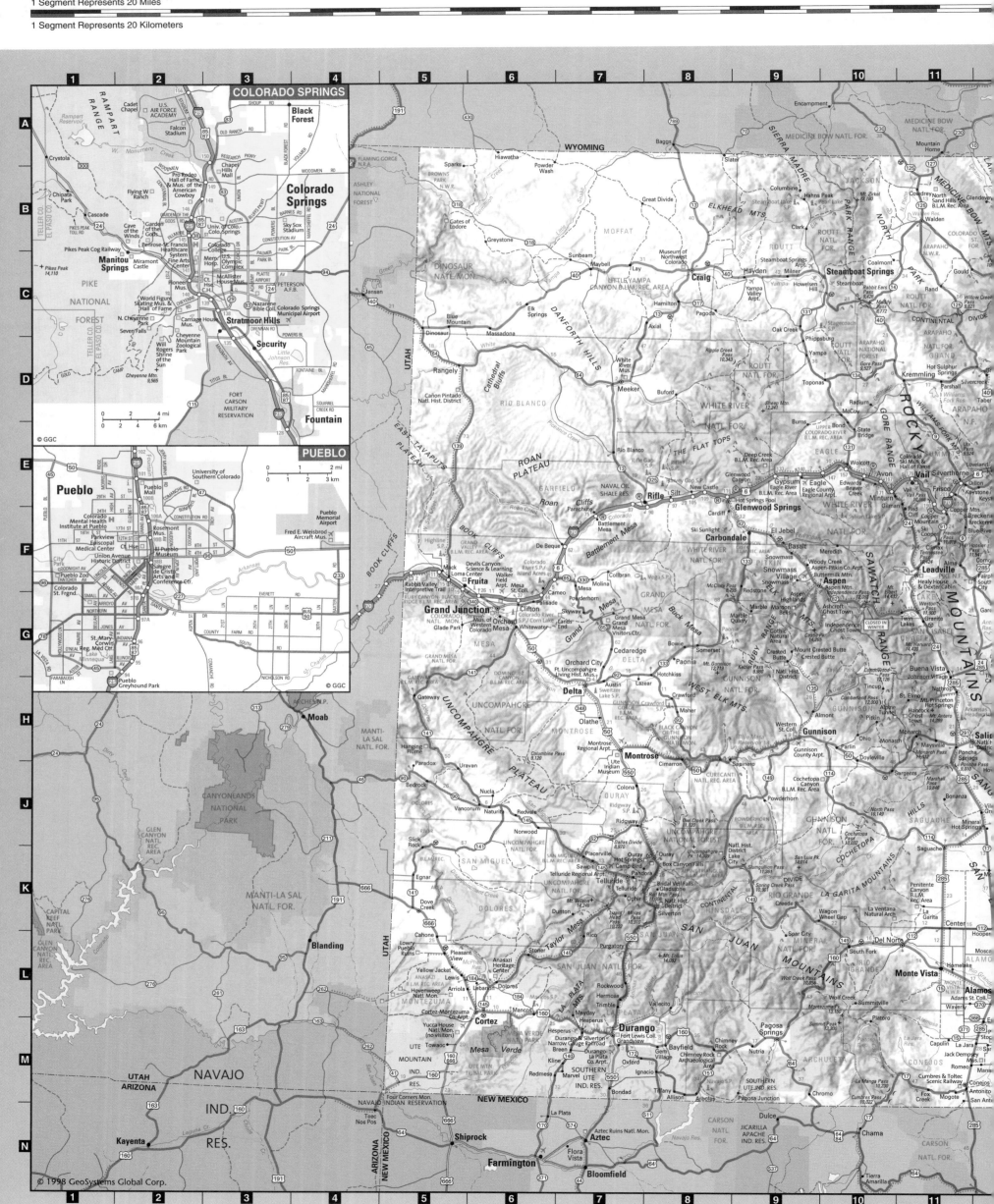

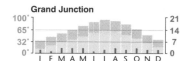

Pueblo

Grand Junction

1 Segment Represents 20 Miles

1 Segment Represents 20 Kilometers

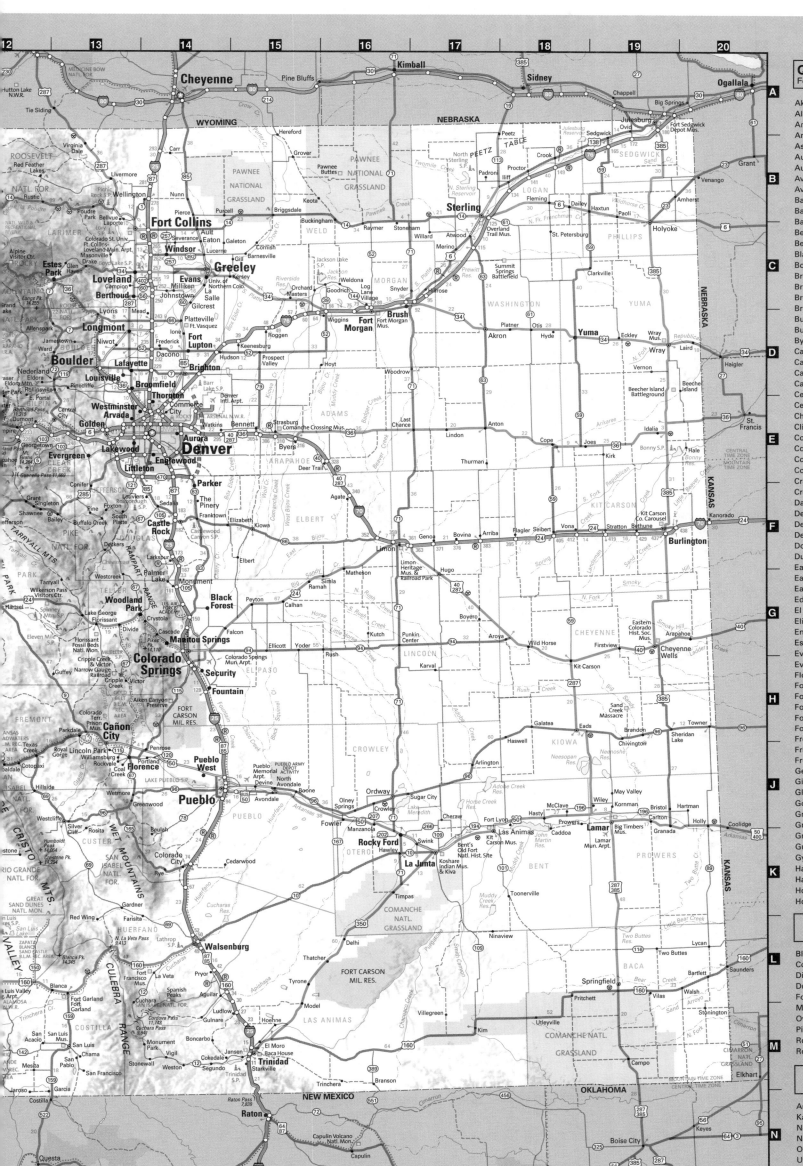

Quick Reference Index

For index to counties and places see page 135.

Akron	D-17	Hotchkiss	G-8
Alamosa	L-12	Hudson	D-14
Antonito	M-11	Ignacio	M-8
Arvada	E-13	Johnstown	C-14
Aspen	F-9	Julesburg	A-19
Ault	C-14	Kersey	C-15
Aurora	E-14	Kremmling	D-11
Avon	E-10	La Jara	M-12
Avondale	J-15	La Junta	K-17
Basalt	F-9	La Salle	C-14
Battlement Mesa	F-7	La Veta	L-14
Bayfield	M-8	Lafayette	D-13
Bennett	E-15	Lakewood	E-13
Berthoud	C-13	Lamar	J-19
Black Forest	G-14	Las Animas	K-17
Boulder	D-13	Leadville	F-11
Breckenridge	F-11	Limon	F-16
Brighton	D-14	Lincoln Park	J-13
Broomfield	D-13	Littleton	E-14
Brush	C-16	Longmont	D-13
Buena Vista	G-11	Louisville	D-13
Burlington	F-19	Loveland	C-13
Byers	E-15	Lyons	D-13
Campion	C-13	Manassa	M-12
Canon City	H-13	Mancos	L-6
Carbondale	F-9	Manitou Springs	G-14
Castle Rock	F-14	Meeker	D-7
Cedaredge	G-7	Milliken	C-14
Center	K-11	Minturn	E-10
Cheyenne Wells	G-19	Monte Vista	L-11
Clifton	G-6	Montrose	H-7
Colorado City	K-14	Monument	G-14
Colorado Springs	G-14	Nederland	D-13
Commerce City	E-14	Niwot	D-13
Cortez	L-6	Olathe	H-7
Craig	C-8	Orchard City	G-7
Crested Butte	G-9	Orchard Mesa	G-6
Dacono	D-14	Ordway	J-16
Del Norte	L-11	Pagosa Springs	M-9
Delta	H-7	Palisade	G-6
Denver	E-14	Palmer Lake	G-14
Dolores	L-6	Paonia	G-8
Durango	M-7	Parker	F-14
Eads	H-18	Penrose	J-13
Eagle	E-10	Pierce	B-14
Eaton	C-14	Platteville	D-14
Edwards	E-10	Pueblo	J-14
El Jebel	F-9	Pueblo West	J-14
Elizabeth	F-14	Rangely	D-5
Englewood	E-14	Rifle	E-7
Estes Park	C-13	Rocky Ford	K-16
Evans	C-14	Salida	H-12
Evergreen	E-13	San Luis	M-13
Florence	J-13	Sanford	M-12
Fort Collins	C-13	Security	H-14
Fort Lupton	D-14	Silt	E-8
Fort Morgan	D-16	Silverthorne	E-11
Fountain	H-14	Snowmass Village	F-9
Fowler	J-16	Springfield	L-19
Frederick	D-14	Steamboat Springs	C-10
Frisco	E-11	Sterling	B-17
Fruita	F-5	Strasburg	E-15
Georgetown	E-12	Telluride	K-7
Gilcrest	C-14	The Pinery	F-14
Glenwood Springs	E-8	Thornton	D-13
Golden	E-13	Trinidad	M-15
Granby	D-12	Vail	E-11
Grand Junction	G-6	Walden	B-11
Greeley	C-14	Walsenburg	L-14
Gunnison	H-9	Wellington	B-14
Gypsum	E-10	Westminster	E-13
Haxtun	B-19	Windsor	C-14
Hayden	C-9	Woodland Park	G-13
Holly	J-20	Wray	D-19
Holyoke	C-19	Yuma	D-18

Selected Attractions

Black Canyon of the Gunnison National Mon.	H-8
Colorado National Monument	G-5
Dinosaur National Monument	C-5
Durango & Silverton Narrow Gauge Railroad	M-7
Four Corners Monument	M-5
Mesa Verde National Park	M-6
Overland Trail Museum	C-17
Pikes Peak	G-14
Rocky Mountain National Park	C-12
Royal Gorge	H-13

Adjacent States

Arizona	8
Kansas	42
Nebraska	68
New Mexico	74
Oklahoma	90
Utah	109
Wyoming	120

"He Who Transplanted Still Sustains"

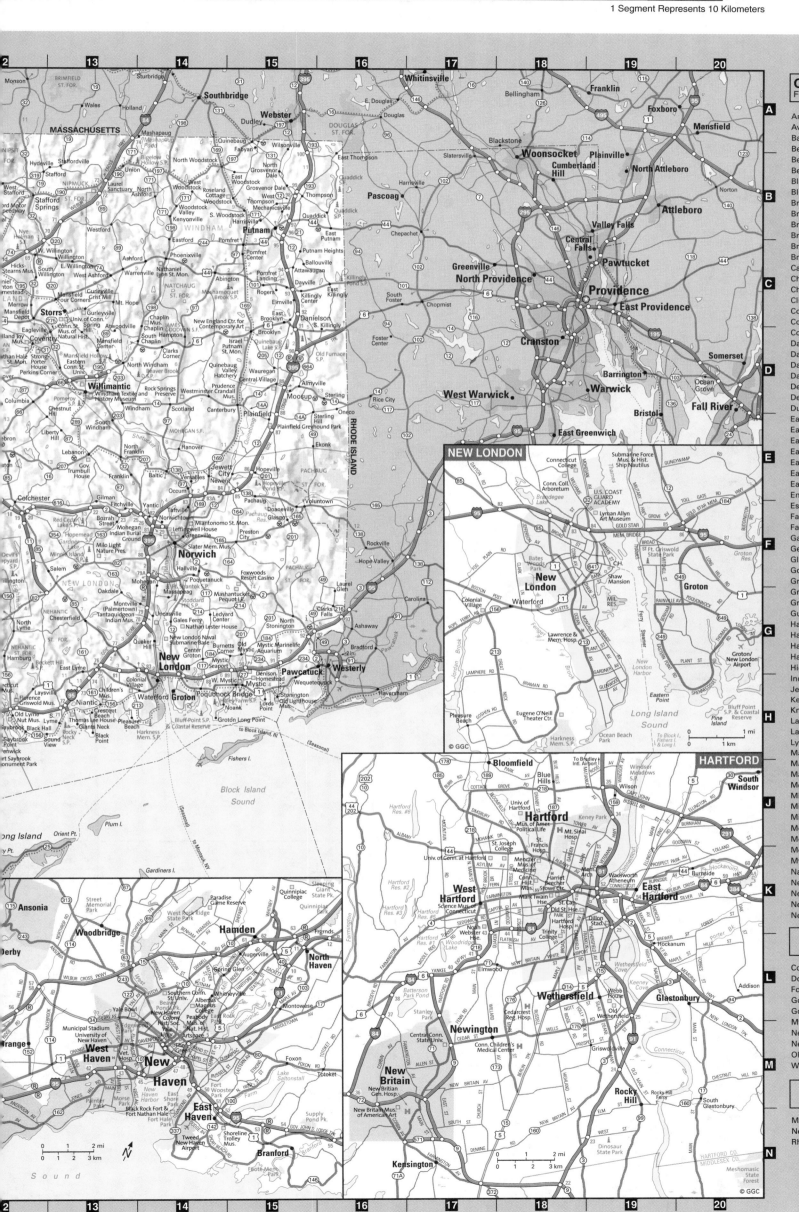

Quick Reference Index

For index to counties and places see page 135.

Ansonia	H-7	New London	H-14
Avon	C-8	New Milford	E-5
Baltic	E-14	Newington	D-9
Beacon Falls	G-7	Newtown	G-5
Bethel	G-4	Niantic	H-13
Bethlehem	E-6	Noank	H-14
Bloomfield	C-9	North Branford	H-9
Blue Hills	C-9	N. Grosvenor Dale	B-15
Branford	H-9	North Haven	G-8
Bridgeport	J-6	Northford	G-9
Bristol	E-8	Norwalk	K-4
Broad Brook	B-11	Norwich	F-14
Brookfield	F-4	Oakville	E-7
Brookfield Center	G-5	Old Saybrook	H-12
Canton	C-8	Orange	H-7
Cheshire	F-8	Pawcatuck	G-16
Chester	G-11	Plainfield	E-15
Clinton	H-11	Plainville	E-8
Colchester	F-12	Plantsville	E-8
Collinsville	C-8	Pleasure Beach	H-13
Coventry	D-12	Poquonock	B-10
Danbury	G-4	Poquonock Bridge	H-14
Danielson	C-15	Portland	F-10
Darien	K-4	Prospect	F-7
Dayville	C-15	Putnam	B-15
Deep River	G-11	Quaker Hill	G-14
Derby	H-7	Quarryville	D-11
Durham	F-9	Ridgefield	H-4
East Brooklyn	C-15	Rockfall	F-9
East Hampton	F-11	Rocky Hill	E-10
East Hartford	D-10	Seymour	G-7
East Hartford Gdns.	D-10	Shelton	H-7
East Haven	H-8	Sherwood Manor	A-10
East Lyme	G-13	Short Beach	H-8
East Village	H-6	Simsbury	C-9
Enfield	B-10	Somers	B-11
Essex	H-12	South Glastonbury	E-10
Fairfield	K-5	South Willington	C-12
Farmington	D-8	South Windham	E-13
Gales Ferry	G-14	Southington	E-8
Georgetown	H-4	Southwood Acres	B-10
Glastonbury	D-10	Stafford Springs	B-12
Goodrich Heights	E-10	Stamford	K-3
Granby	B-9	Storrs	C-13
Greenwich	K-3	Stratford	J-6
Groton	H-14	Talcottville	C-11
Guilford	H-9	Terryville	E-7
Hamden	G-8	Thomaston	E-7
Hartford	D-9	Thompsonville	B-10
Harwinton	D-7	Torrington	C-6
Hazardville	B-11	Trumbull	J-6
Higganum	F-11	Uncasville	G-14
Indian Neck	H-9	Unionville	D-8
Jewett City	E-15	Vernon	C-11
Kensington	E-9	Wallingford	G-9
Knollwood	H-12	Waterbury	F-7
Lake Pocotopaug	E-11	Waterford	H-14
Lanesville	J-4	Watertown	E-6
Lyons Plain	J-5	Weatogue	C-9
Madison	H-10	West Hartford	D-9
Manchester	D-11	West Haven	H-8
Marion	F-8	West Mystic	H-15
Meriden	F-9	West Simsbury	C-8
Middlefield	F-10	Westbrook	H-11
Middletown	F-10	Weston	J-5
Milford	J-7	Westport	J-5
Mohegan	F-14	Wethersfield	D-10
Monroe	H-6	Willimantic	D-13
Moosup	D-15	Wilton	J-4
Mystic	H-15	Windsor	C-10
Naugatuck	F-7	Windsor Locks	B-10
New Britain	E-9	Winsted	B-7
New Canaan	J-4	Wolcott	E-7
New Fairfield	G-4	Woodmont	J-7
New Haven	H-8	Yalesville	F-9

Selected Attractions

Connecticut Yankee Information & Science Ctr.	F-11
Doll and Toy Museum	D-12
Foxwood Resort Casino	F-15
Goodspeed Opera House	G-11
Gov. Trumbull House	E-9
Mystic Seaport	H-15
New England Air Museum	B-9
New London Naval Submarine Base	G-14
Old Lighthouse Museum	H-15
Weir Farm National Historic Site	H-4

Adjacent States

Massachusetts	54
New York	76 & 78
Rhode Island	99

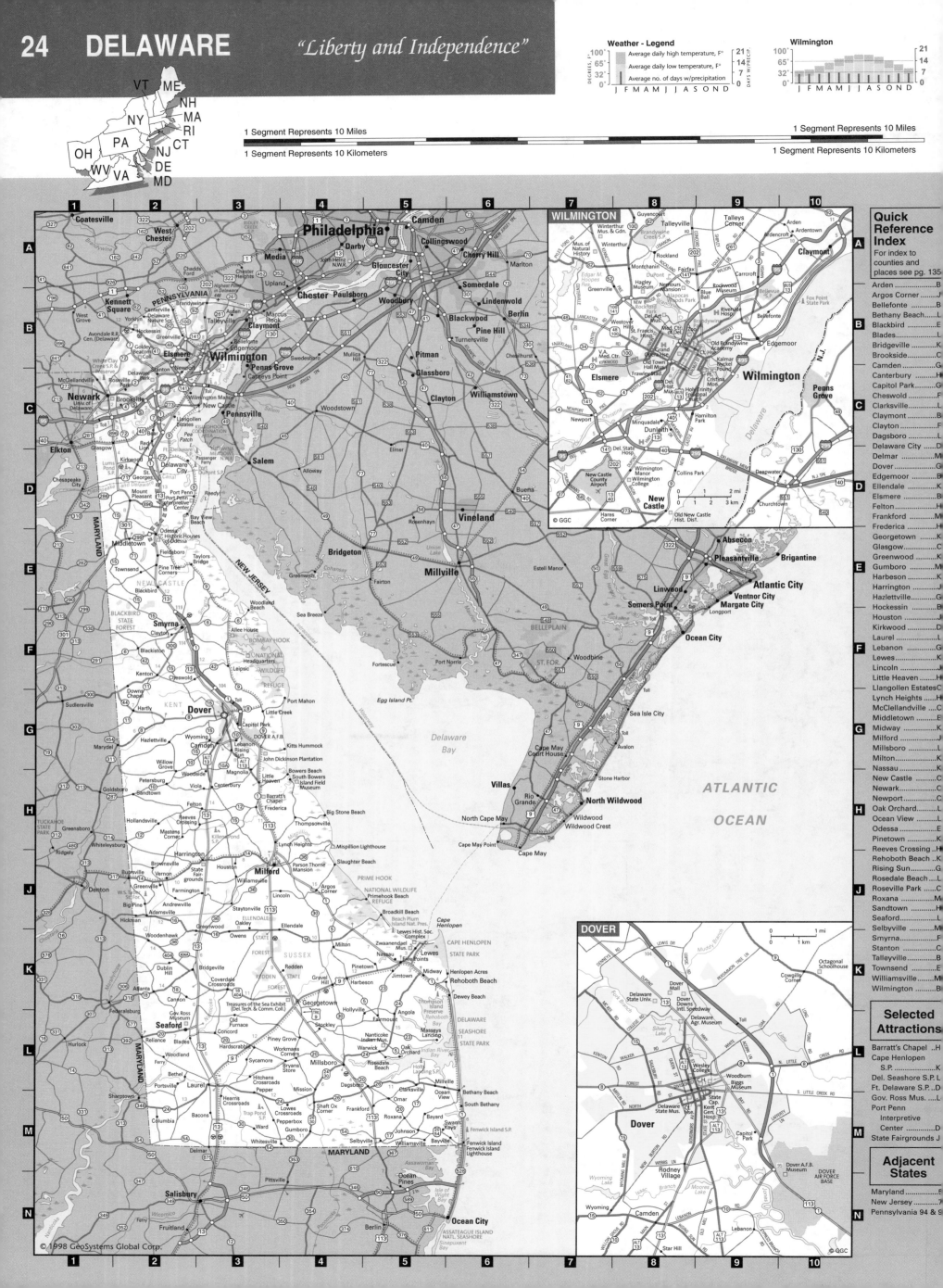

1 Segment Represents 4 Miles (Tampa map)

1 Segment Represents 4 Kilometers map)

1 Segment Represents 4 Miles (Tampa map)

1 Segment Represents 4 Kilometers (Tampa map)

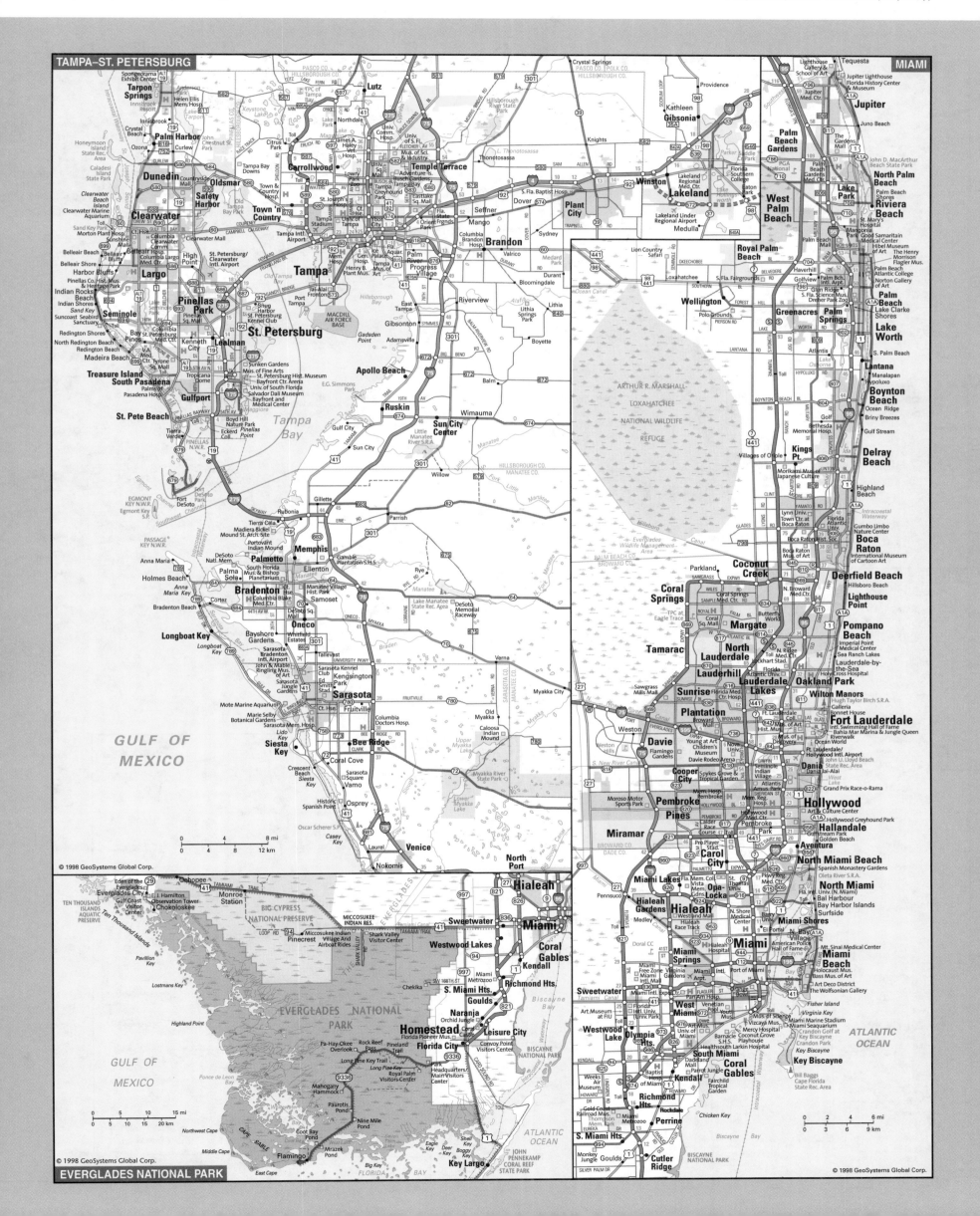

Orlando / Jacksonville climate graphs

1 Segment Represents 20 Miles
1 Segment Represents 20 Kilometers

DAYTONA BEACH

Quick Reference Index
For index to counties and places see page 135.

Alachua	G-14	Melbourne	L-19
Altamonte Springs	K-17	Merritt Island	K-19
Apopka	K-17	Middleburg	F-16
Atlantic Beach	E-17	Milton	D-3
Auburndale	L-16	Mims	E-3
Bayonet Point	K-14	Mount Dora	J-16
Betmar Acres	L-15	Myrtle Grove	E-3
Beverly Hills	J-14	Neptune Beach	E-17
Brandon	L-15	New Port Richey	L-14
Brent	E-3	New Smyrna Beach	J-18
Brooksville	K-15	Niceville	E-5
Butler Beach	G-17	Ocala	H-15
Callaway	F-7	Ocean City	E-4
Campbell	L-17	Ocoee	K-17
Cape Canaveral	K-19	Oldsmar	L-14
Casselberry	K-17	Orange City	J-17
Chattahoochee	D-9	Orange Park	F-16
Chipley	D-7	Orlando	K-17
Clearwater	L-14	Ormond-by-	
Clermont	K-16	the-Sea	H-18
Cocoa	K-19	Ormond Beach	H-18
Cocoa Beach	K-19	Oviedo	K-18
Crestview	D-5	Pace	D-3
Crystal River	J-14	Palatka	G-16
Dade City	K-15	Palm Bay	L-19
Daytona Beach	H-18	Palm Coast	G-18
De Bary	J-17	Palm Harbor	L-14
De Funiak Springs	D-6	Palm Valley	F-17
De Land	J-17	Panama City	F-7
Deltona	J-18	Panama City Beach	F-6
Destin	E-5	Parker	F-7
Dunedin	L-14	Pensacola	E-3
Edgewater	J-18	Perry	F-12
Elfers	L-14	Pine Castle	K-17
Ensley	E-3	Plant City	L-15
Eustis	J-16	Poinciana	L-17
Fernandina Beach	E-17	Port Orange	H-18
Ferry Pass	E-3	Port Saint Joe	G-8
Flagler Beach	H-18	Port Saint John	K-19
Fort Walton Beach	E-4	Quincy	E-9
Fruit Cove	F-17	Ratliff	E-16
Gainesville	G-15	Rockledge	K-19
Gibsonia	L-16	Safety Harbor	L-14
Gonzalez	D-3	St. Augustine	F-17
Green Cove Sprs.	F-16	St. Augustine Bch.	G-17
Gulf Breeze	E-3	St. Augustine	
Haines City	L-17	Shores	G-17
Hiland Park	F-7	St. Cloud	L-17
Holiday	L-14	St. Petersburg	M-14
Holly Hill	H-18	Sanford	J-17
Homosassa Sprs.	J-14	Satellite Beach	L-19
Hudson	K-14	Silver Springs	H-15
Ind. Harbour Beach	L-19	Silver Sprs. Shores	H-15
Inverness	J-15	South Daytona	H-18
Inwood	L-16	S. Patrick Shores	L-19
Jacksonville	E-16	Spring Hill	K-14
Jacksonville Beach	E-17	Springfield	F-7
Jasmine Estates	L-14	Starke	F-15
Kissimmee	L-17	Tallahassee	E-10
Lady Lake	J-16	Tampa	L-14
Lake Alfred	L-16	Tarpon Springs	L-14
Lake City	F-14	Tavares	J-16
Lake Mary	J-17	Titusville	K-19
Lakeland	L-16	Valparaiso	E-5
Land O' Lakes	L-14	Warrington	E-3
Leesburg	J-16	West Melbourne	L-19
Live Oak	E-13	West Pensacola	E-3
Longwood	K-17	Wildwood	J-16
Lutz	L-14	Winston	L-16
Lynn Haven	E-7	Winter Garden	K-17
Macclenny	E-15	Winter Haven	L-16
Maitland	K-17	Winter Park	K-17
Marianna	D-8	Winter Springs	K-17
Mary Esther	E-4	Yulee	E-17
Medulla	L-16	Zephyrhills	L-15

Selected Attractions

Canaveral National Seashore	J-19
Cedar Key State Museum	H-13
Cypress Gardens	L-16
Daytona International Speedway	H-18
Fort Matanzas National Monument	G-18
Gregory House	E-8
Kennedy Space Center	K-19
Marineland of Florida	G-18
Ponce de Leon Inlet Lighthouse	J-18
Walt Disney World	K-17

Adjacent States

Alabama	4
Florida - Southern	28
Georgia	30

Weather - Legend
Average daily high temperature, F°
Average daily low temperature, F°
Average no. of days w/precipitation

Miami

1 Segment Represents 20 Miles
1 Segment Represents 20 Kilometers
1 Segment Represents 20 Miles
1 Segment Represents 20 Kilometers

ATLANTIC OCEAN

GULF OF MEXICO

© 1998 GeoSystems Global Corp.

FORT MYERS–CAPE CORAL

GULF OF MEXICO

Quick Reference Index

For index to counties and places see pg. 135

Altamonte Sprs. ...K-1
Bayonet Point K-1
Belle Glade Q-2
Boca Raton Q-2
Boynton Beach Q-2
Bradenton N-1
Brandon L-1
Cape Coral Q-1
Carol City R-2
Casselberry K-1
Clearwater L-1
Cocoa K-1
Coral Gables S-2
Coral Springs R-2
Cutler Ridge S-2
Davie R-2
Deerfield Beach ...R-2
Delray Beach Q-2
Dunedin L-1
East Naples R-1
Fort Lauderdale ...R-2
Fort Myers Q-1
Fort Pierce N-2
Greenacres Q-2
Hallandale R-2
Hialeah S-2
Holiday L-1
Hollywood R-2
Homestead T-2
Jupiter P-2
Kendall S-2
Key West V-1
Kissimmee K-1
Lake Worth Q-2
Lakeland L-1
Largo M-1
Leisure City T-2
Margate R-2
Melbourne L-1
Merritt Island K-1
Miami S-2
Miami Beach S-2
Miramar R-2
Naples R-1
N. Fort Myers Q-1
N. Miami S-2
N. Miami Beach ...R-2
Orlando K-1
Palm Bay L-1
Palm Harbor L-1
Pinellas Park M-1
Plant City L-1
Plantation R-2
Pompano Beach ..R-2
Port Charlotte P-1
Port St. Lucie P-2
Riviera Beach......P-2
Rockledge K-1
St. Petersburg ...M-1
Sarasota N-1
Spring Hill K-1
Tampa L-1
Tarpon Springs ..L-1
Titusville K-1
Venice N-1
Vero Beach M-2
Wellington Q-2
W. Palm Beach ...P-2
Winter Haven L-1
Winter Park K-1
Winter Springs ..K-1

Selected Attractions

Biscayne N.P. T-2
Canaveral National
  Seashore J-1
Coral Castle T-2
Cypress Gardens L-1
Everglades N.P. ..T-1
Fort De Soto M-1
Kennedy Space
  Center K-1
Miami
  Seaquarium....S-2
Walt Disney
  World K-1

Adjacent States

Alabama ....
Florida - Northern..28
Georgia ....

1 Segment Represents 2 Miles (area map)

1 Segment Represents 2 Kilometers (area map)

1 Segment Represents 2 Miles (area map)

1 Segment Represents 2 Kilometers (area map)

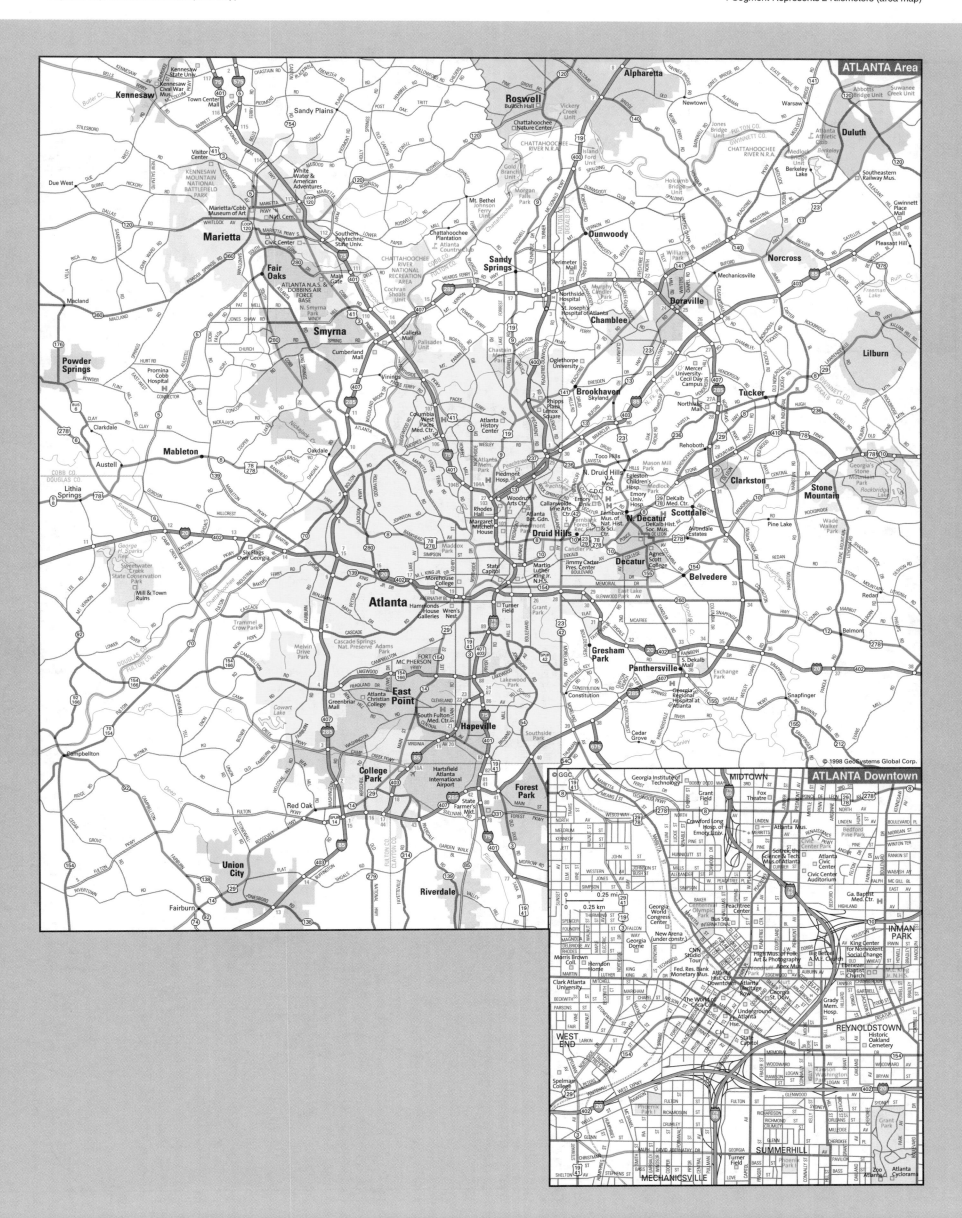

1 Segment Represents 20 Miles

1 Segment Represents 20 Kilometers

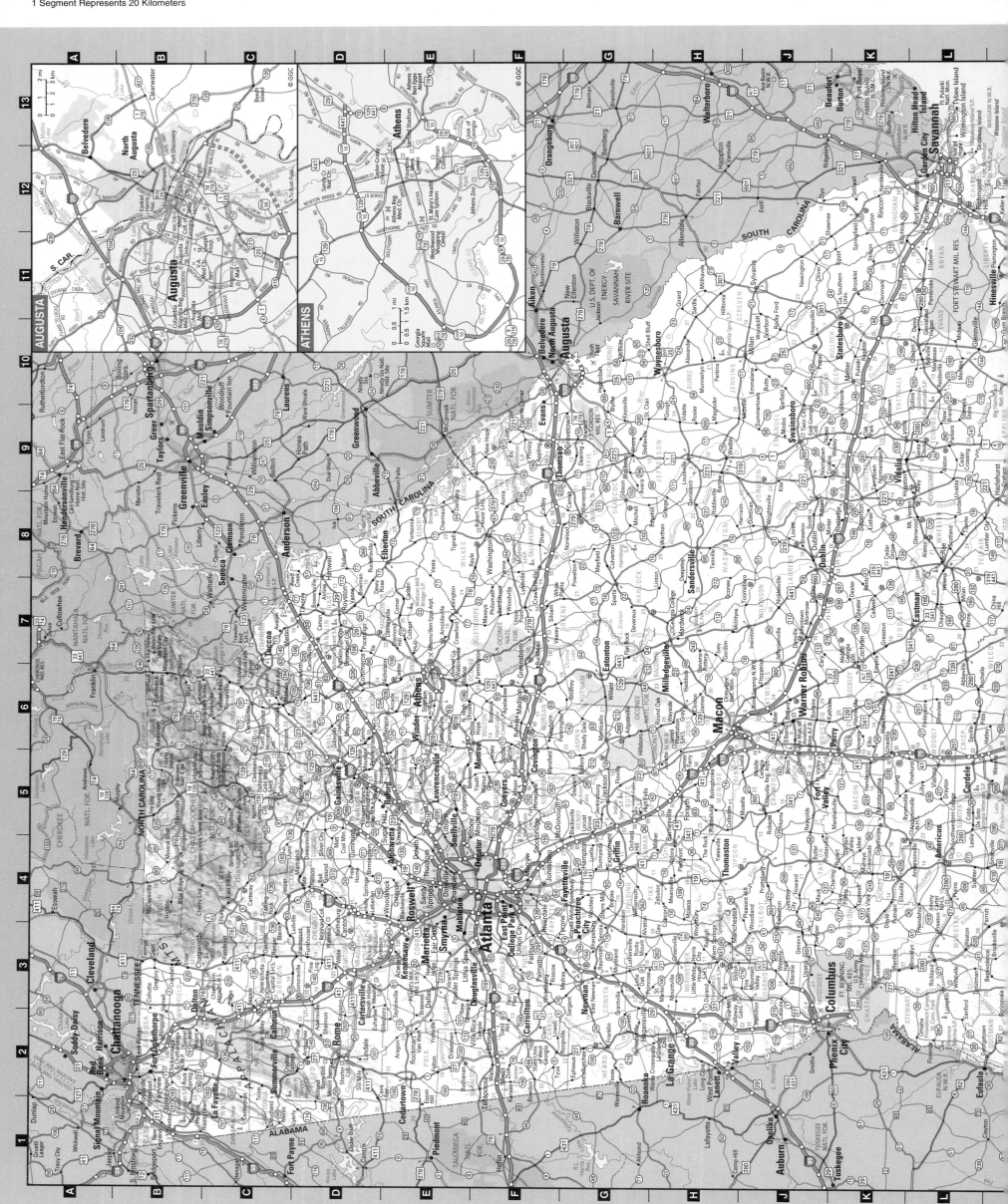

Columbus

100°
65°
32°
0°
J F M A M J J A S O N D

21
14
7
0

Savannah

100°
65°
32°
0°
J F M A M J J A S O N D

21
14
7
0

1 Segment Represents 20 Miles

1 Segment Represents 20 Kilometers

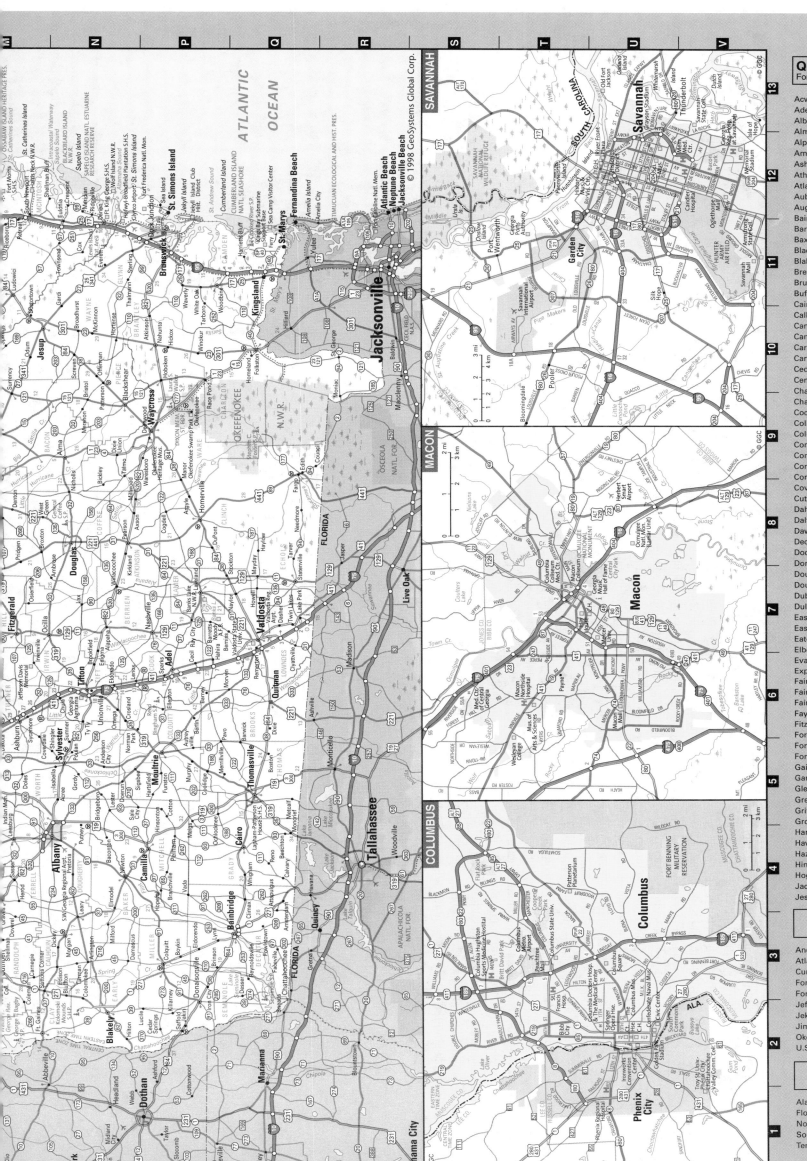

Quick Reference Index

For index to counties and places see page 135.

Acworth	E-3	Jonesboro	F-4
Adel	P-6	Kennesaw	E-3
Albany	N-4	Kingsland	Q-11
Alma	N-9	La Fayette	C-2
Alpharetta	E-4	La Grange	H-2
Americus	L-4	Lawrenceville	E-5
Ashburn	M-6	Lilburn	E-5
Athens	E-6	Lindale	D-2
Atlanta	E-4	Loganville	E-5
Auburn	E-5	Lyons	K-9
Augusta	F-10	Mableton	E-3
Bainbridge	Q-3	Macon	H-6
Barnesville	H-4	Madison	F-6
Baxley	M-9	Manchester	H-3
Blackshear	N-9	Marietta	E-3
Blakely	N-2	McDonough	F-4
Bremen	F-2	McRae	L-8
Brunswick	P-11	Metter	K-10
Buford	E-5	Milledgeville	H-7
Cairo	Q-4	Millen	J-10
Calhoun	C-3	Monroe	F-6
Camilla	P-4	Montezuma	K-5
Canton	D-4	Morrow	F-4
Carrollton	F-2	Moultrie	P-5
Cartersville	D-3	Nashville	P-7
Cedartown	E-2	Newnan	G-3
Centerville	J-6	Norcross	E-4
Chamblee	E-4	Ocilla	M-7
Chatsworth	C-3	Peachtree City	G-3
Cochran	K-6	Pelham	P-4
College Park	F-4	Perry	K-6
Columbus	K-2	Pooler	L-12
Commerce	D-6	Port Wentworth	L-12
Conyers	F-5	Powder Springs	E-3
Cordele	L-5	Putney	N-5
Cornelia	C-6	Quitman	Q-6
Covington	F-5	Richmond Hill	L-12
Cuthbert	M-3	Riverdale	F-4
Dahlonega	C-5	Rockmart	E-2
Dalton	B-2	Rome	D-2
Dawson	M-4	Rossville	B-2
Decatur	F-4	Roswell	E-4
Dock Junction	P-11	St. Marys	Q-11
Doraville	E-4	St.Simons Island	P-12
Douglas	N-8	Sandersville	H-8
Douglasville	E-3	Sandy Springs	E-4
Dublin	J-8	Savannah	L-12
Duluth	E-4	Skidaway Island	L-12
East Point	F-4	Smyrna	E-4
Eastman	L-7	Snellville	E-5
Eatonton	G-6	Statesboro	K-10
Elberton	E-8	Stockbridge	F-4
Evans	F-10	Stone Mountain	E-4
Experiment	G-4	Sugar Hill	E-5
Fair Oaks	E-3	Summerville	C-2
Fairburn	F-3	Swainsboro	J-9
Fairview	B-2	Sylvania	J-11
Fayetteville	G-4	Sylvester	N-5
Fitzgerald	M-7	Thomaston	H-4
Forsyth	H-5	Thomasville	Q-5
Fort Oglethorpe	B-2	Thomson	G-9
Fort Valley	J-5	Tifton	N-6
Gainesville	D-5	Toccoa	C-7
Garden City	L-12	Union City	F-3
Glennville	L-10	Valdosta	Q-7
Greensboro	F-7	Vidalia	K-9
Griffin	G-4	Villa Rica	F-3
Grovetown	G-9	Warner Robins	J-6
Hartwell	D-8	Washington	F-8
Hawkinsville	K-6	Waycross	N-9
Hazlehurst	M-8	Waynesboro	H-10
Hinesville	M-11	West Point	H-2
Hogansville	G-3	Wilmington Island	L-13
Jackson	G-5	Winder	E-6
Jesup	M-10	Woodstock	E-4

Selected Attractions

Andersonville National Historic Site	L-5
Atlanta Motor Speedway	G-4
Cumberland Island National Seashore	Q-12
Fort Frederica National Monument	P-12
Fort Pulaski National Monument	L-13
Jefferson Davis Memorial	M-6
Jekyll Island Club Historic District	P-12
Jimmy Carter National Historic Site	L-4
Okefenokee Swamp Park	P-9
U.S. Army Infantry Museum	K-3

Adjacent States

Alabama	4
Florida	26 & 28
North Carolina	82
South Carolina	100
Tennessee	102

© 1998 GeoSystems Global Corp.

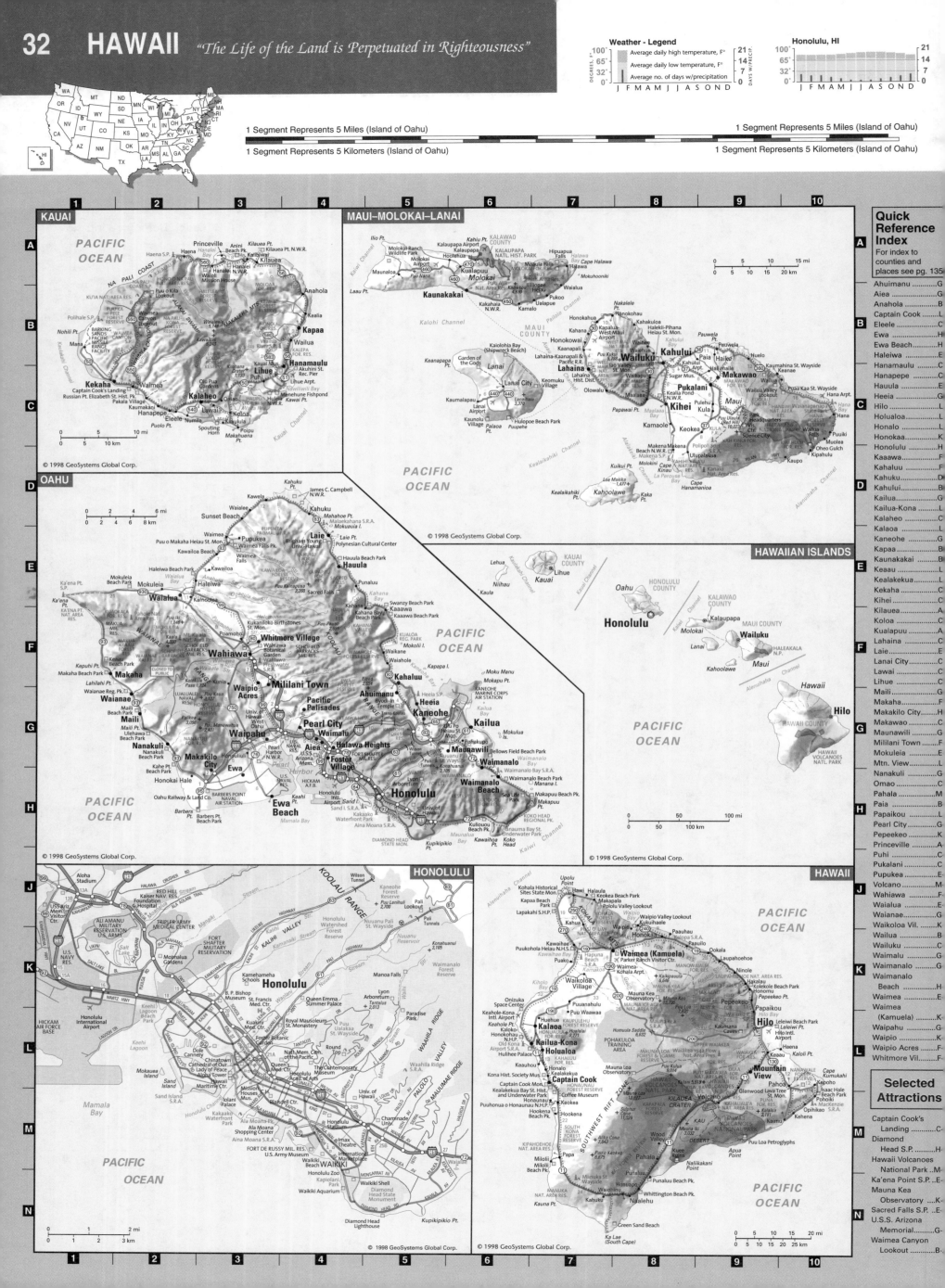

Weather - Legend

Honolulu, HI

1 Segment Represents 5 Miles (Island of Oahu)

1 Segment Represents 5 Kilometers (Island of Oahu)

KAUAI

MAUI–MOLOKAI–LANAI

OAHU

HAWAIIAN ISLANDS

HONOLULU

HAWAII

© 1998 GeoSystems Global Corp.

Quick Reference Index

For index to counties and places see pg. 135

Ahuimanu ....G
Aiea ....G
Anahola ....B
Captain Cook L
Eleele C
Ewa ....H
Ewa Beach ....H
Haleiwa ....E
Hanamaulu C
Hanapepe C
Hauula ....E
Heeia ....G
Hilo L
Holualoa L
Honalo L
Honokaa ....K
Honolulu ....H
Kaaawa ....G
Kahaluu ....G
Kahuku ....D
Kahului C
Kailua ....G
Kailua-Kona L
Kalaheo C
Kalaoa ....K
Kaneohe ....G
Kapaa ....B
Kaunakakai ....B
Keaau L
Kealakekua L
Kekaha C
Kihei C
Kilauea ....A
Koloa C
Kualapuu ....B
Lahaina C
Laie ....E
Lanai City C
Lawai C
Lihue C
Maili ....G
Makaha ....F
Makakilo City ....H
Makawao C
Maunawili ....G
Mililani Town ....F
Mokuleia ....E
Mtn. View L
Nanakuli ....G
Omao C
Pahala ....M
Paia C
Papaikou L
Pearl City ....H
Pepeekeo L
Princeville ....A
Puhi C
Pukalani C
Pupukea ....E
Volcano ....M
Wahiawa ....F
Waialua ....B
Waianae ....G
Waikoloa Vil. ....K
Wailua ....B
Wailuku C
Waimalu ....G
Waimanalo ....G
Waimanalo
   Beach ....G
Waimea ....B
Waimea
   (Kamuela) ....K
Waipahu ....H
Waipio ....K
Waipio Acres ....F
Whitmore Vil. ....F

Selected Attractions

Captain Cook's
   Landing L
Diamond
   Head S.P. ....M
Hawaii Volcanoes
   National Park ..M
Ka'ena Point S.P. ..E
Mauna Kea
   Observatory ...K
Sacred Falls S.P. ..E
U.S.S. Arizona
   Memorial..........G
Waimea Canyon
   Lookout ....B

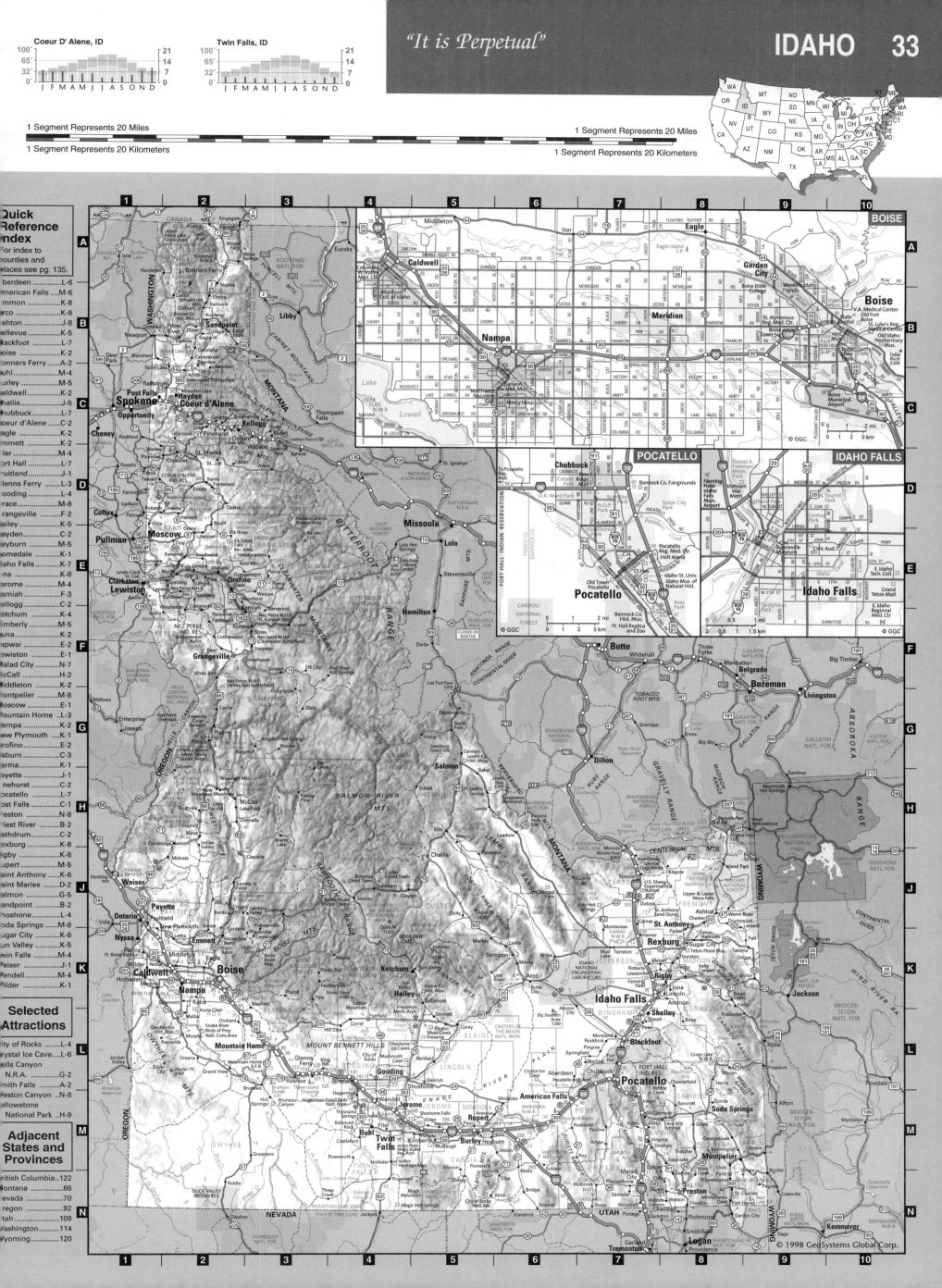

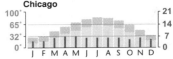

Weather - Legend

Chicago

1 Segment Represents 20 Miles

1 Segment Represents 20 Kilometers

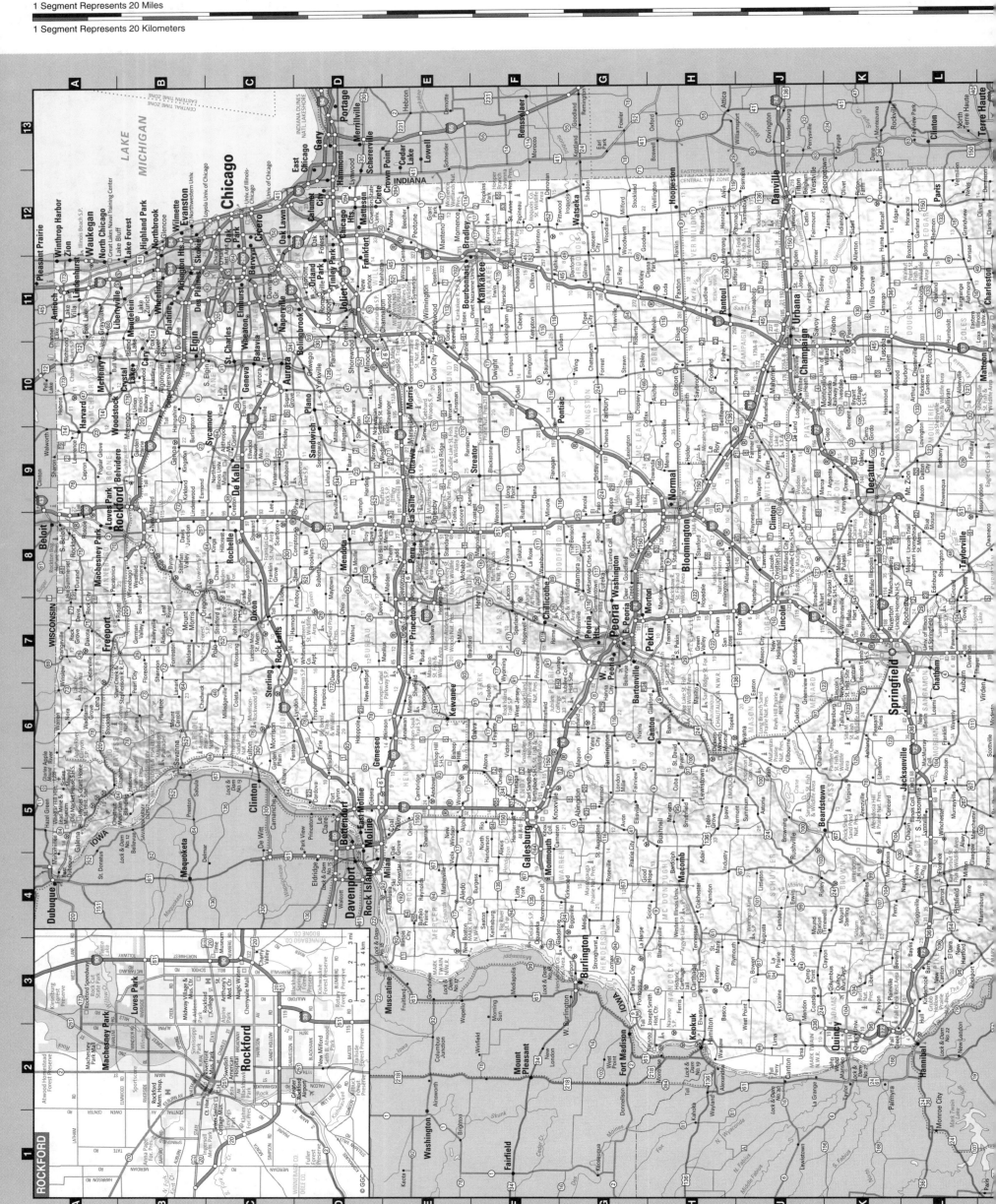

ROCKFORD

Peoria

Springfield

1 Segment Represents 20 Miles

1 Segment Represents 20 Kilometers

© 1996 GeoSystems Global Corp.

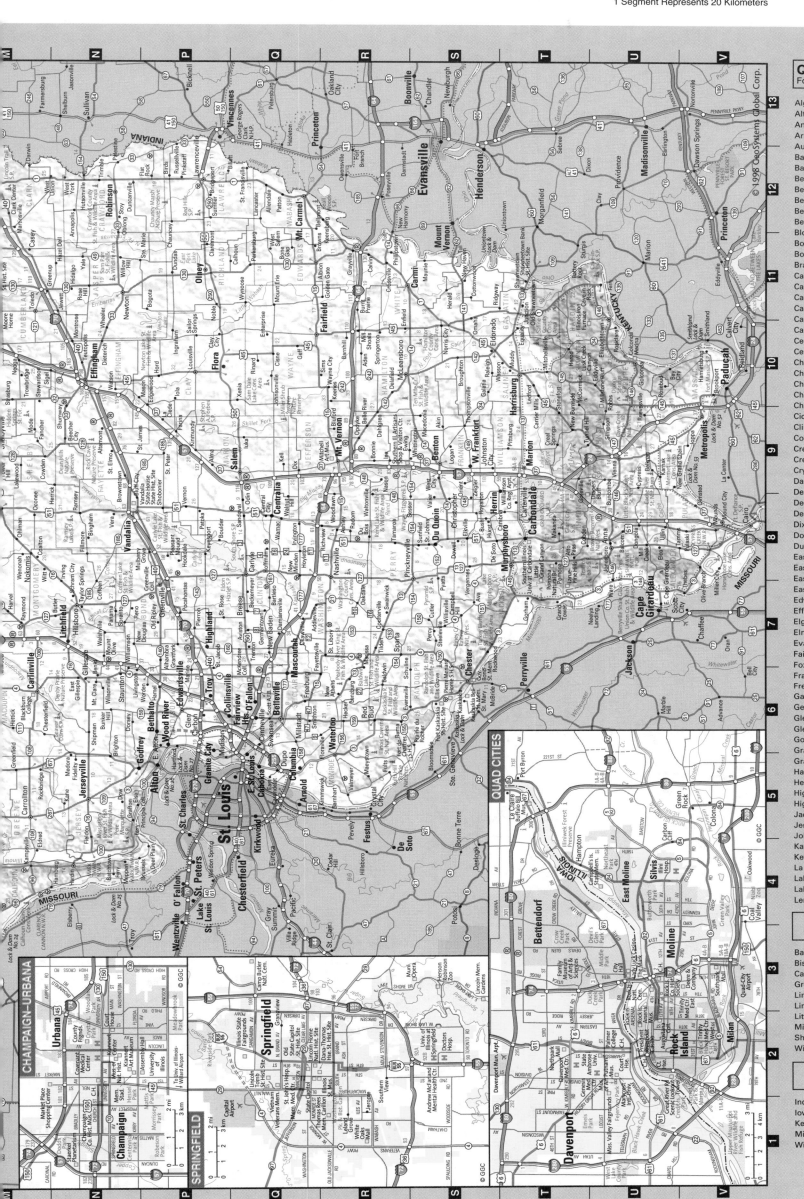

Quick Reference Index

For index to counties and places see page 135.

Algonquin B-10	Libertyville B-11
Alton P-5	Lincoln J-8
Antioch A-11	Lindenhurst A-11
Arlington Heights ...B-11	Litchfield N-7
Aurora C-10	Lockport D-11
Bartonville G-7	Loves Park A-8
Batavia C-10	Lynwood D-12
Belleville..................Q-6	Machesney Park A-8
Belvidere B-9	Macomb H-4
Benton T-9	Marion T-9
Berwyn C-12	Matteson D-12
Bethalto P-6	Mattoon M-10
Bloomington H-9	McHenry A-10
Bolingbrook D-11	Mendota D-8
Bourbonnais E-11	Metropolis V-9
Bradley E-11	Moline D-5
Cahokia Q-5	Monmouth F-4
Calumet City C-12	Morris E-10
Canton H-6	Morton G-7
Carbondale T-8	Mount Carmel Q-12
Carpentersville........B-10	Mount Vernon R-9
Cary B-10	Mundelein B-11
Centralia Q-8	Murphysboro T-8
Centreville Q-6	Naperville C-11
Champaign J-11	New Lenox D-11
Charleston M-11	Normal H-9
Chester S-6	North Chicago A-11
Chicago....................C-12	Northbrook B-12
Chicago Heights D-12	Oak Forest D-12
Cicero C-12	Oak Lawn C-12
Clinton J-9	Oak Park C-12
Collinsville Q-6	O'Fallon Q-6
Crest Hill D-11	Olney P-11
Crete D-12	Orland Park D-11
Crystal Lake B-10	Ottawa E-9
Danville J-12	Palatine B-11
De Kalb C-9	Paris L-12
Decatur K-9	Pekin H-7
Des Plaines B-11	Peoria G-7
Dixon C-7	Peoria Heights G-7
Downers Grove C-11	Peru E-8
Du Quoin S-8	Pontiac F-9
East Alton P-6	Princeton E-7
East Moline D-5	Quincy K-2
East Peoria G-7	Rantoul H-11
East Saint Louis Q-5	Robinson N-12
Edwardsville P-6	Rochelle C-8
Effingham N-10	Rock Falls C-7
Elgin B-10	Rock Island D-4
Elmhurst C-11	Rockford B-8
Evanston B-12	Romeoville D-11
Fairview Heights Q-6	Saint Charles C-10
Fox Lake A-11	Salem Q-9
Frankfort D-11	Shorewood D-11
Freeport B-7	Skokie B-12
Galesburg F-5	South Elgin C-10
Geneva C-10	Springfield K-7
Glen Carbon P-6	Sterling C-7
Glencoe B-12	Streator F-9
Godfrey P-5	Swansea Q-6
Granite City P-6	Sycamore C-9
Grayslake A-11	Taylorville L-8
Harrisburg T-10	Tinley Park D-12
Herrin T-9	Urbana J-11
Highland P-7	Vandalia N-8
Highland Park B-12	Washington G-7
Jacksonville L-5	Waukegan A-11
Jerseyville N-5	West Frankfort S-9
Joliet D-11	Wheaton C-11
Kankakee F-11	Wheeling B-11
Kewanee E-6	Wilmette B-12
La Salle E-8	Winthrop Harbor A-11
Lake Forest B-11	Wood River P-6
Lake Zurich B-11	Woodstock A-10
Lemont D-11	Zion A-11

Selected Attractions

Battery Rock..	U-11
Bishop Hill State Historical Site	E-6
Carl Sandburg Birthplace State Historic Site	F-5
Great Lakes Naval Training Center	A-11
Lincoln Home National Historic Site	K-7
Lincoln Log Cabin State Historic Site	M-11
Little Grand Canyon..	T-8
Mitchell Art Museum	E-8
Shawneetown Bank State Historic Site	T-11
Wild Bill Hickok State Memorial..................................	E-8

Adjacent States

Indiana	38
Iowa	40
Kentucky	44
Missouri	64
Wisconsin	118

1 Segment Represents 4 Miles (area map)

1 Segment Represents 4 Kilometers (area map)

CHICAGO Area

LAKE MICHIGAN

© GeoSystems Global Corp.

1 Segment Represents 4 Miles (area map)

1 Segment Represents 4 Kilometers (area map)

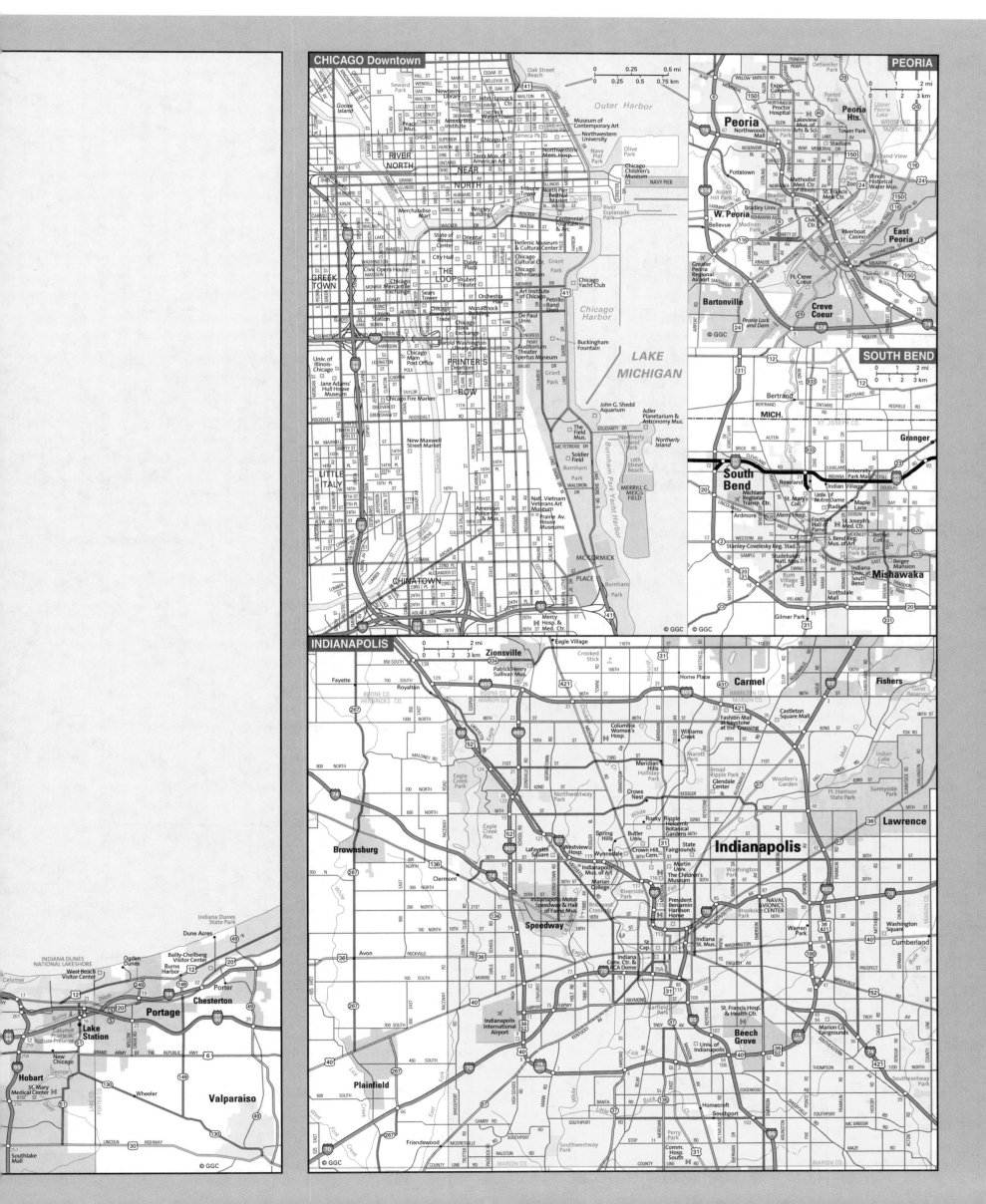

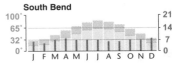

Weather - Legend

South Bend

1 Segment Represents 20 Miles

1 Segment Represents 20 Kilometers

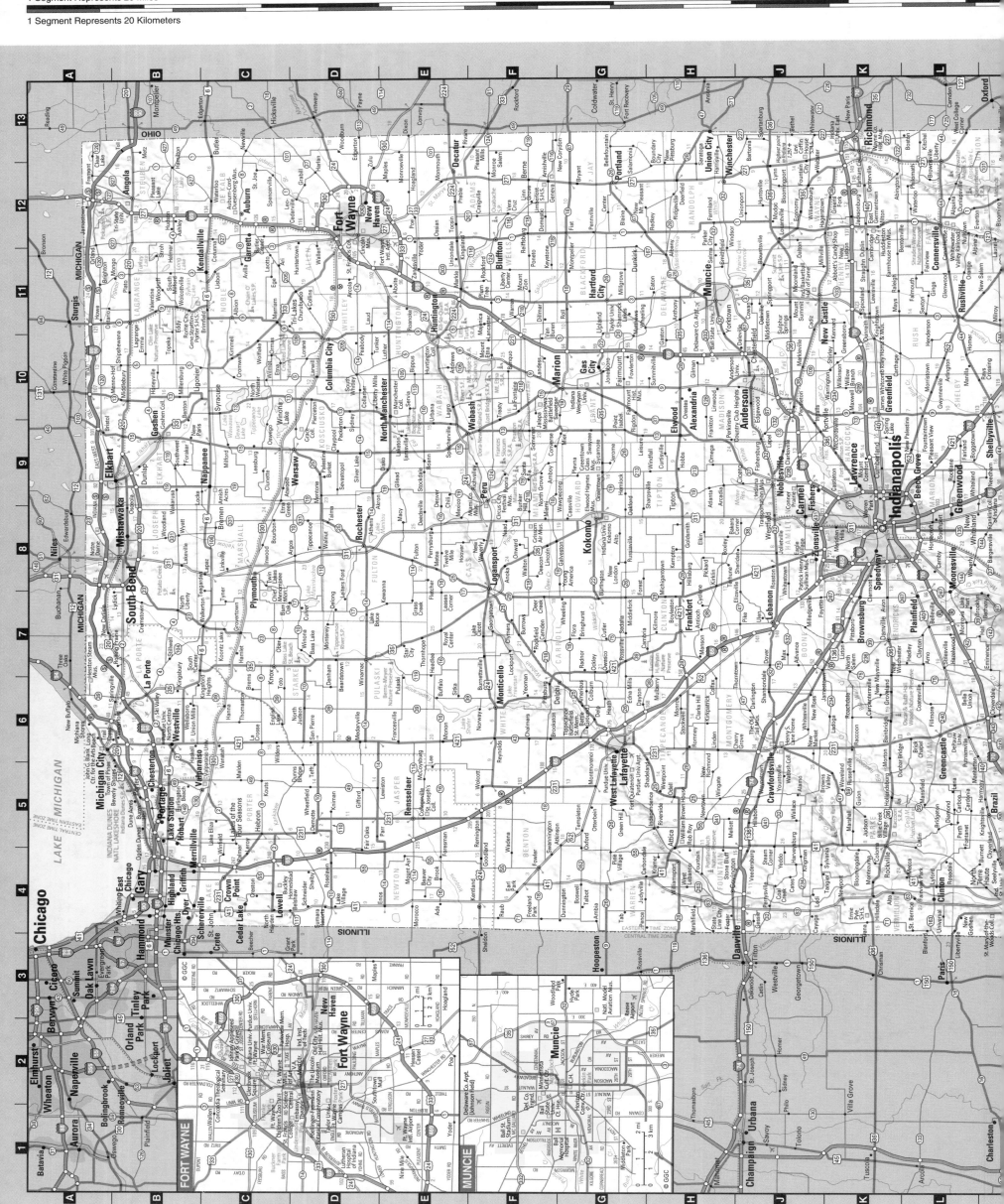

Indianapolis

Evansville

1 Segment Represents 20 Miles

1 Segment Represents 20 Kilometers

Quick Reference Index

For index to counties and places see page 136.

Alexandria	H-10	Lafayette	G-6
Anderson	J-10	Lake Station	B-5
Angola	B-12	Lakes of the Four	
Attica	H-5	Seasons	C-5
Auburn	C-12	Lawrence	K-9
Aurora	P-12	Lawrenceburg	N-13
Austin	Q-9	Lebanon	J-7
Batesville	N-11	Ligonier	B-10
Bedford	Q-7	Linton	P-5
Beech Grove	L-8	Logansport	F-8
Berne	F-12	Lowell	B-5
Bicknell	Q-4	Madison	Q-11
Bloomington	N-7	Marion	G-10
Bluffton	F-12	Martinsville	M-7
Boonville	T-4	Merrillville	B-4
Brazil	M-5	Michigan City	A-6
Bremen	C-8	Mishawaka	B-8
Bright	N-13	Mitchell	Q-7
Brownsburg	K-7	Monticello	F-6
Brownstown	Q-9	Mooresville	L-8
Carmel	J-8	Mount Vernon	U-2
Cedar Lake	C-4	Muncie	H-11
Chandler	T-4	Munster	B-4
Charlestown	R-10	Nappanee	C-9
Chesterton	B-5	New Albany	S-9
Cicero	J-9	New Castle	J-11
Clarksville	S-10	New Haven	D-12
Clinton	L-4	New Whiteland	L-8
Columbia City	D-10	Newburgh	U-4
Columbus	N-9	Noblesville	J-9
Connersville	L-12	North Manchester	E-10
Covington	H-4	North Terre Haute	M-4
Crawfordsville	J-6	North Vernon	P-10
Crown Point	C-4	Oakland City	S-4
Cumberland	K-9	Paoli	R-7
Danville	K-7	Peru	F-9
Decatur	F-12	Plainfield	L-7
Dunlap	B-9	Plymouth	C-8
Dyer	B-4	Portage	B-5
East Chicago	B-4	Porter	B-5
Edinburgh	M-9	Portland	G-12
Elkhart	B-9	Princeton	S-3
Ellettsville	N-7	Rensselaer	E-5
Elwood	H-9	Richmond	K-13
Evansville	U-3	Rochester	D-8
Fairmount	G-10	Rushville	L-11
Fishers	J-9	Saint John	C-4
Fort Wayne	D-12	Salem	R-8
Frankfort	H-7	Schererville	B-4
Franklin	M-9	Scottsburg	Q-10
Garrett	C-12	Sellersburg	S-10
Gary	B-4	Seymour	P-9
Gas City	G-10	Shelbyville	M-10
Goshen	B-9	South Bend	B-8
Greencastle	L-6	Speedway	K-8
Greendale	N-13	Sullivan	P-4
Greenfield	K-10	Tell City	U-6
Greensburg	M-11	Terre Haute	M-4
Greenwood	L-8	Tipton	H-9
Griffith	B-4	Tri-Lakes	C-11
Hammond	B-4	Union City	H-13
Hanover	Q-11	Upland	G-10
Hartford City	G-11	Valparaiso	B-5
Hebron	C-5	Vincennes	Q-3
Highland	B-4	Wabash	E-9
Hobart	B-5	Warsaw	D-9
Huntingburg	S-5	Washington	R-5
Huntington	E-10	West Lafayette	G-6
Indianapolis	K-8	Westfield	J-8
Jasper	S-5	Westville	B-6
Jeffersonville	S-10	Whiting	B-4
Kendallville	C-11	Winchester	H-12
Knox	C-7	Winona Lake	D-9
Kokomo	G-8	Yorktown	H-10
La Porte	B-6	Zionsville	J-8

Selected Attractions

George Rogers Clark National Historic Park	R-3
I.M. Pei Library	N-9
Indiana Basketball Hall of Fame	J-11
Indiana Dunes National Lakeshore	A-5
Indiana Railway Museum	R-6
Lincoln Boyhood National Memorial	T-5
Pigeon Roost State Historic Site	R-10
The Old Jail Museum	J-6
Tippecanoe Battlefield State Memorial	G-6
Wyandotte Caves	T-8

Adjacent States

Illinois	34
Kentucky	44
Michigan	56
Ohio	86 & 88

© 1998 GeoSystems Global Corp.

"Our Liberties We Prize and Our Rights We Will Maintain"

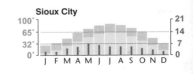

"Our Liberties We Prize and Our Rights We Will Maintain"

Des Moines

Cedar Rapids

1 Segment Represents 20 Miles

1 Segment Represents 20 Kilometers

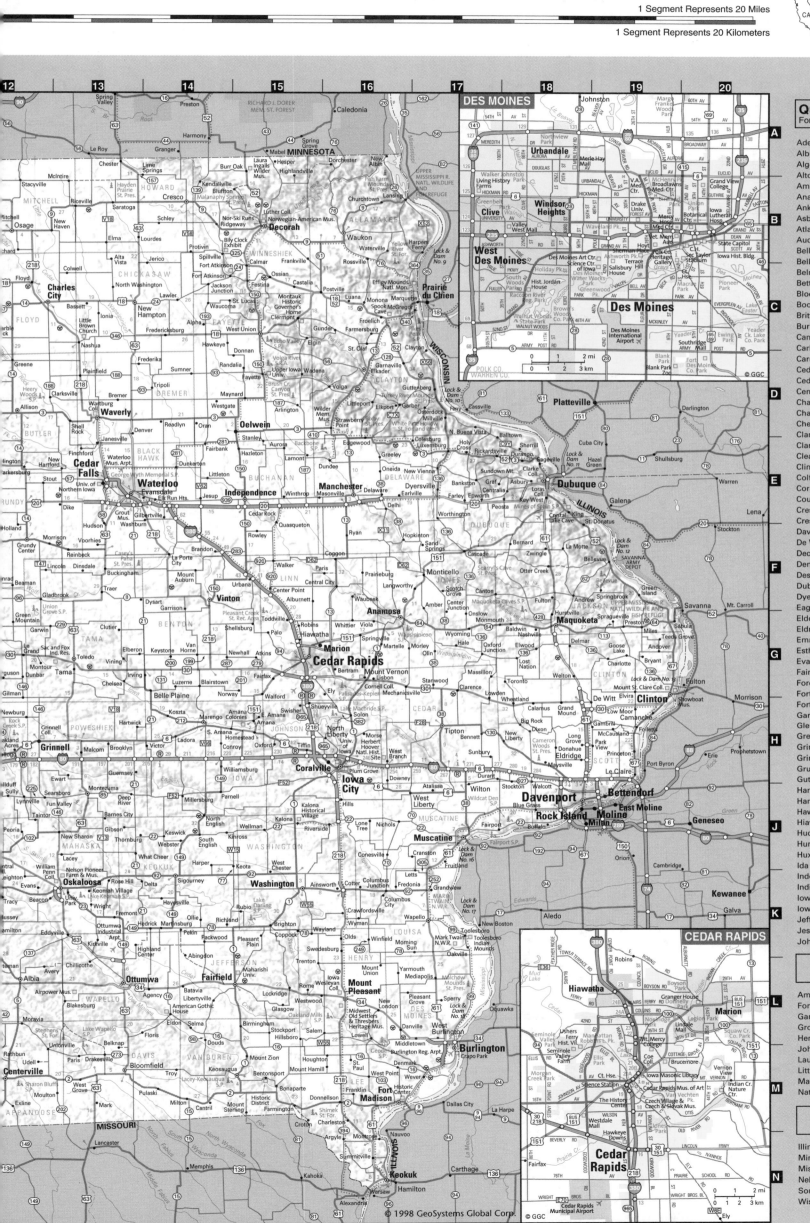

Quick Reference Index

For index to counties and places see page 136.

Adel	H-8	Keokuk	N-16
Albia	L-12	Knoxville	K-11
Algona	C-8	La Porte City	F-14
Altoona	H-10	Lake Mills	B-10
Ames	G-10	Lamoni	M-9
Anamosa	G-16	Le Claire	H-19
Ankeny	H-10	Le Mars	D-2
Asbury	E-18	Leon	M-9
Atlantic	J-6	Madrid	G-9
Audubon	H-6	Manchester	E-16
Belle Plaine	H-14	Maquoketa	G-18
Bellevue	F-19	Marengo	H-14
Belmond	D-10	Marion	G-15
Bettendorf	J-19	Marshalltown	G-12
Bloomfield	M-13	Mason City	C-11
Boone	G-9	Milford	B-5
Britt	C-9	Missouri Valley	J-3
Burlington	M-17	Monticello	F-17
Camanche	H-19	Mount Pleasant	L-16
Carlisle	J-10	Mount Vernon	G-16
Carroll	G-6	Muscatine	J-17
Cedar Falls	E-13	Nevada	G-10
Cedar Rapids	G-15	New Hampton	C-13
Centerville	M-12	Newton	H-11
Chariton	L-11	North Liberty	H-16
Charles City	C-12	Norwalk	J-9
Cherokee	D-4	Oelwein	D-15
Clarinda	M-5	Onawa	G-3
Clarion	D-9	Orange City	C-3
Clear Lake	C-10	Osage	B-12
Clinton	G-19	Osceola	L-9
Colfax	H-11	Oskaloosa	K-13
Coralville	H-16	Ottumwa	L-13
Council Bluffs	K-3	Park View	H-19
Cresco	B-14	Pella	J-12
Creston	L-7	Perry	H-8
Davenport	J-18	Pleasant Hill	J-10
De Witt	H-19	Pocahontas	D-7
Decorah	B-15	Red Oak	L-5
Denison	G-5	Rock Rapids	A-3
Des Moines	J-10	Rock Valley	B-2
Dubuque	E-18	Rockwell City	F-7
Dyersville	E-17	Sac City	E-6
Eagle Grove	D-9	Saylorville	H-10
Eldora	F-11	Sergeant Bluff	E-2
Eldridge	H-18	Sheldon	B-3
Emmetsburg	C-7	Shenandoah	M-5
Estherville	B-6	Sibley	B-4
Evansdale	E-14	Sigourney	K-14
Fairfield	L-15	Sioux Center	C-3
Forest City	B-10	Sioux City	E-2
Fort Dodge	E-8	Spencer	C-5
Fort Madison	M-16	Spirit Lake	B-6
Garner	C-10	Storm Lake	E-5
Glenwood	L-3	Story City	F-10
Greenfield	K-7	Sumner	D-14
Grimes	H-9	Tama	G-13
Grinnell	H-12	Tipton	H-17
Grundy Center	F-12	Toledo	G-13
Guttenberg	D-17	Urbandale	J-9
Hampton	D-11	Vinton	F-14
Harlan	H-5	Wapello	K-17
Hawarden	C-2	Washington	K-15
Hiawatha	G-15	Waterloo	E-13
Hudson	E-13	Waukee	J-9
Humboldt	D-8	Waukon	B-16
Huxley	G-10	Waverly	D-13
Ida Grove	F-4	Webster City	E-9
Independence	E-15	West Burlington	L-17
Indianola	J-10	West Des Moines	J-9
Iowa City	H-16	West Liberty	J-17
Iowa Falls	E-11	West Union	C-15
Jefferson	G-7	Williamsburg	H-14
Jesup	E-14	Wilton	J-17
Johnston	H-9	Winterset	K-8

Selected Attractions

American Gothic House	L-14
Fort Dodge Historic Museum	E-8
Gardner Cabin	B-5
Grotto of the Redemption	D-7
Herbert Hoover National Historic Site	H-16
John Wayne Birthplace	K-8
Laura Ingalls Wilder Museum	A-15
Little Brown Church	C-13
Mamie Doud Eisenhower Birthplace	F-9
National Balloon Museum	J-10

Adjacent States

Illinois	34
Minnesota	60
Missouri	64
Nebraska	68
South Dakota	101
Wisconsin	118

© 1998 GeoSystems Global Corp.

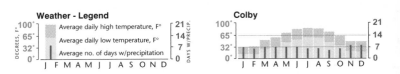

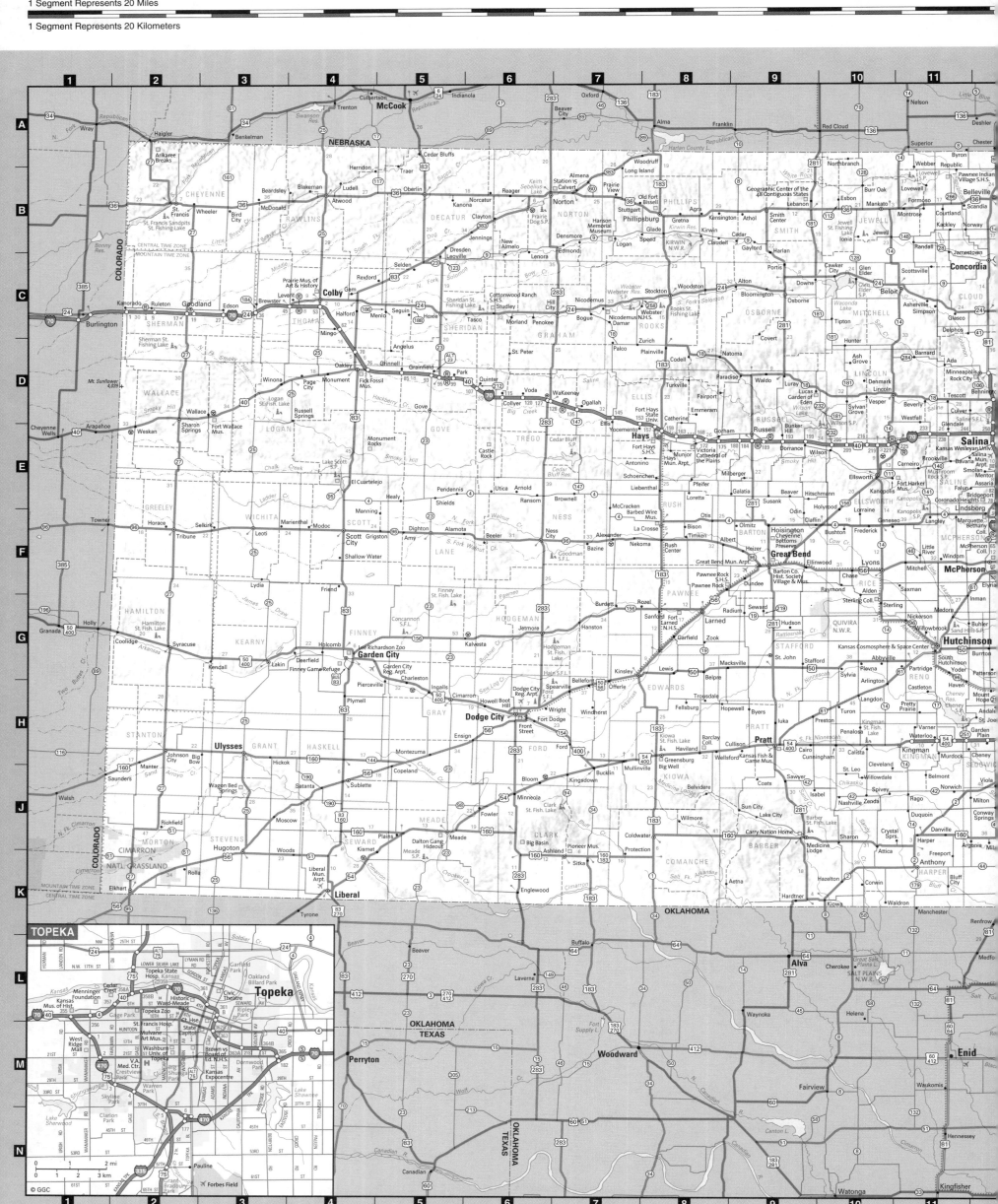

Wichita — climate chart (100°, 65°, 32°, 0° / J F M A M J J A S O N D) scale 21/14/7/0

Topeka — climate chart (100°, 65°, 32°, 0° / J F M A M J J A S O N D) scale 21/14/7/0

1 Segment Represents 20 Miles

1 Segment Represents 20 Kilometers

Quick Reference Index
For index to counties and places see page 136.

Abilene E-13	Kingman................H-11
Andover H-13	Kinsley G-7
Anthony K-11	La Crosse F-8
Arkansas City K-13	Lakin G-3
Arma H-18	Lansing C-18
Atchison C-17	Larned G-8
Atwood B-4	Lawrence D-17
Augusta H-13	Leavenworth C-18
Baldwin City E-17	Lenexa D-18
Basehor D-18	Leoti F-3
Baxter Springs K-18	Liberal K-4
Belle Plaine J-13	Lincoln D-10
Belleville B-12	Lindsborg F-12
Beloit C-11	Louisburg E-18
Bonner Springs D-18	Lyons F-10
Burlington G-16	Maize H-12
Caney K-16	Manhattan D-14
Carbondale E-16	Marion F-13
Chanute H-17	Marysville B-14
Cheney H-11	McPherson F-12
Cherryvale J-17	Meade J-5
Cimarron H-5	Medicine Lodge ...J-9
Clay Center C-13	Minneapolis D-12
Clearwater J-12	Moundridge G-12
Coffeyville K-16	Mulvane J-13
Colby C-4	Neodesha J-16
Columbus K-18	Ness City F-6
Concordia C-12	Newton G-12
Conway Springs ...J-12	Norton B-6
Council Grove E-14	Oakley D-4
De Soto D-18	Oberlin B-5
Derby J-13	Ogden D-14
Dighton F-5	Olathe D-18
Dodge City H-6	Osage City E-16
Douglass J-13	Osawatomie F-18
El Dorado H-14	Osborne C-9
Elkhart K-2	Oswego K-18
Ellinwood F-9	Ottawa E-17
Ellis D-7	Overland Park D-18
Ellsworth E-10	Paola E-18
Emporia F-15	Park City H-13
Eudora D-17	Parsons J-17
Eureka H-15	Phillipsburg B-8
Fort Scott H-18	Pittsburg J-18
Fredonia J-16	Plainville D-8
Frontenac J-19	Pratt H-9
Galena K-19	Rose Hill H-13
Garden City G-4	Russell E-9
Gardner E-18	Sabetha B-16
Garnett F-17	St.Francis B-2
Girard H-18	St. Marys D-15
Goddard H-12	Salina E-12
Goodland C-2	Scott City F-4
Great Bend F-9	Sedgwick G-12
Greensburg H-8	Seneca B-15
Halstead G-12	Shawnee D-18
Harper J-11	Silver Lake D-16
Hays E-8	Smith Center B-9
Haysville H-12	South Hutchinson .G-11
Herington E-13	Spring Hill E-18
Hesston G-12	Sterling G-10
Hiawatha B-16	Stockton C-8
Hill City C-7	Sublette J-4
Hillsboro F-13	Syracuse G-2
Hoisington F-9	Tonganoxie D-17
Holcomb G-4	Topeka D-16
Holton C-16	Ulysses H-3
Horton B-16	Valley Center H-12
Hugoton J-3	WaKeeney D-6
Humboldt H-17	Wamego D-15
Hutchinson G-11	Wellington J-12
Independence J-16	Wellsville E-17
Iola G-17	Wichita H-12
Junction City D-14	Winfield J-13
Kansas City D-18	Yates Center........G-16

Selected Attractions

Barbed Wire Museum F-8
Boot Hill H-6
Cathedral of the Plains E-8
Fort Larned National Historic Site G-8
Fort Scott National Historic Site G-19
International Forest of Friendship C-18
Kaw Mission State Historic Site E-14
Lee Richardson Zoo G-4
Little House on the Prairie K-16
Nicodemus National Historic Site C-7

Adjacent States

Colorado 20
Missouri 64
Nebraska 68
Oklahoma..90

© 1998 GeoSystems Global Corp.

"United We Stand, Divided We Fall"

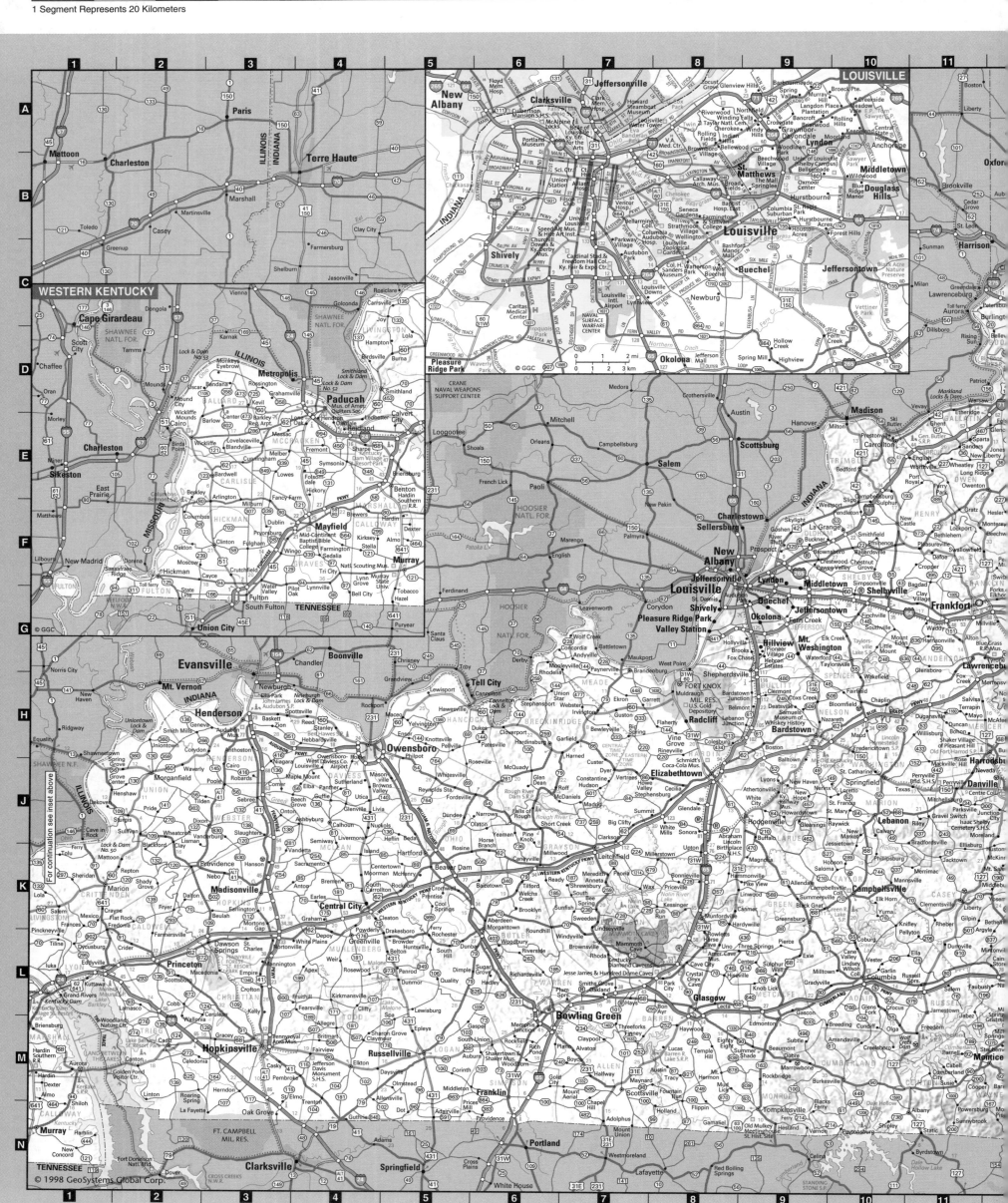

© 1998 GeoSystems Global Corp.

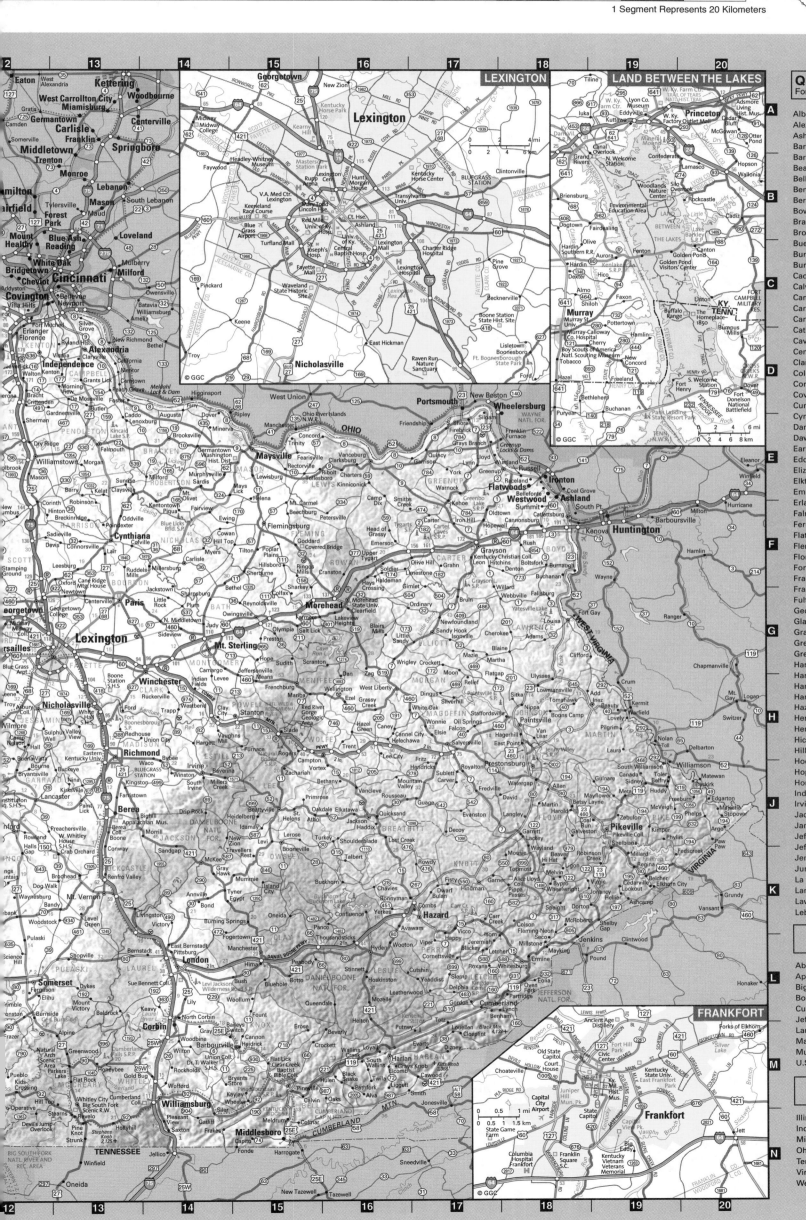

Louisville | Lexington (climate charts)

1 Segment Represents 20 Miles
1 Segment Represents 20 Kilometers

LEXINGTON • LAND BETWEEN THE LAKES • FRANKFORT (inset maps)

Quick Reference Index
For index to counties and places see page 136.

Albany N-11
Alexandria D-13
Ashland F-18
Barbourville M-15
Bardstown H-9
Beaver Dam K-5
Bellevue C-13
Benton E-5
Berea J-13
Bowling Green L-6
Brandenburg G-7
Brooks G-9
Buechel G-9
Burkesville M-10
Burlington C-12
Cadiz M-2
Calvert City E-5
Campbellsville K-10
Carlisle F-14
Carrollton E-10
Catlettsburg F-18
Cave City L-8
Central City L-3
Claryville D-13
Columbia L-10
Corbin M-14
Covington C-12
Cumberland L-17
Cynthiana F-13
Danville J-12
Dawson Springs ...L-3
Earlington K-3
Eddyville L-1
Elizabethtown J-8
Elkton M-4
Eminence F-10
Erlanger C-12
Falmouth E-13
Fern Creek G-9
Flatwoods F-18
Flemingsburg F-15
Florence D-12
Fort Mitchell C-12
Frankfort G-11
Franklin M-6
Fulton G-3
Georgetown G-12
Glasgow L-8
Grayson F-17
Greensburg K-9
Greenville L-4
Hardinsburg H-6
Harlan M-16
Harrodsburg H-12
Hartford J-5
Hazard K-17
Henderson H-3
Hendron E-4
Hickman F-2
Hillview G-9
Hodgenville J-9
Hopkinsville M-3
Horse Cave L-8
Independence D-12
Irvine J-14
Jackson J-16
Jamestown L-11
Jeffersontown G-9
Jeffersonville G-15
Jenkins L-18
Junction City J-12
La Grange F-10
Lancaster J-12
Lawrenceburg G-11
Lebanon J-10

Lebanon Junction H-9
Ledbetter E-4
Leitchfield K-7
Lewisport H-5
Lexington G-12
Liberty K-11
London L-14
Louisa G-18
Louisville G-8
Lyndon F-9
Madisonville K-3
Marion K-1
Massac E-3
Mayfield F-4
Maysville E-15
Middlesboro N-15
Middletown G-9
Monticello M-12
Morehead G-16
Morganfield J-2
Morgantown K-6
Mount Sterling G-14
Mount Vernon K-13
Mount Washington ..G-9
Murray N-1
Newport C-13
Nicholasville H-12
Oak Grove N-3
Oakdale E-4
Okolona G-9
Olive Hill F-17
Owensboro H-5
Paducah D-4
Paintsville H-18
Paris G-13
Pikeville J-19
Pineville M-15
Pleasure Ridge Park ..G-8
Prestonsburg J-18
Princeton L-2
Prospect F-9
Providence K-2
Raceland E-18
Radcliff H-8
Reidland E-4
Richmond H-13
Russell E-18
Russell Springs L-11
Russellville M-5
Saint Dennis G-8
Salyersville H-17
Scottsville M-7
Shelbyville G-10
Shepherdsville G-9
Shively G-8
Somerset L-12
Springfield J-10
Stanford J-12
Stanton H-15
Sturgis J-2
Summit F-18
Tompkinsville N-9
Valley Station G-8
Vanceburg E-16
Versailles G-12
Villa Hills C-12
Vine Grove H-8
Walton D-12
West Liberty H-16
Westwood F-18
Whitesburg L-18
Williamsburg M-14
Williamstown E-12
Wilmore H-12
Winchester G-14

Selected Attractions

Abraham Lincoln Birthplace National Historic Site J-8
Appalachian Museum J-13
Big Bone Lick State Park D-12
Boone Station State Historic Site H-13
Cumberland Gap National Historic Park N-16
Jefferson Davis Monument State Historic Site .M-4
Land Between the Lakes M-1
Mammoth Cave National Park L-7
Museum of Whisky History H-9
U.S. Gold Depository H-8

Adjacent States

Illinois 34
Indiana 38
Missouri 64
Ohio ....86 & 88
Tennessee 102
Virginia 112
West Virginia 117

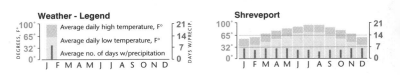

© 1998 GeoSystems Global Corp.

Baton Rouge

New Orleans

1 Segment Represents 20 Miles

1 Segment Represents 20 Kilometers

Quick Reference Index

For index to counties and places see page 137.

Abbeville	K-9	Lake Arthur	K-8
Alexandria	F-8	Lake Charles	K-6
Amelia	L-12	Lake Providence	B-12
Amite	H-14	Laplace	K-14
Arcadia	C-7	Larose	M-14
Avondale	L-15	Leesville	G-6
Baker	J-12	Lockport	L-14
Baldwin	L-11	Lutcher	K-13
Ball	F-9	Mamou	H-9
Bastrop	B-10	Mandeville	J-15
Baton Rouge	J-12	Mansfield	D-5
Bawcomville	C-9	Many	E-6
Bayou Cane	L-13	Marksville	G-9
Bayou Vista	L-12	Marrero	L-15
Belle Chasse	L-15	Mathews	L-14
Berwick	L-12	Meraux	L-15
Bogalusa	H-16	Metairie	K-15
Bossier City	C-5	Minden	B-6
Boutte	L-14	Monroe	C-9
Breaux Bridge	K-10	Morgan City	L-12
Broussard	K-10	Moss Bluff	J-7
Bunkie	G-9	Natchitoches	E-7
Carencro	J-10	New Iberia	K-10
Carlyss	K-6	New Llano	G-6
Chackbay	L-13	New Orleans	K-15
Chalmette	K-15	New Roads	H-11
Chauvin	M-14	Norco	K-14
Church Point	J-9	Oak Grove	B-12
Cottonport	G-10	Oakdale	H-8
Covington	J-15	Opelousas	J-9
Crowley	K-9	Patterson	L-12
Cut Off	M-14	Pierre Part	L-12
De Quincy	J-6	Pineville	F-9
De Ridder	H-6	Plaquemine	J-12
Delhi	C-11	Ponchatoula	J-14
Denham Springs	J-13	Port Allen	J-12
Des Allemands	K-14	Port Barre	J-10
Destrehan	K-14	Port Sulphur	M-16
Donaldsonville	K-13	Poydras	L-16
Dulac	M-13	Raceland	L-14
Eastwood	B-6	Rayne	K-9
Edgard	K-14	Rayville	C-10
Empire	M-16	Reserve	K-14
Erath	K-10	Ruston	C-8
Eunice	J-9	St. Gabriel	K-12
Farmerville	B-9	St. Martinville	K-10
Ferriday	E-11	St. Rose	K-14
Franklin	L-11	Schriever	L-13
Franklinton	H-15	Scott	K-9
Galliano	M-14	Seymourville	J-12
Garyville	K-14	Shreveport	C-5
Gonzales	K-13	Simmesport	G-10
Grambling	C-8	Slidell	K-16
Gramercy	K-13	Springhill	A-6
Gray	L-13	Sulphur	K-6
Greenwood	C-5	Sunset	J-9
Gretna	L-15	Swartz	B-10
Hahnville	K-14	Tallulah	C-12
Hammond	J-14	Terrytown	L-15
Haynesville	A-7	Thibodaux	L-13
Homer	B-7	Vidalia	F-11
Houma	M-13	Ville Platte	H-9
Iowa	K-7	Vinton	K-5
Jackson	H-12	Violet	L-15
Jeanerette	L-11	Vivian	A-5
Jena	E-9	Walker	J-13
Jennings	K-8	Welsh	K-7
Jonesboro	C-8	West Monroe	C-9
Jonesville	E-10	Westlake	K-6
Kaplan	K-9	Westminster	G-20
Kenner	K-15	Westwego	L-15
Kentwood	G-14	White Castle	K-12
Kinder	J-7	Winnfield	D-8
Lacombe	J-15	Winnsboro	D-11
Lafayette	K-10	Zachary	H-12

Selected Attractions

Antebellum Homes	H-10
Bayou Sauvage National Wildlife Refuge	K-16
Cane River Creole National Historic Park	F-7
DeQuincy Railroad Museum	J-6
Fort Polk Military Museum	G-7
Jean Lafitte National Historic Park & Preserve	L-15
Nibletts Bluff Park	K-5
Pontchartrain Causeway	K-15
Poverty Point National Monument	B-12
Shell Keys National Wildlife Refuge	M-10

Adjacent States

Arkansas	10
Mississippi	62
Texas	104 & 106

"I Direct"

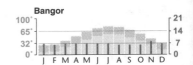

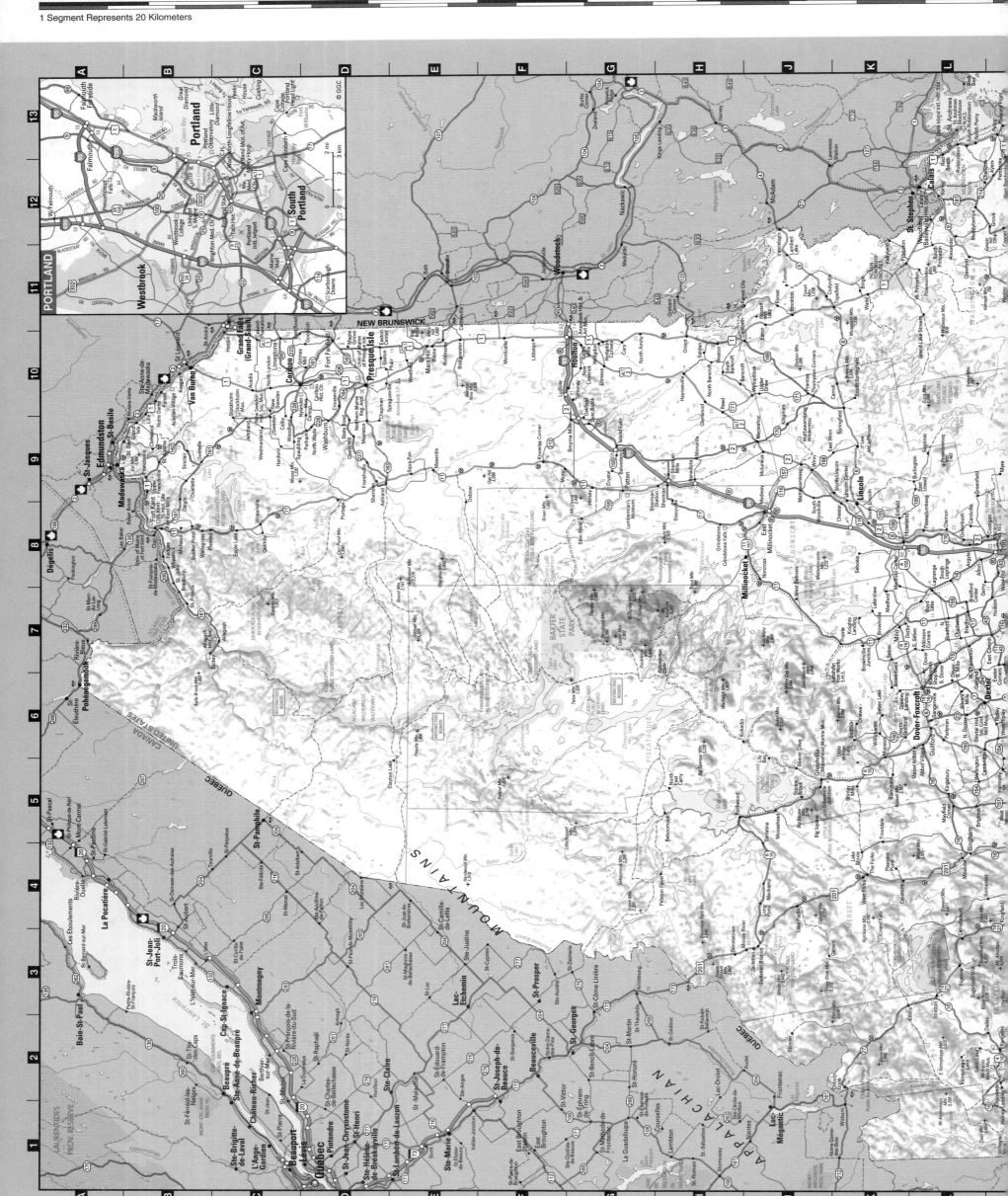

Portland

Presque Isle

1 Segment Represents 20 Miles

1 Segment Represents 20 Kilometers

© 1998 GeoSystems Global Corp.

ACADIA NATIONAL PARK

Quick Reference Index

For index to counties and places see page 137.

Selected Attractions

Adjacent States and Provinces

ATLANTIC OCEAN

Gulf of Maine

Casco Bay

NEW HAMPSHIRE

CRANBERRY ISLES

MOUNT DESERT ISLAND

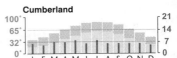

1 Segment Represents 10 Miles

1 Segment Represents 10 Kilometers

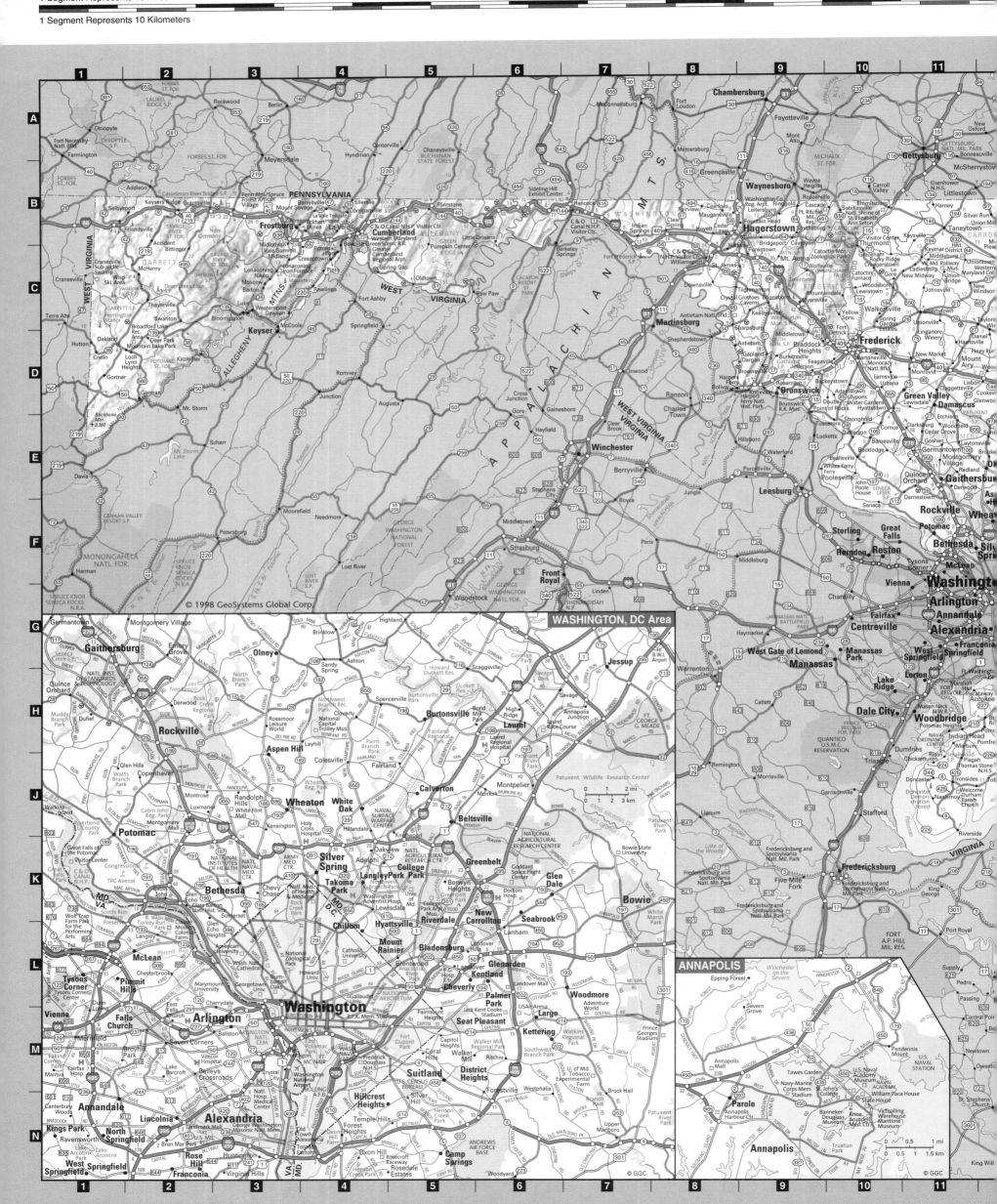

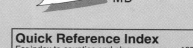

1 Segment Represents 10 Miles

1 Segment Represents 10 Kilometers

Quick Reference Index

For index to counties and places see page 137.

Place	Grid	Place	Grid
Aberdeen	C-15	Hyattsville	F-12
Accokeek	H-12	Indian Head	H-11
Annapolis	F-14	Jarrettsville	C-14
Arnold	F-14	Jessup	E-13
Aspen Hill	F-12	Joppatowne	D-15
Baltimore	D-13	La Plata	J-12
Bay Ridge	F-14	La Vale	B-4
Bel Air	C-15	Lake Shore	E-14
Beltsville	F-12	Laurel	F-13
Berlin	K-20	Lexington Park	K-14
Bethesda	F-11	Lochearn	D-13
Boonsboro	C-9	Londontown	F-14
Bowie	F-13	Lutherville	D-14
Bowleys Quarters	D-15	Manchester	B-12
Bowling Green	C-4	Marlton	G-13
Boxhill North	C-15	Marywood	C-15
Braddock Heights	D-9	Maugansville	B-8
Bridgeport	B-9	Mayo	G-14
Brunswick	D-9	Middle River	D-14
Bryans Road	H-12	Montgomery Vil.	E-11
Burtonsville	F-12	Mount Aetna	C-9
California	K-14	Mount Airy	D-11
Calverton	F-12	Mountain	
Cambridge	H-16	Lake Park	D-2
Camp Springs	G-12	New Carrollton	F-12
Cape Saint Claire	F-14	Oakland	D-12
Catonsville	E-13	Ocean City	K-20
Centreville	F-16	Ocean Pines	J-20
Charlotte Hall	J-13	Odenton	F-13
Chesapeake Beach	H-14	Olney	E-12
Chestertown	E-16	Overlea	D-14
Cheverly	F-12	Owings Mills	D-13
Clinton	G-12	Oxon Hill	G-12
Cockeysville	C-13	Parkville	D-14
Colesville	F-12	Perry Hall	D-14
Columbia	E-12	Perryman	C-15
Cresaptown	B-4	Perryville	C-16
Crisfield	M-17	Pikesville	D-13
Crofton	F-13	Pleasant Hills	C-14
Cumberland	B-4	Pocomoke City	L-18
Damascus	D-11	Poolesville	E-10
Deale	G-14	Potomac	F-11
Denton	G-17	Quince Orchard	E-11
Dundalk	E-14	Randallstown	D-13
Easton	G-16	Redland	E-11
Edgemere	E-14	Reisterstown	D-13
Eldersburg	D-12	Riviera Beach	E-14
Elkridge	E-13	Rockdale	D-13
Elkton	C-17	Rockville	F-11
Ellicott City	E-13	Rosaryville	G-13
Essex	D-14	Rosedale	D-14
Fairland	F-12	Saint Charles	H-12
Fallston	C-14	Salisbury	K-18
Federalsburg	H-17	Savage	E-13
Frederick	D-10	Severn	E-13
Friendly	G-12	Severna Park	F-14
Frostburg	B-3	Shady Side	G-14
Fruitland	K-18	Silver Spring	F-12
Gaithersburg	E-11	Snow Hill	L-19
Germantown	E-11	Spr. Gdn. Estates	C-10
Glen Burnie	E-13	Suitland	G-12
Glenarden	F-12	Sunnybrook	C-14
Glenn Dale	F-13	Sykesville	D-12
Golden Beach	J-13	Taneytown	B-11
Grasonville	F-15	Thurmont	C-10
Great Mills	K-14	Tonytank	K-18
Green Haven	E-14	Towson	D-14
Green Valley	D-11	Waldorf	H-12
Greenbelt	F-12	Walkersville	C-10
Hagerstown	B-9	Westernport	C-3
Halfway	C-8	Westminster	C-12
Hampstead	C-12	Wheaton	F-12
Harewood Park	D-15	White Plains	H-12
Havre de Grace	C-16	Williamsport	C-8
Hillcrest Heights	G-12	Woodfield	E-11

Selected Attractions

Attraction	Grid
Adventure World	G-13
Antietam National Battlefield	C-8
Assateague Island National Seashore	L-20
Catoctin Mountain Park	B-10
Chesapeake Bay Maritime Museum	G-15
Chesapeake Railroad	F-17
Dr. Samuel A. Mudd House Museum	H-13
Ladew Topiary Gardens	C-14
Ocean City Boardwalk	K-20
Thomas Stone National Historic Site	J-12

Adjacent States

State	Page
Delaware	24
Pennsylvania	94 & 96
Virginia	112
West Virginia	117

1 Segment Represents 2 Miles (area map)

1 Segment Represents 2 Kilometers (area map)

1 Segment Represents 2 Miles (area map)

1 Segment Represents 2 Kilometers (area map)

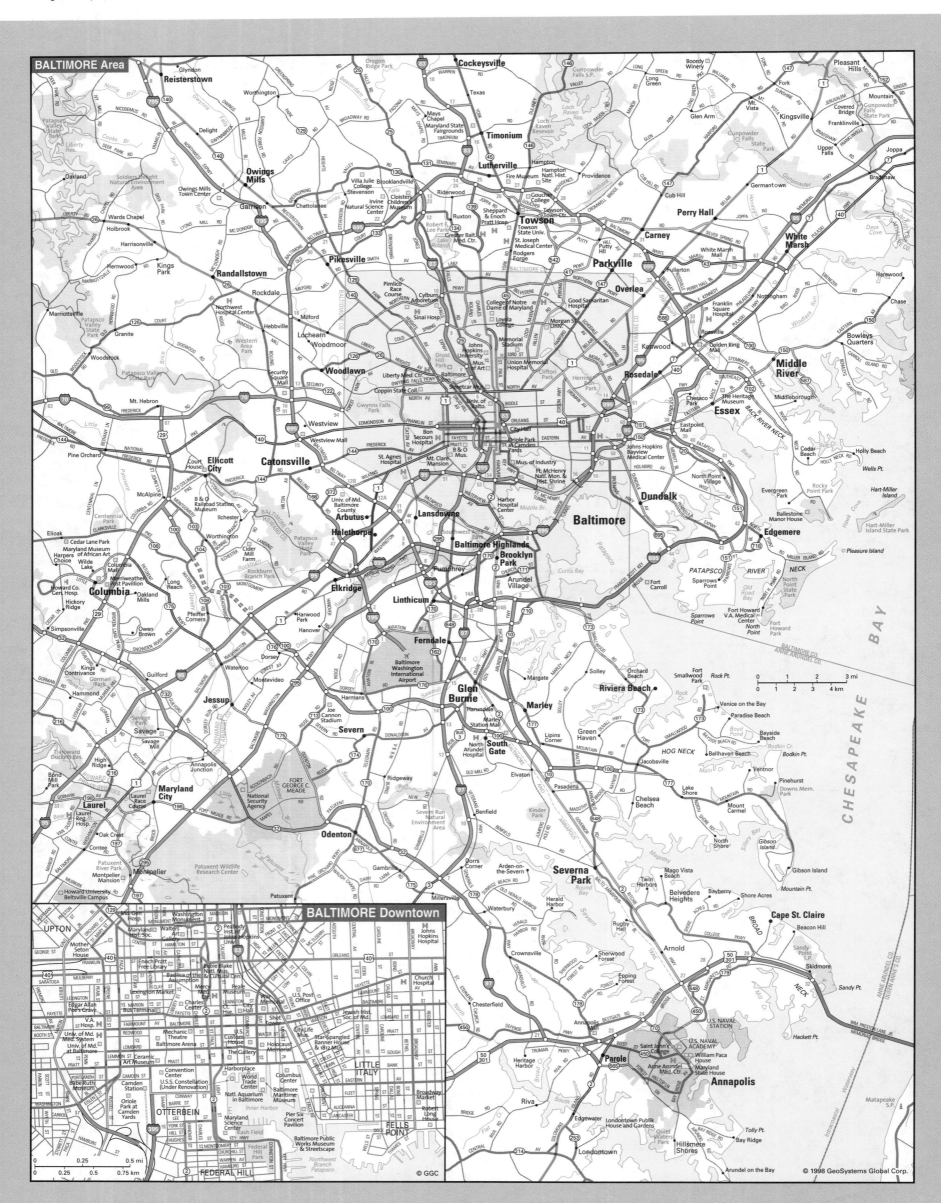

© 1998 GeoSystems Global Corp.

1 Segment Represents 2 Miles (area map)
1 Segment Represents 2 Kilometers (area map)

1 Segment Represents 2 Miles (area map)
1 Segment Represents 2 Kilometers (area map)

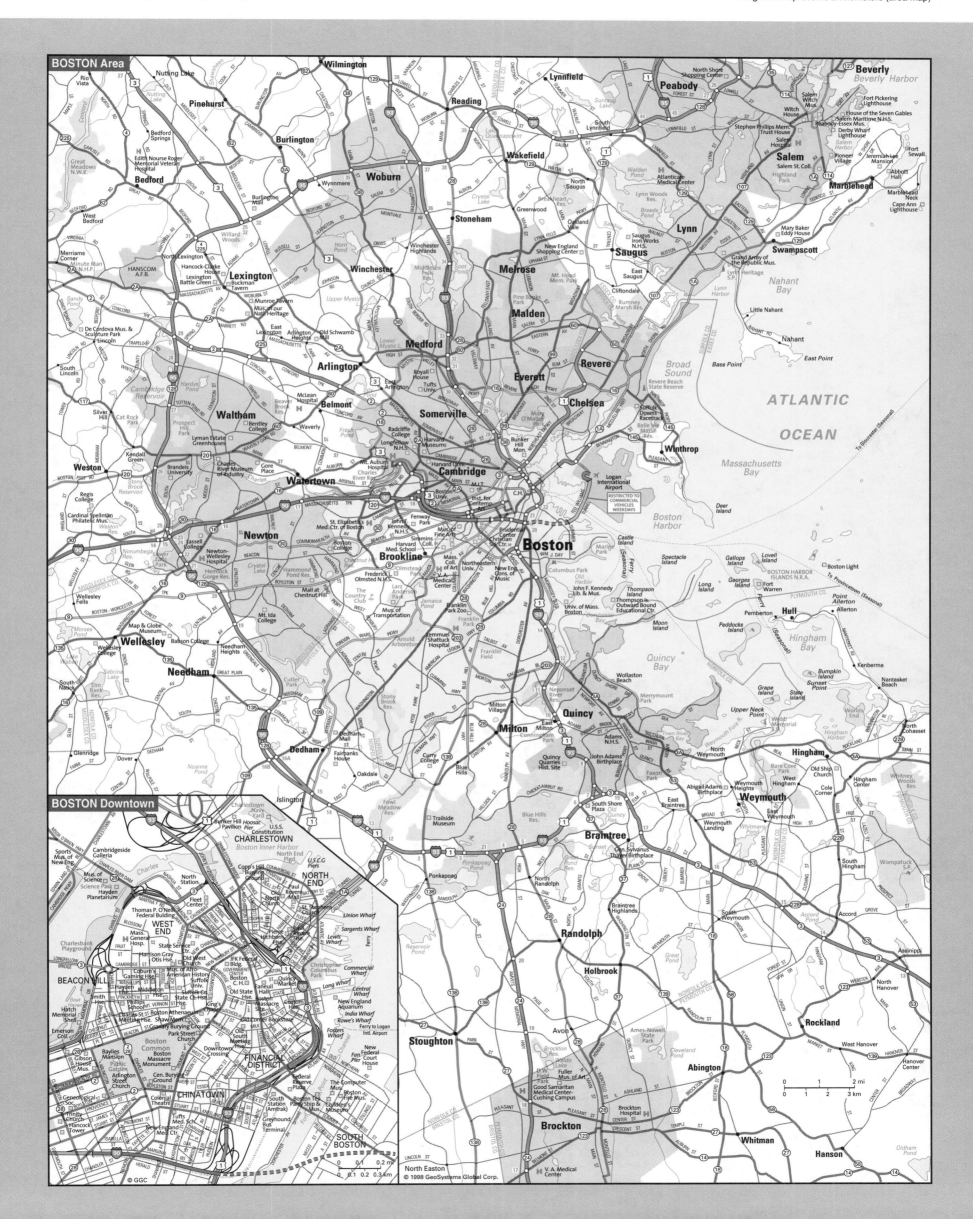

© GGC
© 1998 GeoSystems Global Corp.

*"By the Sword
We Seek Peace, but Peace
Only Under Liberty"*

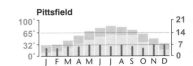

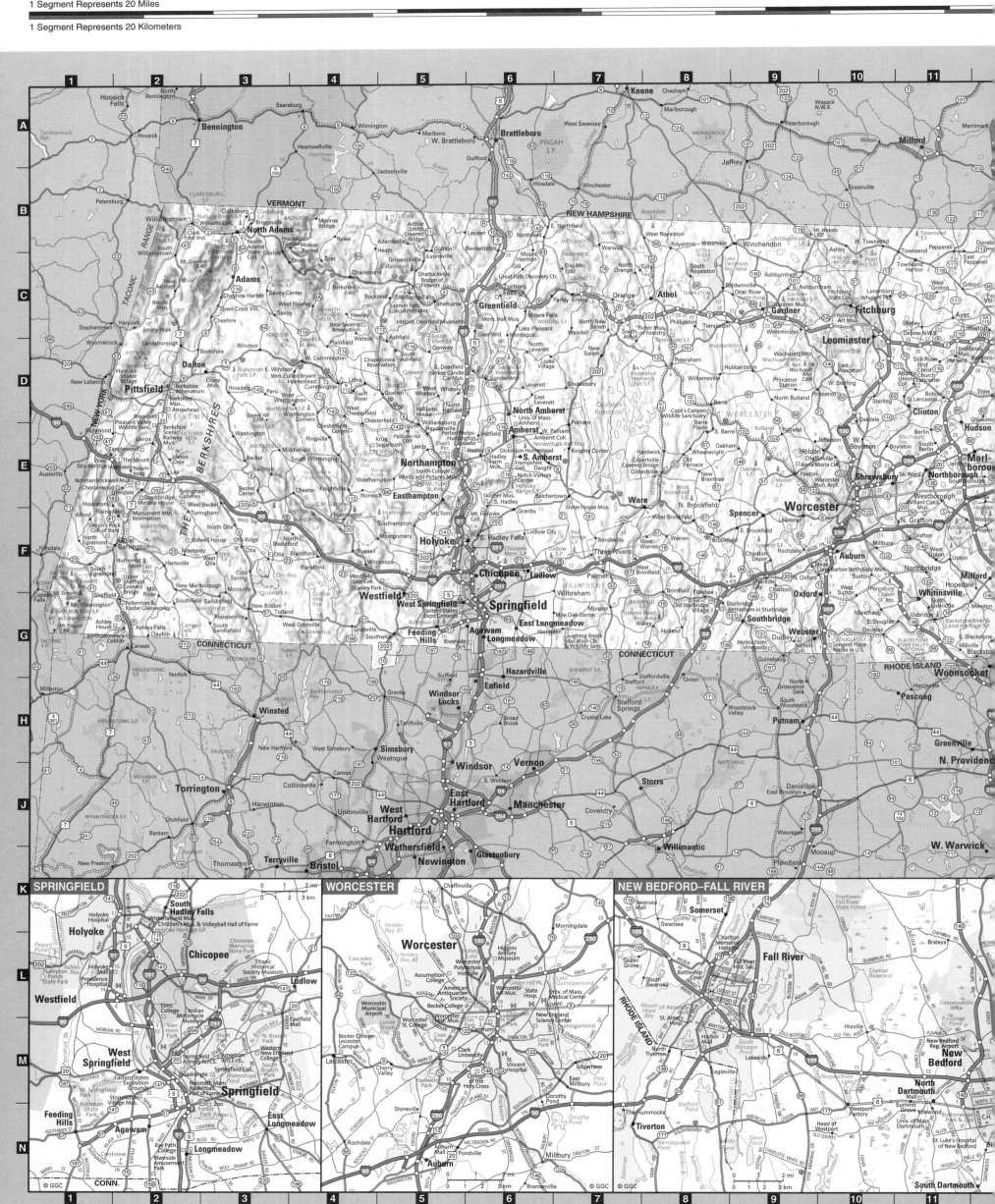

1 Segment Represents 20 Miles

1 Segment Represents 20 Kilometers

"By the Sword
We Seek Peace, but Peace
Only Under Liberty"

Worcester

100°
65°
32°
0°
J F M A M J J A S O N D

21
14
7

Boston

100°
65°
32°
0°
J F M A M J J A S O N D

21
14
7

1 Segment Represents 20 Miles

1 Segment Represents 20 Kilometers

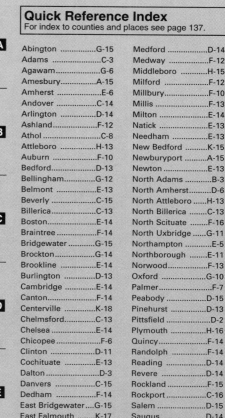

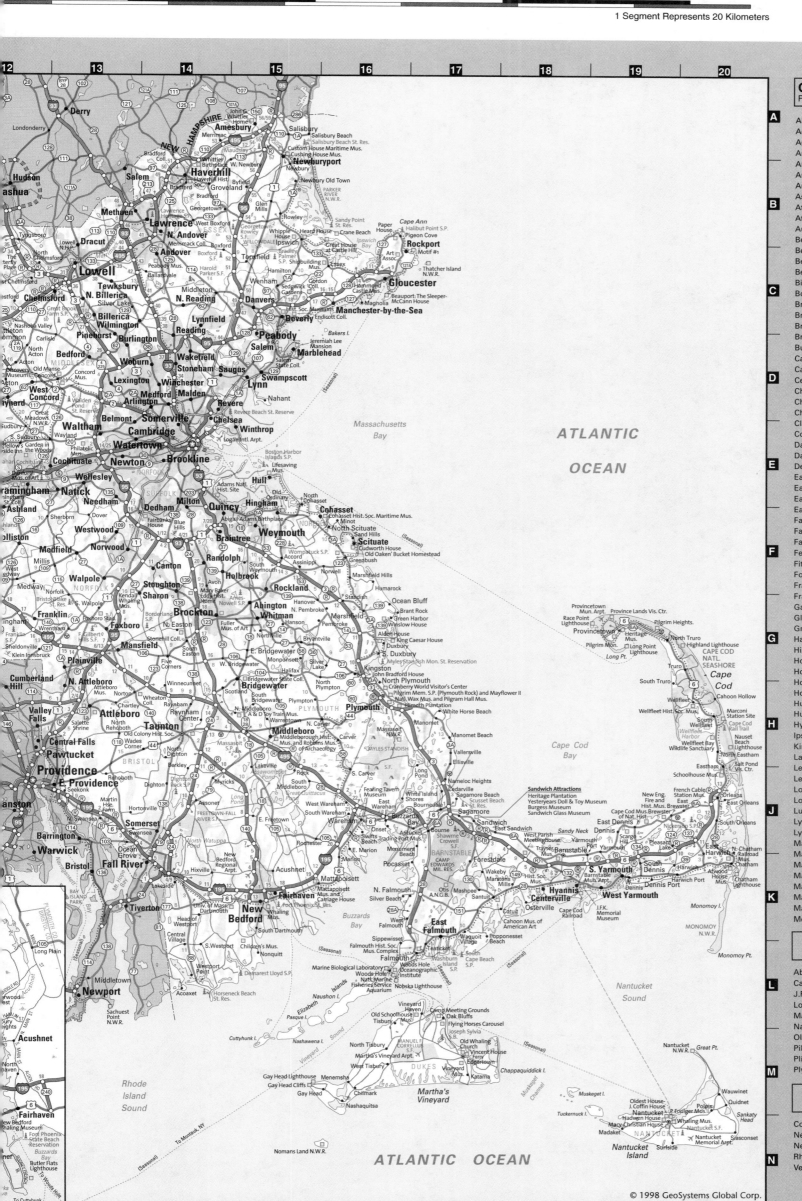

Quick Reference Index

For index to counties and places see page 137.

Abington	G-15	Medford	D-14
Adams	C-3	Medway	F-12
Agawam	G-6	Middleboro	H-15
Amesbury	A-15	Milford	F-12
Amherst	E-6	Millbury	F-10
Andover	C-14	Millis	F-13
Arlington	D-14	Milton	E-14
Ashland	F-12	Natick	E-13
Athol	C-8	Needham	E-13
Attleboro	H-13	New Bedford	K-15
Auburn	F-10	Newburyport	A-15
Bedford	D-13	Newton	E-13
Bellingham	G-12	North Adams	B-3
Belmont	E-13	North Amherst	D-6
Beverly	C-15	North Attleboro	H-13
Billerica	C-13	North Billerica	C-13
Boston	E-14	North Scituate	F-16
Braintree	F-14	North Uxbridge	G-11
Bridgewater	G-15	Northampton	E-5
Brockton	G-14	Northborough	E-11
Brookline	E-14	Norwood	F-13
Burlington	D-13	Oxford	G-10
Cambridge	E-14	Palmer	F-7
Canton	F-14	Peabody	D-15
Centerville	K-18	Pinehurst	D-13
Chelmsford	C-13	Pittsfield	D-2
Chelsea	E-14	Plymouth	H-16
Chicopee	F-6	Quincy	F-14
Clinton	D-11	Randolph	F-14
Cochituate	E-13	Reading	D-14
Dalton	D-3	Revere	D-14
Danvers	C-15	Rockland	F-15
Dedham	F-14	Rockport	C-16
East Bridgewater	G-15	Salem	D-15
East Falmouth	K-17	Saugus	D-14
East Longmeadow	G-6	Scituate	F-16
Easthampton	E-5	Sharon	F-13
Fairhaven	K-15	Shrewsbury	E-10
Fall River	K-14	Somerset	J-14
Falmouth	L-17	Somerville	E-14
Feeding Hills	G-5	South Amherst	E-6
Fitchburg	C-10	South Hadley Falls	F-6
Foxboro	G-13	South Yarmouth	K-19
Framingham	E-12	Southbridge	G-9
Franklin	G-12	Spencer	F-9
Gardner	C-9	Springfield	G-6
Gloucester	C-16	Stoneham	D-14
Greenfield	C-6	Stoughton	F-14
Haverhill	B-14	Swampscott	D-15
Hingham	F-15	Taunton	H-14
Holbrook	F-14	Tewksbury	C-13
Holden	E-10	Turners Falls	C-6
Holyoke	F-6	Wakefield	D-14
Hopedale	F-12	Walpole	F-13
Hudson	E-11	Waltham	E-13
Hull	E-15	Ware	F-8
Hyannis	K-18	Watertown	E-13
Ipswich	B-15	Webster	G-9
Kingston	G-16	Wellesley	E-13
Lawrence	B-14	West Concord	D-12
Leominster	D-10	West Springfield	G-5
Lexington	D-13	West Yarmouth	K-19
Longmeadow	G-6	Westfield	G-5
Lowell	C-13	Westwood	F-13
Ludlow	F-6	Weymouth	F-15
Lynn	D-15	Whitinsville	G-11
Lynnfield	C-14	Whitman	G-15
Malden	D-14	Williamstown	B-2
Mansfield	G-13	Wilmington	C-13
Marblehead	D-15	Winchendon	B-9
Marlborough	E-12	Winchester	D-14
Marshfield	G-16	Winthrop	E-15
Marstons Mills	K-18	Woburn	D-14
Maynard	D-12	Worcester	F-10
Medfield	F-13	Yarmouth Port	K-18

Selected Attractions

Abigail Adams Birthplace	F-15
Cape Cod National Seashore	G-20
J.F.K. Memorial Museum	K-19
Lowell National Historic Park	C-13
Martha's Vineyard	M-17
Nantucket Island	N-19
Old Sturbridge Village	G-8
Pilgrim Monument	G-19
Plimoth Plantation	H-16
Plymouth Rock	H-16

Adjacent States

Connecticut	22
New Hampshire	71
New York	76 & 78
Rhode Island	99
Vermont	110

© 1998 GeoSystems Global Corp.

"If You Seek a Pleasant Peninsula, Look About You"

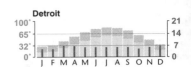

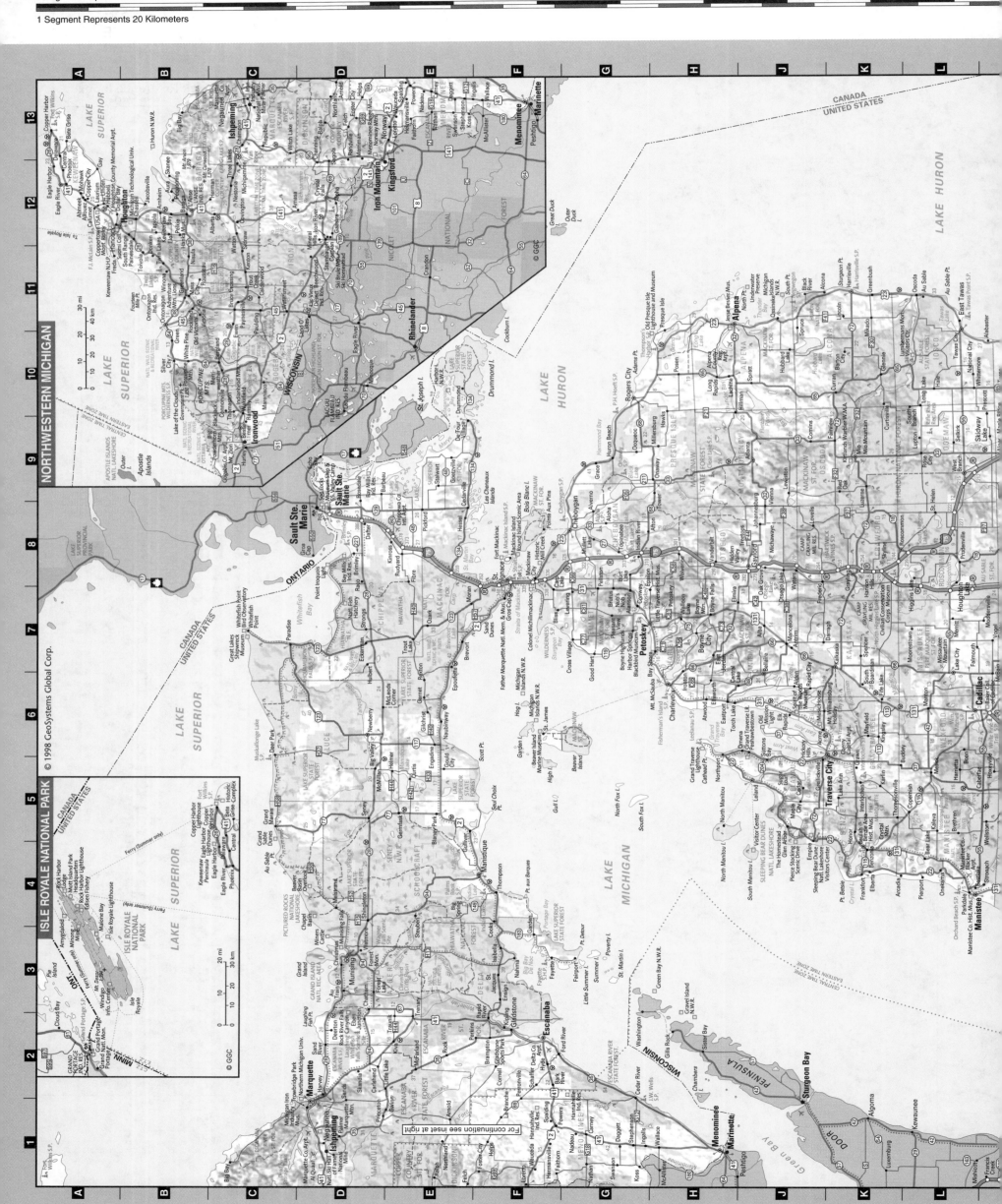

"If You Seek a Pleasant Peninsula, Look About You"

Grand Rapids / **Marquette** (climate graphs)

1 Segment Represents 20 Miles

1 Segment Represents 20 Kilometers

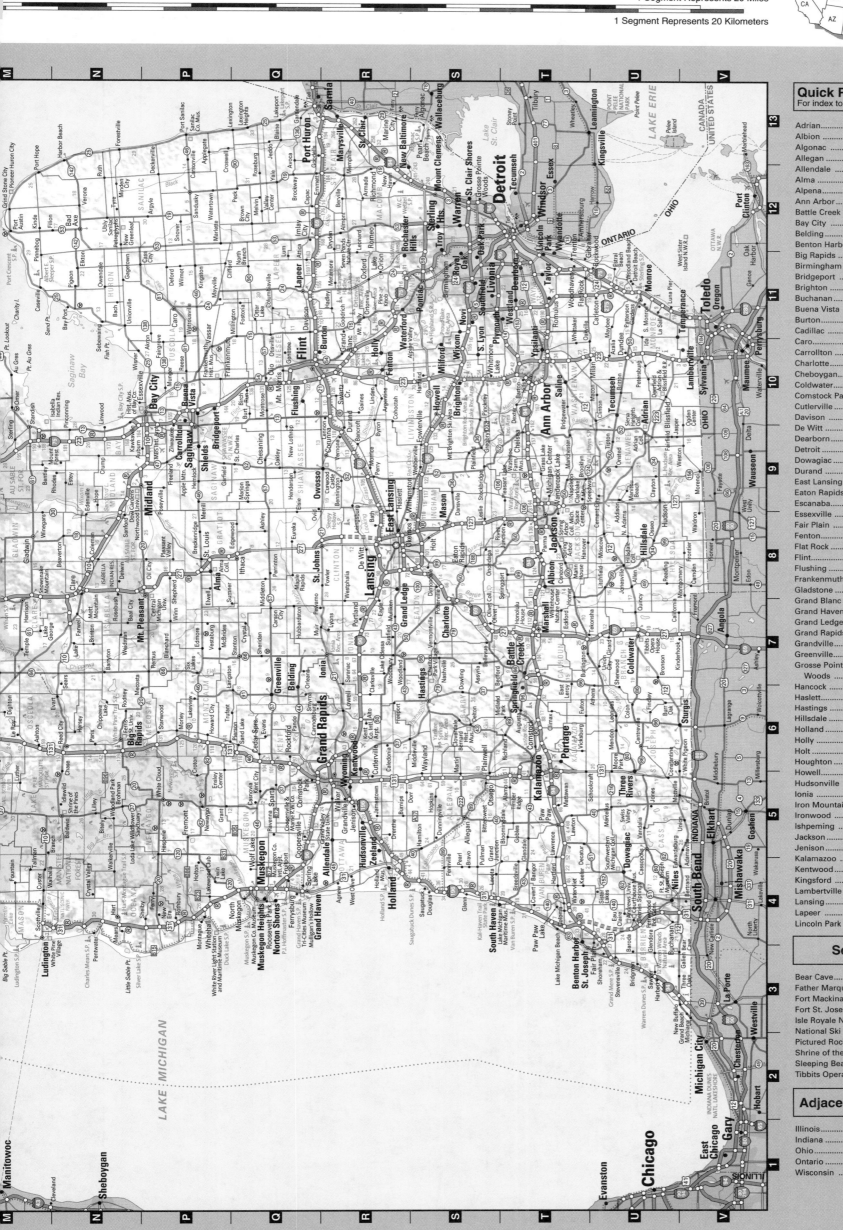

Quick Reference Index
For index to counties and places see page 137.

Adrian	U-10	Livonia	S-11
Albion	T-8	Lowell	R-6
Algonac	S-13	Ludington	M-4
Allegan	S-5	Manistee	M-4
Allendale	R-5	Marine City	R-13
Alma	P-8	Marquette	D-1
Alpena	J-11	Marshall	T-7
Ann Arbor	T-10	Marysville	R-13
Battle Creek	T-7	Mason	S-8
Bay City	P-10	Menominee	H-1
Belding	Q-6	Michigan Center	T-9
Benton Harbor	T-4	Midland	P-9
Big Rapids	N-6	Milan	U-10
Birmingham	S-11	Milford	S-10
Bridgeport	P-10	Monroe	U-11
Brighton	S-10	Mount Clemens	S-12
Buchanan	U-4	Mount Pleasant	P-7
Buena Vista	P-10	Muskegon	Q-4
Burton	R-10	Muskegon Heights	Q-4
Cadillac	M-6	Negaunee	D-1
Caro	P-11	New Baltimore	R-12
Carrollton	P-9	Niles	U-4
Charlotte	S-7	North Muskegon	Q-4
Cheboygan	G-8	Norton Shores	Q-4
Coldwater	U-7	Novi	S-11
Comstock Park	Q-5	Oak Park	S-11
Cutlerville	R-5	Okemos	S-8
Davison	Q-10	Otsego	S-5
De Witt	R-8	Owosso	R-9
Dearborn	T-11	Petoskey	G-7
Detroit	T-12	Plainwell	S-5
Dowagiac	U-4	Plymouth	S-11
Durand	R-9	Pontiac	S-11
East Lansing	R-8	Port Huron	Q-13
Eaton Rapids	S-8	Portage	T-6
Escanaba	F-2	Richmond	R-12
Essexville	P-10	Rochester Hills	R-11
Fair Plain	U-3	Romulus	T-11
Fenton	R-10	Royal Oak	S-11
Flat Rock	T-11	Saginaw	P-9
Flint	Q-10	St. Clair	R-13
Flushing	Q-10	St. Clair Shores	S-12
Frankenmuth	P-10	St. Johns	Q-8
Gladstone	F-2	St. Joseph	T-3
Grand Blanc	R-10	Saline	T-10
Grand Haven	R-4	Sault Ste. Marie	D-8
Grand Ledge	R-8	Shields	P-9
Grand Rapids	R-6	South Haven	S-4
Grandville	R-5	South Lyon	S-10
Greenville	Q-6	South Monroe	U-11
Grosse Pointe Woods	S-12	Southfield	S-11
Hancock	A-12	Sparta	Q-5
Haslett	R-9	Springfield	T-6
Hastings	S-6	Sterling Heights	S-12
Hillsdale	U-8	Sturgis	V-6
Holland	R-4	Swartz Creek	R-10
Holly	R-10	Taylor	T-11
Holt	S-8	Tecumseh	U-10
Houghton	A-12	Temperance	V-11
Howell	S-10	Three Rivers	U-5
Hudsonville	R-5	Traverse City	K-5
Ionia	R-7	Trenton	T-11
Iron Mountain	D-12	Troy	S-11
Ironwood	A-12	Vandercook Lake	T-9
Ishpeming	D-1	Walker	R-5
Jackson	T-8	Warren	S-12
Jenison	R-5	Waterford	R-11
Kalamazoo	T-6	Westland	T-11
Kentwood	R-5	Wixom	S-11
Kingsford	E-12	Wolf Lake	Q-4
Lambertville	V-10	Woodhaven	T-11
Lansing	R-8	Wyandotte	T-11
Lapeer	Q-11	Wyoming	R-5
Lincoln Park	T-11	Ypsilanti	T-10
		Zeeland	R-5

Selected Attractions

Bear Cave	U-3
Father Marquette National Memorial & Museum	F-7
Fort Mackinac	F-8
Fort St. Joseph Museum	U-4
Isle Royale National Park	B-2
National Ski Hall of Fame	D-1
Pictured Rocks National Lakeshore	C-4
Shrine of the Pines	N-5
Sleeping Bear Dunes National Lakeshore	J-4
Tibbits Opera House	U-7

Adjacent States and Provinces

Illinois	34
Indiana	38
Ohio	86 & 88
Ontario	126
Wisconsin	118

1 Segment Represents 2 Miles

1 Segment Represents 2 Miles

1 Segment Represents 2 Kilometers

1 Segment Represents 2 Kilometers

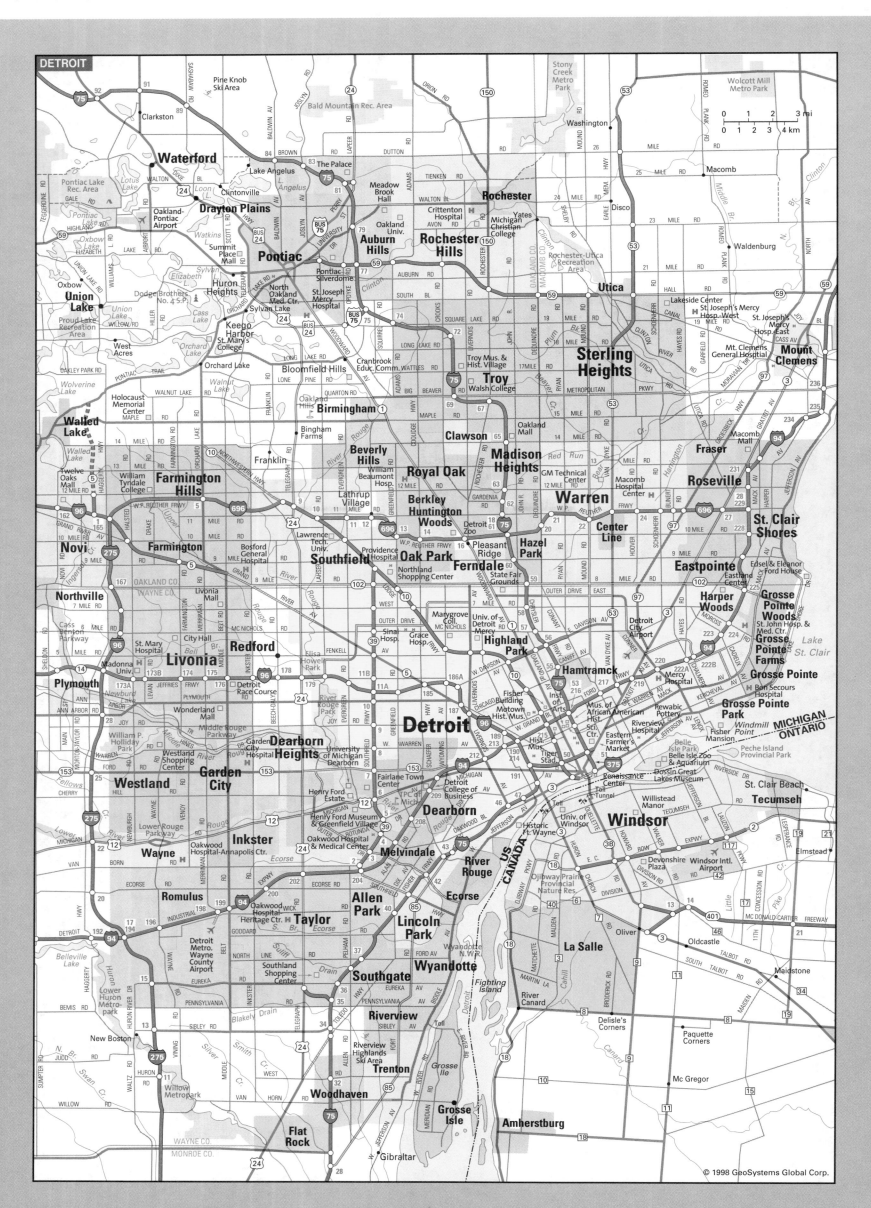

© 1998 GeoSystems Global Corp.

1 Segment Represents 2 Miles (Minneapolis–St. Paul map)

1 Segment Represents 2 Kilometers (Minneapolis–St. Paul map)

1 Segment Represents 2 Miles (Minneapolis–St. Paul map)

1 Segment Represents 2 Kilometers Minneapolis–St. Paul map)

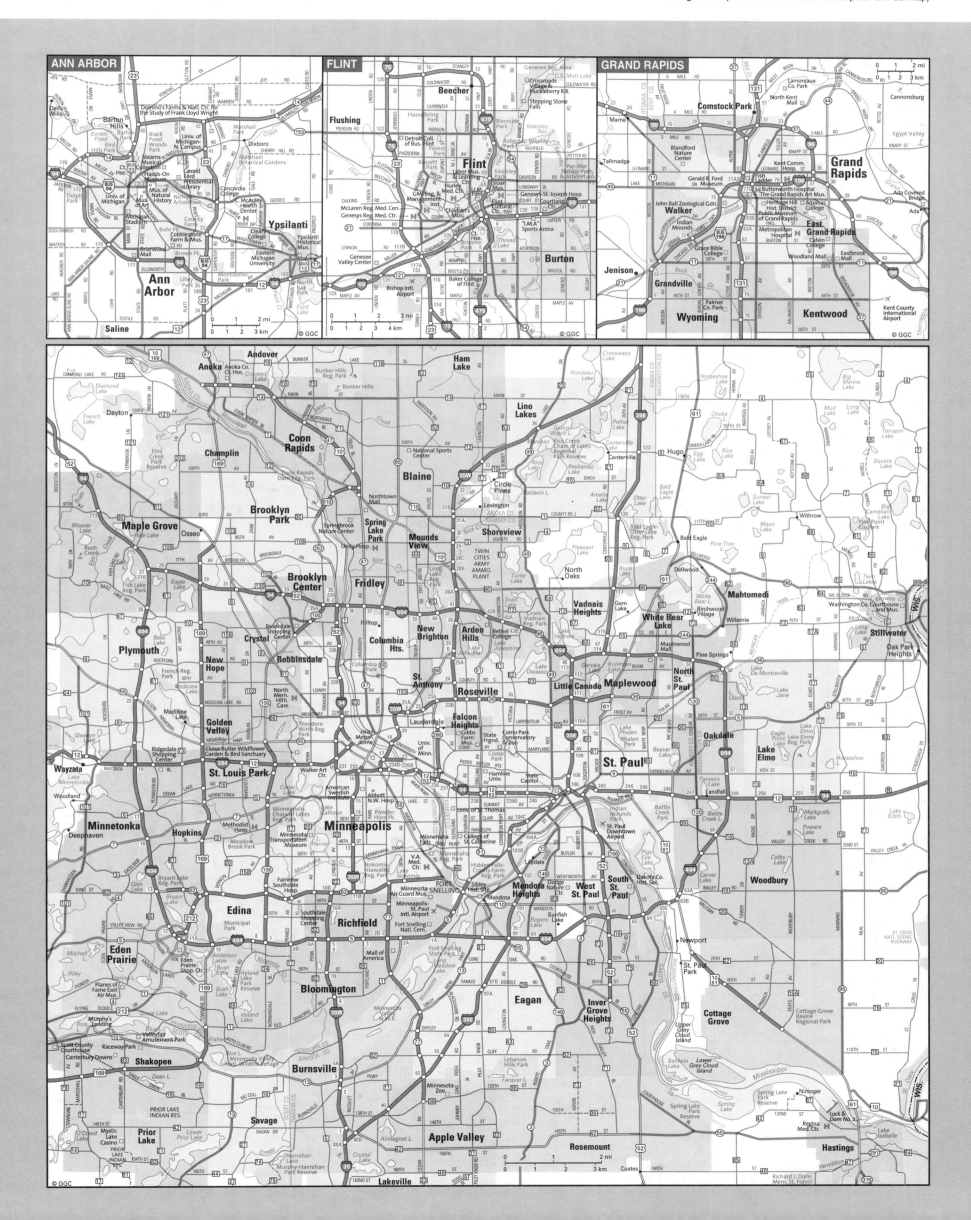

Weather - Legend

International Falls

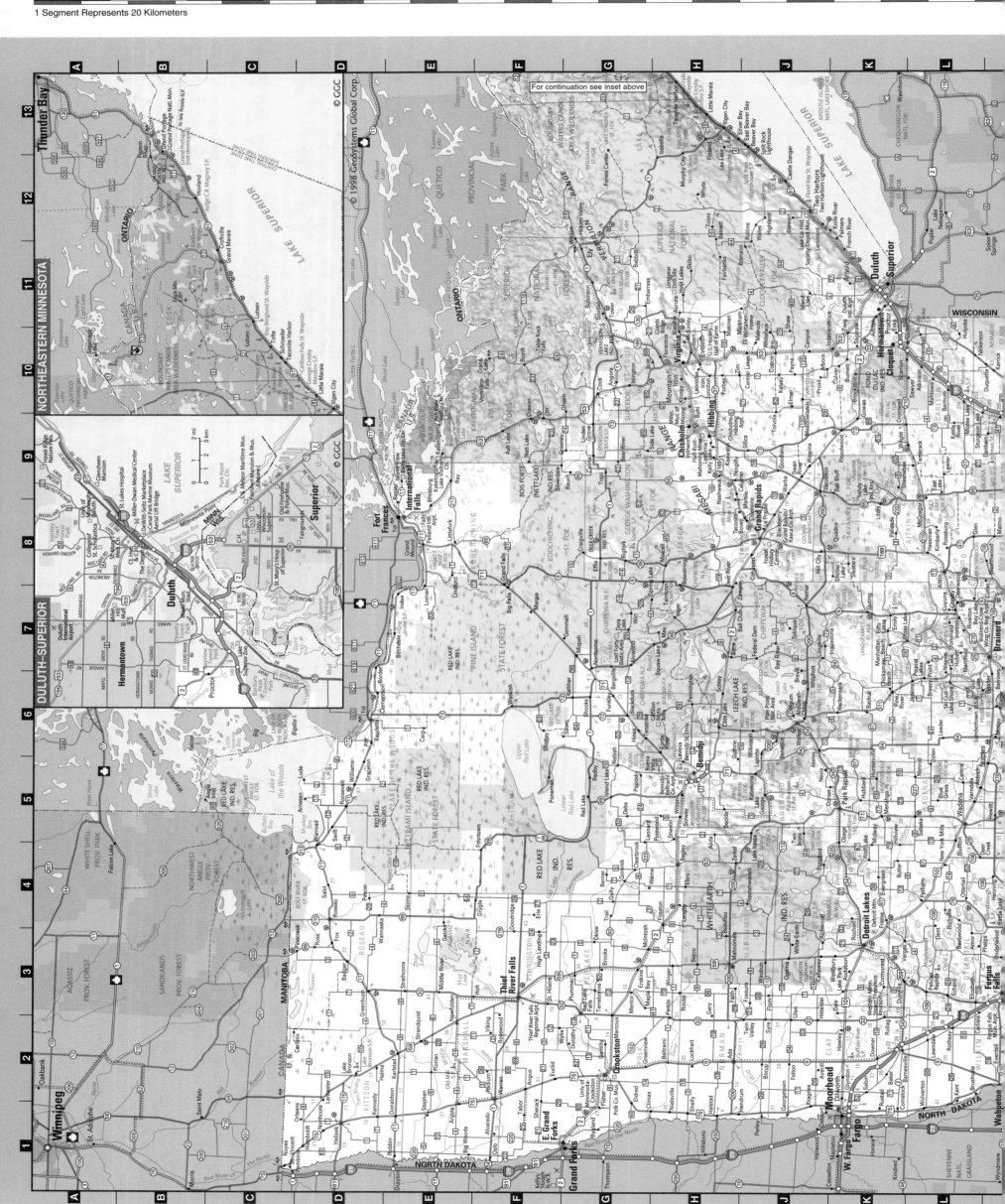

1 Segment Represents 20 Miles

1 Segment Represents 20 Kilometers

Duluth

Minneapolis

1 Segment Represents 20 Miles

1 Segment Represents 20 Kilometers

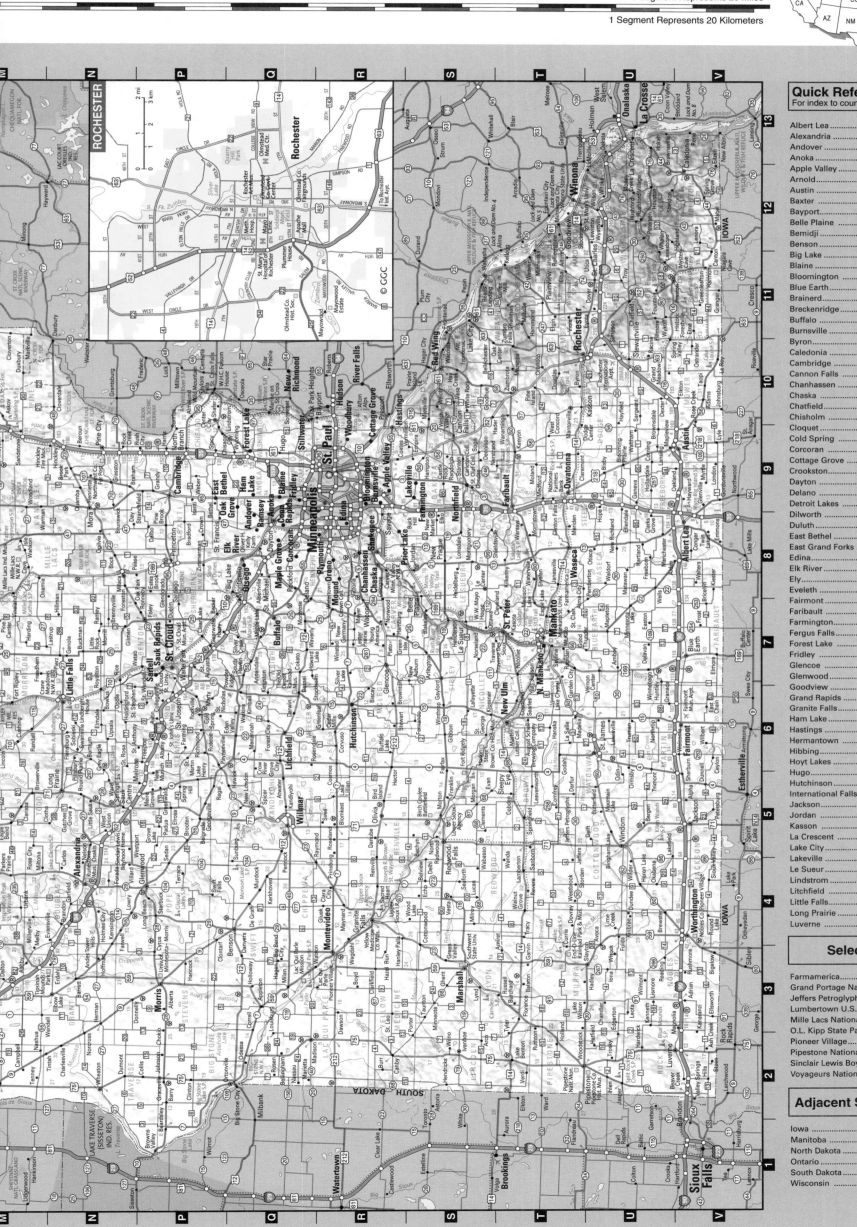

Quick Reference Index

For index to counties and places see page 137.

Albert Lea	V-8	Madelia	T-6
Alexandria	N-4	Mankato	T-7
Andover	Q-8	Maple Grove	Q-8
Anoka	Q-9	Marshall	S-3
Apple Valley	R-9	Melrose	P-5
Arnold	K-11	Minneapolis	R-9
Austin	V-9	Montevideo	R-3
Baxter	M-6	Montgomery	S-8
Bayport	Q-10	Monticello	Q-7
Belle Plaine	S-8	Moorhead	K-1
Bemidji	H-5	Mora	N-9
Benson	Q-4	Morris	P-3
Big Lake	Q-8	Mound	R-8
Blaine	Q-9	Mountain Iron	H-10
Bloomington	R-9	New Prague	S-8
Blue Earth	V-7	New Ulm	T-6
Brainerd	M-7	North Branch	P-9
Breckenridge	M-2	North Mankato	T-7
Buffalo	Q-7	Northfield	S-9
Burnsville	R-9	Oak Grove	Q-9
Byron	T-10	Oak Park Heights	Q-10
Caledonia	V-12	Olivia	R-5
Cambridge	P-9	Orono	R-8
Cannon Falls	S-9	Otsego	Q-8
Chanhassen	R-8	Owatonna	T-9
Chaska	R-8	Park Rapids	K-5
Chatfield	U-11	Paynesville	P-6
Chisholm	H-9	Pine City	N-9
Cloquet	K-10	Pipestone	T-2
Cold Spring	P-6	Plainview	T-11
Corcoran	Q-8	Plymouth	R-8
Cottage Grove	R-9	Princeton	P-8
Crookston	G-2	Prior Lake	R-8
Dayton	Q-8	Proctor	K-11
Delano	Q-7	Ramsey	Q-8
Detroit Lakes	K-3	Red Wing	S-10
Dilworth	K-2	Redwood Falls	S-5
Duluth	K-11	Rochester	T-10
East Bethel	P-9	Rockford	Q-8
East Grand Forks	F-1	Roseau	D-4
Edina	R-8	Saint Charles	U-11
Elk River	Q-8	Saint Cloud	P-7
Ely	G-11	Saint Francis	P-8
Eveleth	H-10	Saint James	U-6
Fairmont	V-6	Saint Joseph	P-6
Faribault	T-9	Saint Michael	Q-8
Farmington	S-9	Saint Paul	R-9
Fergus Falls	M-3	Saint Peter	T-7
Forest Lake	P-7	Sartell	P-7
Fridley	R-9	Sauk Centre	N-5
Glencoe	R-7	Sauk Rapids	P-7
Glenwood	P-4	Savage	R-8
Goodview	T-12	Shakopee	R-8
Grand Rapids	J-8	Sleepy Eye	T-5
Granite Falls	R-4	Spring Valley	U-10
Ham Lake	Q-9	Staples	M-5
Hastings	S-9	Stewartville	U-10
Hermantown	K-11	Stillwater	Q-10
Hibbing	H-9	Thief River Falls	F-3
Hoyt Lakes	H-11	Two Harbors	J-12
Hugo	Q-9	Victoria	R-8
Hutchinson	R-6	Virginia	H-10
International Falls	E-8	Wabasha	S-11
Jackson	V-5	Waconia	R-7
Jordan	S-8	Wadena	L-5
Kasson	T-10	Waite Park	P-7
La Crescent	U-13	Waseca	T-8
Lake City	S-11	Watertown	R-7
Lakeville	S-9	Wells	U-8
Le Sueur	S-7	Willmar	Q-5
Lindstrom	P-9	Windom	U-5
Litchfield	Q-6	Winona	T-12
Little Falls	N-6	Woodbury	R-9
Long Prairie	N-5	Worthington	V-4
Luverne	U-2	Zumbrota	T-10

Selected Attractions

Farmamerica	T-8
Grand Portage National Monument	B-13
Jeffers Petroglyphs	T-5
Lumbertown U.S.A.	L-6
Mille Lacs National Wildlife Refuge	M-8
O.L. Kipp State Park	U-12
Pioneer Village	R-3
Pipestone National Monument	T-2
Sinclair Lewis Boyhood Home	N-5
Voyageurs National Park	E-9

Adjacent States and Provinces

Iowa	40
Manitoba	125
North Dakota	85
Ontario	126
South Dakota	101
Wisconsin	118

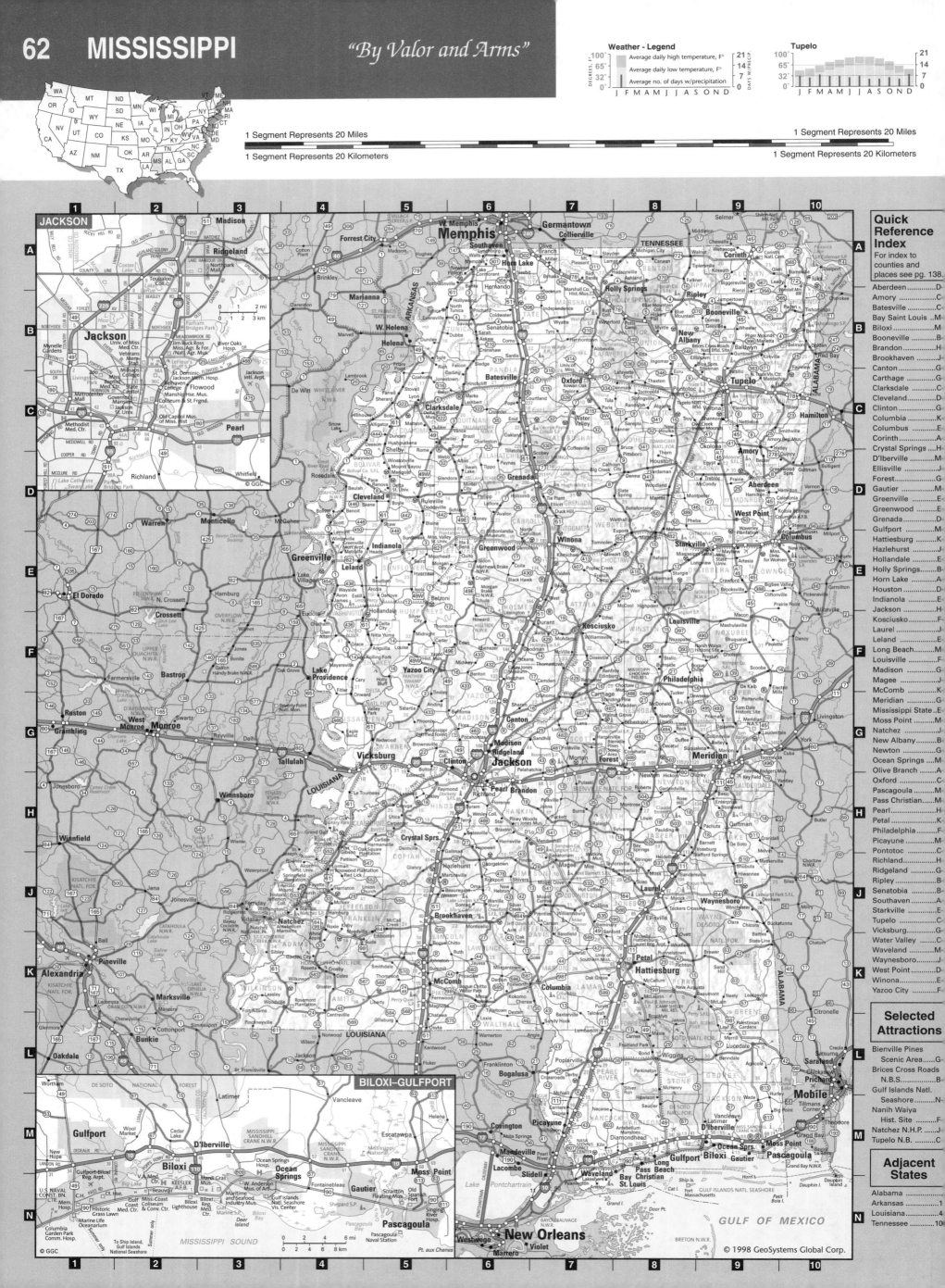

1 Segment Represents 2 Miles (Kansas City map)
1 Segment Represents 2 Kilometers (Kansas City map)
1 Segment Represents 2 Miles (Kansas City map)
1 Segment Represents 2 Kilometers (Kansas City map)

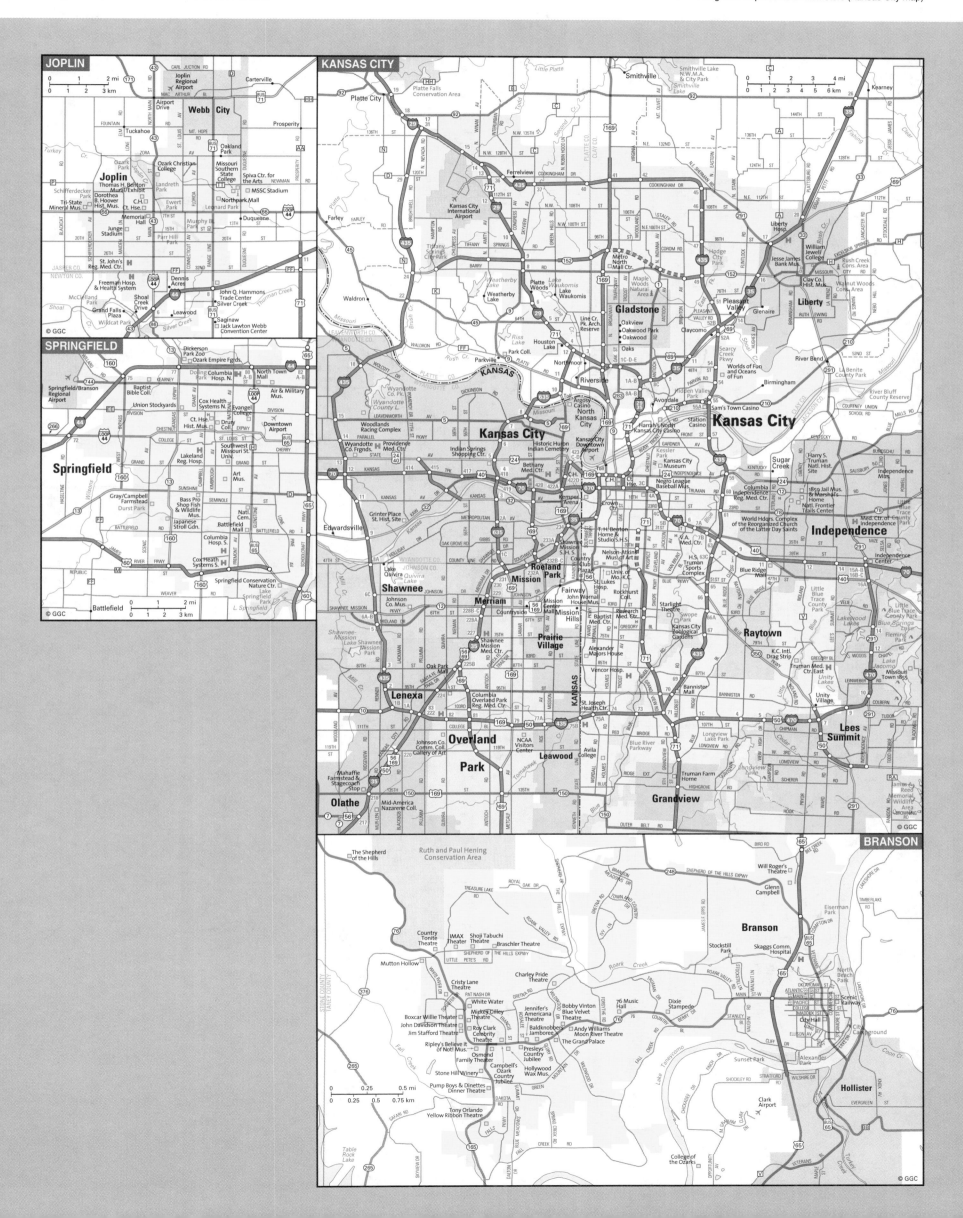

"The Welfare of the People Shall Be the Supreme Law"

Weather - Legend

Kansas City

1 Segment Represents 20 Miles

1 Segment Represents 20 Kilometers

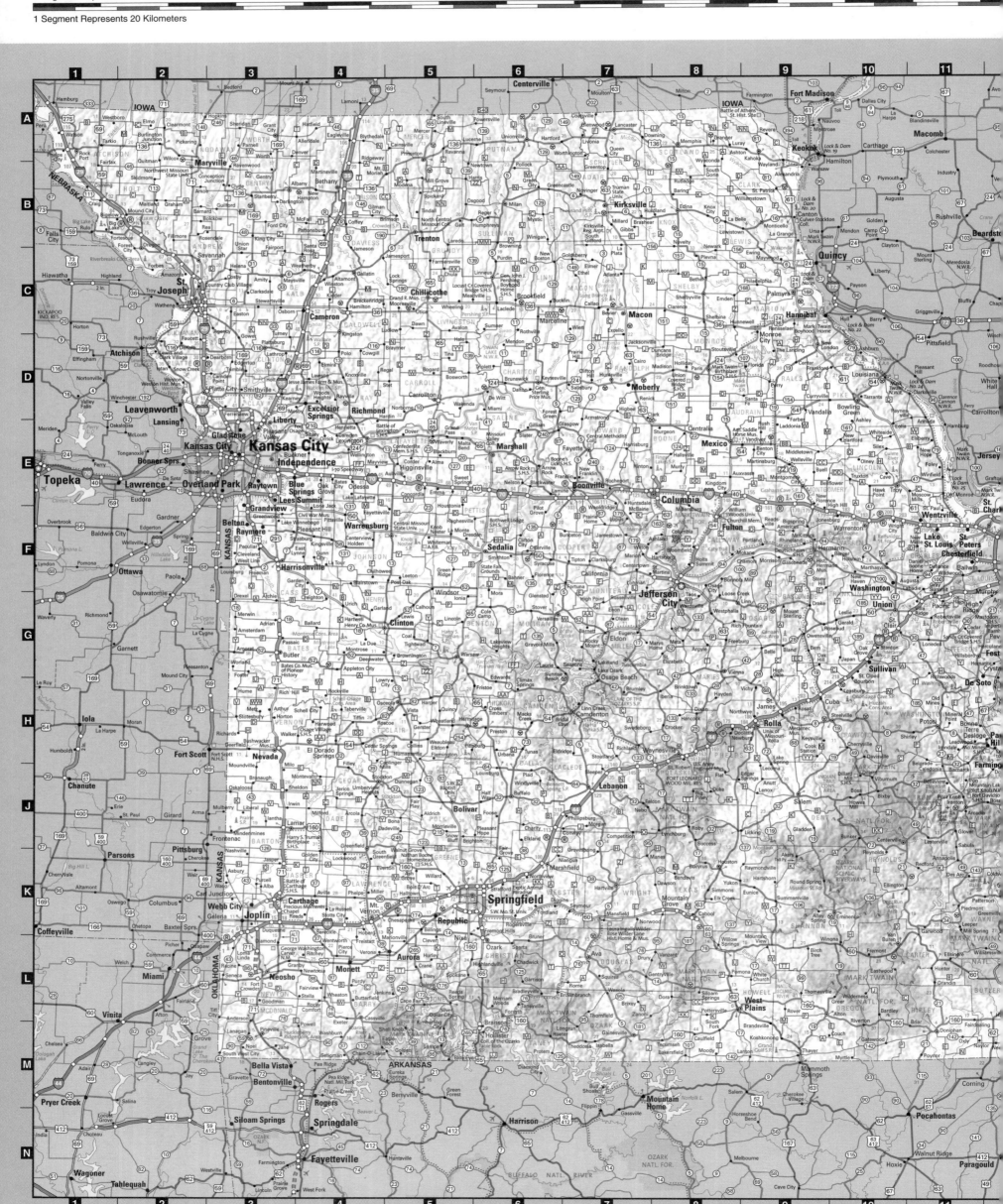

Springfield

St. Louis

1 Segment Represents 20 Miles

1 Segment Represents 20 Kilometers

Quick Reference Index

For index to counties and places see page 138.

Arnold	G-12	Lees Summit	E-3
Aurora	L-5	Lexington	E-4
Ava	L-7	Liberty	E-3
Ballwin	F-11	Louisiana	D-10
Barnhart	G-12	Macon	C-7
Belton	F-3	Malden	M-13
Bethany	B-4	Marceline	C-6
Blue Springs	E-3	Marshall	E-6
Bolivar	J-5	Marshfield	K-6
Bonne Terre	H-11	Maryville	B-2
Boonville	E-7	Mehlville	F-12
Bowling Green	D-10	Mexico	E-8
Branson	M-6	Moberly	D-7
Brookfield	C-6	Monett	L-4
Buckner	E-4	Monroe City	D-9
Buffalo	J-6	Montgomery City	D-9
Butler	G-3	Mount Vernon	K-4
California	F-7	Mountain Grove	K-8
Camdenton	H-7	Murphy	G-12
Cameron	C-4	Neosho	L-3
Canton	B-9	Nevada	H-3
Cape Girardeau	K-14	New Madrid	M-14
Carl Junction	K-3	Nixa	K-5
Carrollton	D-5	Oak Grove	E-4
Carthage	K-3	Oakville	G-12
Caruthersville	N-14	Odessa	E-4
Cassville	L-4	Osage Beach	H-7
Centralia	E-8	Owensville	G-9
Chaffee	K-13	Ozark	L-6
Charleston	L-14	Pacific	G-11
Chesterfield	F-11	Palmyra	C-9
Chillicothe	C-5	Park Hills	H-12
Clayton	F-12	Perryville	J-13
Clinton	G-4	Pevely	G-12
Columbia	E-8	Platte City	D-2
Crystal City	G-12	Pleasant Hill	F-3
Cuba	H-9	Pleasant Valley	E-3
De Soto	H-11	Poplar Bluff	L-12
Desloge	H-12	Portageville	M-13
Dexter	L-13	Potosi	H-11
East Prairie	L-14	Raymore	F-3
El Dorado Springs	H-4	Raytown	E-3
Eldon	G-7	Republic	K-5
Excelsior Springs	D-4	Richmond	D-4
Farmington	J-12	Rolla	H-9
Fayette	E-7	St. Charles	F-12
Festus	G-12	St. Clair	G-10
Florissant	F-12	St. James	H-9
Fredericktown	J-12	St. Joseph	C-2
Fulton	F-8	St. Louis	F-12
Gladstone	E-3	St. Peters	F-11
Grandview	F-3	Ste. Genevieve	H-12
Gray Summit	G-11	Salem	J-9
Hannibal	C-9	Savannah	C-2
Harrisonville	F-3	Scott City	K-14
Hayti	N-13	Sedalia	F-6
Herculaneum	G-12	Sikeston	L-14
Hermann	F-9	Smithville	D-3
Higginsville	E-5	Springfield	K-5
High Ridge	G-11	Steele	N-13
Holden	F-4	Sullivan	G-10
Hollister	M-6	Trenton	B-5
Holts Summit	F-8	Troy	E-10
Imperial	G-12	Union	G-10
Independence	E-3	Vandalia	D-9
Jackson	J-13	Versailles	G-6
Jefferson City	F-8	Warrensburg	F-5
Joplin	K-3	Warrenton	F-10
Kansas City	E-3	Washington	F-10
Kennett	N-13	Waynesville	H-8
Kirksville	B-7	Webb City	K-3
Knob Noster	F-5	Wentzville	F-11
Lake St. Louis	F-11	West Plains	L-9
Lamar	J-3	Wildwood	F-11
Lebanon	J-7	Windsor	F-5

Selected Attractions

Battle of Athens State Historic Site	A-9
Churchill Memorial	F-8
Daniel Boone Home	F-11
Dillard Mill State Historic Site	J-10
George Washington Carver National Monument	L-3
Harry S. Truman State Park	G-5
Mark Twain Boyhood Home	C-9
Nathan Boone Homestead State Historic Site	K-5
Roaring River State Park	M-4
U.S. Army Engineer Museum	J-8

Adjacent States

Arkansas	10
Illinois	34
Iowa	40
Kansas	42
Kentucky	44
Nebraska	68
Oklahoma	90
Tennessee	102

© 1998 GeoSystems Global Corp.

"Gold and Silver"

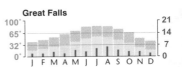

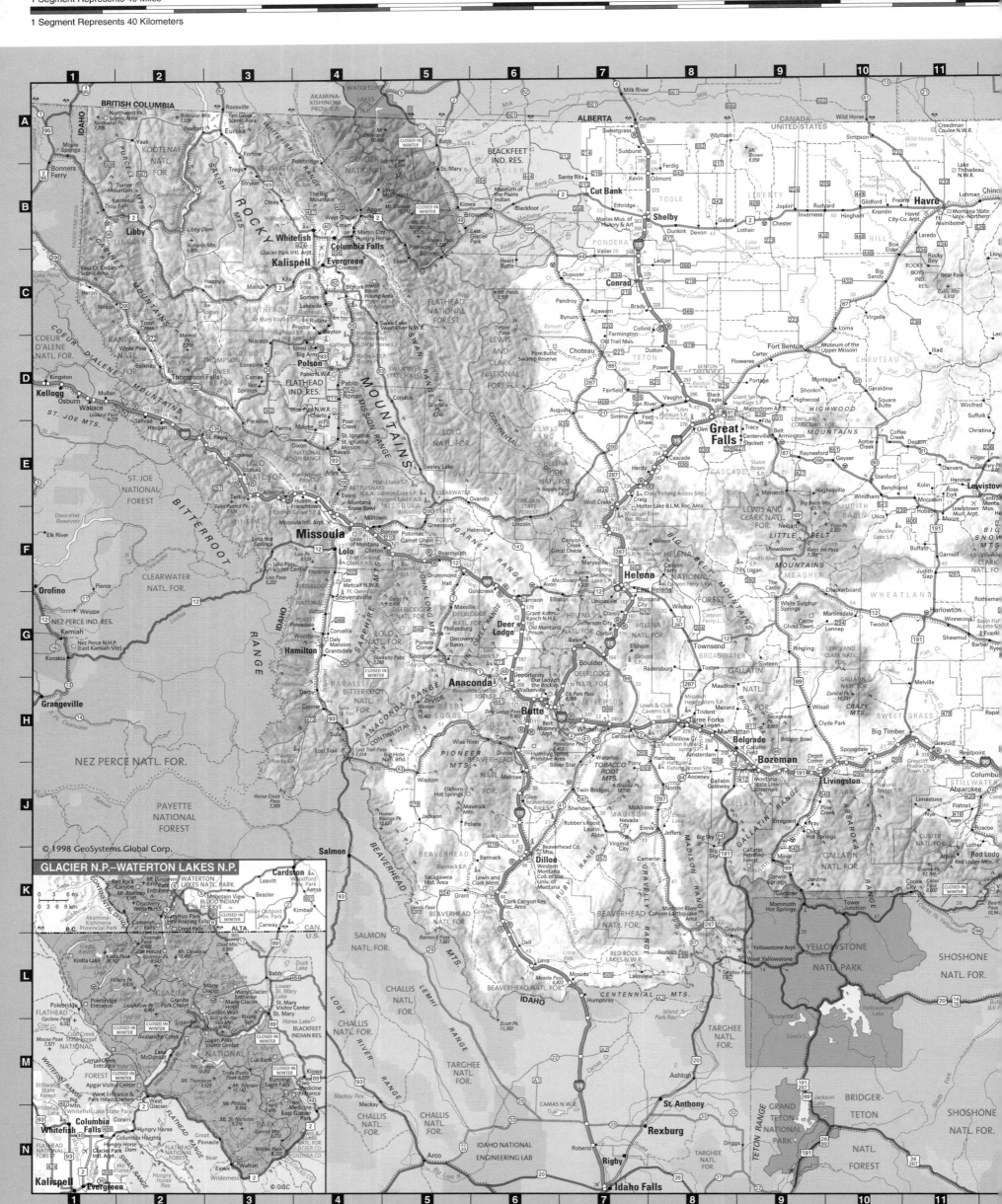

© 1998 GeoSystems Global Corp.

"Gold and Silver"

Helena

Billings

1 Segment Represents 40 Miles

1 Segment Represents 40 Kilometers

Quick Reference Index

For index to counties and places see page 138.

Absarokee	J-12	Hays	C-13
Alberton	E-3	Heart Butte	C-6
Anaconda	H-5	Helena	F-7
Arlee	E-4	Hot Springs	D-3
Ashland	J-17	Hungry Horse	B-4
Augusta	D-7	Huntley	H-13
Baker	G-20	Hysham	G-15
Ballantine	H-14	Joliet	J-12
Belgrade	H-8	Jordan	E-15
Belt	E-9	Kalispell	C-4
Big Sandy	C-10	Lakeside	C-4
Big Timber	H-11	Lame Deer	J-16
Bigfork	C-4	Laurel	J-13
Billings	J-13	Lewistown	E-12
Black Eagle	D-8	Libby	B-2
Bonner	F-4	Lima	L-6
Boulder	G-7	Lincoln	F-6
Box Elder	C-10	Livingston	J-9
Bozeman	J-9	Lodge Grass	J-15
Bridger	J-12	Lolo	F-4
Broadus	J-18	Malta	B-14
Brockton	C-18	Manhattan	H-8
Browning	B-6	Medicine Lake	B-19
Busby	J-15	Miles City	G-17
Butte	H-6	Missoula	F-4
Cascade	E-8	Nashua	C-16
Charlo	D-4	Pablo	D-4
Chester	B-9	Park City	J-12
Chinook	B-12	Philipsburg	G-5
Choteau	D-7	Pinesdale	G-4
Circle	D-17	Plains	D-3
Clinton	F-5	Plentywood	A-19
Clyde Park	H-9	Polson	D-4
Colstrip	H-16	Poplar	C-18
Columbia Falls	B-4	Pryor	J-13
Columbus	J-12	Red Lodge	K-12
Conrad	C-7	Richey	D-18
Corvallis	G-4	Ronan	D-4
Crow Agency	J-15	Roundup	G-13
Culbertson	C-19	Rudyard	B-9
Cut Bank	B-7	Ryegate	G-12
Darby	H-4	Saco	B-15
Deer Lodge	G-6	Saint Ignatius	E-4
Denton	E-11	Saint Regis	E-2
Dillon	K-6	Scobey	A-18
Drummond	F-5	Seeley Lake	E-5
Dutton	D-8	Shelby	B-8
East Glacier Park	B-5	Shepherd	H-13
East Helena	F-7	Sheridan	J-7
Ekalaka	H-19	Sidney	D-20
Ennis	J-8	Somers	C-4
Eureka	A-3	Stanford	E-10
Evergreen	C-4	Stevensville	G-4
Fairfield	D-7	Sunburst	A-7
Fairview	C-20	Superior	E-3
Florence	F-4	Terry	F-18
Forsyth	G-16	Thompson Falls	D-2
Fort Belknap		Three Forks	H-8
Agency	B-12	Townsend	G-8
Fort Benton	D-9	Troy	B-1
Fort Peck	C-16	Twin Bridges	J-7
Frazer	C-17	Valier	C-7
Fromberg	J-12	Vaughn	D-8
Gallatin Gateway	J-8	Victor	G-4
Gardiner	K-9	Walkerville	H-6
Geraldine	D-10	West Yellowstone	L-9
Glasgow	C-16	Westby	A-20
Glendive	E-19	White Sulphur	
Grantsdale	G-4	Springs	G-9
Great Falls	D-8	Whitefish	B-4
Hamilton	G-4	Whitehall	H-7
Hardin	H-14	Wibaux	E-20
Harlem	B-12	Wilsall	H-9
Harlowton	G-11	Wolf Point	C-17
Havre	B-11	Worden	H-14

Selected Attractions

Big Hole National Battlefield	J-5
Bighorn Canyon National Recreation Area	J-14
Fort Peck Dam	C-16
Gallatin Petrified Forest	K-9
Glacier National Park	B-4
Lewis and Clark Memorial	K-6
Little Bighorn Battlefield National Monument	J-15
Museum of the Plains Indian	B-6
Sacagawea Historic Area	K-5
Yellowstone National Park	L-9

Adjacent States and Provinces

Alberta	123
British Columbia	122
Idaho	33
North Dakota	85
Saskatchewan	124
South Dakota	101
Wyoming	120

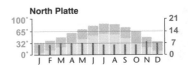

Weather - Legend

North Platte

68 NEBRASKA

1 Segment Represents 20 Miles

1 Segment Represents 20 Kilometers

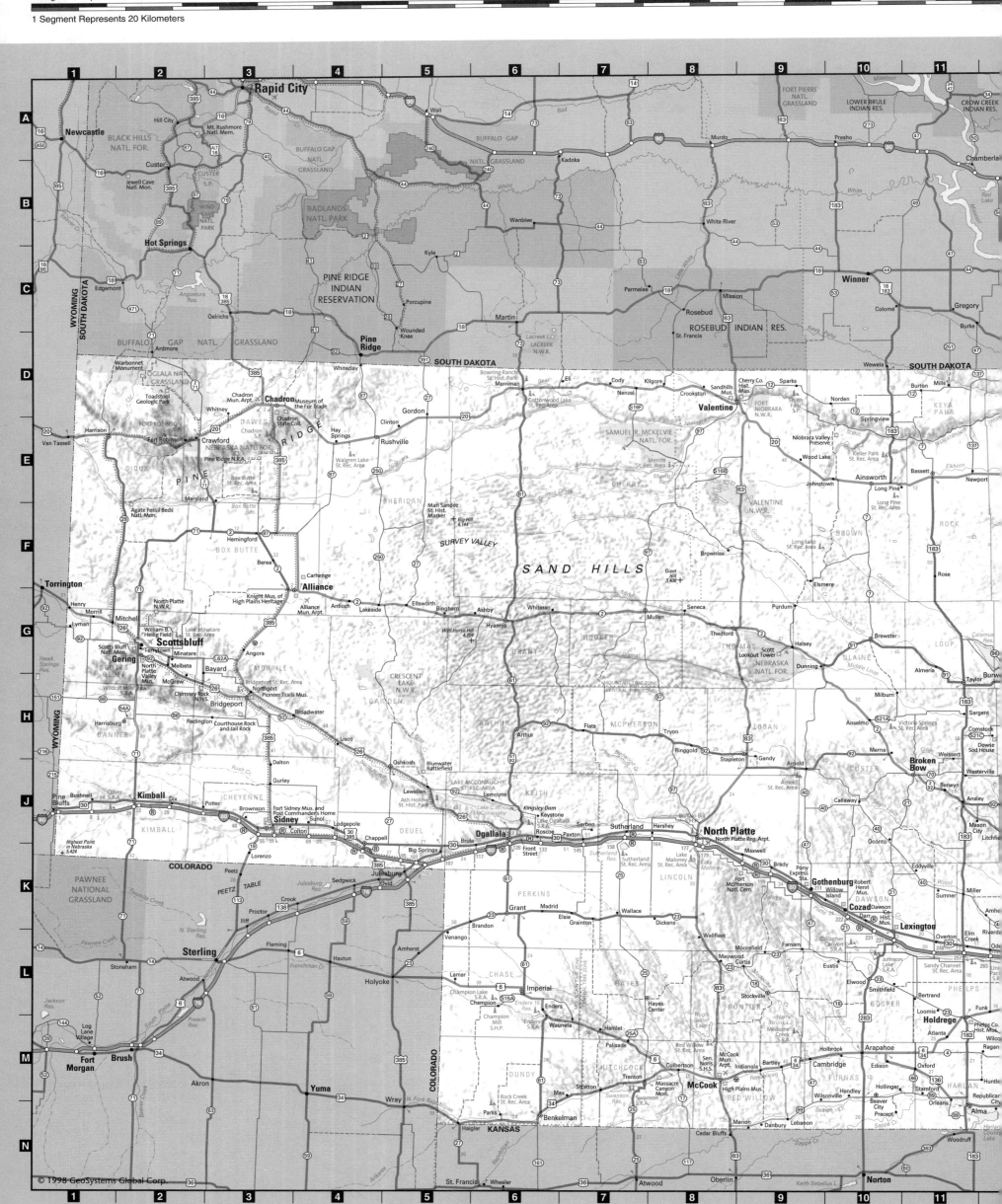

© 1998 GeoSystems Global Corp.

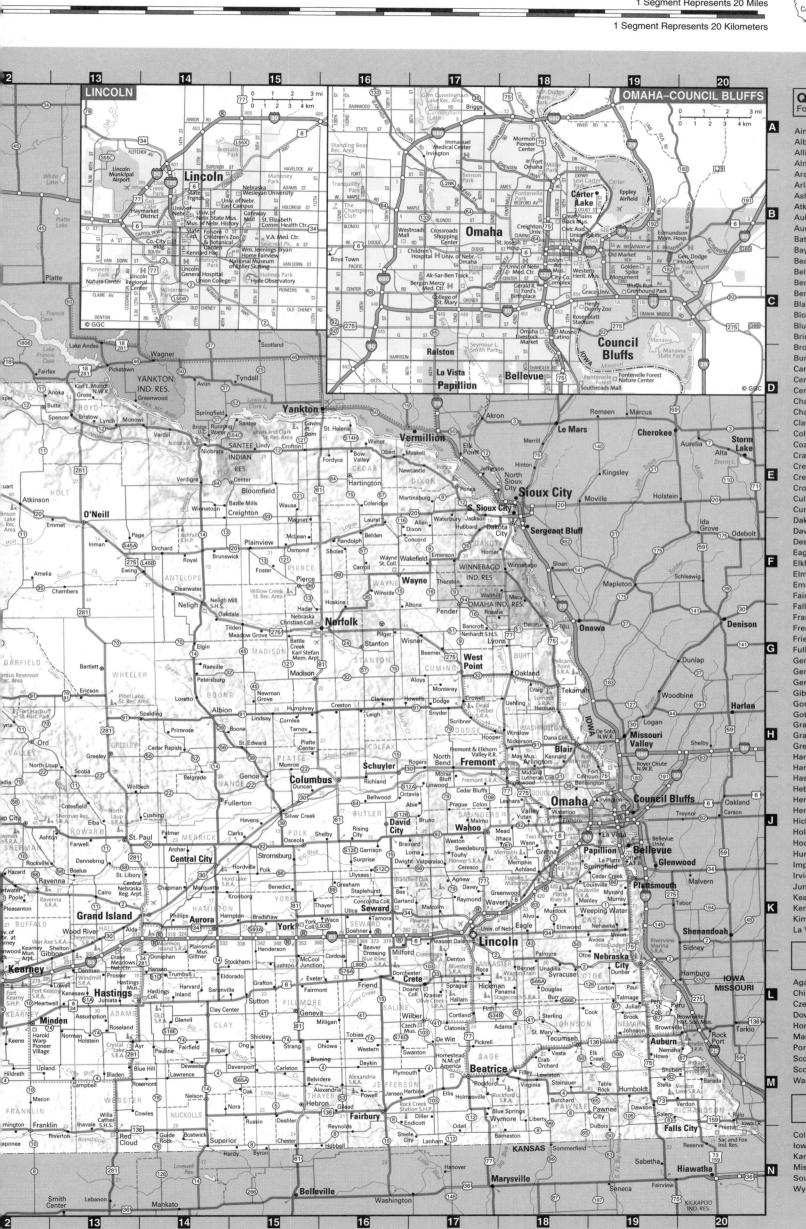

Quick Reference Index
For index to counties and places see page 138.

Ainsworth	E-10	Laurel	F-16
Albion	H-14	Lexington	L-10
Alliance	G-4	Lincoln	K-17
Alma	N-11	Louisville	K-18
Arapahoe	M-10	Loup City	J-12
Arlington	H-18	Lyons	J-18
Ashland	K-18	Macy	F-18
Atkinson	E-12	Madison	G-15
Auburn	L-19	McCook	M-8
Aurora	K-14	Milford	K-16
Battle Creek	G-15	Minatare	G-2
Bayard	G-2	Minden	L-12
Beatrice	M-17	Mitchell	G-1
Bellevue	J-19	Morrill	G-1
Benkelman	N-6	Nebraska City	L-19
Bennington	H-18	Neligh	G-14
Blair	H-18	Newman Grove	H-15
Bloomfield	E-15	Norfolk	G-16
Blue Hill	M-13	North Bend	H-17
Bridgeport	H-3	North Platte	J-8
Broken Bow	J-11	O'Neill	F-13
Burwell	H-12	Oakland	G-18
Cambridge	M-9	Ogallala	J-6
Central City	K-14	Omaha	J-19
Ceresco	K-17	Ord	H-12
Chadron	D-3	Osceola	J-15
Chappell	J-4	Oshkosh	J-5
Clay Center	L-14	Osmond	F-15
Columbus	J-16	Oxford	M-11
Cozad	K-10	Palmer	J-14
Crawford	E-2	Papillion	J-19
Creighton	F-14	Pawnee City	M-19
Crete	L-17	Pender	G-17
Crofton	E-15	Peru	L-19
Culbertson	M-8	Pierce	F-15
Curtis	M-8	Plainview	F-15
Dakota City	F-18	Plattsmouth	K-19
David City	J-16	Ponca	E-17
Deshler	M-15	Randolph	F-16
Eagle	K-18	Ravenna	K-12
Elkhorn	J-18	Red Cloud	N-13
Elm Creek	L-11	Rushville	E-4
Emerson	F-17	Saint Edward	H-15
Fairbury	M-16	Saint Paul	J-13
Falls City	M-20	Schuyler	H-16
Franklin	N-12	Scottsbluff	G-2
Fremont	H-18	Scribner	H-17
Friend	L-16	Seward	K-16
Fullerton	J-14	Shelton	K-13
Geneva	L-15	Sidney	J-3
Genoa	J-15	South Sioux City	E-18
Gering	G-2	Springfield	K-19
Gibbon	L-13	Stanton	G-16
Gordon	D-5	Stromsburg	J-15
Gothenburg	K-9	Superior	N-14
Grand Island	K-14	Sutherland	J-7
Grant	K-6	Sutton	L-15
Gretna	J-18	Syracuse	L-18
Hartington	E-16	Tecumseh	M-18
Harvard	L-14	Tekamah	G-18
Hastings	L-13	Tilden	G-15
Hebron	M-15	Valentine	D-8
Hemingford	F-3	Valley	J-18
Henderson	K-15	Wahoo	J-17
Hickman	L-17	Wakefield	F-17
Holdrege	M-11	Walthill	F-18
Hooper	H-17	Waverly	K-18
Humboldt	M-19	Wayne	F-16
Imperial	L-6	Weeping Water	K-18
Irvington	J-19	West Point	G-17
Juniata	L-13	Wilber	L-17
Kearney	L-12	Wisner	G-17
Kenesaw	L-13	Wood River	K-13
Kimball	J-2	Wymore	M-17
La Vista	J-19	York	K-15

Selected Attractions

Agate Fossil Beds National Monument	F-2
Chimney Rock National Historic Site	H-2
Czech Museum	L-17
Dowse Sod House	H-12
Homestead National Monument of America	M-17
Massacre Canyon Monument	M-8
Pony Express Station	K-9
Scott Lookout Tower	G-9
Scotts Bluff National Monument	G-2
Warbonnet Monument	D-2

Adjacent States

Colorado	20
Iowa	40
Kansas	42
Missouri	64
South Dakota	101
Wyoming	120

"All for Our Country"

Weather - Legend
Average daily high temperature, F°
Average daily low temperature, F°
Average no. of days w/precipitation

Las Vegas, NV

1 Segment Represents 30 Miles
1 Segment Represents 30 Kilometers
1 Segment Represents 30 Miles
1 Segment Represents 30 Kilometers

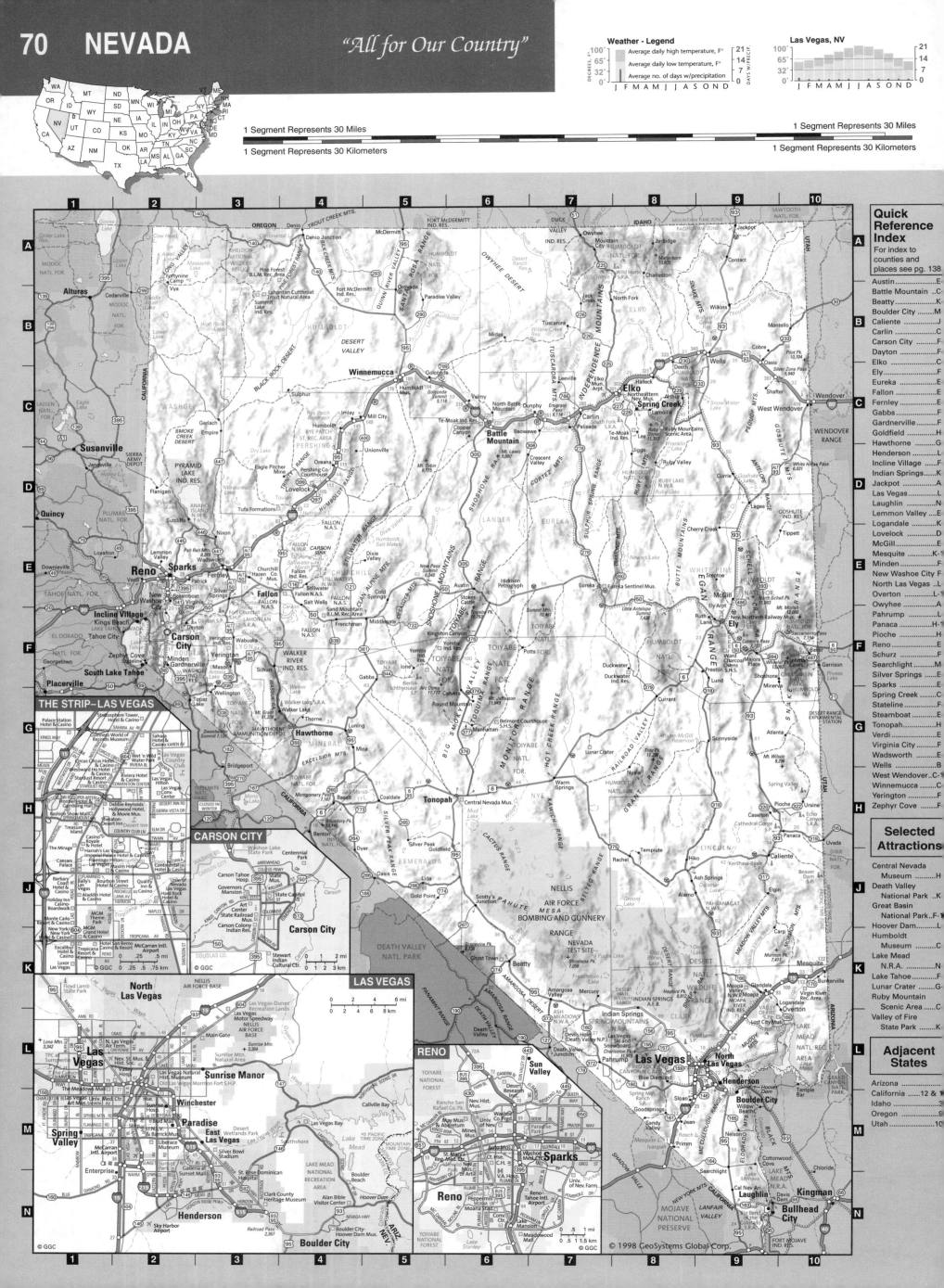

Quick Reference Index

For index to counties and places see pg. 138

Selected Attractions

Adjacent States

© 1998 GeoSystems Global Corp.

Berlin, NH

Manchester, NH

1 Segment Represents 10 Miles
1 Segment Represents 10 Kilometers

1 Segment Represents 10 Miles
1 Segment Represents 10 Kilometers

Quick Reference Index

For index to counties and places see pg. 138.

Amherst M-7
Antrim M-6
Atkinson M-8
Berlin E-8
Bristol J-6
Canobie Lake N-8
Claremont K-5
Colebrook C-7
Concord L-7
Contoocook L-7
Conway G-9
Derry M-8
Dover L-9
Durham L-9
East Hampstead .. M-9
Enfield J-5
Epping L-9
Exeter M-9
Farmington K-9
Franklin K-7
Goffstown M-7
Gorham E-8
Hampton M-10
Hampton Beach ... M-10
Hanover H-5
Henniker L-6
Hillsboro L-6
Hinsdale N-4
Hooksett L-8
Hudson N-8
Jaffrey N-6
Keene M-5
Kingston M-9
Laconia J-7
Lancaster E-7
Lebanon J-5
Littleton F-6
Londonderry M-8
Manchester M-7
Meredith J-7
Merrimack M-7
Milford M-7
Nashua N-7
Newmarket L-9
Newport K-5
North Conway G-9
North Salem N-8
Northfield K-7
Pelham N-8
Peterborough M-6
Pinardville M-7
Pittsfield K-8
Plaistow M-9
Plymouth H-7
Portsmouth L-10
Raymond L-8
Reeds Ferry M-7
Rochester K-9
Rollinsford L-10
Salem M-8
Seabrook M-10
Somersworth K-9
South Hooksett M-8
South Merrimack .. N-7
Suncook L-8
Tilton K-7
West Rye M-10
Westville M-9
Winchester N-4
Windham N-8
Wolfeboro J-8

Selected Attractions

Daniel Webster
  Birthplace
  S.H.S. K-7
Franklin Pierce
  Homestead L-6
Mt. Washington Cog
  Railway F-8
Old Man of the
  Mountain F-7

Adjacent States and Provinces

Maine 48
Massachusetts 54
Québec 128
Vermont 110

MANCHESTER

NASHUA

© 1998 GeoSystems Global Corp.

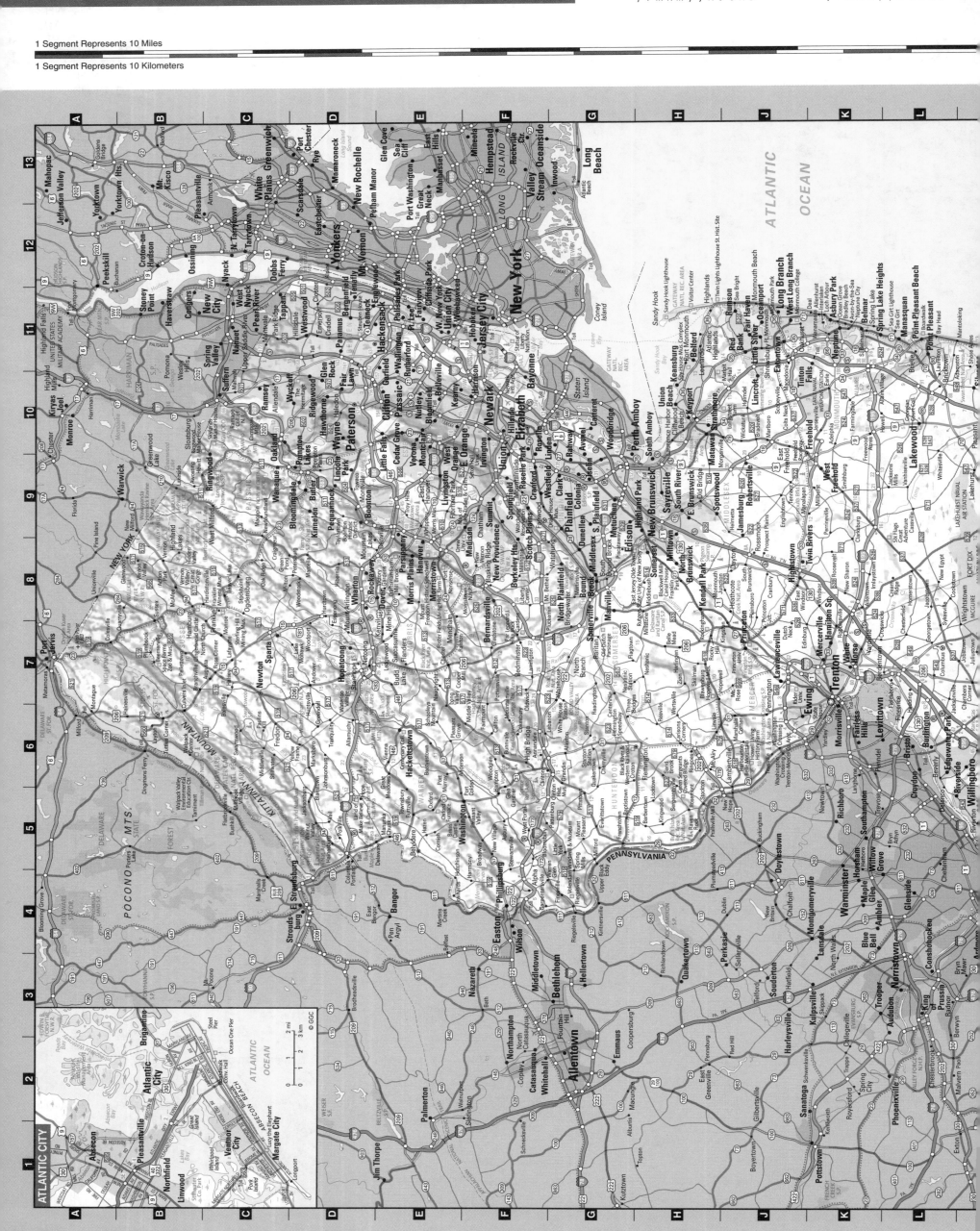

Trenton

Atlantic City

1 Segment Represents 10 Miles

1 Segment Represents 10 Kilometers

© 1998 GeoSystems Global Corp.

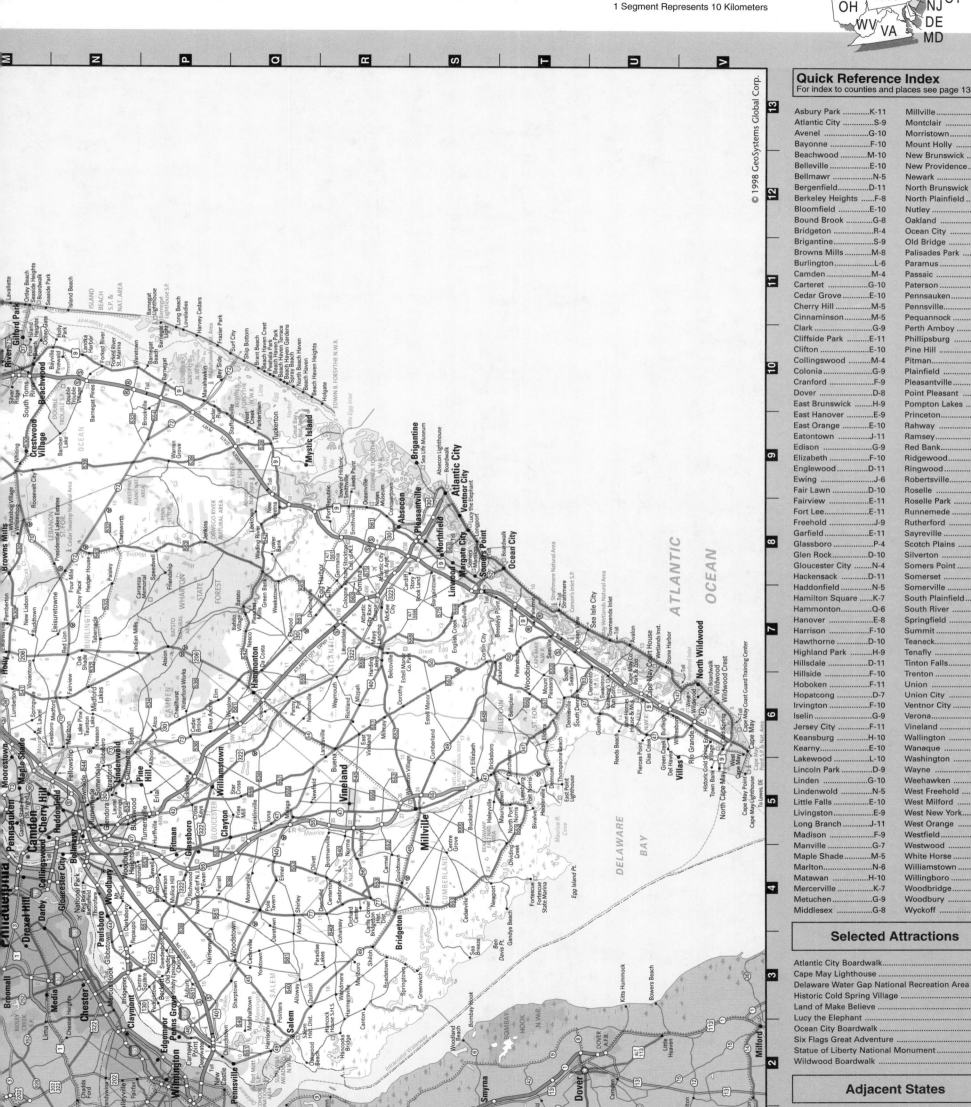

Quick Reference Index

For index to counties and places see page 138.

Asbury Park K-11	Millville S-5
Atlantic City S-9	Montclair E-10
Avenel G-10	Morristown E-8
Bayonne F-10	Mount Holly M-6
Beachwood M-10	New Brunswick H-8
Belleville E-10	New Providence F-9
Bellmawr N-5	Newark F-10
Bergenfield D-11	North Brunswick H-8
Berkeley Heights F-8	North Plainfield G-8
Bloomfield E-10	Nutley E-10
Bound Brook G-8	Oakland C-10
Bridgeton R-4	Ocean City T-8
Brigantine S-9	Old Bridge H-9
Browns Mills M-8	Palisades Park E-11
Burlington L-6	Paramus D-11
Camden M-4	Passaic E-10
Carteret G-10	Paterson D-10
Cedar Grove E-10	Pennsauken M-5
Cherry Hill M-5	Pennsville Q-2
Cinnaminson M-5	Pequannock D-9
Clark G-9	Perth Amboy H-9
Cliffside Park E-11	Phillipsburg F-4
Clifton E-10	Pine Hill N-5
Collingswood M-4	Pitman P-4
Colonia G-9	Plainfield G-9
Cranford F-9	Pleasantville S-8
Dover D-8	Point Pleasant L-11
East Brunswick H-9	Pompton Lakes D-9
East Hanover E-9	Princeton J-7
East Orange E-10	Rahway G-9
Eatontown J-11	Ramsey C-10
Edison G-9	Red Bank J-11
Elizabeth F-10	Ridgewood D-10
Englewood D-11	Ringwood C-9
Ewing J-6	Robertsville J-9
Fair Lawn D-10	Roselle F-9
Fairview E-11	Roselle Park F-10
Fort Lee E-11	Runnemede N-5
Freehold J-9	Rutherford E-10
Garfield E-11	Sayreville H-9
Glassboro P-4	Scotch Plains F-9
Glen Rock D-10	Silverton M-10
Gloucester City N-4	Somers Point S-8
Hackensack D-11	Somerset H-8
Haddonfield N-5	Somerville G-8
Hamilton Square K-7	South Plainfield G-9
Hammonton Q-6	South River H-9
Hanover E-9	Springfield F-9
Harrison F-10	Summit F-9
Hawthorne D-10	Teaneck D-11
Highland Park H-9	Tenafly D-11
Hillsdale D-11	Tinton Falls K-11
Hillside F-10	Trenton K-7
Hoboken F-11	Union F-9
Hopatcong D-7	Union City E-11
Irvington F-10	Ventnor City S-8
Iselin G-9	Verona E-10
Jersey City F-11	Vineland R-5
Keansburg H-10	Wallington E-10
Kearny F-10	Wanaque C-9
Lakewood L-10	Washington E-5
Lincoln Park D-9	Wayne D-10
Linden G-10	Weehawken E-11
Lindenwold N-5	West Freehold K-9
Little Falls E-10	West Milford C-9
Livingston E-9	West New York E-11
Long Branch J-11	West Orange E-10
Madison E-9	Westfield F-9
Manville G-7	Westwood D-11
Maple Shade M-5	White Horse K-7
Marlton N-6	Williamstown P-5
Matawan H-10	Willingboro M-6
Mercerville K-7	Woodbridge G-9
Metuchen G-9	Woodbury N-4
Middlesex G-8	Wyckoff D-10

Selected Attractions

Atlantic City Boardwalk	S-9
Cape May Lighthouse	V-5
Delaware Water Gap National Recreation Area	C-6
Historic Cold Spring Village	V-6
Land of Make Believe	D-5
Lucy the Elephant	S-8
Ocean City Boardwalk	T-8
Six Flags Great Adventure	K-9
Statue of Liberty National Monument	F-11
Wildwood Boardwalk	V-6

Adjacent States

Delaware	24
New York	76 & 78
Pennsylvania	94 & 96

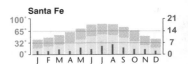

Weather - Legend
Average daily high temperature, F°
Average daily low temperature, F°
Average no. of days w/precipitation

Santa Fe

1 Segment Represents 20 Miles

1 Segment Represents 20 Kilometers

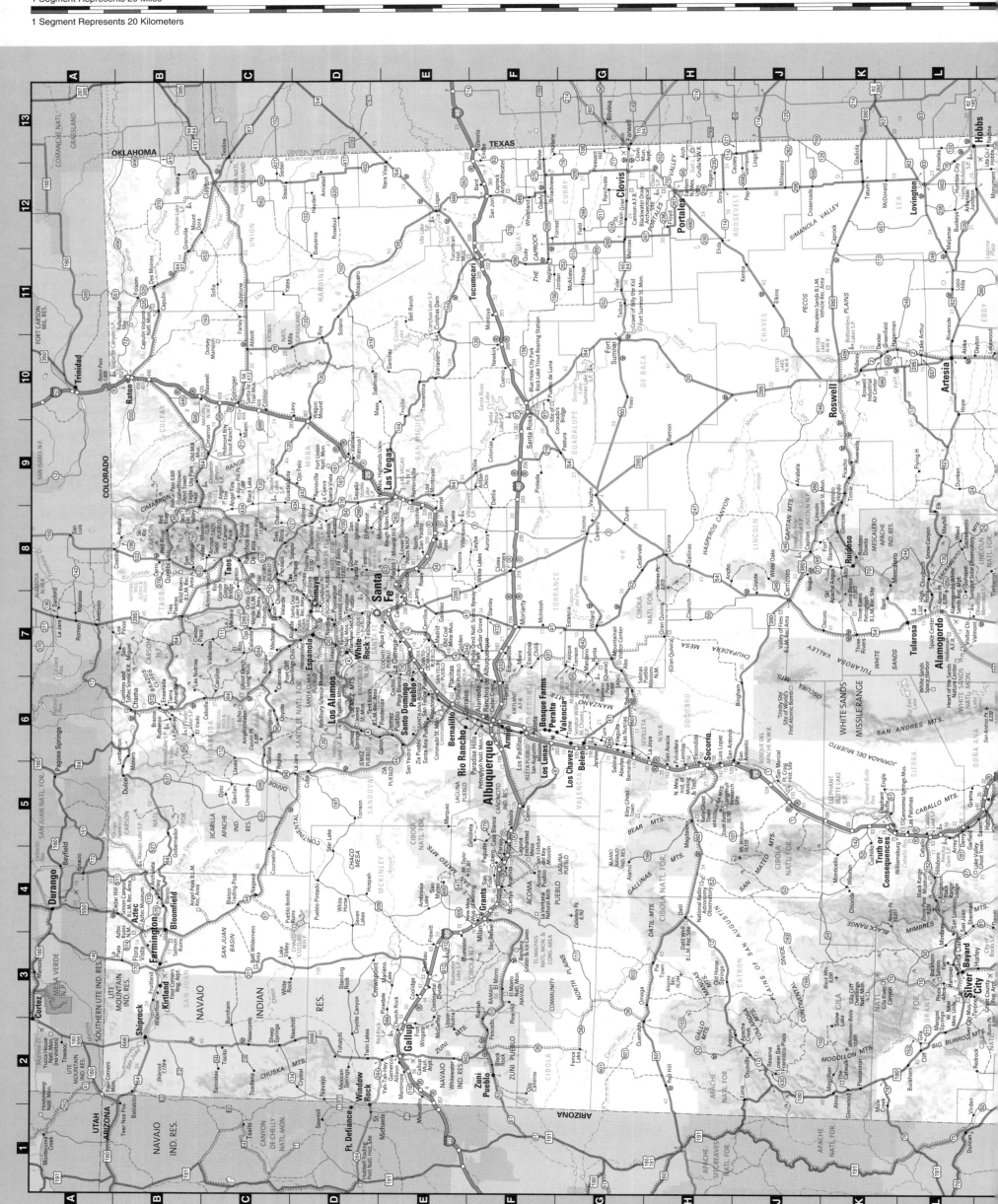

Albuquerque

Las Cruces

1 Segment Represents 20 Miles

1 Segment Represents 20 Kilometers

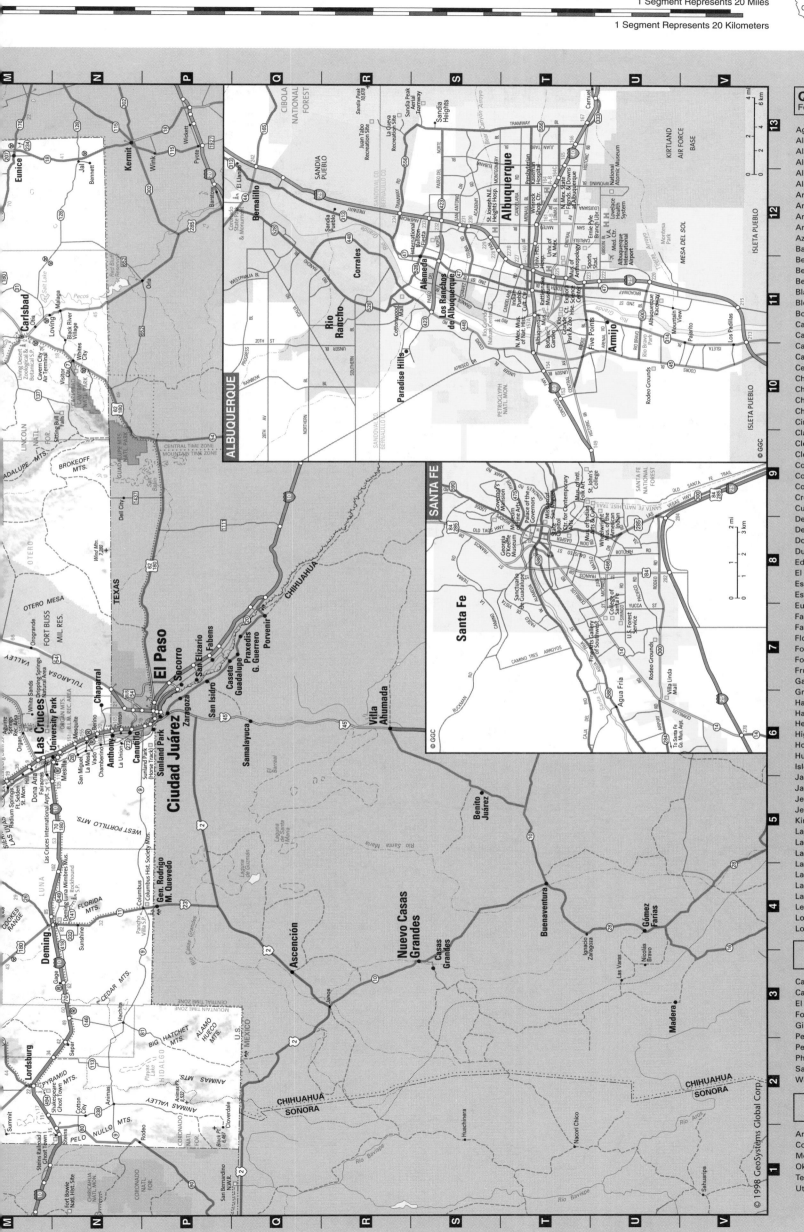

Quick Reference Index

For index to counties and places see page 138.

Place	Grid	Place	Grid
Agua Fria	E-7	Los Alamos	D-7
Alameda	F-6	Los Chavez	G-6
Alamo	G-4	Los Lunas	F-6
Alamogordo	L-7	Los Padillas	F-6
Albuquerque	F-6	Los Ranchos de	
Algodones	E-6	Albuquerque	F-6
Armijo	F-6	Loving	M-11
Arroyo Hondo	C-8	Lovington	L-12
Arroyo Seco	C-8	Magdalena	H-5
Artesia	L-10	Medanales	C-7
Aztec	B-4	Melrose	G-12
Bayard	L-3	Mescalero	K-8
Belen	G-6	Mesilla	N-6
Berino	N-6	Mesita	F-5
Bernalillo	E-6	Mesquite	N-6
Black Rock	F-2	Midway	K-10
Bloomfield	B-4	Milan	F-4
Bosque Farms	F-6	Mora	D-8
Capitan	J-8	Moriarty	F-7
Carlsbad	M-11	Mountainair	G-7
Carrizozo	J-7	Nambe	D-7
Casa Blanca	F-4	Navajo	D-2
Central	L-3	Paguate	F-5
Chama	B-6	Paradise Hills	F-6
Chamberino	N-6	Paraje	F-4
Chaparral	N-6	Pecos	E-8
Chimayo	D-7	Penasco	C-8
Cimarron	C-9	Peralta	F-6
Clayton	C-12	Placitas	E-6
Cloudcroft	L-8	Pojoaque	D-7
Clovis	G-12	Portales	H-12
Cochiti	E-7	Questa	B-8
Columbus	P-4	Ranchos De Taos	C-8
Corrales	E-6	Raton	B-10
Crownpoint	D-3	Rio Rancho	E-6
Cuba	D-5	Roswell	K-10
Deming	N-4	Ruidoso	K-8
Dexter	K-10	Ruidoso Downs	K-8
Dona Ana	M-6	Salem	M-5
Dulce	B-5	San Felipe Pueblo	E-6
Edgewood	F-7	San Miguel	N-6
El Rito	C-7	Sandia Park	F-6
Espanola	D-7	Sanostee	C-2
Estancia	G-7	Santa Ana Pueblo	E-6
Eunice	M-13	Santa Fe	D-7
Fairacres	M-6	Santa Rosa	F-10
Farmington	B-3	Santo Domingo Pueblo	
Flora Vista	B-3		E-6
Fort Sumner	G-10	Shiprock	B-2
Fort Wingate	E-2	Silver City	L-3
Fruitland	B-3	Socorro	H-5
Gallup	E-2	Springer	C-10
Grants	F-4	Sunland Park	P-6
Hagerman	K-10	Taos	C-8
Hatch	M-5	Tatum	K-12
Hernandez	D-7	Tesuque	D-7
High Rolls	L-7	Texico	G-13
Hobbs	L-13	Thoreau	E-3
Hurley	M-3	Tohatchi	D-2
Isleta	F-6	Tome	E-6
Jal	N-13	Truth or Consequences	
Jarales	G-6		K-5
Jemez Pueblo	E-6	Tucumcari	F-11
Jemez Springs	D-6	Tularosa	L-7
Kirtland	B-3	Turley	B-4
La Cienega	E-7	Twin Lakes	D-2
La Luz	L-7	Tyrone	M-3
La Mesa	N-6	University Park	N-6
La Union	N-6	Vado	N-6
Laguna	F-5	Valencia	G-6
Las Cruces	N-6	Vaughn	G-9
Las Vegas	E-9	White Rock	D-7
Lemitar	H-6	Williamsburg	K-5
Logan	E-12	Zia Pueblo	E-6
Lordsburg	M-2	Zuni Pueblo	F-2

Selected Attractions

Capulin Volcano National Monument	B-11
Carlsbad Caverns National Park	N-10
El Malpais Natl. Mon. & Conservation Area	F-3
Four Corners Monument	A-2
Gila Cliff Dwellings National Monument	K-3
Pecos National Historic Park	E-8
Petroglyph National Monument	F-6
Philmont Boy Scout Ranch	C-9
Sandia Crest National Scenic Byway	F-7
White Sands National Monument	M-6

Adjacent States

Arizona	8
Colorado	20
Mexico	132
Oklahoma	90
Texas	104 & 106
Utah	109

© 1998 GeoSystems Global Corp.

© 1998 GeoSystems Global Corp.

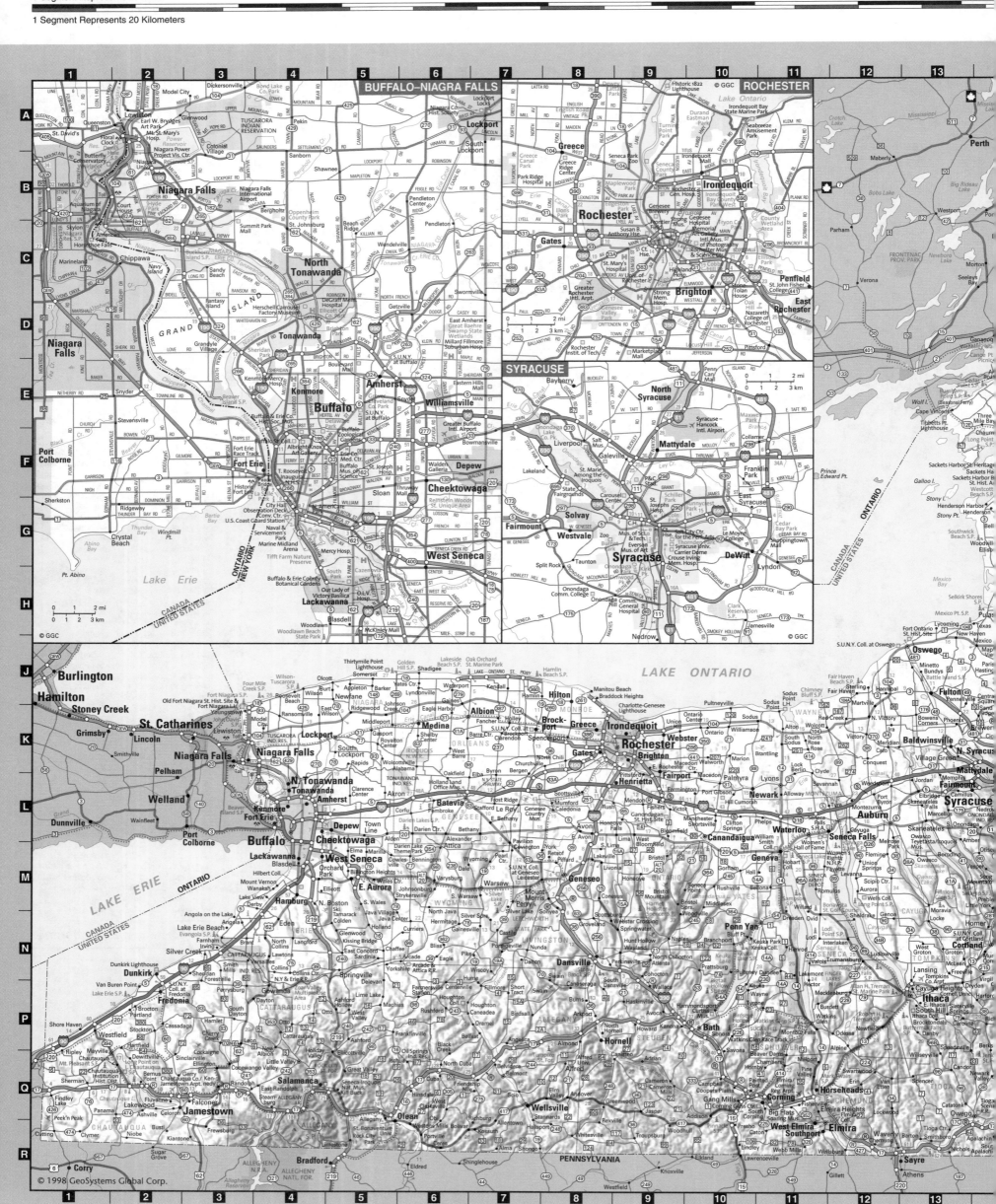

Rochester | Syracuse

1 Segment Represents 20 Miles
1 Segment Represents 20 Kilometers

Quick Reference Index
For index to counties and places see page 138.

Albany	N-23	Lake Erie Beach	N-3
Albion	K-6	Lakewood	Q-2
Alfred	Q-8	Lansing	N-13
Amherst	L-4	Le Roy	L-7
Amsterdam	L-21	Lewiston	K-3
Auburn	L-12	Little Falls	L-19
Baldwinsville	K-13	Lockport	K-5
Ballston Spa	L-22	Loudonville	M-23
Batavia	L-6	Lowville	G-16
Bath	P-10	Lyons	L-11
Binghamton	Q-15	Malone	B-20
Brighton	K-9	Manlius	L-15
Brockport	K-7	Massena	A-18
Buffalo	L-4	Mattydale	K-14
Canandaigua	L-10	Mechanicville	L-23
Canastota	L-15	Medina	K-6
Canton	C-17	Minoa	L-14
Carthage	F-16	Mount Morris	M-8
Catskill	Q-22	Mount Vernon	M-4
Cayuga Heights	P-13	Newark	L-10
Cheektowaga	K-4	Niagara Falls	K-3
Chenango Bridge	Q-15	North Chili	K-8
Chittenango	L-15	North Syracuse	K-14
Clifton Park	L-23	North Tonawanda	L-4
Cobleskill	M-20	Norwich	N-16
Cohoes	M-23	Ogdensburg	B-16
Colonie	M-22	Olean	Q-5
Corning	Q-11	Oneida	K-16
Cortland	N-14	Oneonta	P-18
Dannemora	B-22	Orchard Park	M-4
Dansville	N-8	Oswego	J-13
De Witt	L-14	Owego	Q-14
Delhi	Q-18	Palmyra	L-10
Delmar	N-22	Penn Yan	N-11
Depew	L-5	Perry	M-7
Dunkirk	N-2	Plattsburgh	B-23
East Aurora	M-5	Potsdam	B-18
East Glenville	L-22	Ravena	N-22
East Rochester	K-9	Rensselaer	N-23
Eden	N-4	Rochester	K-9
Elmira Heights	Q-11	Rome	K-16
Endicott	Q-14	Rotterdam	M-22
Endwell	Q-14	Salamanca	Q-4
Fairmount	L-14	Saranac Lake	D-21
Fairport	K-9	Saratoga Springs	K-22
Fayetteville	L-14	Saugerties	Q-22
Fort Edward	J-23	Schenectady	M-22
Fredonia	P-2	Scotia	M-22
Fulton	J-13	Seneca Falls	L-12
Gates	K-8	Sidney	P-17
Geneseo	M-8	South Hill	P-13
Geneva	M-11	South Lockport	K-5
Glens Falls	J-23	Spencerport	K-8
Gloversville	L-20	Springville	N-5
Gouverneur	D-16	Syracuse	L-14
Greece	K-8	Tonawanda	L-4
Hamburg	M-4	Troy	M-23
Hamilton	M-16	Tupper Lake	E-20
Henrietta	L-9	Utica	K-17
Herkimer	L-18	Village Green	K-13
Hilton	K-8	Voorheesville	N-22
Homer	N-14	Walton	Q-18
Hoosick Falls	L-24	Wanakah	M-4
Hornell	P-8	Warrensburg	H-22
Horseheads	Q-11	Warsaw	M-7
Hudson	Q-23	Waterloo	L-11
Hudson Falls	J-23	Watertown	F-15
Ilion	L-18	Webster	K-9
Irondequoit	K-9	Wellsville	Q-7
Ithaca	P-13	West Glens Falls	J-23
Jamestown	Q-2	West Seneca	M-4
Johnson City	Q-15	Westfield	P-1
Johnstown	L-20	Westmere	M-22
Kenmore	L-4	Whitehall	H-24
Lackawanna	M-4	Whitesboro	K-17

Selected Attractions

Adirondack Park	E-21
Catskill Park	R-20
Corning Glass Center	Q-11
Fort Ticonderoga	G-24
National Baseball Hall of Fame & Museum	M-18
Robert H. Treman State Park	P-12
Van Buren National Historic Site	P-23
Watkins Glen State Park	P-11
Women's Rights National Historic Park	L-11

Adjacent States and Provinces

Connecticut	22
Massachusetts	54
New Jersey	72
New York - Southern	78
Ontario	126
Pennsylvania	94 & 96
Québec	128
Rhode Island	99
Vermont	110

Weather - Legend

Average daily high temperature, F°
Average daily low temperature, F°
Average no. of days w/precipitation

Binghamton

1 Segment Represents 10 Miles

1 Segment Represents 10 Kilometers

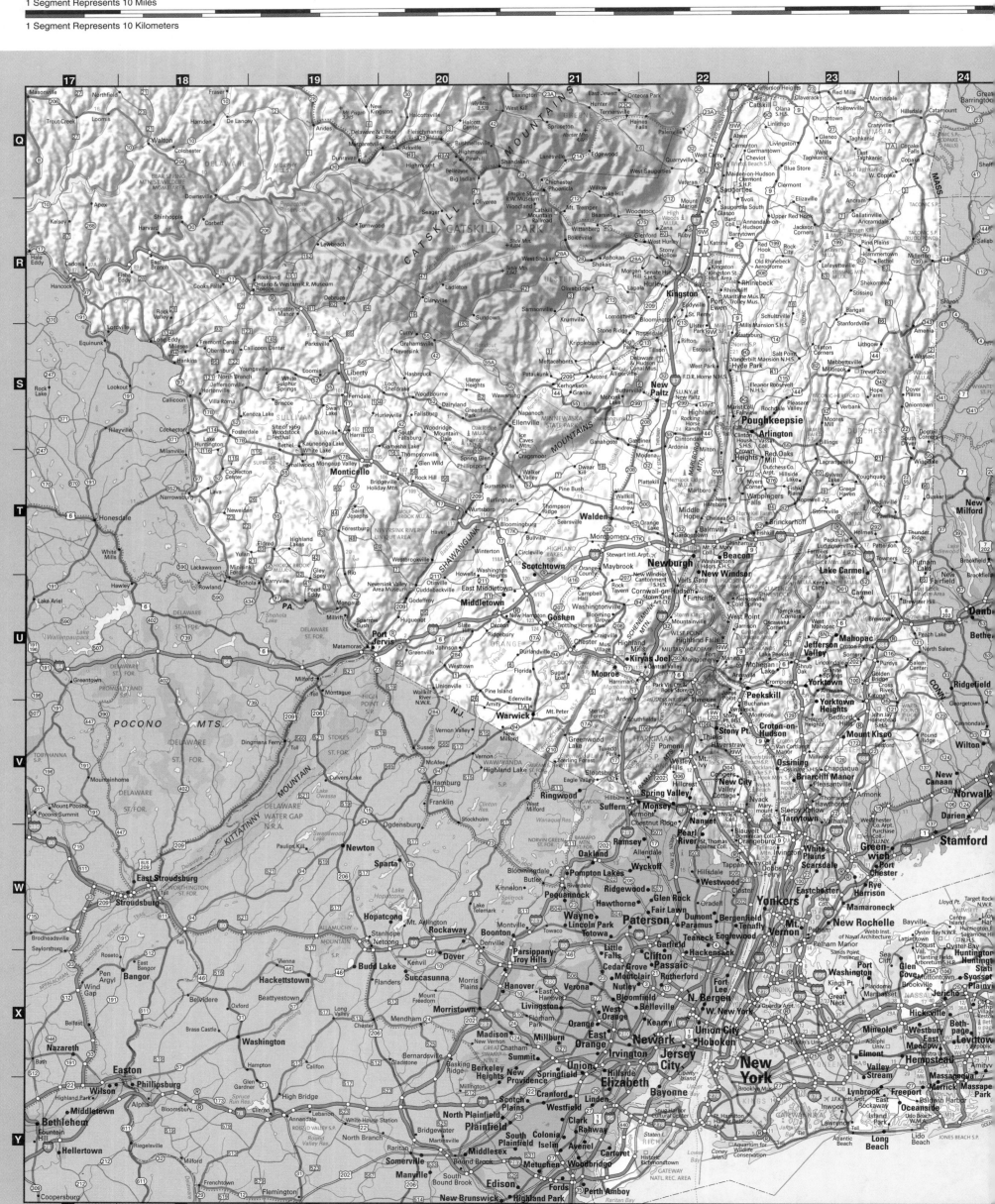

Albany

New York City

1 Segment Represents 10 Miles

1 Segment Represents 10 Kilometers

ALBANY–SCHENECTADY–TROY

Quick Reference Index
For index to counties and places see page 138.

Airmont	V-22	Merrick	Y-24
Amityville	X-24	Middle Island	W-26
Arlington	S-22	Middletown	U-20
Babylon	X-25	Miller Place	W-26
Baldwin Harbor	Y-24	Mineola	X-23
Bay Shore	X-25	Mohegan Lake	U-23
Bayport	X-26	Monroe	U-21
Bayville	W-24	Monsey	V-22
Beacon	T-22	Monticello	T-19
Bethpage	X-24	Mount Ivy	V-22
Binghamton	Q-15	Mount Kisco	V-23
Brentwood	X-25	Mount Sinai	W-26
Briarcliff Manor	V-23	Mount Vernon	W-23
Center Moriches	X-27	Nanuet	V-22
Centereach	W-26	Nesconset	X-25
Central Islip	X-25	New City	V-22
Chestnut Ridge	V-22	New Rochelle	W-23
Commack	X-25	New Windsor	U-22
Congers	V-22	New York	V-22
Copiague	X-24	Newburgh	T-22
Coram	W-26	North Bellport	X-26
Corning	Q-11	Northport	W-25
Croton-on-Hudson	V-22	Nyack	V-22
Deer Park	X-25	Oakdale	X-26
Dobbs Ferry	W-23	Oceanside	Y-24
East Islip	X-25	Olean	Q-5
East Meadow	X-24	Ossining	V-23
East Northport	W-25	Oyster Bay	W-24
East Patchogue	X-26	Patchogue	X-26
East Rockaway	Y-23	Pearl River	W-22
Eastchester	W-23	Peekskill	U-22
Elmira	R-11	Pelham	W-23
Elmont	X-23	Plainview	X-24
Endicott	Q-14	Pleasantville	V-23
Endwell	Q-14	Port Chester	W-23
Farmingdale	X-26	Port Jefferson	W-26
Fort Salonga	W-25	Port Jefferson Sta.	W-26
Freeport	Y-24	Port Jervis	U-19
Glen Cove	X-24	Port Washington	X-23
Great Neck	X-23	Poughkeepsie	S-22
Hampton Bays	W-28	Ridge	W-26
Harrison	W-23	Riverhead	W-27
Hauppauge	X-25	Rocky Point	W-26
Haverstraw	V-22	Ronkonkoma	X-25
Hempstead	X-24	Rye	W-23
Hicksville	X-24	Salamanca	Q-4
Hillcrest	V-22	Sayville	X-26
Holbrook	X-26	Scarsdale	W-23
Horseheads	Q-11	Scotchtown	T-21
Hudson	Q-23	Selden	W-26
Huntington	W-24	Shirley	X-26
Huntington Station	X-24	Sleepy Hollow	V-23
Inwood	Y-23	Smithtown	X-25
Irvington	W-23	Sound Beach	W-26
Jamestown	Q-2	Southport	R-11
Jericho	X-24	Spring Valley	V-22
Johnson City	Q-15	St. James	W-25
Kings Park	W-25	Stony Brook	W-25
Kingston	R-22	Stony Point	V-22
Kiryas Joel	U-21	Suffern	V-22
Lake Carmel	T-23	Syosset	X-24
Lawrence	Y-23	Tappan	W-22
Levittown	X-24	Tarrytown	V-23
Lindenhurst	X-24	Terryville	W-26
Long Beach	Y-23	Thornwood	V-23
Lynbrook	Y-23	Valley Cottage	V-22
Mahopac	U-23	Valley Stream	X-23
Mamaroneck	W-23	Walden	T-21
Manhasset	X-23	Warwick	U-21
Manorville	W-27	West Babylon	X-24
Massapequa	X-24	West Islip	X-25
Massapequa Park	Y-24	Westbury	X-24
Mastic	X-26	White Plains	W-23
Mastic Beach	X-26	Yonkers	W-22
Medford	X-26	Yorktown Heights	V-23

Selected Attractions

Catskill Park	R-21
Eleanor Roosevelt National Historic Site	S-22
F.D.R. Home National Historic Site	S-22
Fire Island National Seashore	X-26
Gateway National Recreation Area	Y-22
Historic Richmondtown	Y-22
Vanderbilt Mansion National Historic Site	S-22
Washington Headquarters State Historic Site	T-22
West Point Military Academy	U-22

Adjacent States and Provinces

Connecticut	22
Massachusetts	54
New Jersey	72
New York - Northern	76
Ontario	126
Pennsylvania	94 & 96
Québec	128
Rhode Island	99
Vermont	110

© 1998 GeoSystems Global Corp.

1 Segment Represents 2 Miles (area map)

1 Segment Represents 2 Kilometers (area map)

1 Segment Represents 2 Miles (area map)

1 Segment Represents 2 Kilometers (area map)

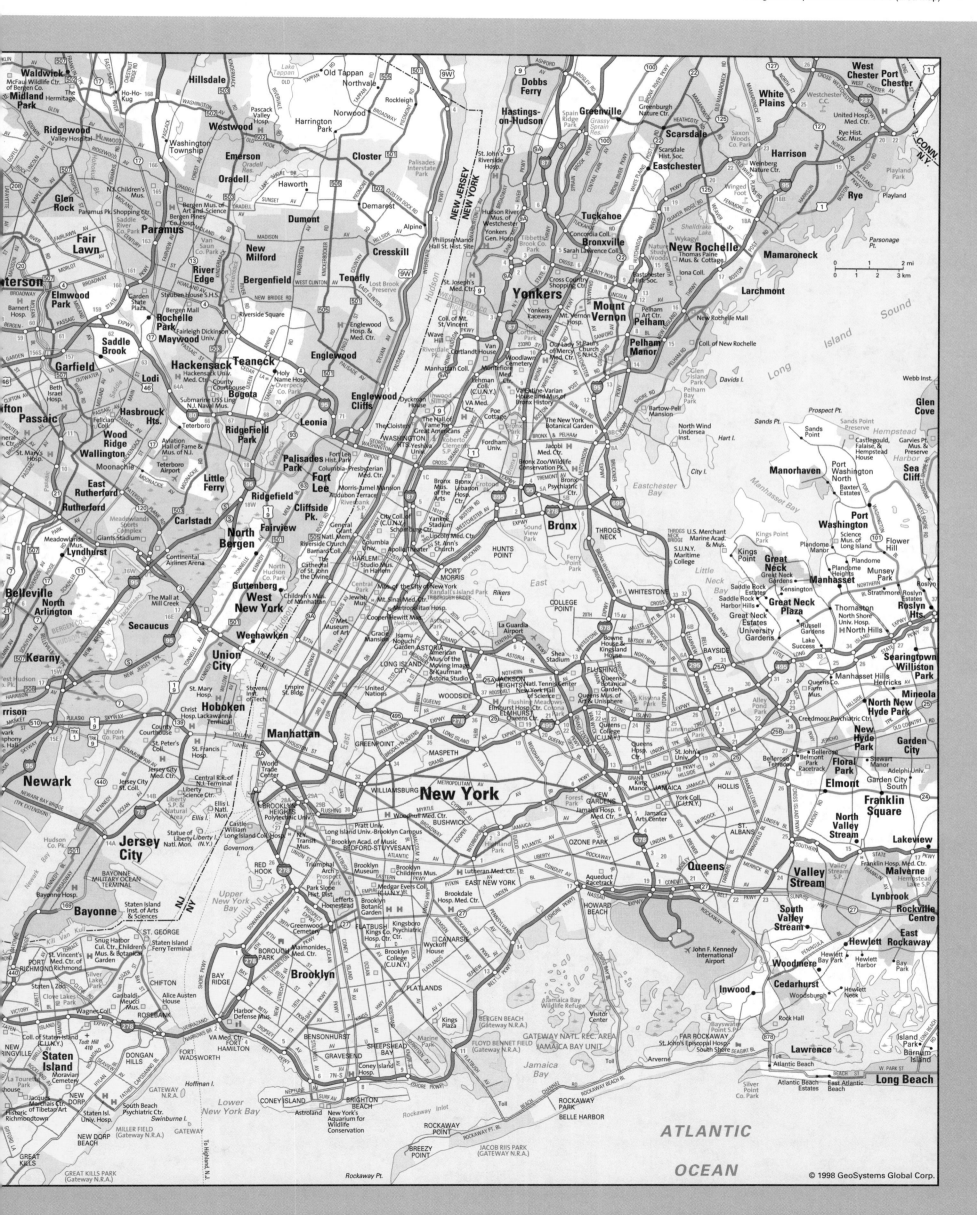

"To Be, Rather than to Seem"

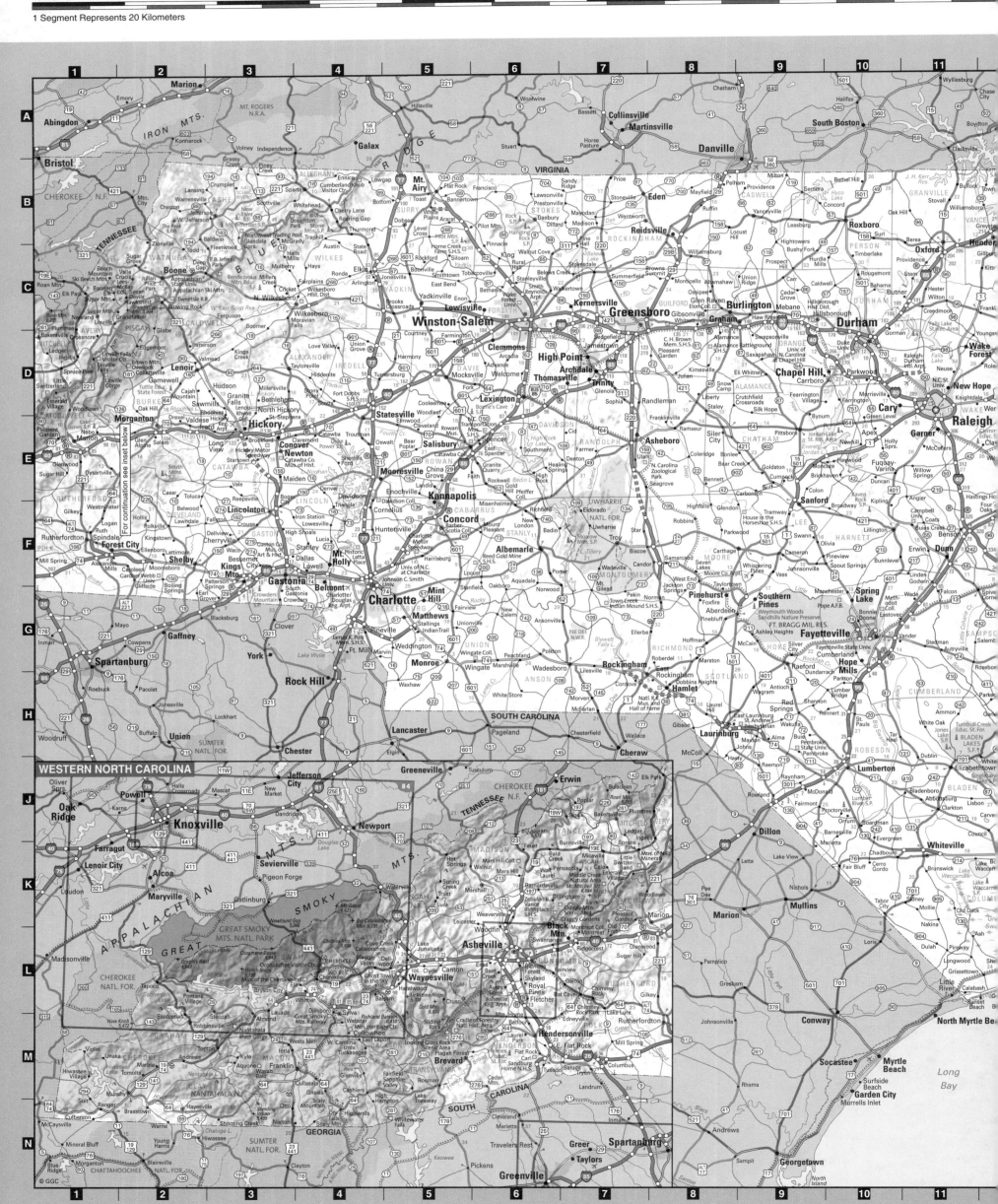

1 Segment Represents 20 Miles

1 Segment Represents 20 Kilometers

WESTERN NORTH CAROLINA

1 Segment Represents 20 Miles

1 Segment Represents 20 Kilometers

Quick Reference Index
For index to counties and places see page 139.

Ahoskie	C-16	Long Beach	L-13
Albemarle	F-6	Louisburg	C-12
Apex	E-10	Lumberton	J-10
Archdale	D-7	Mar-Mac	F-13
Asheboro	E-7	Marion	E-1
Asheville	L-6	Masonboro	K-13
Ayden	F-15	Matthews	G-5
Beaufort	H-17	Mebane	C-9
Belmont	F-4	Mint Hill	G-5
Bessemer City	F-3	Mocksville	D-5
Black Mountain	L-6	Monroe	G-5
Bonnie Doone	F-10	Mooresville	E-4
Boone	C-2	Morehead City	H-17
Brevard	M-5	Morganton	E-2
Burlington	C-8	Mount Airy	B-5
Butner	C-11	Mount Holly	F-4
Canton	L-5	Mount Olive	G-13
Carolina Beach	K-13	Myrtle Grove	K-13
Carrboro	D-9	Nashville	D-13
Cary	D-10	New Bern	G-16
Chapel Hill	D-10	New Hope	D-11
Charlotte	G-4	New Hope	F-13
Cherryville	F-3	Newton	E-3
Clayton	E-12	North Hickory	D-3
Clemmons	D-6	North Wilkesboro	C-4
Clinton	G-12	Oxford	C-11
Concord	F-5	Parkwood	D-10
Conover	E-3	Pinehurst	F-8
Cornelius	F-4	Piney Green	H-15
Cullowhee	M-5	Plymouth	D-17
Davidson	E-4	Raeford	G-9
Dunn	F-11	Raleigh	E-11
Durham	D-10	Red Springs	H-9
East Rockingham	H-8	Reidsville	B-8
Eden	B-7	Roanoke Rapids	B-14
Edenton	C-17	Rockingham	H-7
Elizabeth City	B-18	Rocky Mount	D-14
Elizabethtown	J-11	Roxboro	B-10
Elkin	C-4	Royal Pines	L-6
Erwin	F-11	Rutherfordton	F-1
Farmville	E-14	St. Stephens	E-3
Fayetteville	G-10	Salisbury	E-5
Forest City	F-1	Sanford	F-9
Fuquay-Varina	E-10	Sawmills	D-3
Gamewell	D-2	Seagate	K-13
Garner	E-11	Selma	E-12
Gastonia	F-3	Shelby	F-2
Gibsonville	C-8	Siler City	E-8
Goldsboro	F-13	Silver Lake	K-13
Graham	C-8	Smithfield	E-12
Greensboro	C-7	South Gastonia	G-3
Greenville	E-15	Southern Pines	G-9
Half Moon	H-14	Spindale	F-1
Hamlet	H-8	Spring Lake	G-10
Havelock	H-16	Statesville	E-4
Henderson	B-12	Swannanoa	L-6
Hendersonville	M-6	Tarboro	D-14
Hickory	E-3	Thomasville	D-7
High Point	D-7	Trent Woods	G-15
Hillsborough	C-9	Trinity	D-7
Hope Mills	G-10	Troy	F-7
Huntersville	F-4	Valdese	E-2
Jacksonville	H-15	Wadesboro	G-6
James City	G-16	Wake Forest	D-11
Kannapolis	F-5	Washington	E-16
Kernersville	C-7	Waynesville	L-5
Kill Devil Hills	C-20	Weddington	G-5
King	C-6	Welcome	D-6
Kings Mountain	F-3	Whiteville	K-11
Kinston	F-14	Williamston	D-16
Laurinburg	H-8	Wilmington	K-13
Lenoir	D-2	Wilson	E-13
Lewisville	C-6	Windemere	K-13
Lexington	D-6	Winston-Salem	C-6
Lincolnton	F-3	Wrightsboro	K-13

Selected Attractions

Blue Ridge Parkway	B-4
Camp Lejeune Marine Corps Base	H-15
Cape Hatteras National Seashore	F-20
Cape Lookout Lighthouse	J-17
Cape Lookout National Seashore	H-18
Great Smoky Mountains National Park	L-3
Hickory Motor Speedway	E-3
Ocracoke Island Visitor Center	G-19
The Country Doctor Museum	D-12
Wright Brothers National Memorial	C-20

Adjacent States

Georgia	30
South Carolina	100
Tennessee	102
Virginia	112

© 1998 GeoSystems Global Corp.

Charlotte, NC
Great Smoky
 Mountains N.P., NC/TN Area
Raleigh–Durham, NC

Winston-Salem–
 Greensboro, NC

1 Segment Represents 8 Miles (Smoky Mts. map)

1 Segment Represents 8 Kilometers (Smoky Mts. map)

1 Segment Represents 8 Miles (Smoky Mts. map)

1 Segment Represents 8 Kilometers (Smoky Mts. map)

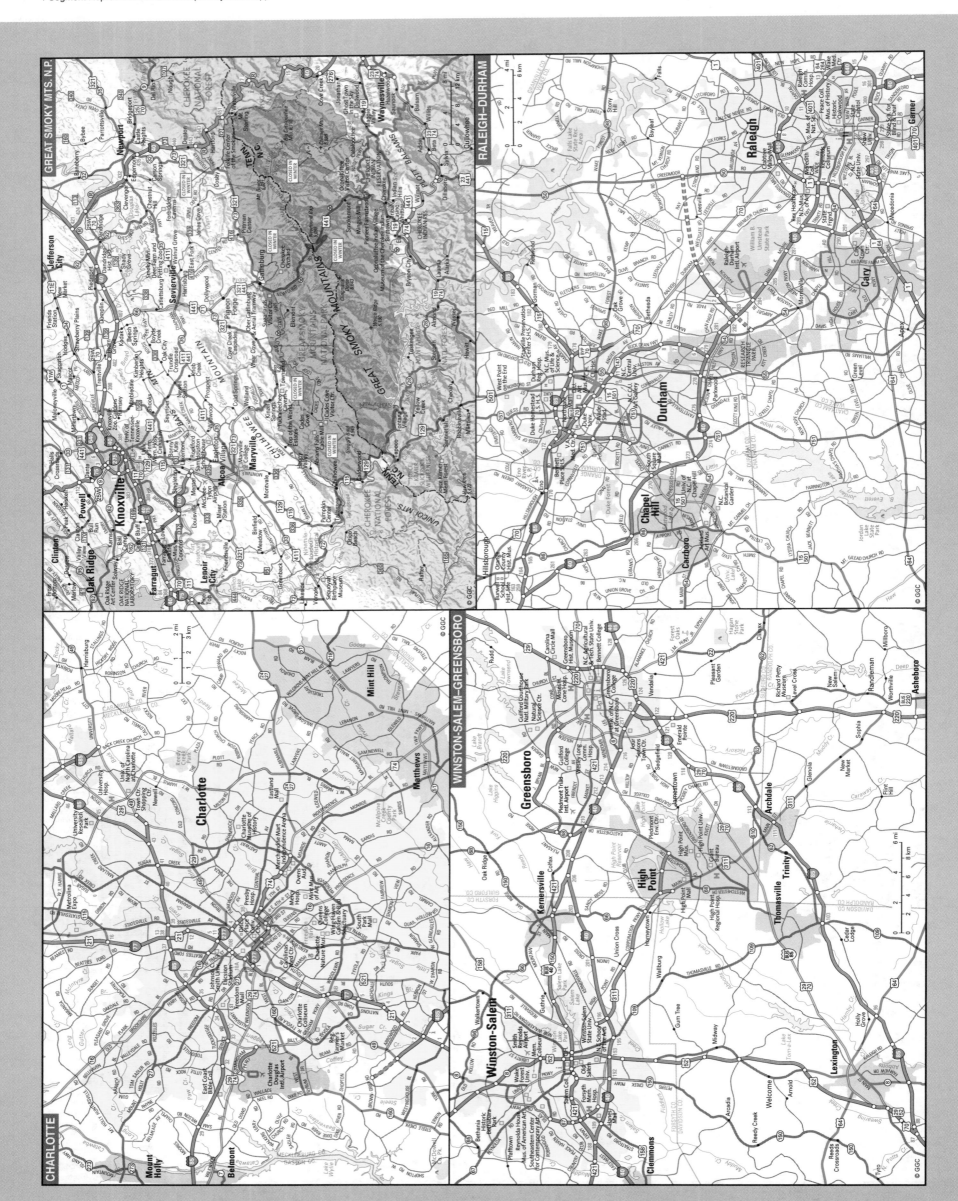

"Liberty and Union,
Now and Forever,
One and Inseparable"

Weather - Legend

- Average daily high temperature, F°
- Average daily low temperature, F°
- Average no. of days w/precipitation

J F M A M J J A S O N D

Bismarck

J F M A M J J A S O N D

1 Segment Represents 20 Miles

1 Segment Represents 20 Kilometers

1 Segment Represents 20 Miles

1 Segment Represents 20 Kilometers

Quick Reference Index

For index to counties and places see pg. 139.

Selected Attractions

Adjacent States and Provinces

© 1998 GeoSystems Global Corp.

"With God All Things are Possible"

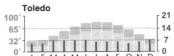

1 Segment Represents 10 Miles

1 Segment Represents 10 Kilometers

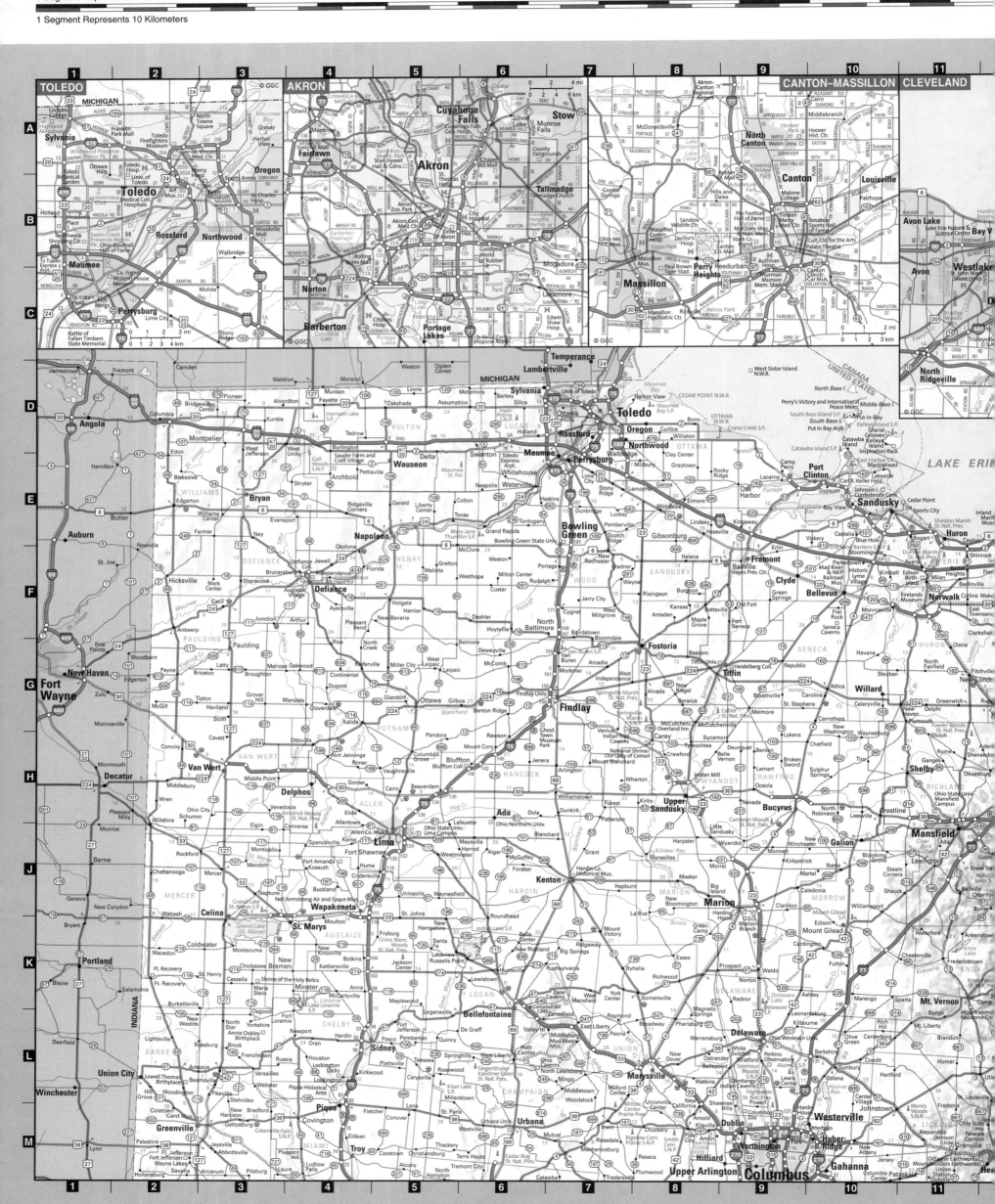

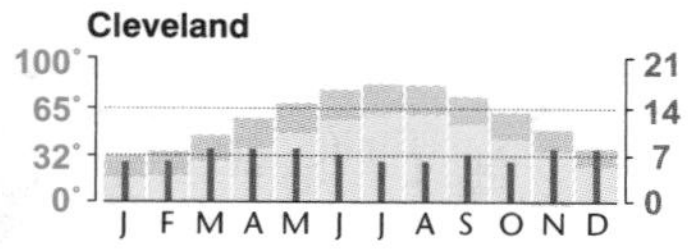

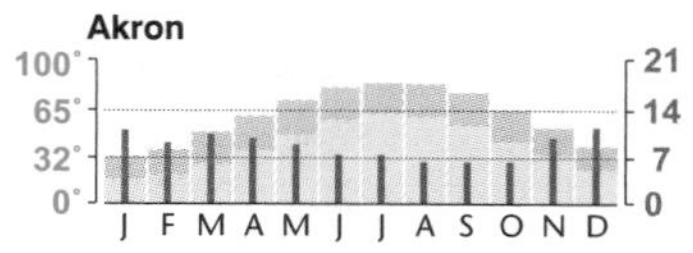

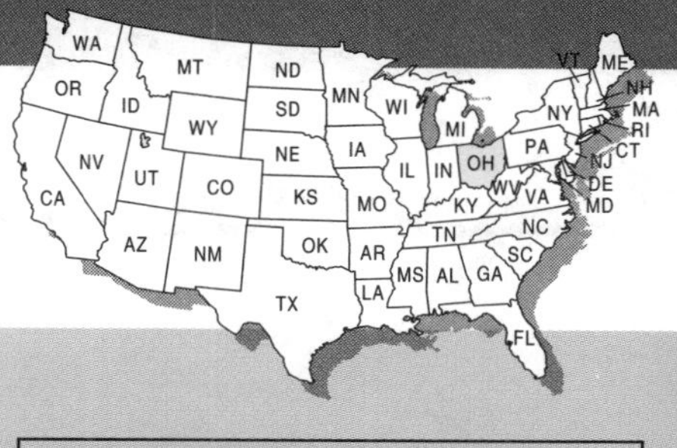

"With God All Things are Possible"

© 1998 GeoSystems Global Corp.

1 Segment Represents 10 Miles

1 Segment Represents 10 Kilometers

Cleveland

Akron

LAKE ERIE

Quick Reference Index

For index to counties and places see page 139.

Place	Ref	Place	Ref
Ada	H-6	Mayfield Heights	E-16
Akron	G-15	Medina	G-14
Alliance	H-17	Mentor	D-16
Amherst	E-12	Mentor-on-the-Lake	D-16
Ashland	H-12	Mount Vernon	K-11
Ashtabula	C-18	Napoleon	E-5
Aurora	F-16	New Carlisle	M-5
Austintown	G-19	New Philadelphia	K-16
Avon	E-13	Newark	M-12
Avon Lake	E-13	Niles	F-18
Barberton	G-15	North Canton	H-16
Bay Village	E-14	North Olmsted	E-14
Bedford	E-15	North Ridgeville	E-13
Bellaire	M-19	North Royalton	F-14
Bellefontaine	L-6	Northbridge	M-6
Bellevue	F-10	Northwood	D-7
Berea	F-14	Norton	G-15
Boardman	G-19	Norwalk	F-11
Bowling Green	E-7	Oberlin	F-12
Brunswick	F-14	Oregon	D-8
Bryan	E-3	Orrville	H-14
Bucyrus	H-9	Painesville	D-16
Cambridge	M-15	Parma	E-14
Campbell	G-19	Parma Heights	F-15
Canton	H-16	Perry Heights	H-16
Celina	J-3	Perrysburg	E-7
Cleveland	E-15	Piqua	M-4
Cleveland Heights	E-15	Port Clinton	D-10
Clyde	F-9	Ravenna	G-16
Columbus	M-9	Richmond Heights	E-15
Conneaut	C-19	Rittman	G-14
Cortland	F-19	Rocky River	E-14
Coshocton	L-14	Rossford	D-7
Cuyahoga Falls	G-15	Saint Marys	K-4
Defiance	F-4	Salem	H-18
Delaware	L-9	Sandusky	E-11
Delphos	H-4	Shaker Heights	E-15
Dover	K-16	Sheffield Lake	E-13
Dublin	M-9	Shelby	H-11
East Cleveland	E-15	Sidney	L-4
East Liverpool	J-19	Solon	E-16
Eastlake	D-16	Steubenville	K-19
Elyria	F-13	Stow	G-16
Euclid	D-15	Streetsboro	F-16
Fairlawn	G-15	Strongsville	F-14
Findlay	G-7	Struthers	G-19
Fostoria	G-8	Sylvania	D-6
Fremont	F-9	Tallmadge	G-16
Gahanna	M-10	Tiffin	G-9
Galion	J-10	Tipp City	M-4
Garfield Heights	E-15	Toledo	D-7
Geneva	C-18	Toronto	K-19
Girard	G-19	Troy	M-4
Green	H-16	Twinsburg	F-15
Greenville	M-2	Uhrichsville	K-16
Heath	M-12	Upper Arlington	M-9
Hilliard	M-9	Upper Sandusky	H-8
Hubbard	F-19	Urbana	M-6
Hudson Village	F-16	Van Wert	H-3
Huron	E-11	Vermilion	E-12
Kent	G-16	Wadsworth	G-15
Kenton	J-7	Wapakoneta	J-4
Kirtland	D-16	Warren	H-18
Lakewood	E-14	Warrensville Hts.	E-15
Lima	J-5	Wauseon	E-5
Lorain	E-13	Westerville	M-10
Louisville	H-16	Westlake	E-14
Macedonia	F-15	Wickliffe	D-15
Mansfield	J-11	Willard	G-10
Maple Heights	E-15	Willoughby	D-16
Marion	J-9	Willoughby Hills	D-16
Martins Ferry	M-19	Willowick	D-15
Marysville	L-8	Wooster	H-14
Massillon	H-15	Worthington	M-9
Maumee	E-7	Youngstown	G-19

Selected Attractions

Anne Oakley Birthplace	L-3
Cedar Point	E-11
Columbus Zoo	M-9
Fort Laurens	J-15
Gnadenhutten Monument	L-16
Museum of Ceramics	J-19
Neil Armstrong Air and Space Museum	J-4
Perry's Victory and International Peace Mem.	D-10
Sea World of Ohio	J-16
Zoar Village	J-16

Adjacent States

Indiana	38
Kentucky	44
Michigan	56
Ohio - Southern	88
Ontario	126
Pennsylvania	94 & 96
West Virginia	117

"With God All Things are Possible"

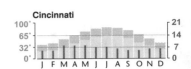

1 Segment Represents 10 Miles

1 Segment Represents 10 Kilometers

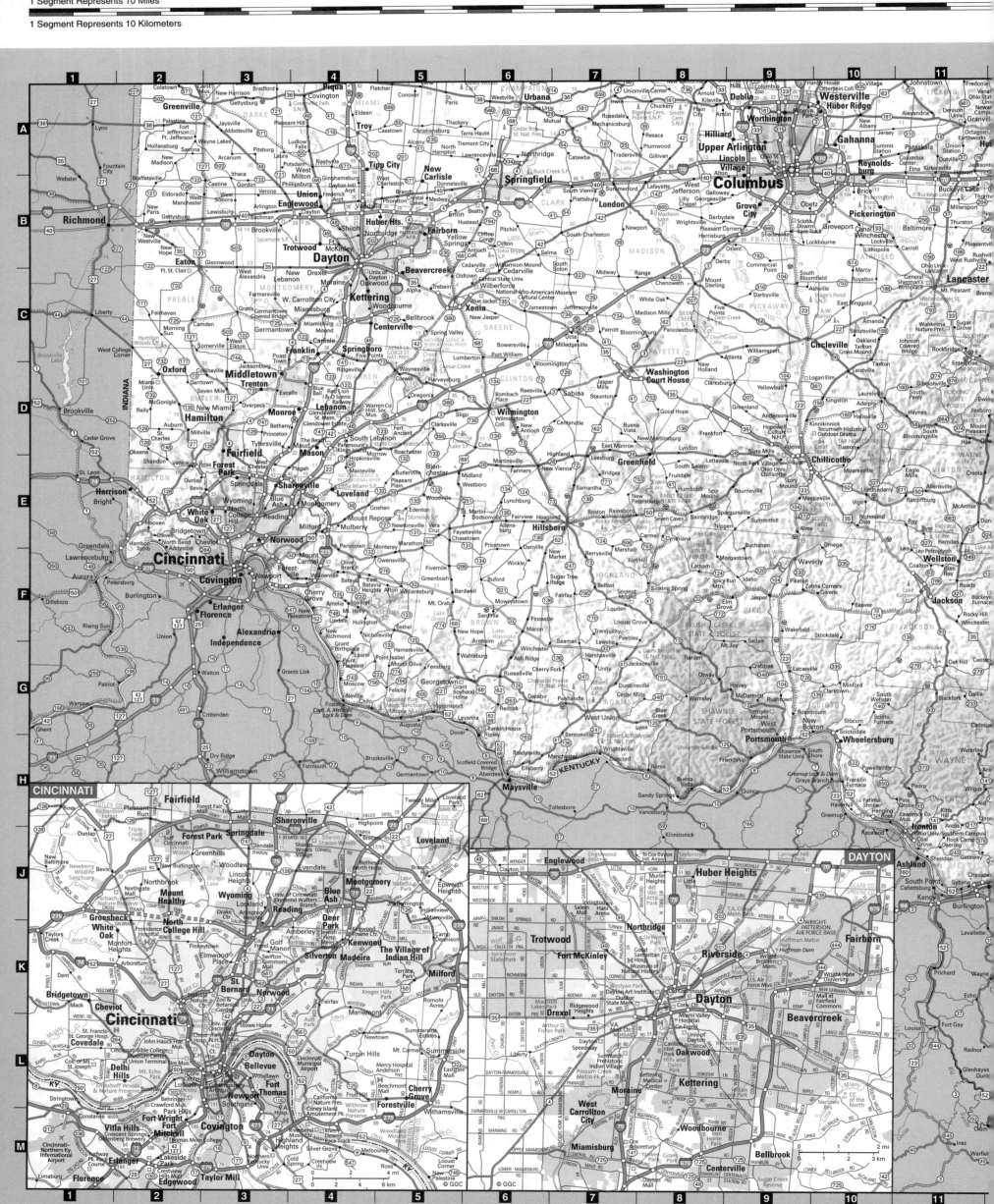

"With God All Things are Possible"

1 Segment Represents 10 Miles

1 Segment Represents 10 Kilometers

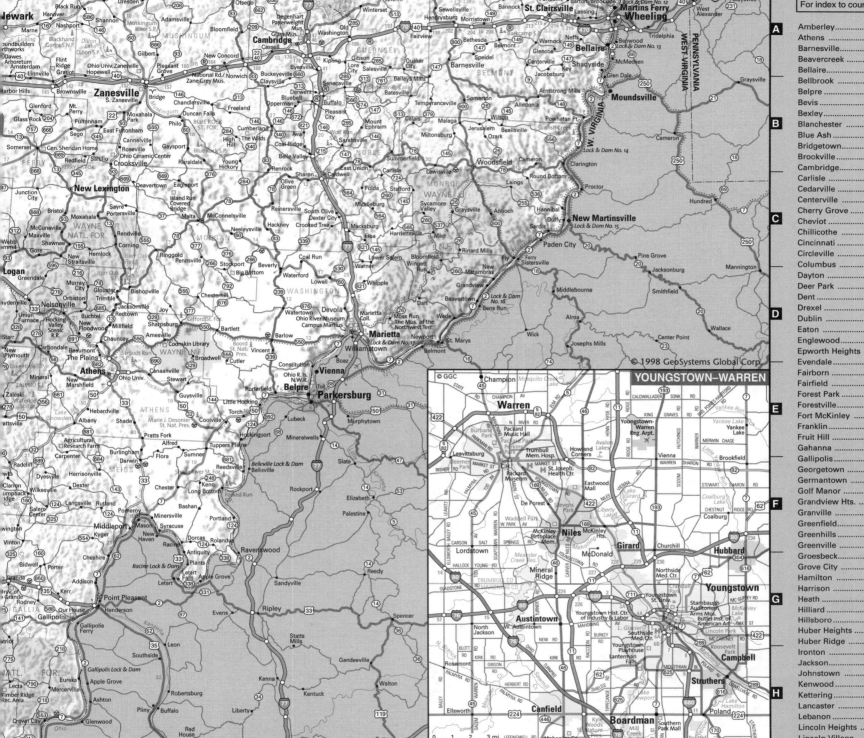

© 1998 GeoSystems Global Corp.

Quick Reference Index

For index to counties and places see page 139.

Amberley	W-4	Mason	Q-4
Athens	R-13	Maud	Q-4
Barnesville	M-17	Miamisburg	P-4
Beavercreek	P-5	Middletown	Q-3
Bellaire	M-19	Milford	R-4
Bellbrook	P-5	Monfort Heights	W-2
Belpre	R-15	Monroe	Q-4
Bevis	R-3	Montgomery	R-4
Bexley	X-19	Moraine	P-4
Blanchester	R-5	Mount Carmel	S-4
Blue Ash	R-3	Mount Healthy	V-2
Bridgetown	R-2	Mount Repose	S-4
Brookville	N-3	Nelsonville	Q-12
Cambridge	M-15	New Carlisle	M-5
Carlisle	P-4	New Lebanon	N-3
Cedarville	P-6	New Lexington	P-13
Centerville	P-4	Newark	N-11
Cherry Grove	S-4	North College Hill	R-3
Cheviot	R-2	Northbrook	V-2
Chillicothe	R-9	Northridge	N-4
Cincinnati	S-3	Northridge	M-6
Circleville	P-9	Norwood	R-3
Columbus	M-9	Oakwood	P-4
Dayton	N-4	Obetz	N-9
Deer Park	V-4	Oxford	Q-2
Dent	W-1	Page Manor	W-9
Drexel	P-4	Pataskala	M-11
Dublin	M-9	Pickerington	N-10
Eaton	N-2	Piqua	M-4
Englewood	N-4	Pleasant Run	U-2
Epworth Heights	V-5	Portsmouth	U-9
Evendale	V-4	Reading	R-3
Fairborn	V-5	Reynoldsburg	N-10
Fairfield	Q-3	Riverside	W-9
Fairfield	Q-3	St. Bernard	W-3
Forest Park	R-3	St. Clairsville	M-18
Forestville	S-4	Shadyside	M-19
Fort McKinley	N-4	Sharonville	R-3
Franklin	P-4	Shiloh	N-4
Fruit Hill	X-4	Silverton	W-4
Gahanna	M-10	South Point	V-11
Gallipolis	T-13	Springboro	P-4
Georgetown	T-5	Springdale	R-3
Germantown	P-4	Springfield	N-6
Golf Manor	W-3	Summerside	X-5
Grandview Hts.	X-18	The Village of	
Granville	F-11	Indian Hill	W-5
Greenfield	R-8	Tipp City	M-4
Greenhills	V-2	Trenton	Q-3
Greenville	M-2	Trotwood	N-4
Groesbeck	V-2	Troy	M-4
Grove City	N-9	Turpin Hills	X-4
Hamilton	Q-3	Union	N-4
Harrison	R-2	Upper Arlington	M-9
Heath	M-12	Urbana	M-6
Hilliard	M-9	Vandalia	N-4
Hillsboro	R-7	Washington C.H.	Q-7
Huber Heights	N-5	Waverly	S-9
Huber Ridge	M-10	Wellston	S-11
Ironton	V-11	West Carrollton City	P-4
Jackson	S-11	West Jefferson	N-8
Johnstown	M-10	West Milton	M-4
Kenwood	W-4	West Portsmouth	T-9
Kettering	P-4	West Union	T-7
Lancaster	P-11	Westerville	M-10
Lebanon	Q-4	Wheelersburg	U-10
Lincoln Heights	V-3	White Oak	R-3
Lincoln Village	N-9	Whitehall	X-20
Lockland	V-3	Wilmington	Q-6
Logan	Q-12	Woodbourne	P-4
London	N-7	Worthington	M-9
Loveland	R-4	Wyoming	R-3
Madeira	W-4	Xenia	P-5
Mariemont	W-4	Yellow Springs	N-6
Marietta	Q-16	Zanesville	N-13
Martins Ferry	M-19		

Selected Attractions

Fort Ancient	Q-5
General Sherman's Birthplace	P-11
Grant Boyhood Home	T-6
Hopewell Culture National Historic Park	Q-9
Miamisburg	P-4
National Afro-American Museum Cultural Center	P-6
Ohio River Museum	Q-16
Paint Creek State Park	R-8
Serpent Mound	S-7
Timber Ridge Recreation Area	U-12

Adjacent States

Indiana	38
Kentucky	44
Michigan	56
Ohio - Northern	86
Ontario	126
Pennsylvania	94 & 96
West Virginia	117

"Labor Conquers All Things"

Weather - Legend

Oklahoma City

1 Segment Represents 20 Miles

1 Segment Represents 20 Kilometers

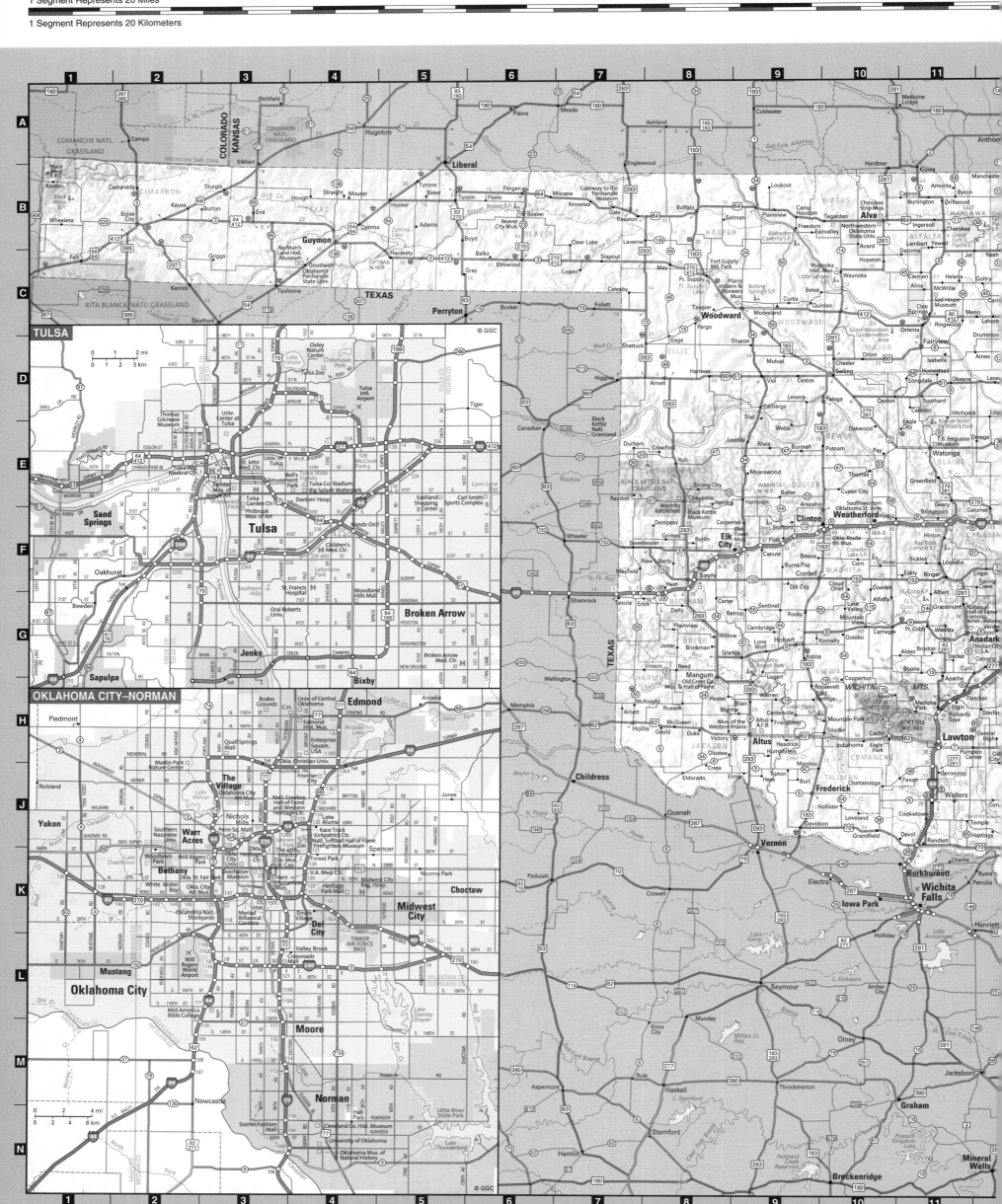

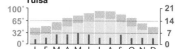

1 Segment Represents 20 Miles

1 Segment Represents 20 Kilometers

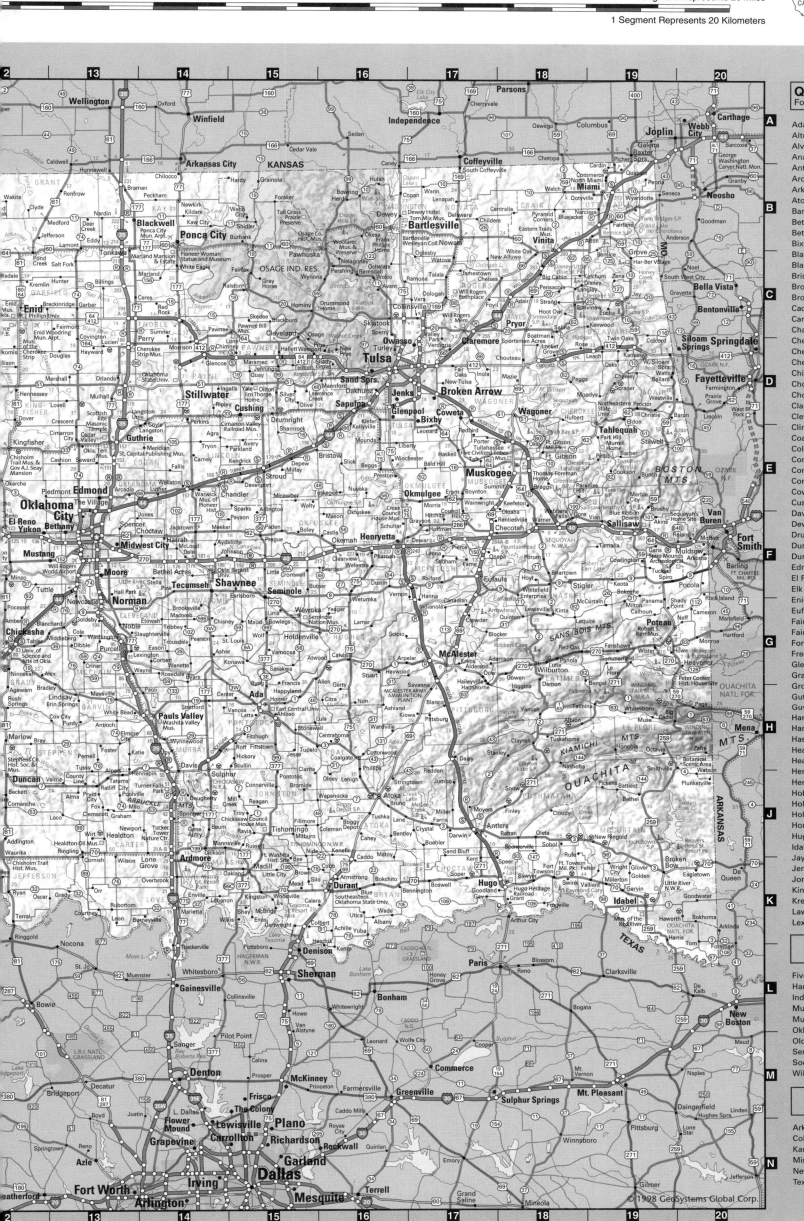

Quick Reference Index

For index to counties and places see page 139.

Ada	H-15	Lindsay	H-13
Altus	H-9	Lone Grove	J-14
Alva	B-10	Madill	K-15
Anadarko	G-11	Mangum	G-8
Antlers	J-17	Mannford	D-16
Ardmore	J-14	Marietta	K-14
Arkoma	F-20	Marlow	H-12
Atoka	J-16	McAlester	G-17
Bartlesville	B-16	McLoud	F-14
Bethany	F-13	Miami	B-19
Bethel Acres	F-14	Midwest City	F-13
Bixby	D-17	Moore	F-13
Blackwell	B-13	Muldrow	F-20
Blanchard	G-13	Muskogee	E-18
Bristow	E-16	Mustang	F-13
Broken Arrow	D-17	Newcastle	F-13
Broken Bow	K-19	Newkirk	B-14
Cache	H-10	Noble	G-13
Carnegie	G-10	Norman	G-13
Chandler	E-14	Nowata	B-17
Checotah	F-18	Oakhurst	D-16
Chelsea	C-17	Okemah	F-16
Cherokee	B-11	Oklahoma City	F-13
Chickasha	G-12	Okmulgee	E-16
Choctaw	F-14	Owasso	D-17
Chouteau	D-18	Pauls Valley	H-14
Claremore	C-17	Pawhuska	B-16
Cleveland	D-15	Pawnee	C-15
Clinton	F-10	Perkins	D-14
Coalgate	H-16	Perry	D-13
Collinsville	C-17	Picher	A-19
Comanche	J-12	Piedmont	E-12
Commerce	B-19	Pocola	F-20
Cordell	F-9	Ponca City	B-14
Coweta	D-17	Poteau	G-19
Cushing	D-15	Prague	F-15
Davis	H-14	Pryor	C-18
Dewey	B-16	Purcell	G-13
Drumright	D-15	Roland	F-20
Duncan	J-12	Sallisaw	F-20
Durant	K-16	Sand Springs	D-16
Edmond	E-13	Sapulpa	D-16
El Reno	F-12	Sayre	F-8
Elk City	F-8	Seminole	F-15
Enid	C-12	Shawnee	F-14
Eufaula	F-17	Skiatook	C-16
Fairfax	C-15	Slaughterville	G-13
Fairview	D-11	Snyder	H-10
Fort Gibson	E-18	Spencer	F-13
Frederick	J-9	Spiro	F-19
Glenpool	D-16	Stigler	F-18
Granite	G-9	Stillwater	D-14
Grove	C-19	Stilwell	E-19
Guthrie	E-13	Stroud	E-15
Guymon	B-4	Sulphur	H-14
Harrah	F-14	Tahlequah	D-19
Hartshorne	G-17	Tecumseh	F-14
Haskell	E-17	The Village	F-13
Healdton	J-13	Tishomingo	J-15
Heavener	G-20	Tonkawa	C-13
Hennessey	D-12	Tulsa	D-16
Henryetta	F-16	Turley	D-16
Hobart	G-9	Tuttle	F-13
Holdenville	G-16	Vinita	B-18
Hollis	H-7	Wagoner	D-18
Hominy	C-16	Walters	J-11
Hugo	K-18	Watonga	E-11
Idabel	K-19	Waurika	J-12
Jay	C-19	Weatherford	F-10
Jenks	D-16	Wewoka	G-15
Jones	F-14	Wilburton	G-18
Kingfisher	E-12	Wilson	J-13
Krebs	G-17	Woodward	C-9
Lawton	H-11	Wynnewood	H-14
Lexington	G-13	Yukon	F-12

Selected Attractions

Five Civilized Tribes Museum	E-18
Har-Ber Village	C-19
Indian City U.S.A.	G-12
Museum of the Red River	K-19
Museum of the Western Prairie	H-9
Oklahoma Route 66 Museum	F-10
Old Town Museum	F-9
Seminole Nation Museum	G-16
Sod House Museum	C-11
Will Rogers Birthplace	C-17

Adjacent States

Arkansas	10
Colorado	20
Kansas	42
Missouri	64
New Mexico	74
Texas	104 & 106

© 1998 GeoSystems Global Corp.

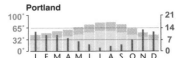

1 Segment Represents 20 Miles

1 Segment Represents 20 Kilometers

PACIFIC OCEAN

© 1998 GeoSystems Global Corp.

1 Segment Represents 20 Miles

1 Segment Represents 20 Kilometers

Quick Reference Index

For index to counties and places see page 140.

Place	Ref	Place	Ref
Albany	E-4	Lincoln City	E-2
Aloha	C-4	Madras	F-8
Altamont	M-6	McMinnville	D-4
Amity	D-4	Medford	M-4
Ashland	M-4	Mill City	E-5
Astoria	A-3	Milton-Freewater	B-13
Aumsville	E-4	Molalla	D-5
Baker City	E-14	Monmouth	E-4
Bandon	K-1	Mount Angel	D-4
Barview	J-1	Myrtle Creek	K-3
Bay City	C-2	Myrtle Point	K-2
Beaverton	C-4	Newberg	D-4
Bend	G-7	Newport	E-2
Boardman	B-11	North Albany	E-4
Brookings	N-1	North Bend	J-1
Brownsville	F-4	Nyssa	G-16
Bunker Hill	J-1	Oakridge	H-5
Burns	H-12	Odell	C-7
Canby	D-5	Ontario	G-16
Cannon Beach	B-2	Oregon City	D-5
Canyonville	K-3	Pendleton	C-12
Carlton	D-4	Philomath	F-3
Cave Junction	M-2	Phoenix	M-4
Central Point	M-4	Pilot Rock	C-12
Chenoweth	C-7	Port Orford	L-1
Clatskanie	A-4	Portland	C-5
Coos Bay	J-1	Prairie City	F-13
Coquille	J-2	Prineville	F-8
Cornelius	C-4	Rainier	B-4
Corvallis	F-3	Redmond	G-8
Cottage Grove	H-4	Reedsport	H-2
Creswell	G-4	Riddle	K-3
Dallas	E-3	Rogue River	L-3
Dayton	D-4	Rose Lodge	D-2
Drain	H-3	Roseburg	J-3
Dundee	D-4	Saint Helens	B-4
Dunes City	G-2	Salem	E-4
Eagle Point	L-4	Sandy	C-5
Elgin	C-14	Santa Clara	G-4
Enterprise	C-15	Scappoose	B-4
Estacada	D-5	Seaside	B-2
Eugene	G-4	Shady Cove	L-4
Fairview	C-5	Sheridan	D-3
Florence	G-2	Sherwood	D-4
Forest Grove	C-4	Silverton	D-4
Four Corners	E-4	Springfield	G-4
Gearhart	B-2	Stanfield	B-12
Gold Beach	M-1	Stayton	E-4
Grants Pass	M-3	Sublimity	E-4
Green	K-3	Sutherlin	J-3
Gresham	C-5	Sweet Home	F-4
Harbor	N-1	Talent	M-4
Harrisburg	F-4	Terrebonne	F-8
Hayesville	D-4	The Dalles	C-8
Heppner	D-11	Tigard	C-4
Hermiston	B-11	Tillamook	C-2
Hillsboro	C-4	Toledo	E-2
Hines	H-12	Tri City	K-3
Hood River	C-7	Troutdale	C-5
Hubbard	D-4	Tualatin	C-4
Independence	E-4	Turner	E-4
Jacksonville	M-4	Umatilla	B-11
Jefferson	E-4	Union	D-14
John Day	F-12	Vale	G-16
Joseph	C-15	Veneta	G-3
Junction City	G-4	Vernonia	B-4
Keizer	D-4	Waldport	F-2
Klamath Falls	M-6	Warm Springs	E-7
La Grande	D-14	Warrenton	A-2
Lafayette	D-4	West Linn	C-5
Lake Oswego	C-5	White City	M-4
Lakeside	H-2	Willamina	D-3
Lakeview	M-9	Wilsonville	D-4
Lebanon	F-4	Winston	K-3
Lincoln Beach	E-2	Woodburn	D-4

Selected Attractions

Attraction	Ref
Cape Blanco Lighthouse	K-1
Columbia River Maritime Museum	A-3
Crater Lake National Park	K-6
Hells Canyon National Recreation Area	C-16
Hole-in-the-Ground	J-7
John Day Fossil Beds National Monument	F-11
Natural Bridge	K-5
Oregon Caves National Monument	M-3
Oregon Coast Aquarium	E-2
Oregon Trail Interpretive Site	F-15

Adjacent States

State	Page
California	12 & 14
Idaho	33
Nevada	70
Washington	114

"Virtue, Liberty and Independence"

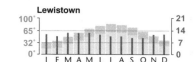

Pittsburgh

Lewistown

1 Segment Represents 20 Miles

1 Segment Represents 20 Kilometers

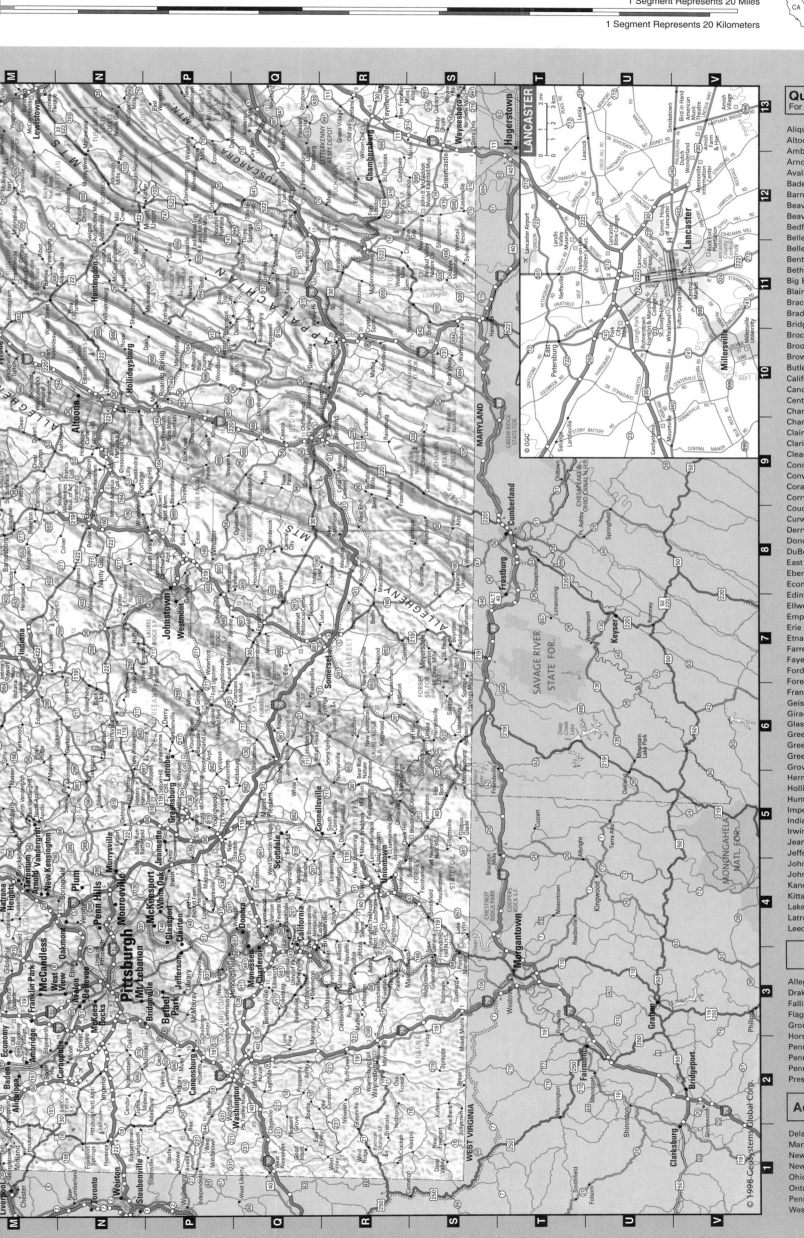

Quick Reference Index

For index to counties and places see page 140.

Aliquippa	M-2	Lewistown	M-13
Altoona	N-10	Library	P-3
Ambridge	M-2	Lyndora	L-3
Arnold	M-4	Masontown	R-3
Avalon	N-3	McCandless	M-3
Baden	M-2	McDonald	N-2
Barnesboro	M-8	McKees Rocks	N-3
Beaver	M-2	McKeesport	P-4
Beaver Falls	L-2	McMurray	P-3
Bedford	R-9	Meadville	F-3
Bellefonte	L-12	Mercer	J-2
Bellevue	N-3	Meridian	L-3
Bentleyville	Q-3	Meyersdale	S-7
Bethel Park	P-3	Midland	M-1
Big Beaver	L-2	Monaca	M-2
Blairsville	N-6	Monessen	Q-3
Brackenridge	M-4	Monongahela	P-3
Bradford	E-9	Monroeville	N-4
Bridgeville	P-3	Mount Lebanon	N-3
Brockway	J-8	Mount Pleasant	Q-5
Brookville	J-7	Mount Union	P-12
Brownsville	Q-3	Murrysville	N-4
Butler	L-4	Nanty Glo	N-8
California	Q-4	Natrona Heights	M-4
Canonsburg	P-2	New Brighton	L-2
Centerville	Q-3	New Castle	K-2
Chambersburg	R-13	New Kensington	M-4
Charleroi	Q-3	New Wilmington	J-2
Clairton	R-4	North East	C-4
Clarion	J-6	Oakmont	N-4
Clearfield	K-10	Oakwood	K-2
Connellsville	R-5	Ohioville	M-1
Conway	M-2	Oil City	G-4
Coraopolis	N-2	Oliver	R-4
Corry	E-5	Penn Hills	N-4
Coudersport	F-11	Philipsburg	L-11
Curwensville	K-9	Pittsburgh	N-3
Derry	P-6	Plum	N-4
Donora	Q-4	Port Allegany	E-10
DuBois	J-8	Portage	P-9
East Uniontown	R-4	Punxsutawney	K-7
Ebensburg	N-8	Reynoldsville	J-8
Economy	M-2	Ridgway	H-8
Edinboro	E-3	Roaring Spring	P-10
Ellwood City	L-2	Rochester	M-2
Emporium	G-11	Saint Marys	H-9
Erie	C-3	Scottdale	Q-5
Etna	N-4	Sharon	H-1
Farrell	J-1	Sharpsville	H-1
Fayetteville	R-13	Shippensburg	Q-13
Ford City	L-5	Slippery Rock	K-3
Forest Grove	N-3	Somerset	R-7
Franklin Park	M-3	South Greensburg	P-5
Geistown	P-8	Springdale	N-4
Girard	D-2	State College	L-12
Glassport	P-4	Sugarcreek	H-4
Greencastle	S-12	Tarentum	M-4
Greensburg	P-5	Titusville	F-5
Greenville	H-2	Tyrone	M-10
Grove City	J-3	Union City	E-4
Hermitage	J-1	Uniontown	R-4
Hollidaysburg	N-10	Vandergrift	M-5
Huntingdon	N-11	Verona	N-4
Imperial	N-2	Warren	E-7
Indiana	M-7	Washington	Q-2
Irwin	P-4	Waynesboro	S-13
Jeannette	P-5	Waynesburg	R-2
Jefferson	P-3	Wesleyville	C-3
Johnsonburg	G-9	West View	N-3
Johnstown	P-7	Westmont	P-7
Kane	F-8	White Oak	P-4
Kittanning	L-5	Windber	P-8
Lake City	D-2	Wolfdale	P-2
Latrobe	P-6	Youngwood	P-5
Leechburg	M-5	Zelienople	L-3

Selected Attractions

Allegheny National Recreation Area	E-7
Drake Well Museum	G-5
Fallingwater	R-5
Flagship Niagara	C-3
Groundhog Zoo	K-7
Horseshoe Curve	N-10
Penn's Cave	L-13
Pennsylvania State University	L-12
Pennsylvania Trolley Museum	Q-2
Presque Isle State Park	C-3

Adjacent States and Provinces

Delaware	24
Maryland	50
New Jersey	72
New York	76 & 78
Ohio	86 & 88
Ontario	126
Pennsylvania - Eastern	96
West Virginia	117

© 1998 GeoSystems Global Corp.

"Virtue, Liberty and Independence"

Weather - Legend

Average daily high temperature, F°
Average daily low temperature, F°
Average no. of days w/precipitation

Harrisburg

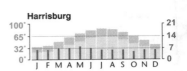

1 Segment Represents 20 Miles

1 Segment Represents 20 Kilometers

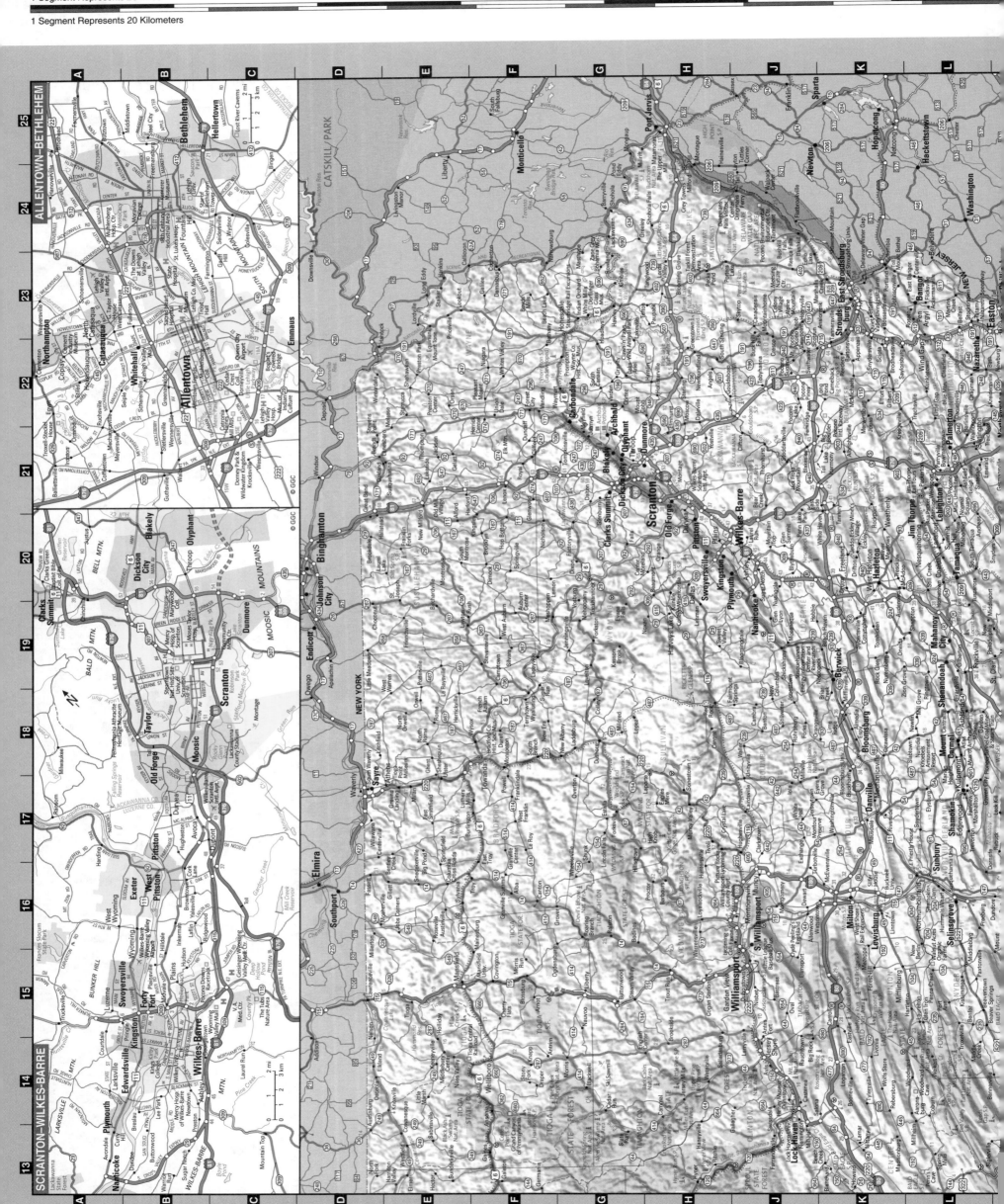

"Virtue, Liberty and Independence"

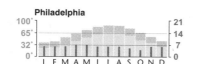

Allentown

Philadelphia

1 Segment Represents 20 Miles

1 Segment Represents 20 Kilometers

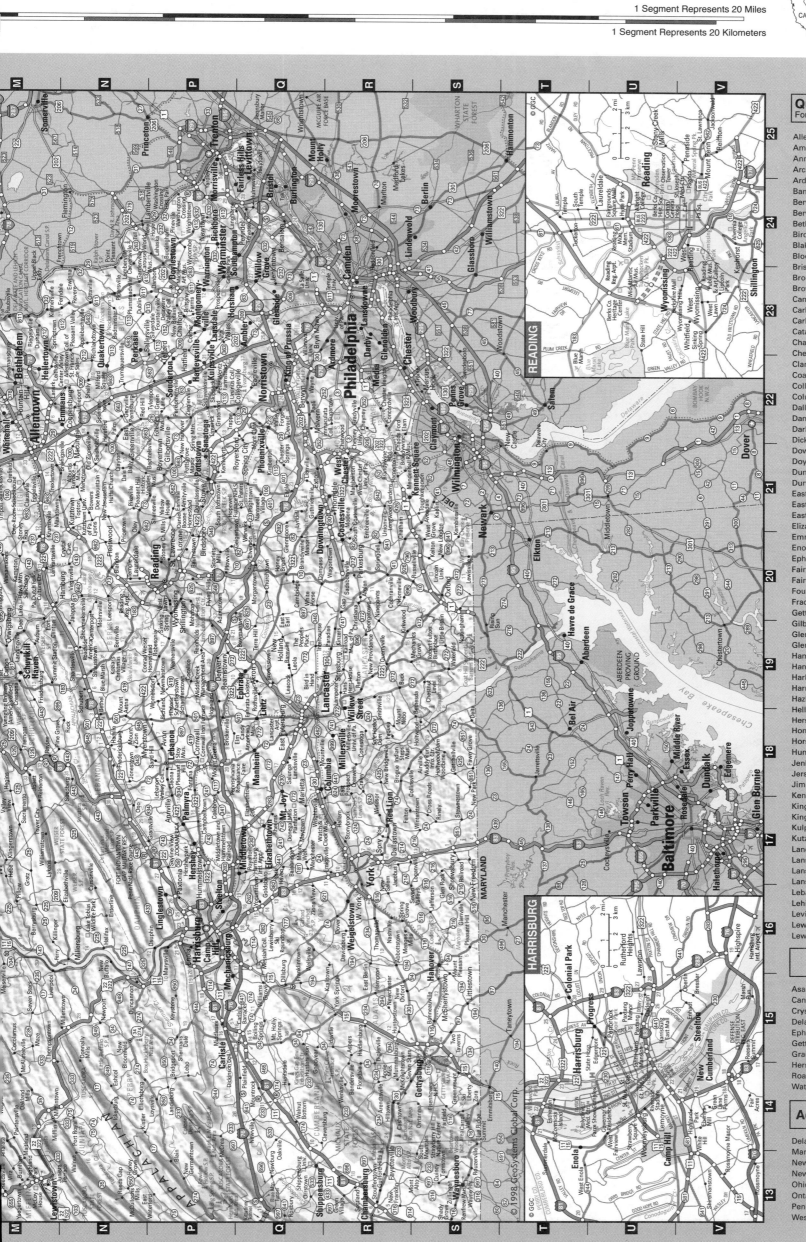

Quick Reference Index

For index to counties and places see page 140.

Allentown	M-22	Linglestown	P-16
Ambler	Q-23	Lititz	Q-18
Annville	P-17	Lock Haven	J-14
Archbald	G-21	Mahanoy City	L-19
Ardmore	R-23	Manheim	Q-18
Bangor	L-23	Mechanicsburg	P-15
Berwick	K-19	Media	R-22
Berwyn	Q-22	Middletown	Q-17
Bethlehem	M-22	Millersville	R-18
Birdsboro	P-20	Milton	K-16
Blakely	G-21	Minersville	M-18
Bloomsburg	K-18	Montgomeryville	P-23
Bristol	Q-24	Montoursville	J-16
Brookside	H-14	Morrisville	Q-25
Brownstown	Q-19	Mount Carmel	L-18
Camp Hill	P-16	Mount Joy	Q-18
Carbondale	G-22	Nanticoke	J-20
Carlisle	P-15	Nazareth	L-22
Catasauqua	M-22	New Holland	Q-19
Chambersburg	R-13	Norristown	Q-22
Chester	R-22	Northampton	M-22
Clarks Summit	G-21	Old Forge	H-21
Coatesville	R-20	Olyphant	G-21
Collegeville	Q-22	Palmerton	L-21
Columbia	R-18	Palmyra	P-17
Dallastown	R-17	Paoli	Q-22
Danville	K-17	Paxtonia	P-16
Darby	R-23	Perkasie	N-23
Dickson City	G-21	Philadelphia	R-23
Downingtown	R-20	Phoenixville	Q-22
Doylestown	P-23	Pittston	H-20
Dunmore	H-21	Plains	H-20
Duryea	H-20	Plymouth	J-20
East Petersburg	Q-18	Pottstown	P-21
East Stroudsburg	K-23	Pottsville	M-19
Easton	M-23	Quakertown	N-22
Elizabethtown	Q-17	Reading	P-20
Emmaus	N-22	Red Lion	R-17
Enola	P-16	Richboro	P-24
Ephrata	Q-19	Royersford	Q-22
Fairless Hills	Q-24	Sanatoga	P-21
Fairview	L-17	Sayre	D-17
Fountain Hill	M-22	Schuylkill Haven	M-19
Frackville	L-19	Scranton	H-21
Gettysburg	S-15	Selinsgrove	L-16
Gilbertsville	P-21	Sellersville	S-23
Glenolden	R-23	Shamokin	L-17
Glenside	Q-23	Shenandoah	L-19
Hamburg	M-20	Shillington	P-20
Hanover	S-16	Shippensburg	Q-13
Harleysville	P-22	Slatington	L-21
Harrisburg	P-16	Souderton	P-22
Hazleton	K-20	South Williamsport	J-16
Hellertown	M-22	Spry	R-17
Hershey	P-17	Steelton	P-16
Honesdale	G-23	Stonybrook	R-17
Horsham	P-23	Stroudsburg	K-23
Hummelstown	P-17	Sunbury	L-16
Jenkintown	Q-23	Swoyersville	H-20
Jersey Shore	J-14	Tamaqua	L-20
Jim Thorpe	L-21	Telford	P-22
Kennett Square	R-21	Throop	G-21
King of Prussia	Q-22	Waynesboro	S-13
Kingston	H-20	Weigelstown	R-16
Kulpsville	P-22	West Chester	R-21
Kutztown	N-21	West Hazleton	K-20
Lancaster	Q-18	West York	R-16
Lansdale	P-23	Whitehall	M-22
Lansdowne	R-23	Wilkes-Barre	J-20
Lansford	L-20	Williamsport	J-15
Lebanon	P-18	Willow Grove	Q-23
Lehighton	L-21	Willow Street	R-18
Levittown	Q-24	Wilson	M-23
Lewisburg	K-16	Wyomissing	P-20
Lewistown	M-13	York	R-17

Selected Attractions

Asa Packer Mansion	L-20
Candy Americana Museum	Q-18
Crystal Cave	N-10
Delaware Water Gap National Recreation Area	J-24
Ephrata Cloister	Q-19
Gettysburg National Military Park	S-14
Grand Canyon of Pennsylvania	P-14
Hersheypark	P-17
Roadside America	N-19
Watch & Clock Museum	R-18

Adjacent States and Provinces

Delaware	24
Maryland	50
New Jersey	72
New York	76 & 78
Ohio	86 & 88
Ontario	126
Pennsylvania - Western	94
West Virginia	117

© 1998, GeoSystems Global Corp.

1 Segment Represents 2 Miles (Philadelphia area map)

1 Segment Represents 2 Kilometers (Philadelphia area map)

1 Segment Represents 2 Miles (Philadelphia area map)

1 Segment Represents 2 Kilometers (Philadelphia area map)

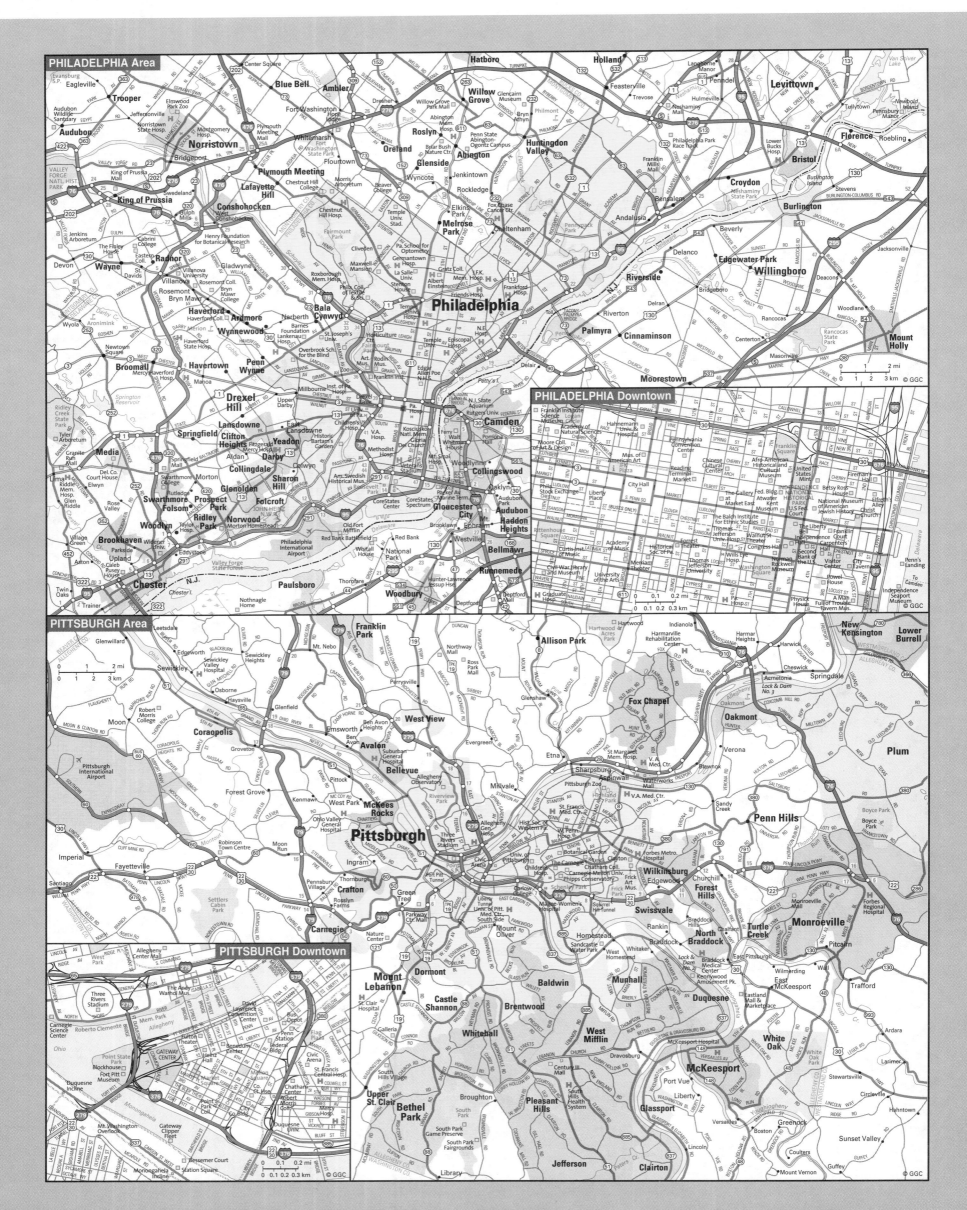

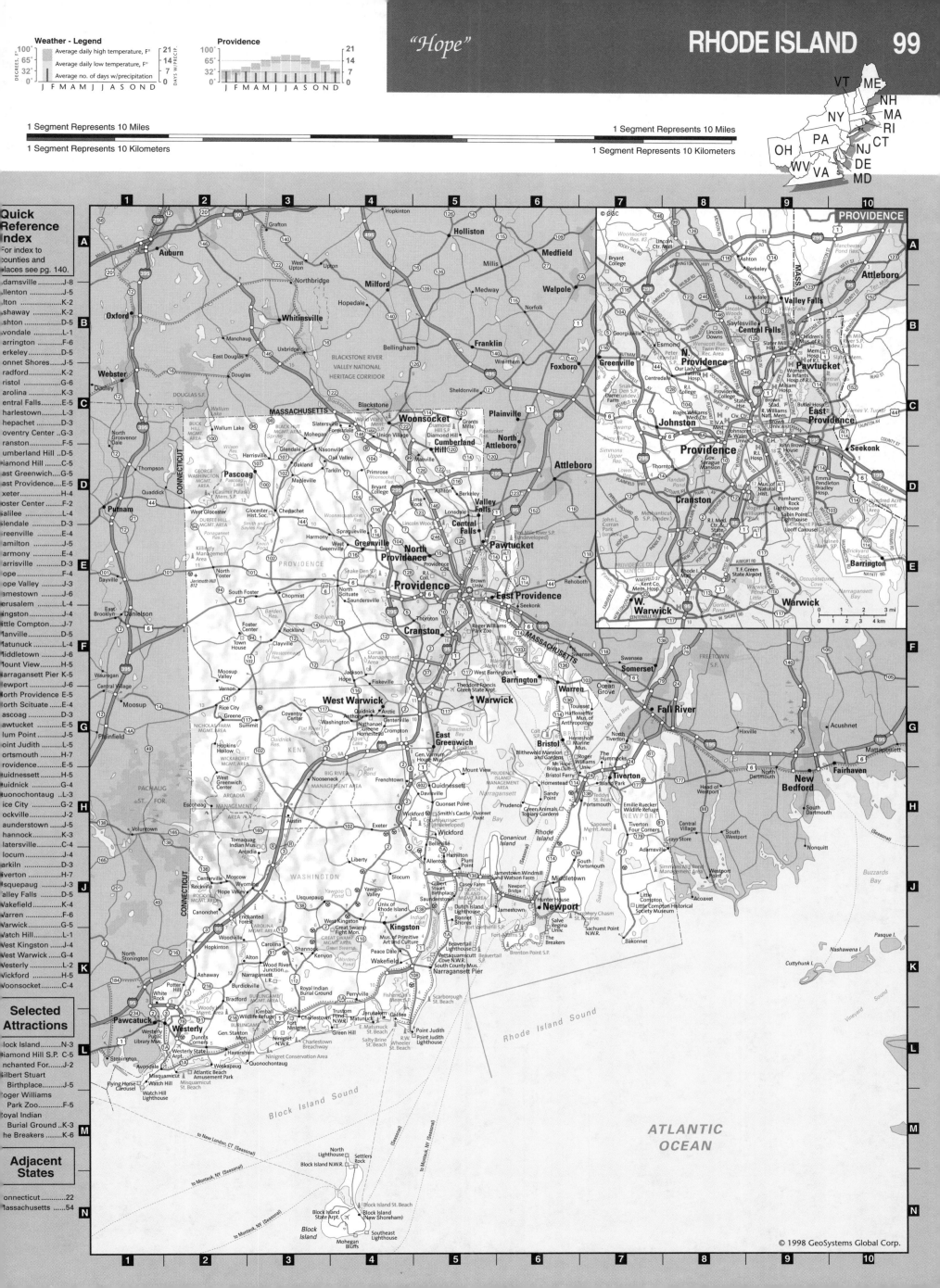

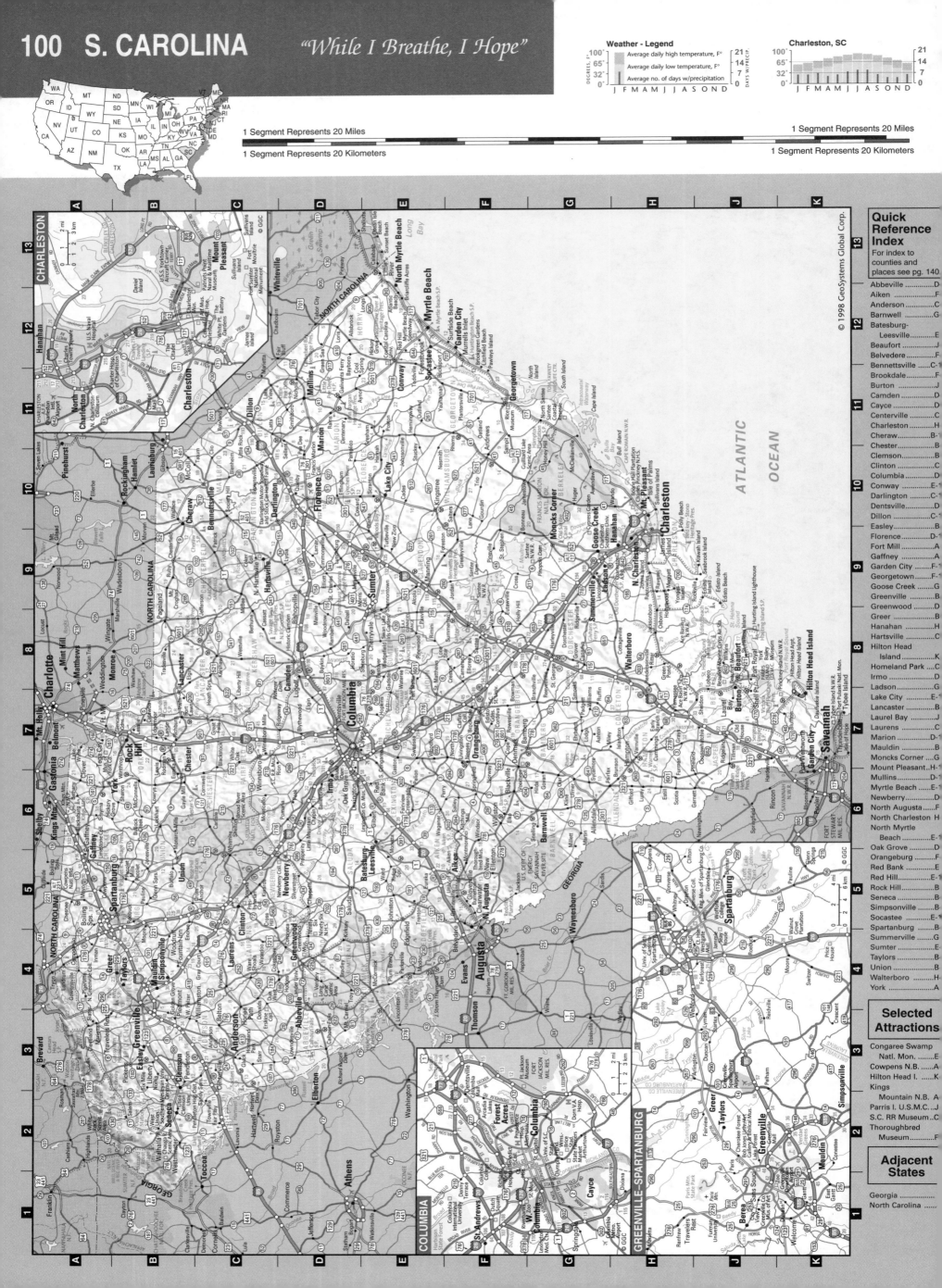

Weather - Legend
Average daily high temperature, F°
Average daily low temperature, F°
Average no. of days w/precipitation

Charleston, SC

1 Segment Represents 20 Miles
1 Segment Represents 20 Kilometers
1 Segment Represents 20 Miles
1 Segment Represents 20 Kilometers

© 1998 GeoSystems Global Corp.

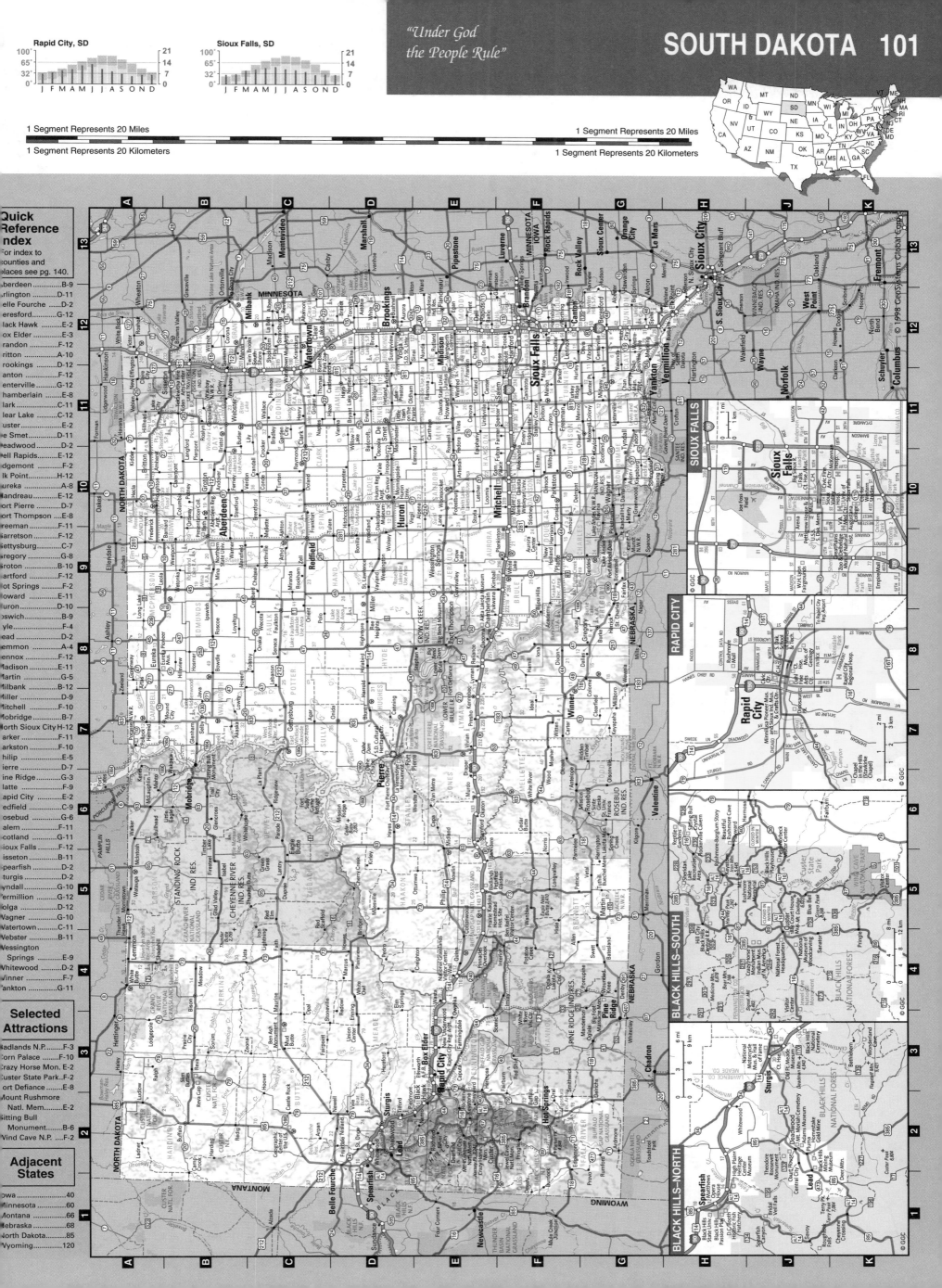

Weather - Legend
Average daily high temperature, F°
Average daily low temperature, F°
Average no. of days w/precipitation

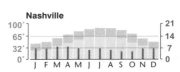

Nashville

1 Segment Represents 20 Miles

1 Segment Represents 20 Kilometers

© 1998 GeoSystems Global Corp.

MEMPHIS

NASHVILLE

Memphis
100° 65° 32° 0° —21 14 7 0
J F M A M J J A S O N D

Bristol–Johnson City–Kingsport
100° 65° 32° 0° —21 14 7 0
J F M A M J J A S O N D

1 Segment Represents 20 Miles

1 Segment Represents 20 Kilometers

Quick Reference Index

For index to counties and places see page 140.

Alamo	D-4
Alcoa	D-19
Algood	C-15
Ashland City	B-10
Athens	E-17
Bartlett	F-2
Bloomingdale	K-14
Blountville	K-15
Bolivar	F-4
Brentwood	C-11
Bristol	J-15
Brownsville	E-4
Camden	C-7
Carthage	B-14
Centerville	D-9
Central	K-15
Chattanooga	G-15
Church Hill	K-13
Clarksville	A-9
Cleveland	F-17
Clinton	C-19
Collegedale	G-16
Collierville	G-2
Colonial Heights	K-14
Columbia	E-10
Cookeville	C-15
Cordova	F-2
Covington	E-3
Crossville	D-16
Dayton	E-16
Decherd	F-13
Dickson	C-9
Dresden	B-5
Dunlap	F-15
Dyer	C-3
Dyersburg	C-3
Eagleton Village	D-19
East Ridge	G-16
Elizabethton	K-15
Erwin	L-14
Etowah	F-18
Fairfield Glade	C-17
Fairview	C-10
Farragut	D-19
Fayetteville	F-12
Franklin	D-11
Gallatin	C-11
Gatlinburg	N-11
Germantown	F-2
Goodlettsville	B-11
Green Hill	C-12
Greenbrier	B-11
Greeneville	L-13
Greenfield	C-5
Halls	D-3
Harriman	D-18
Harrison	G-16
Hartsville	B-13
Henderson	E-5
Hendersonville	B-12
Hohenwald	E-9
Hopewell	F-17
Humboldt	D-5
Huntingdon	C-6
Jackson	E-5
Jasper	G-14
Jefferson City	L-11
Jellico	A-19
Johnson City	K-14
Jonesborough	L-14
Kingsport	K-14
Kingston	D-18
Knoxville	C-19
La Follette	C-19
La Vergne	C-12

Lafayette	B-13
Lake City	C-19
Lawrenceburg	F-9
Lebanon	C-13
Lenoir City	D-19
Lewisburg	E-11
Lexington	E-6
Livingston	B-15
Loudon	D-18
Lynchburg	F-12
Madisonville	E-18
Manchester	E-13
Martin	B-5
Maryville	D-19
Mascot	C-20
McKenzie	C-6
McMinnville	E-14
Memphis	F-1
Middle Valley	F-16
Milan	D-5
Millersville	B-11
Millington	E-2
Monterey	C-16
Morristown	L-12
Mount Carmel	K-14
Mount Juliet	C-12
Mount Pleasant	E-10
Mountain City	K-16
Munford	E-3
Murfreesboro	D-12
Nashville	C-11
Newbern	C-4
Newport	M-12
Oak Grove	K-14
Oak Ridge	C-18
Oliver Springs	C-18
Oneida	B-18
Ooltewah	G-16
Paris	B-6
Pigeon Forge	M-11
Portland	A-12
Powell	C-19
Pulaski	F-10
Red Bank	G-16
Ripley	D-3
Rockwood	D-17
Rogersville	K-13
Ryall Springs	G-16
Savannah	G-7
Selmer	F-6
Sevierville	D-20
Sewanee	F-14
Seymour	C-20
Shawanee	A-20
Shelbyville	E-12
Signal Mountain	G-15
Smithville	D-14
Smyrna	D-12
Soddy-Daisy	F-16
South Fulton	A-5
South Pittsburg	G-14
Sparta	D-15
Spring City	E-17
Springfield	B-11
Sweetwater	E-18
Tazewell	B-20
Tiptonville	B-3
Trenton	C-5
Tullahoma	F-13
Union City	B-4
Walnut Hill	K-15
Waverly	C-8
White House	B-12
Winchester	F-13
Woodbury	D-13

Selected Attractions

Abraham Lincoln Museum	A-20
Alex Haley House Museum	D-3
Casey Jones Home & Railroad Museum	D-5
David Crockett Cabin & Museum	F-9
Dollywood	M-11
Great Smoky Mountains National Park	E-20
James K. Polk Home	E-10
Land Between the Lakes	A-7
Museum of Science & Energy	C-18
Unaka Mountain Scenic Area	L-15

Adjacent States

Alabama	4
Arkansas	10
Georgia	30
Kentucky	44
Mississippi	60
Missouri	64
North Carolina	82
Virginia	112

EASTERN TENNESSEE

KNOXVILLE

CHATTANOOGA

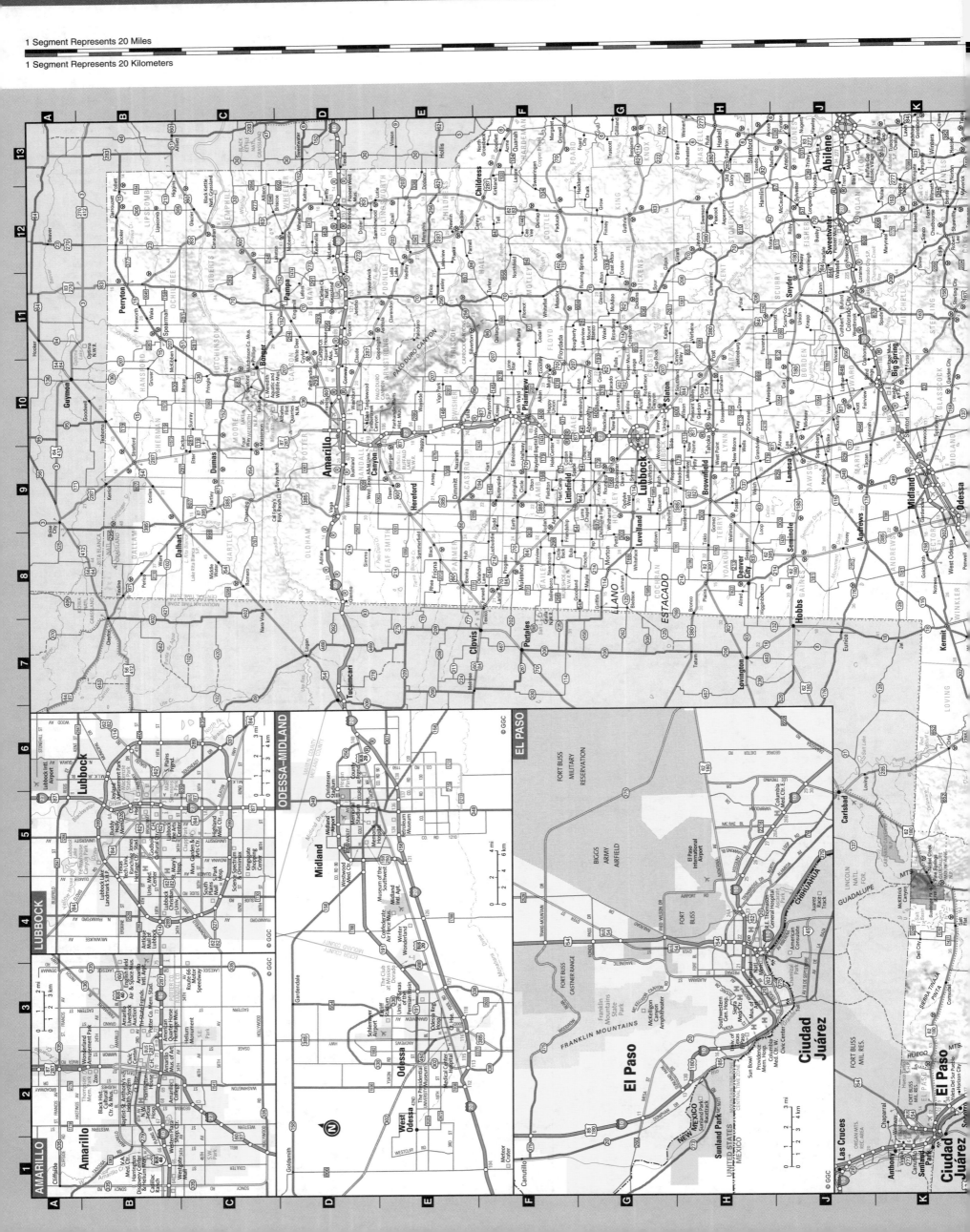

Lubbock

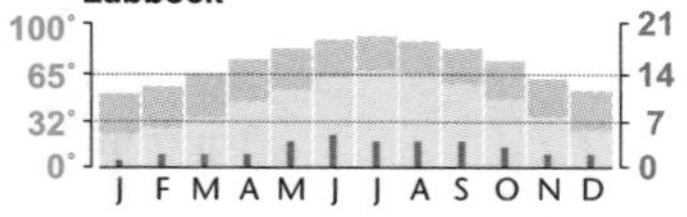

El Paso

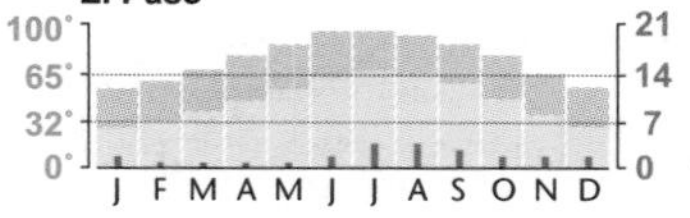

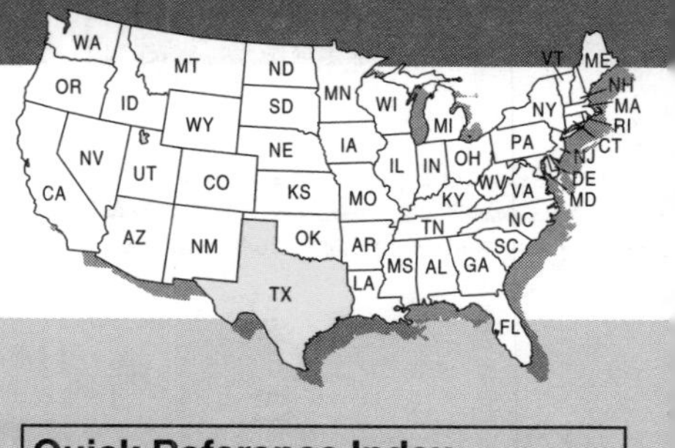

1 Segment Represents 20 Miles

1 Segment Represents 20 Kilometers

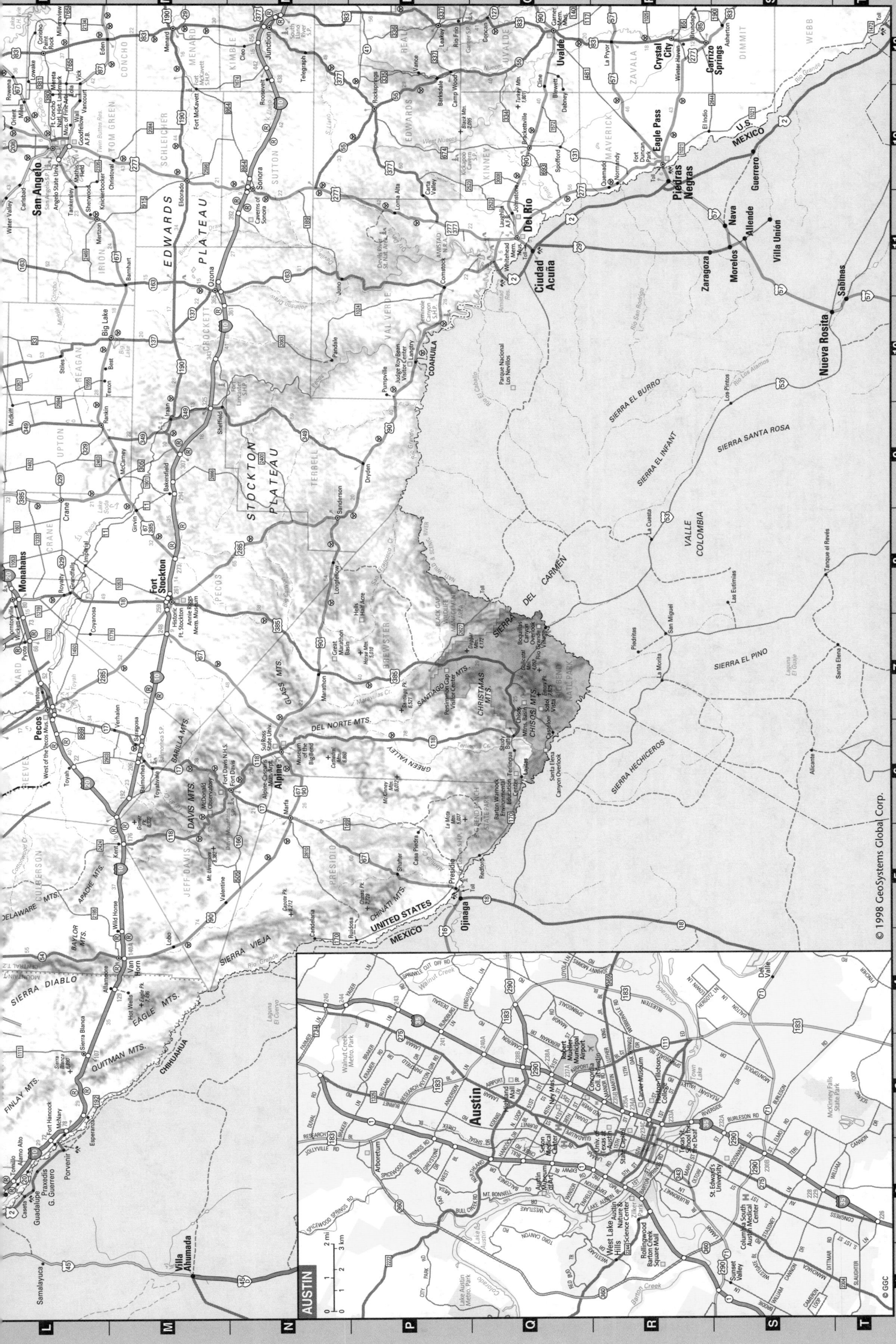

Quick Reference Index

For index to counties and places see page 141.

Selected Attractions

Adjacent States

© 1998 GeoSystems Global Corp.

AUSTIN

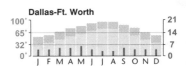

1 Segment Represents 20 Miles

1 Segment Represents 20 Kilometers

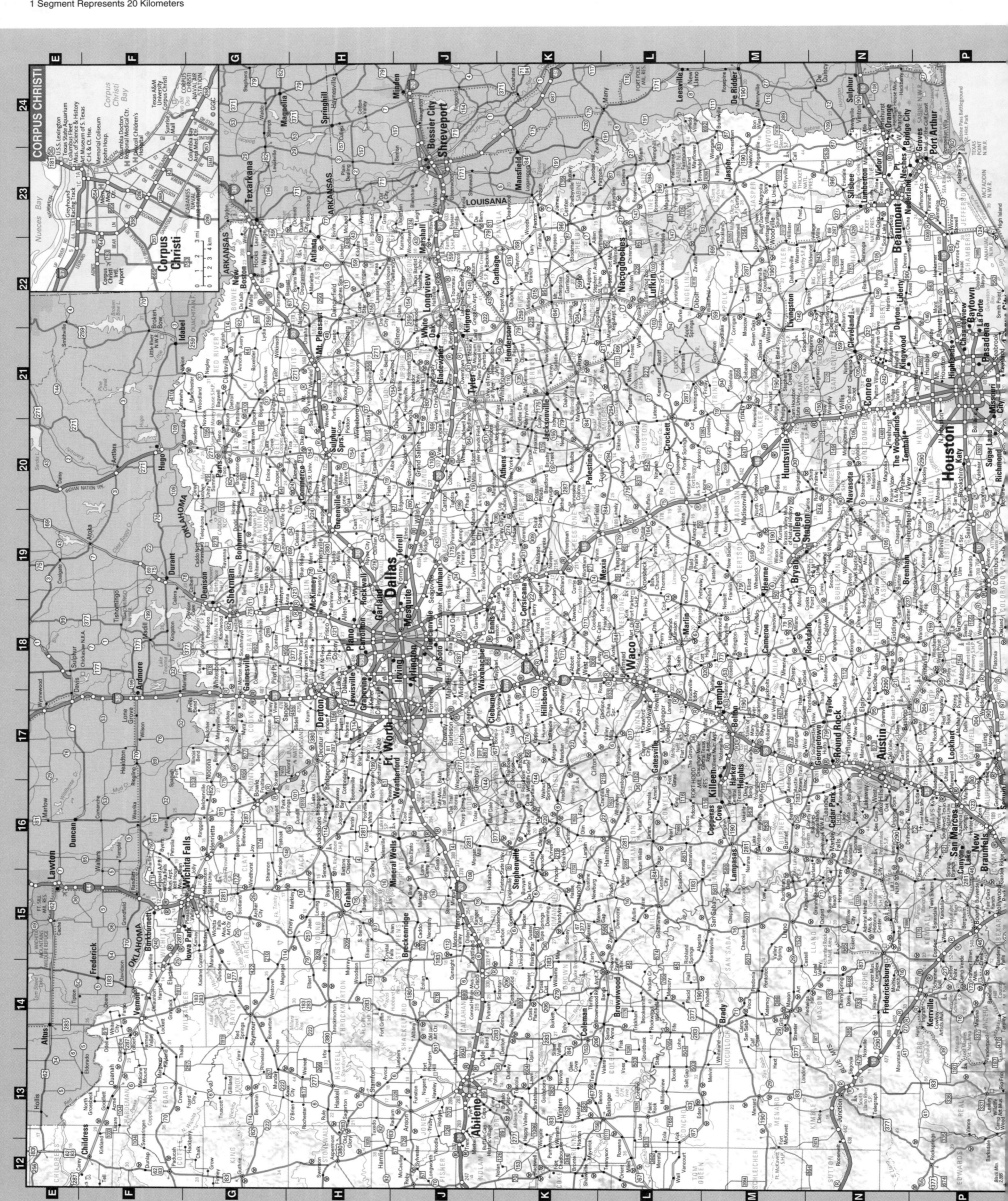

Houston

Corpus Christi

1 Segment Represents 20 Miles

1 Segment Represents 20 Kilometers

Quick Reference Index
For index to counties and places see page 141.

Place	Grid	Place	Grid
Abilene	J-13	Lake Jackson	Q-21
Alice	T-16	Lancaster	J-18
Allen	H-18	Laredo	T-14
Alvin	Q-21	League City	P-21
Angleton	Q-21	Leon Valley	Q-15
Arlington	J-18	Lewisville	H-18
Athens	K-20	Live Oak	Q-16
Austin	N-17	Lockhart	P-17
Azle	H-17	Longview	J-22
Bay City	R-20	Lufkin	L-22
Baytown	P-22	Mansfield	J-17
Beaumont	N-23	Marshall	J-22
Beeville	S-17	McAllen	W-16
Bellaire	P-21	McKinney	H-18
Bellmead	L-18	Mercedes	W-16
Belton	M-17	Mesquite	J-18
Brenham	N-19	Mineral Wells	J-16
Brownsville	W-17	Mission	W-16
Brownwood	L-14	Missouri City	P-21
Bryan	M-19	Mount Pleasant	H-21
Burkburnett	F-15	Nacogdoches	L-22
Burleson	J-17	Nederland	N-23
Canyon Lake	P-16	New Braunfels	P-16
Carrollton	H-18	Orange	N-24
Channelview	P-21	Palestine	K-20
Cleburne	J-17	Paris	G-20
Clute	Q-21	Pasadena	P-21
College Station	M-19	Pearland	P-21
Colleyville	H-18	Pharr	W-16
Conroe	N-21	Plano	H-18
Copperas Cove	M-16	Port Arthur	P-23
Corpus Christi	T-17	Port Lavaca	R-19
Corsicana	K-19	Port Neches	N-23
Dallas	J-18	Portland	T-17
De Soto	J-18	Raymondville	V-17
Denison	G-19	Richmond	P-20
Denton	H-17	Rio Grande City	V-15
Dickinson	Q-21	Robstown	T-17
Donna	W-16	Rockwall	H-19
Duncanville	J-18	Rosenberg	P-20
Eagle Pass	R-12	Round Rock	N-17
Edinburg	V-16	San Angelo	L-12
El Campo	Q-19	San Antonio	Q-15
Ennis	J-18	San Benito	W-17
Forest Hill	J-17	San Marcos	P-16
Fort Worth	J-17	Santa Fe	Q-21
Freeport	R-21	Seagoville	J-18
Friendswood	P-21	Seguin	Q-16
Gainesville	G-17	Sherman	G-18
Galveston	Q-22	Spring	N-21
Garland	H-18	Stephenville	K-16
Gatesville	L-17	Sugar Land	P-20
Georgetown	N-17	Sulphur Springs	H-20
Graham	H-15	Sweetwater	J-12
Grapevine	H-18	Taylor	N-17
Greenville	H-19	Temple	M-17
Groves	P-23	Terrell	J-19
Harker Heights	M-17	Texarkana	G-23
Harlingen	W-17	Texas City	Q-22
Henderson	K-22	The Colony	H-18
Hewitt	L-17	The Woodlands	N-21
Houston	P-20	Tyler	J-21
Humble	P-21	Universal City	Q-16
Huntsville	M-20	Uvalde	Q-13
Irving	J-18	Vernon	F-14
Jacksonville	K-21	Victoria	R-18
Jollyville	N-17	Vidor	N-23
Keller	H-17	Waco	L-18
Kerrville	P-14	Waxahachie	J-18
Kilgore	J-21	Weatherford	J-16
Killeen	M-17	Weslaco	W-16
Kingsville	T-16	Wharton	Q-20
Kingwood	N-21	Wichita Falls	G-15
La Marque	Q-22	Woodway	L-17
La Porte	P-21	Wylie	H-19

Selected Attractions

Attraction	Grid
Big Thicket National Preserve	N-22
Blanco State Park	P-15
Buescher State Park	P-18
Conrad Hilton Museum	J-14
Matagorda Lighthouse	S-19
Museum of East Texas	J-22
Padre Island National Seashore	U-18
Sabine Pass Battleground State Historic Park	P-13
Texas Air Museum	W-17
Texas Zoo	R-18

Adjacent States

State	Page
Arkansas	10
Louisiana	46
Mexico	132
New Mexico	74
Oklahoma	90
Texas - Western	104

© 1998 GeoSystems/Global Corp.

108 TEXAS CITY MAPS: Dallas – Houston

Dallas–
Ft. Worth, TX
Dallas, TX Downtown

Houston–
Galveston, TX
Houston, TX Downtown

1 Segment Represents 4 Miles (area maps)

1 Segment Represents 4 Kilometers (area maps)

1 Segment Represents 4 Miles (area maps)

1 Segment Represents 4 Kilometers (area maps)

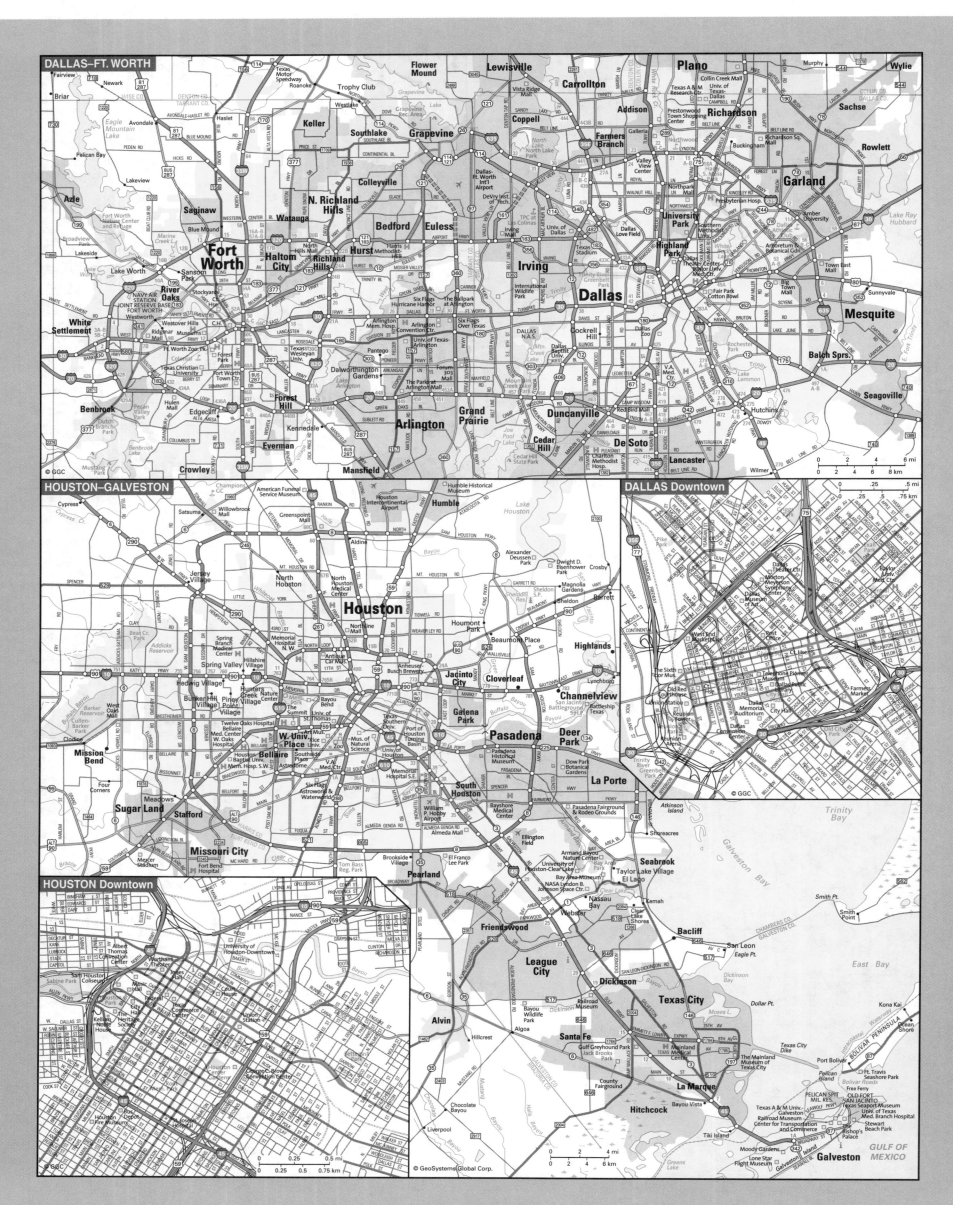

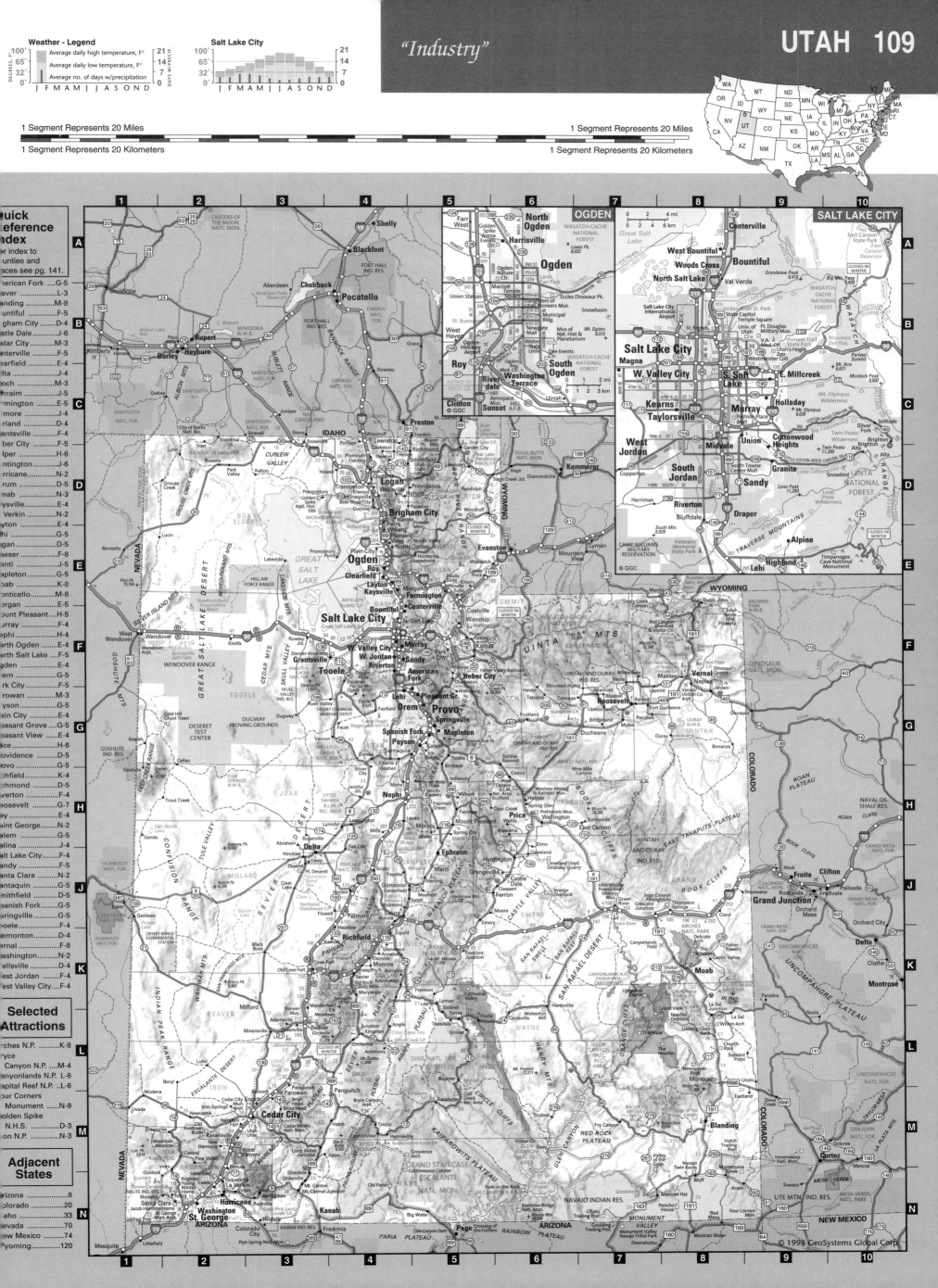

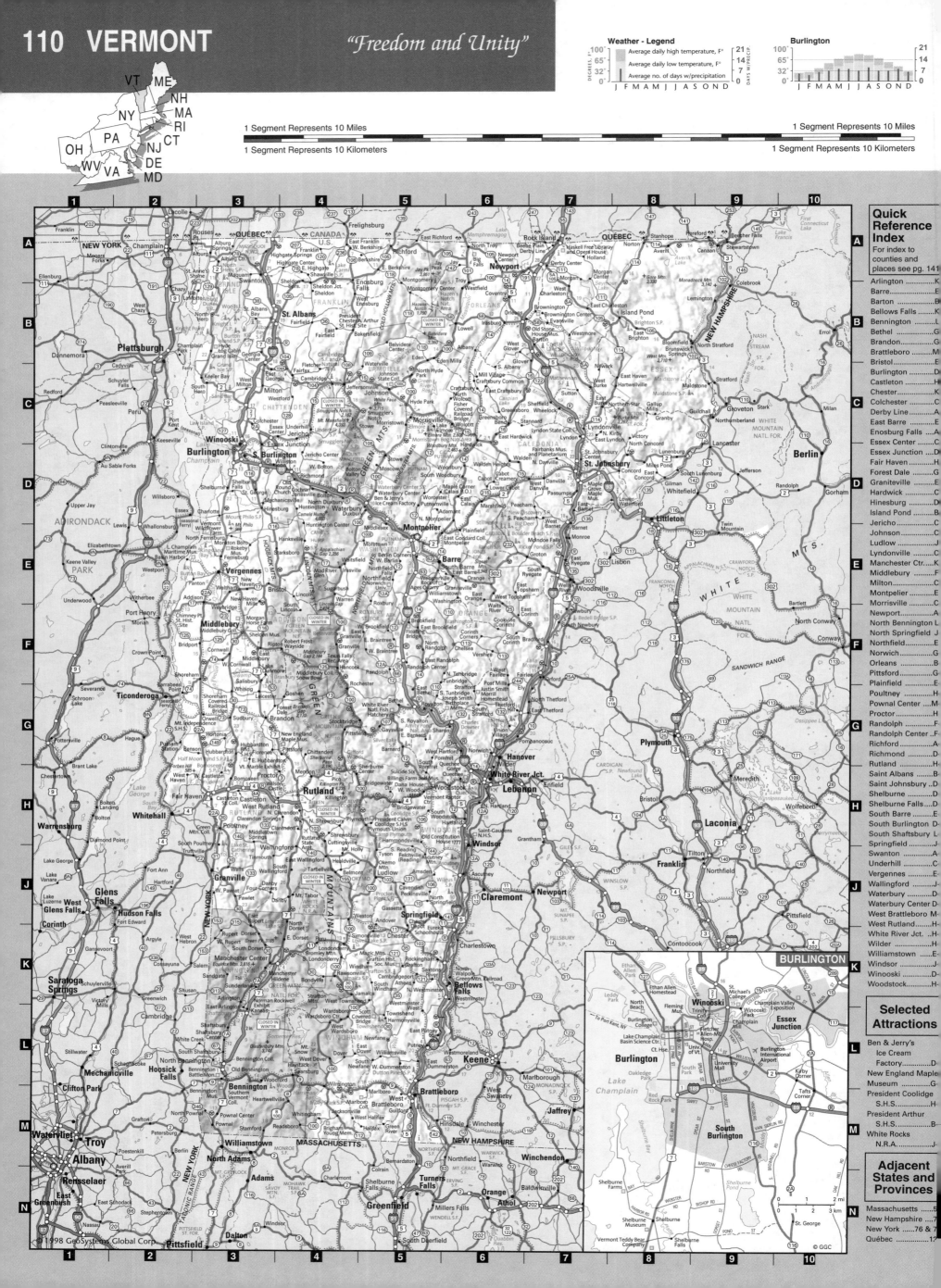

1 Segment Represents 10 Miles

1 Segment Represents 10 Kilometers

1 Segment Represents 10 Miles

1 Segment Represents 10 Kilometers

Weather - Legend

Average daily high temperature, F°
Average daily low temperature, F°
Average no. of days w/precipitation

Burlington

Charlottesville, VA
Norfolk–Virginia Beach–
  Newport News, VA

Petersburg, VA
Washington, DC Area

CITY MAPS: Charlottesville – Washington, DC Area **111**

1 Segment Represents 4 Miles (Norfolk map)

1 Segment Represents 4 Kilometers (Norfolk map)

1 Segment Represents 4 Miles (Norfolk map)

1 Segment Represents 4 Kilometers (Norfolk map)

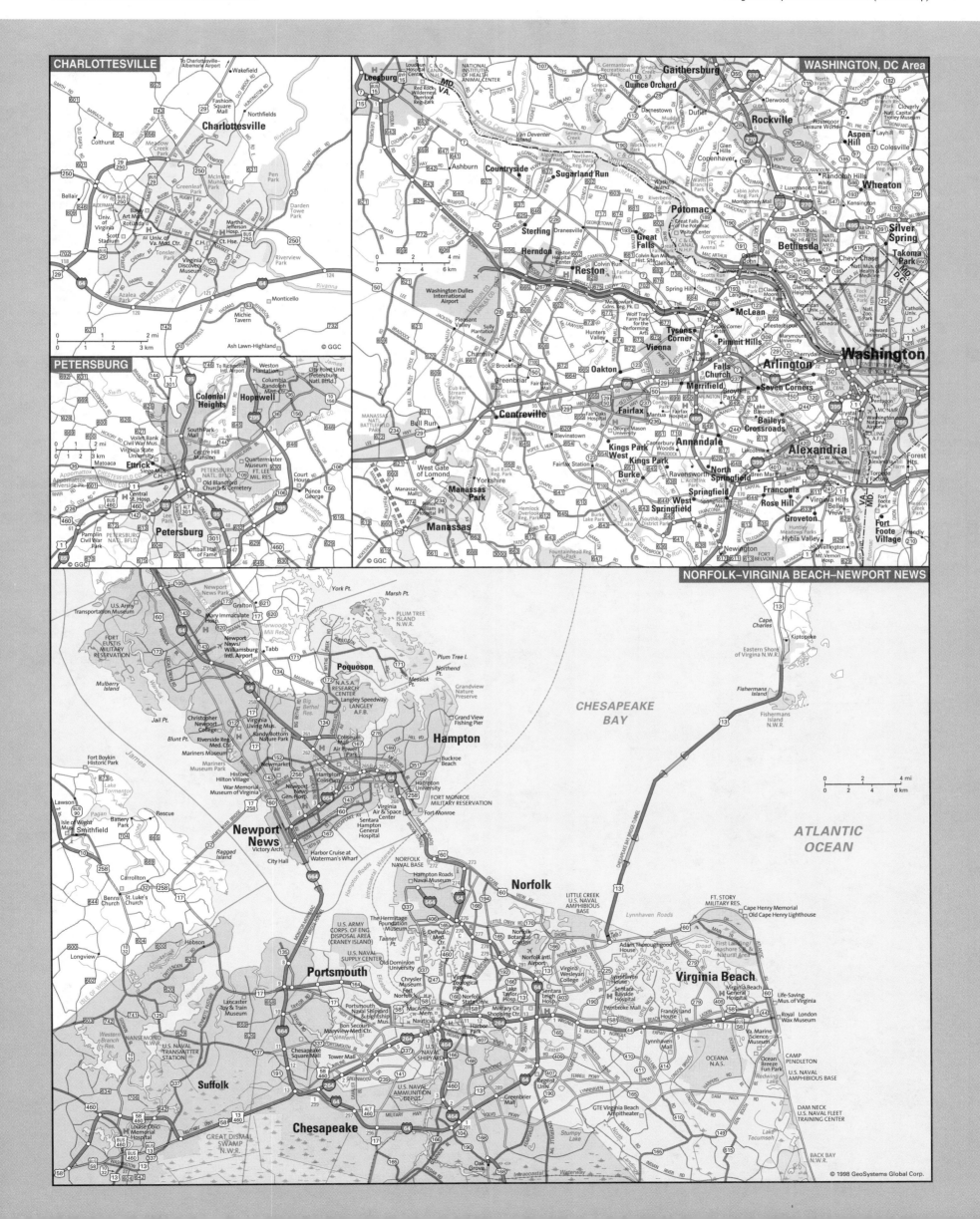

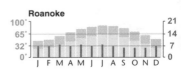

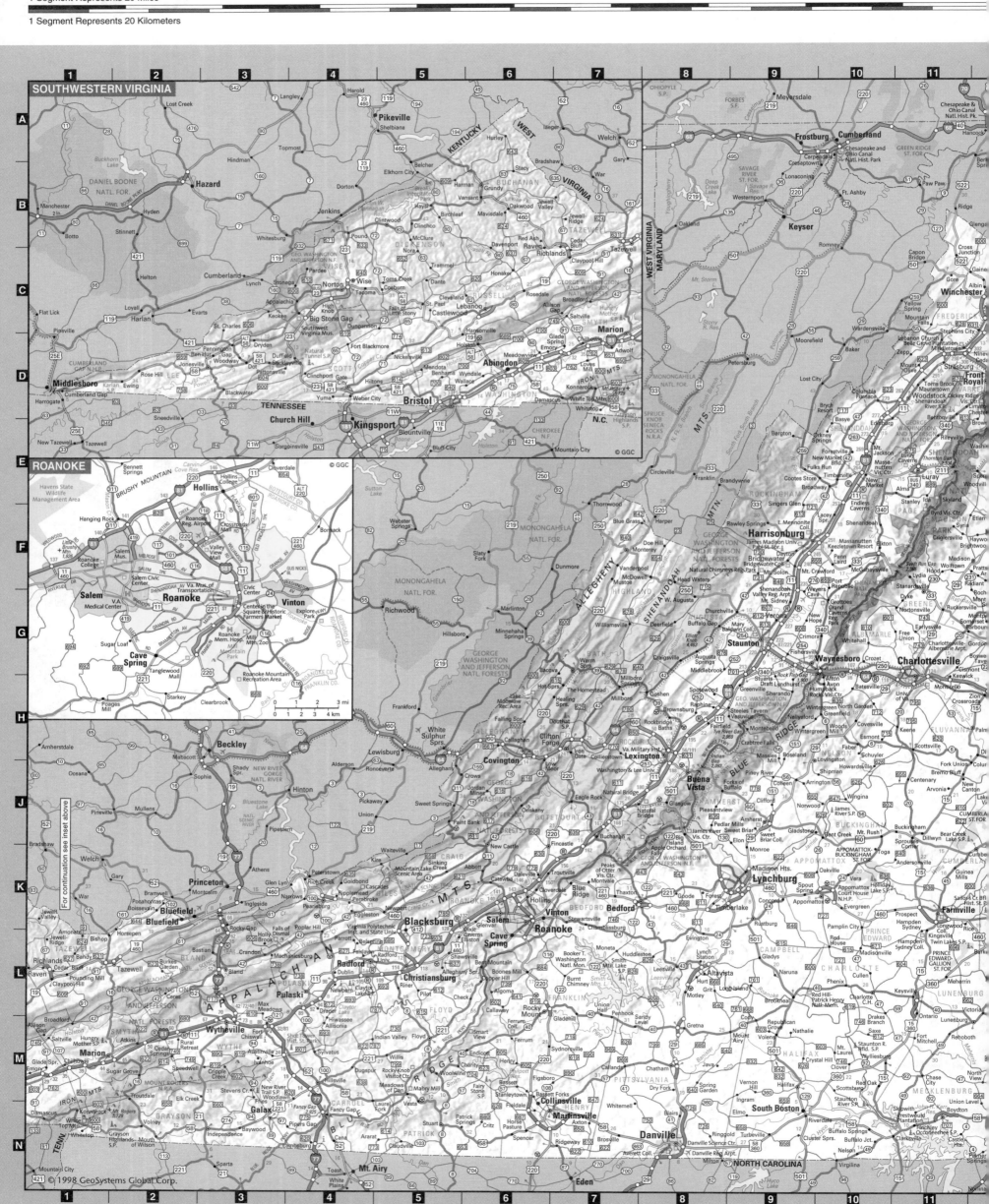

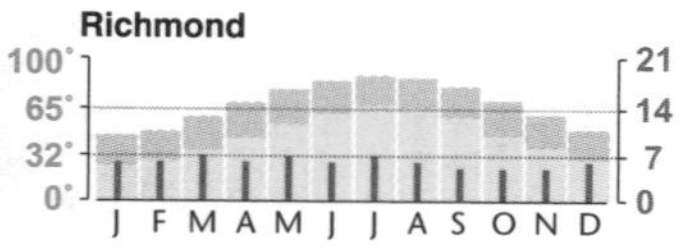

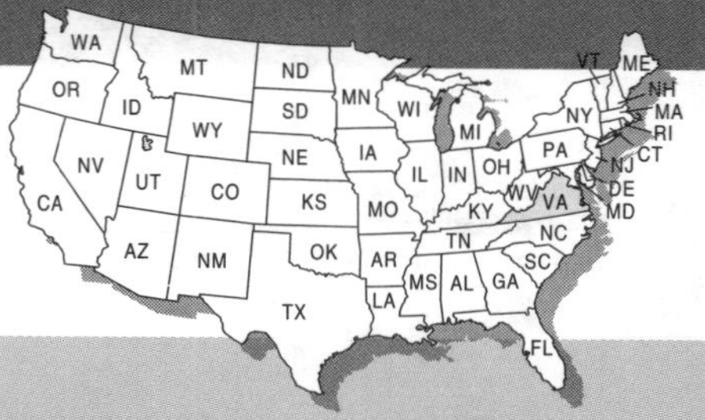

Richmond
Norfolk

1 Segment Represents 20 Miles
1 Segment Represents 20 Kilometers

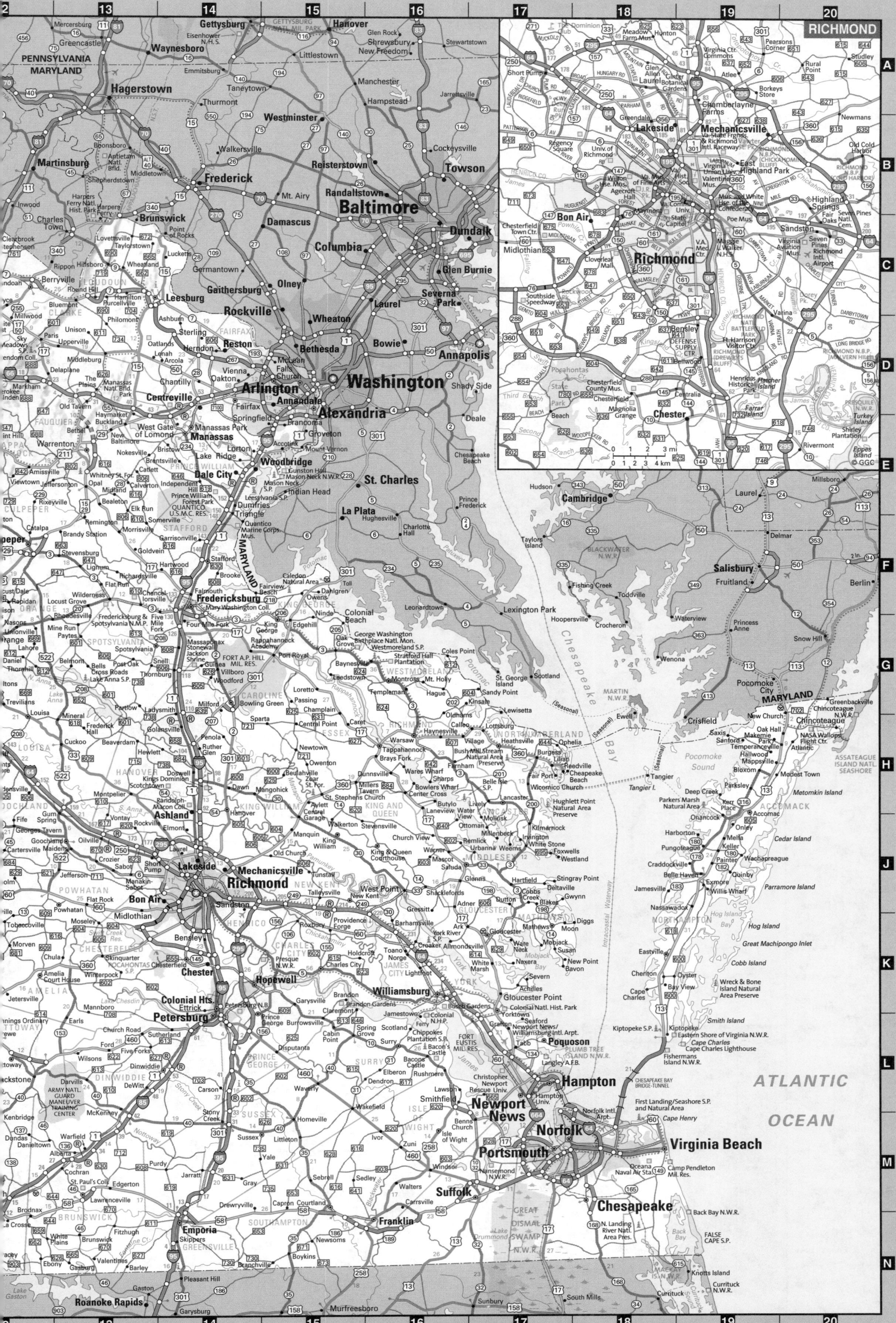

RICHMOND

Quick Reference Index

For index to counties and places see page 141.

Place	Ref	Place	Ref
Abingdon	D-6	Horse Pasture	N-6
Alexandria	D-15	Lake Ridge	E-14
Altavista	L-8	Lakeside	J-14
Annandale	D-15	Laurel	J-14
Appalachia	C-4	Lebanon	C-6
Arlington	D-15	Leesburg	C-13
Ashburn	D-14	Lexington	H-8
Ashland	H-14	Lorton	E-14
Bealeton	E-13	Luray	E-11
Bedford	K-8	Lynchburg	K-9
Bensley	K-14	Madison Heights	K-9
Berryville	C-12	Manassas	E-14
Big Stone Gap	C-4	Manassas Park	E-14
Blacksburg	K-5	Marion	M-1
Blackstone	L-12	Martinsville	N-7
Blue Ridge	K-7	McLean	D-15
Bluefield	K-2	Mechanicsville	J-14
Bon Air	J-14	Midlothian	K-13
Bridgewater	F-9	Mount Vernon	E-15
Bristol	D-5	Narrows	K-4
Buena Vista	J-8	Newport News	L-17
Castlewood	C-5	Norfolk	M-17
Cave Spring	L-6	Norton	C-4
Centreville	D-14	Oakton	D-14
Chantilly	D-14	Orange	G-12
Charlottesville	G-11	Pearisburg	K-4
Chase City	M-11	Pennington Gap	D-3
Chesapeake	M-18	Petersburg	L-14
Chester	K-14	Poquoson	L-17
Chesterfield	K-14	Portsmouth	M-17
Chilhowie	M-1	Pulaski	L-4
Chincoteague	H-20	Purcellville	C-13
Christiansburg	L-5	Radford	L-4
Clifton Forge	H-7	Raven	L-1
Coeburn	C-5	Reston	D-14
Collinsville	N-6	Richlands	L-1
Colonial Beach	G-15	Richmond	J-14
Colonial Heights	K-14	Roanoke	K-6
Covington	H-6	Rocky Mount	L-6
Crewe	L-12	Salem	K-6
Crimora	G-10	Saltville	M-1
Crozet	G-10	Sandston	J-14
Culpeper	F-12	Seaford	L-17
Dale City	E-14	Shenandoah	F-10
Danville	N-8	Short Pump	J-13
Dublin	L-4	Smithfield	L-16
Dumfries	E-14	South Boston	N-9
Elkton	F-10	South Hill	M-12
Emporia	N-14	Spotsylvania	G-13
Ettrick	K-14	Springfield	E-15
Fairfax	D-14	Stafford	F-14
Fairlawn	L-4	Staunton	G-9
Falls Church	D-15	Sterling	D-14
Falmouth	F-14	Strasburg	D-11
Farmville	K-11	Stuarts Draft	H-9
Fishersville	G-9	Suffolk	M-17
Five Mile Fork	F-14	Tazewell	L-2
Forest	K-8	Timberlake	K-8
Four Mile Fork	G-14	Triangle	F-14
Franconia	E-15	Verona	G-9
Franklin	N-16	Victoria	L-12
Fredericksburg	F-14	Vienna	D-14
Front Royal	D-12	Vinton	K-6
Galax	N-3	Virginia Beach	M-18
Garrisonville	E-14	Warrenton	E-13
Gate City	D-4	Waverly	L-15
Gloucester	K-17	Waynesboro	G-9
Gloucester Point	K-17	W. Gate of Lomond	E-14
Groveton	E-15	West Point	J-16
Hampton	L-17	Williamsburg	K-16
Harrisonburg	F-9	Winchester	C-12
Herndon	D-14	Wise	C-4
Hillsville	M-4	Woodbridge	E-14
Hollins	K-6	Woodstock	D-11
Hopewell	K-14	Wytheville	M-3

Selected Attractions

Attraction	Ref
Booker T. Washington National Monument	L-7
Bush Gardens	K-16
Chesapeake Bay Bridge-Tunnel	L-18
Claytor Lake State Park	L-4
False Cape State Park	N-19
George Washington Birthplace Natl. Monument	G-15
Manassas National Battlefield Park	D-13
Monticello	H-11
Mount Rogers National Recreation Area	M-2
Shenandoah National Park	E-11

Adjacent States

State	Page
Kentucky	44
Maryland	50
North Carolina	82
Tennessee	102
West Virginia	117

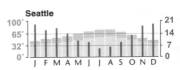

1 Segment Represents 20 Miles

1 Segment Represents 20 Kilometers

"By and By"

Spokane

Walla Walla

1 Segment Represents 20 Miles

1 Segment Represents 20 Kilometers

Quick Reference Index

For index to counties and places see page 141.

Selected Attractions

Adjacent States and Provinces

SPOKANE

© GGC

1 Segment Represents 2 Miles (area map)

1 Segment Represents 2 Kilometers (area map)

1 Segment Represents 2 Miles (area map)

1 Segment Represents 2 Kilometers (area map)

WASHINGTON, DC Area

Watkins Island · Potomac · Riverbend County Park · Great Falls of the Potomac · Visitor Center · C&O Canal National Historical Park · Great Falls Park · TPC Avenel · Congressional · Randolph Hills · Watts Branch Park · Cabin John Reg. Park · White Flint Mall · Garrett Park · Wheaton · Wheaton Regional Park · Calverton · Howard University Beltsville Campus · Patuxent Wildlife Research Center

Luxmanor · Montgomery Mall · Kensington · Chevy Chase View · White Oak · Naval Surface Warfare Center · Hillandale · Knollwood · Beltsville · National Agricultural Research Center

Potomac · Great Falls National Historical Park · National Institutes of Health · Suburban Hospital · Naval Naval Med Center · Washington Mormon Temple · Holy Cross Hospital · Oakview · Adelphi · Greenbelt · Goddard Space Flight Center

Wolf Trap Farm Park for the Performing Arts · Spring Hill · Claude Moore Colonial Farm · Glen Echo · Bethesda · Chevy Chase · National Museum of Health & Medicine · Silver Spring · Takoma Park · Washington Adventist Hospital · Langley Park · College Park · University of Maryland · College Park Airport Mus. · Berwyn Heights · Glenn Dale · Doctors Community Hospital

McLean · Scotts Run Nature Preserve · Turkey Run Park · Glen Echo Heights · Rock Creek Park · Walter Reed Army Medical Center · University Park · Lewisdale · Riverdale · Seabrook · Lanham

Tysons Corner Center · Pimmit Hills · Idylwood · Marymount University · Potomac Overlook Regional Park · University of the District of Columbia · American University · Sibley Memorial Hospital · Washington National Cathedral · National Zoological Park · Howard University · National Shrine of the Immaculate Conception · Providence Hospital · Catholic University of America · Trinity College · Colmar Manor · Hyattsville · Chillum · Mount Rainier · Brentwood · Cottage City · Bladensburg · Landover Hills · Landover · New Carrollton

Vienna · Falls Church · East Falls Church · Arlington · Cherrydale · Rosslyn · Newseum · G.W. Univ. · The White House · The Phillips Collection · Georgetown University & Hospital · Dumbarton Oaks · Washington · Gallaudet University · National Arboretum · Anacostia River Park · Cheverly · Kentland · Glenarden · Landover Mall · Palmer Park · Largo

Merrifield · Seven Corners · Westover · Ballston · Clarendon · Lincoln Mem. · Constitution · The Mall · U.S. Capitol · R.F.K. Mem. Stadium · Fairmount Heights · Jack Kent Cooke Stadium · USAir Arena · Seat Pleasant

Broyhill Park · Vencor Hospital Barcroft · The Pentagon · Washington Monument · Jefferson Memorial · WASH. NAVY YARD · D.C. Gen. Hosp. · Fort Dupont Park · Capitol Heights · Walker Mill · Walker Mill Reg. Park · Ritchie · Southwest Branch Park · Watkins Regional Park

Fairfax · Fairfax Hospital · Lake Barcroft · Baileys Crossroads · Pentagon City Mall · Crystal City · Fort McNair · East Potomac Park · Bolling A.F.B. · St. Elizabeths Hospital · Frederick Douglass Natl. Hist. Site · Suitland · U.S. Census Bureau · Coral Hills · District Heights · Forestville · Westphalia

Annandale · Lincolnia · National Hospital Medical Center · Washington National Airport · Greater S.E. Community Hospital · Hillcrest Heights · Silver Hill · Marlow Heights · Morningside · Henson Creek Park

Kings Park · Ravensworth · North Springfield · Alexandria Hospital · George Washington Masonic Natl. Mem. · Christ Church · Old Town Alexandria · Torpedo Factory · Forest Heights · Glassmanor · Oxon Hill · Rosecroft Raceway · Temple Hills · Camp Springs · Andrews Air Force Base

Springfield · Franconia · West Springfield · Springfield Mall · Bren Mar Park · U.S. Mil. Res. · Rose Hill · Belle Haven · Virginia Hills · Huntington · Oxon Hill Farm · Rosedale Estates

Groveton · Belle View · VIRGINIA / MARYLAND · Fort Foote Park · Fort Foote Village · Oaklawn · Rosaryville State Park · Marlton

WASHINGTON, DC Downtown

GEORGETOWN · Rock Creek Park · St. Matthew's Cathedral · B'nai B'rith Klutznick National Jewish Mus. · Thomas Circle · Washington Post · Bus Depot · Washington Coliseum

FOGGY BOTTOM · George Washington Univ. Hosp. · National Geographic Society & Explorers Hall · Strayer College · Wilderness Society · Edward R. Murrow Park · Farragut Square · McPherson Square · Franklin Park · National Convention Center · CHINATOWN · Friendship Archway · Tech 2000 · Mt. Vernon Place · Capital Children's Museum

George Washington University · Decatur House · Lafayette Square · Dept. of Veterans Affairs · Claims Court Bldg. · D.C. Convention Center · National Museum of Women in the Arts · Martin Luther King Jr. Memorial Library · MCI Center · National Building Museum · National Postal Museum · Union Station · Georgetown University Law Center

Octagon House · Blair House · Renwick Gallery · The White House · Dept. of the Treasury · National Theatre · Ford's Theatre · National Portrait Gallery · Judiciary Square

Corcoran Gallery of Art · Zero Milestone · The Ellipse · National Aquarium · J. Edgar Hoover FBI Building · Navy Memorial · D.C. Ct. Hse. · U.S. Dist. Ct. Hse. · Dept. of Labor · Union Station Plaza · Taft Memorial Carillon · Sewall-Belmont House · Stanton Park

U.S. Bureau of Medicine and Surgery · Dept. of State · Department of the Interior · D.A.R. · Constitution Hall · Organization of American States · Interstate Commerce Commission · I.R.S. · Dept. of Justice · National Archives · National Gallery of Art · John Marshall Park · Grant Memorial · U.S. Capitol · The Supreme Court · Folger Shakespeare Library

John F. Kennedy Center for the Performing Arts · Vietnam Veterans Memorial · Constitution Gardens · Signers of the Declaration of Independence Memorial · Washington Monument · Natl. Mus. of Natural History · Arts & Industries Building · Smithsonian Institution Castle · Hirshhorn Museum & Sculpture Garden · National Air & Space Museum · East Wing National Gallery of Art · Grant Monument · U.S. Botanic Gardens · The Library of Congress

Lincoln Memorial · Reflecting Pool · West Potomac Park · Korean War Veterans Memorial · D.C. War Memorial · National Museum of American History · Freer Gallery of Art · Dept. of Independence · Arthur M. Sackler Gallery · Natl. Mus. of African Art · Dept. of Agriculture · Dept. of Energy · Dept. of Education · Dept. of Health & Human Services

THEODORE ROOSEVELT MEMORIAL · Theodore Roosevelt Island · ROSSLYN · Marine Corps War Memorial (Iwo Jima) · The Netherlands Carillon · ARLINGTON NATIONAL CEMETERY · Columbia Island · Lady Bird Johnson Park · Tidal Basin · Bureau of Engraving & Printing · U.S. Holocaust Memorial Museum · L'Enfant Plaza · Department of H.U.D. · U.S. Postal Service Headquarters · Dept. of Transportation · School of Engineering & Architecture · Southeastern University

John F. Kennedy Gravesite · Franklin Delano Roosevelt Memorial · Thomas Jefferson Memorial · Benjamin Banneker Park · Washington Channel · NORTH PARKING AREA FOR THE PENTAGON · Lyndon B. Johnson Memorial Grove · Navy and Marine Memorial · Kreeger Theatre · East Potomac Park · WASHINGTON NAVY YARD

© GGC

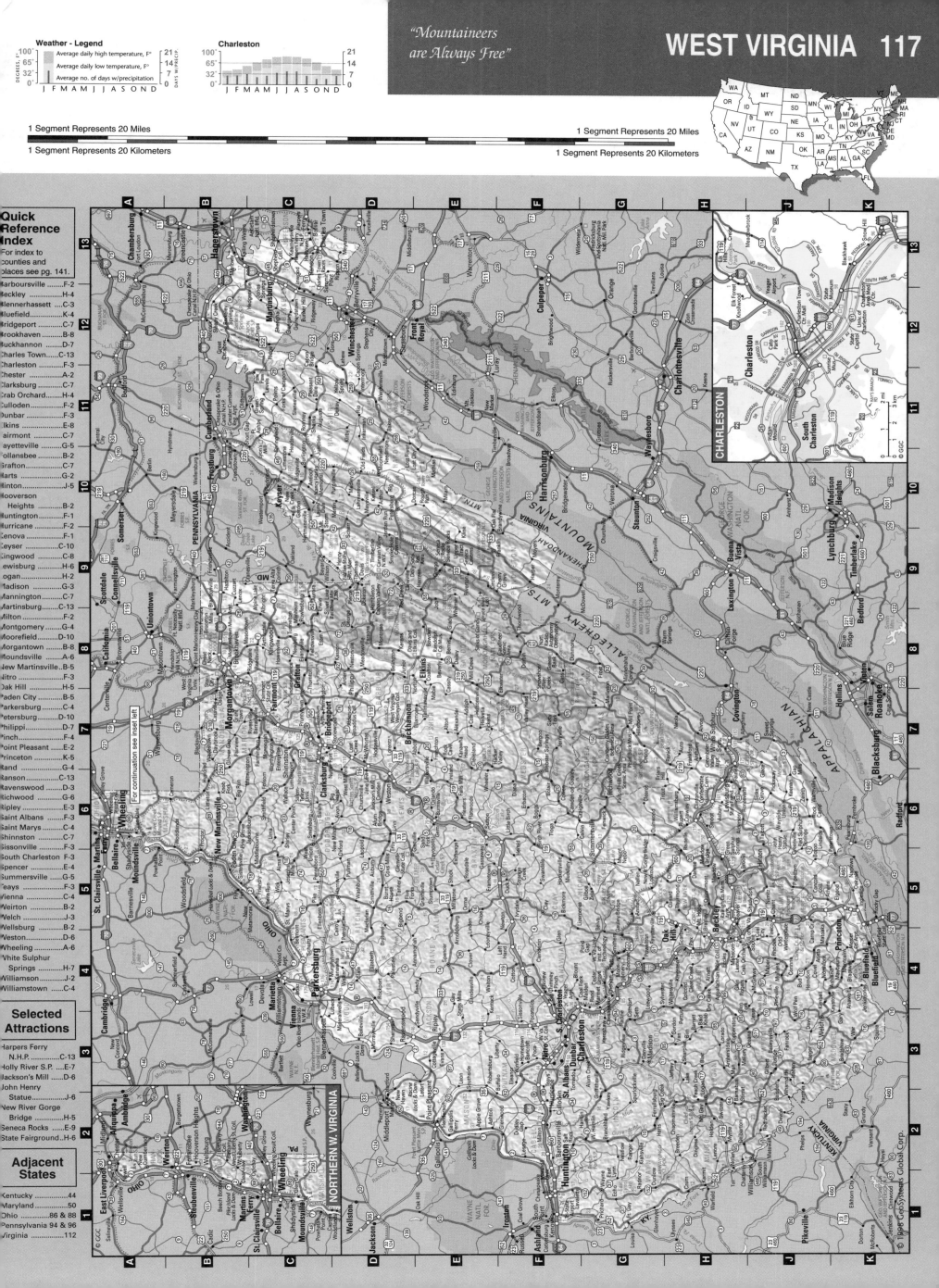

Weather - Legend

Average daily high temperature, F°
Average daily low temperature, F°
Average no. of days w/precipitation

J F M A M J J A S O N D

Charleston

J F M A M J J A S O N D

1 Segment Represents 20 Miles
1 Segment Represents 20 Kilometers

1 Segment Represents 20 Miles
1 Segment Represents 20 Kilometers

Quick Reference Index

For index to counties and places see pg. 141.

Barboursville F-2
Beckley H-4
Blennerhassett C-3
Bluefield K-4
Bridgeport C-7
Brookhaven B-8
Buckhannon D-7
Charles Town C-13
Charleston F-3
Chester A-2
Clarksburg C-7
Crab Orchard H-4
Culloden F-2
Dunbar F-3
Elkins E-8
Fairmont C-7
Fayetteville G-5
Follansbee B-2
Grafton C-7
Harts G-2
Hinton J-5
Hooverson
   Heights B-2
Huntington F-2
Hurricane F-2
Kenova F-1
Keyser C-10
Kingwood C-8
Lewisburg H-6
Logan H-2
Madison G-3
Mannington C-7
Martinsburg C-13
Milton F-2
Montgomery G-4
Moorefield D-10
Morgantown B-8
Moundsville A-6
New Martinsville ...B-5
Nitro F-3
Oak Hill H-5
Paden City B-5
Parkersburg C-4
Petersburg D-10
Philippi D-7
Pinch F-4
Point Pleasant E-2
Princeton K-5
Rand G-4
Ranson C-13
Ravenswood D-3
Richwood G-6
Ripley E-3
Saint Albans F-3
Saint Marys C-4
Shinnston C-7
Sissonville E-3
South Charleston ...F-3
Spencer E-4
Summersville G-5
Teays F-3
Vienna C-4
Weirton B-2
Welch J-3
Wellsburg B-2
Weston D-6
Wheeling A-6
White Sulphur
   Springs H-7
Williamson J-2
Williamstown C-4

Selected Attractions

Harpers Ferry
   N.H.P. C-13
Holly River S.P. E-7
Jackson's Mill D-6
John Henry
   Statue J-6
New River Gorge
   Bridge H-5
Seneca Rocks E-9
State Fairground ...H-6

Adjacent States

Kentucky 44
Maryland 50
Ohio ....86 & 88
Pennsylvania 94 & 96
Virginia 112

"Forward"

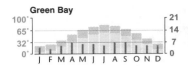

Weather - Legend
Average daily high temperature, F°
Average daily low temperature, F°
Average no. of days w/precipitation

Green Bay

1 Segment Represents 20 Miles

1 Segment Represents 20 Kilometers

Madison

Milwaukee

1 Segment Represents 20 Miles

1 Segment Represents 20 Kilometers

© 1998 GeoSystems Global Corp.

Quick Reference Index
For index to counties and places see page 141.

Algoma	K-12	Middleton	P-8
Altoona	J-4	Milton	Q-9
Antigo	H-9	Milwaukee	Q-11
Appleton	L-10	Monona	Q-8
Ashland	D-5	Monroe	R-8
Ashwaubenon	K-11	Mosinee	J-7
Baraboo	N-7	Mount Horeb	Q-7
Barron	H-3	Mukwonago	Q-10
Beaver Dam	N-9	Muskego	Q-11
Bellevue	K-11	Neenah	L-10
Beloit	R-9	New Berlin	Q-11
Berlin	M-9	New Holstein	M-11
Black River Falls	L-6	New London	L-9
Bloomer	H-4	New Richmond	H-2
Brillion	L-11	North Fond du Lac	M-10
Brodhead	R-8	Oak Creek	Q-11
Brookfield	Q-11	Oconomowoc	P-10
Brown Deer	P-11	Oconto	J-11
Burlington	R-10	Omro	M-9
Cedarburg	P-11	Onalaska	M-4
Chilton	M-11	Oregon	Q-8
Chippewa Falls	J-4	Oshkosh	M-10
Clintonville	K-9	Park Falls	F-6
Columbus	P-9	Peshtigo	J-11
Cudahy	Q-11	Platteville	R-6
De Forest	Q-8	Pleasant Prairie	R-11
De Pere	K-11	Plover	K-8
Delafield	Q-10	Plymouth	N-11
Delavan	R-10	Port Washington	P-11
Dodgeville	Q-7	Portage	N-8
Eau Claire	J-4	Prairie du Chien	Q-5
Edgerton	Q-9	Prescott	J-1
Elkhorn	R-10	Racine	Q-12
Evansville	Q-8	Reedsburg	N-7
Fitchburg	Q-8	Rhinelander	G-8
Fond du Lac	M-10	Rice Lake	G-3
Fort Atkinson	Q-9	Richland Center	P-6
Fox Point	P-11	Ripon	M-9
Franklin	Q-11	River Falls	J-2
Germantown	P-11	Rothschild	J-8
Glendale	P-11	Sauk City	P-7
Grafton	P-11	Saukville	P-11
Green Bay	K-11	Seymour	K-10
Hales Corners	Q-11	Shawano	J-10
Hartford	P-10	Sheboygan	N-12
Hartland	P-10	Sheboygan Falls	N-11
Holmen	M-4	South Milwaukee	Q-11
Horicon	N-10	Sparta	M-5
Howard	K-11	Stevens Point	K-8
Hudson	J-1	Stoughton	Q-8
Janesville	Q-9	Sturgeon Bay	J-12
Jefferson	Q-9	Sturtevant	R-11
Kaukauna	L-10	Sun Prairie	P-9
Kenosha	R-11	Superior	D-3
Kewaunee	K-12	Sussex	P-11
Kiel	M-11	Tomah	M-6
La Crosse	M-4	Tomahawk	G-7
Ladysmith	G-5	Twin Lakes	R-11
Lake Geneva	R-10	Two Rivers	L-12
Lake Mills	Q-9	Union Grove	R-11
Lancaster	Q-5	Verona	Q-8
Little Chute	L-10	Viroqua	N-5
Madison	Q-8	Watertown	P-9
Manitowoc	M-12	Waukesha	Q-11
Marinette	H-12	Waunakee	P-8
Marshfield	K-7	Waupaca	L-9
Mauston	M-7	Waupun	N-9
Mayville	N-10	Wausau	J-8
McFarland	Q-8	West Allis	Q-11
Medford	H-6	West Bend	N-11
Menasha	L-10	West Salem	M-5
Menomonee Falls	P-11	Whitefish Bay	P-11
Menomonie	J-3	Whitewater	Q-9
Mequon	P-11	Wind Lake	Q-11
Merrill	H-8	Wisconsin Rapids	L-7

Selected Attractions

Apostle Island National Lakeshore	C-5
Beyer House Museum	J-11
Circus World Museum	N-8
First Capital	Q-6
Little Norway	Q-7
Logging Museum	G-8
Octagon House	P-10
Red Cedar State Trail	J-3
St. Croix National Scenic Riverway	G-1
Whitefish Dunes State Park	J-13

Adjacent States

Illinois	34
Iowa	40
Michigan	56
Minnesota	60

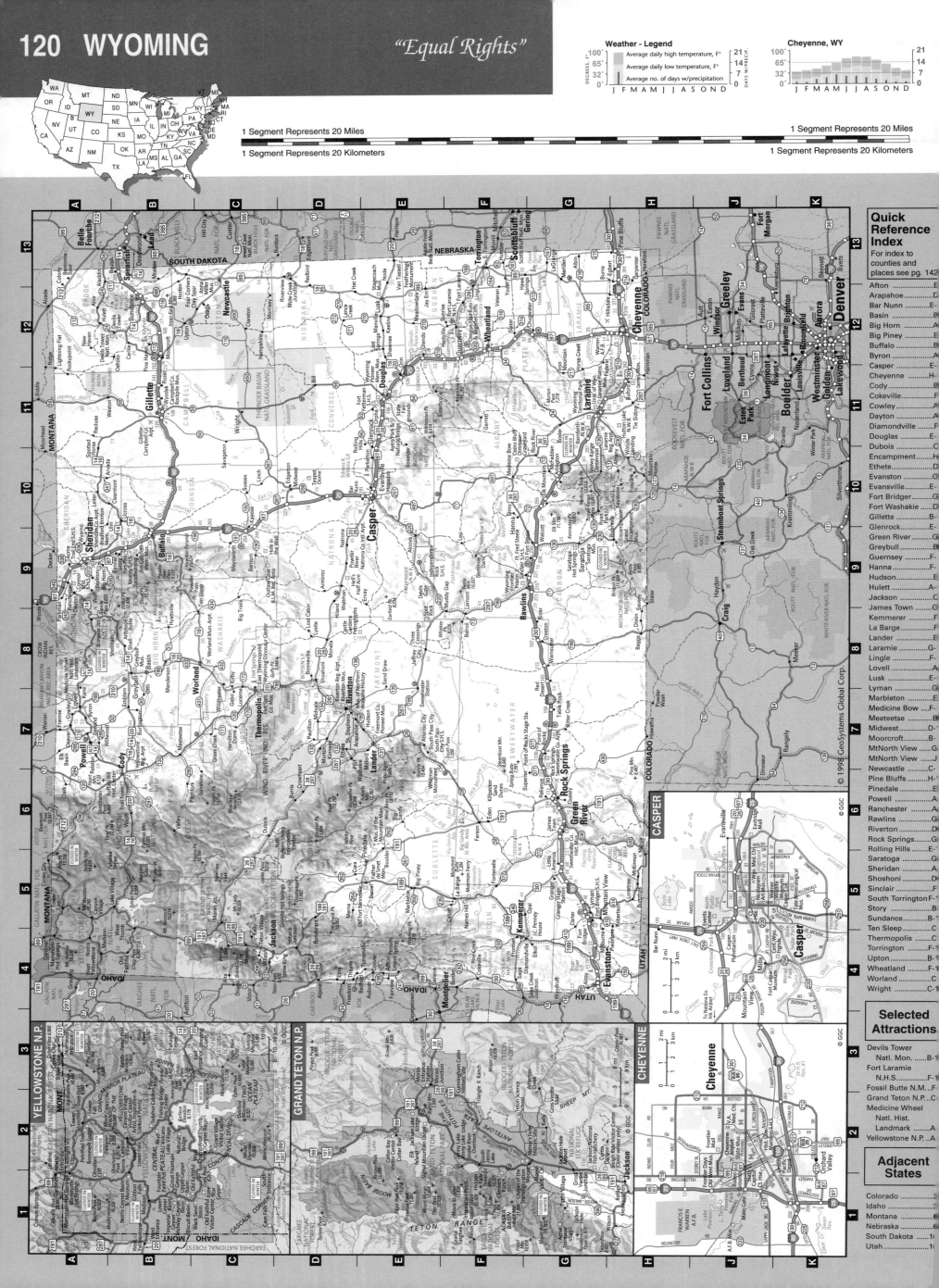

Prince George, BC

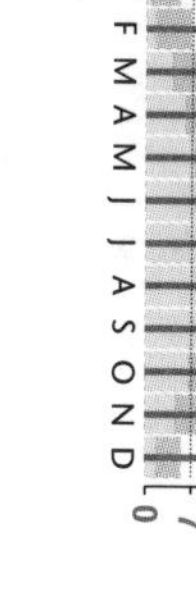

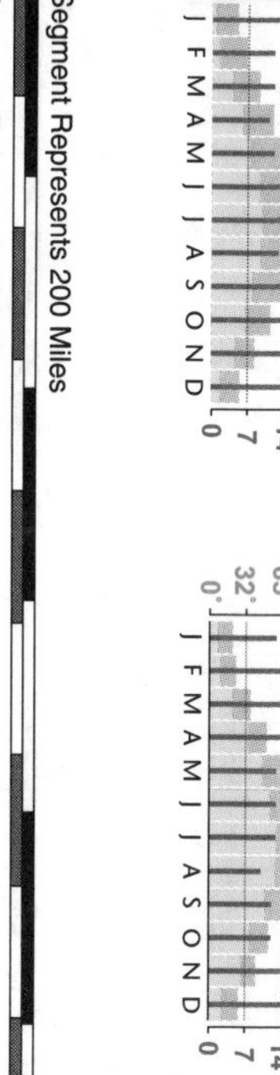

J F M A M J J A S O N D

Montréal, PQ

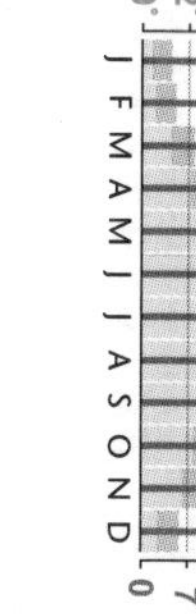

100° 65° 32°

J F M A M J J A S O N D

1 Segment Represents 200 Miles

1 Segment Represents 200 Kilometers

1 Segment Represents 200 Miles

1 Segment Represents 200 Kilometers

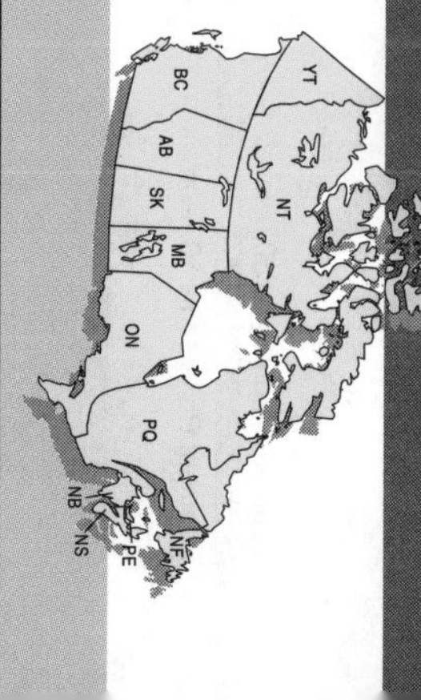

DISTANCES BETWEEN CITIES ARE COMPUTED IN KILOMETERS OVER MAIN HIGHWAYS AND INCLUDE FERRY DISTANCES

To convert kilometers to miles, multiply the distance in kilometers by 0.622.
Example: Toronto, ON to Québec, PQ = 809 kilometers, or 503 miles (809 x 0.622)

© GGC.

Distance table city labels (diagonal): WINNIPEG, MB; WINDSOR, ON; WHITEHORSE, YT; VICTORIA, BC; VANCOUVER, BC; TORONTO, ON; THUNDER BAY, ON; SEATTLE, WA; SAULT STE. MARIE, ON; SASKATOON, SK; ST. JOHN'S, NF; REGINA, SK; QUÉBEC, PQ; PRINCE GEORGE, BC; OTTAWA, ON; NORTH BAY, ON; NEW YORK, NY; MONTREAL, PQ; MINNEAPOLIS, MN; KENORA, ON; HALIFAX, NS; FREDERICTON, NB; EDMONTON, AB; DAWSON CREEK, BC; CHICAGO, IL; CHARLOTTETOWN, PE; CALGARY, AB; BRANDON, MB; BOSTON, MA; BANFF, AB

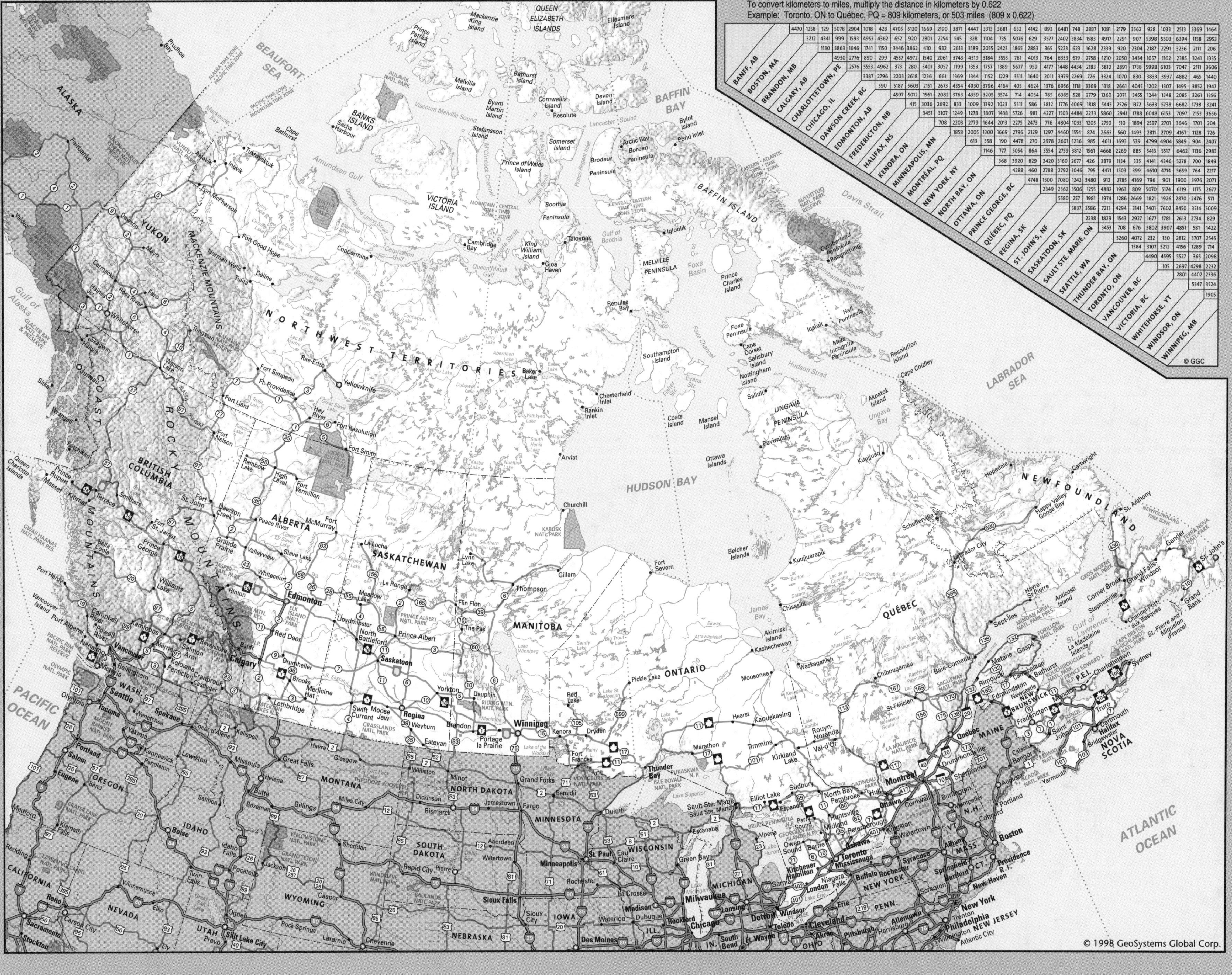

© 1998 GeoSystems Global Corp.

Map region and place labels include: ATLANTIC OCEAN, PACIFIC OCEAN, BEAUFORT SEA, LABRADOR SEA, Davis Strait, Gulf of Alaska, HUDSON BAY, Foxe Basin, Foxe Channel, BAFFIN BAY, BAFFIN ISLAND, VICTORIA ISLAND, BANKS ISLAND, Ellesmere Island, QUEEN ELIZABETH ISLANDS, MELVILLE PENINSULA, UNGAVA PENINSULA, NEWFOUNDLAND, LABRADOR, QUÉBEC, ONTARIO, MANITOBA, SASKATCHEWAN, ALBERTA, BRITISH COLUMBIA, NORTHWEST TERRITORIES, YUKON, ALASKA, ROCKY MOUNTAINS, MACKENZIE MOUNTAINS, COAST MOUNTAINS, NOVA SCOTIA, NEW BRUNSWICK, MAINE, MINNESOTA, NORTH DAKOTA, SOUTH DAKOTA, MONTANA, WYOMING, IDAHO, NEBRASKA, IOWA, WISCONSIN, MICHIGAN, OHIO, NEW YORK, UTAH, NEVADA, CALIFORNIA, OREGON, WASHINGTON, MASS., VT., N.H., CONN., PENN., NEW JERSEY

Cities labeled: Winnipeg, Edmonton, Calgary, Regina, Saskatoon, Prince Albert, Yellowknife, Fort Smith, Fort McMurray, Whitehorse, Prince George, Vancouver, Victoria, Thunder Bay, Toronto, Ottawa, Montréal, Québec, Halifax, Fredericton, Boston, New York, Philadelphia, Chicago, Minneapolis, St. Paul, Milwaukee, Detroit, Cleveland, Seattle, Portland, Salt Lake City

Inset locator map of Canada with provinces: YT, NT, BC, AB, SK, MB, ON, PQ, NB, NS, PE, NF

"Splendor Without Diminishment"

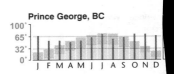

Prince George, BC

1 Segment Represents 50 Miles

1 Segment Represents 50 Kilometers

© 1998 GeoSystems Global Corp.

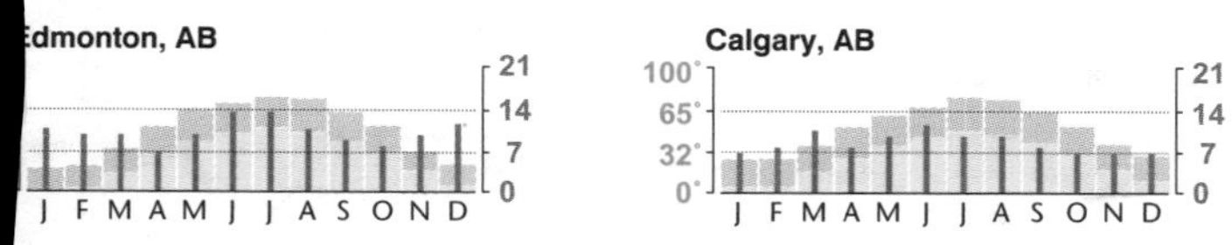

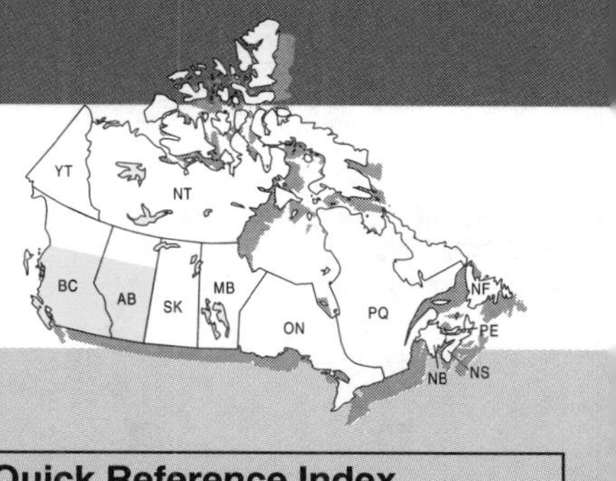

"Strong and Free"

Edmonton, AB

Calgary, AB

1 Segment Represents 50 Miles

1 Segment Represents 50 Kilometers

Quick Reference Index

For index to places see page 142.

ALBERTA

Airdrie J-16
Athabasca............E-16
Banff J-15
Barrhead E-15
Beaumont F-16
Bonnyville..........E-19
Brooks K-18
Calgary K-16
Camrose.............G-17
Canmore J-15
Cardston M-17
Claresholm L-16
Coaldale L-17
Cochrane J-16
Cold Lake E-19
Crowsnest Pass L-16
Devon F-16
Didsbury J-16
Drayton Valley G-15
Drumheller J-17
Edmonton F-16
Edson F-14
Fairview C-12
Fox Cr. E-13
Ft. Macleod L-17
Ft. McMurray B-17
Ft. Saskatchewan F-17
Gibbons F-16
Grand Centre E-19
Grande Cache F-11
Grande Prairie D-12
Grimshaw C-13
Hanna J-18
High Prairie D-14
High River K-16
Hinton F-13
Innisfail H-16
Jasper G-12
Lac La Biche D-18
Lacombe G-16
Leduc F-16
Lethbridge L-17
Lloydminster F-19
Medicine Hat L-19
Morinville F-16
Okotoks..............K-16
Olds J-16
Peace River C-13
Pincher Cr. M-16
Ponoka G-16
Raymond M-17
Red Deer H-16
Redcliff L-19
Redwater F-17
Rimbey G-16
Rocky Mtn. House H-15
Slave Lake D-15
Spruce Gr. F-16
St. Albert F-16
St. Paul E-18
Stettler H-17
Stony Plain F-16
Strathmore K-17
Swan Hills E-15
Sylvan Lake H-16
Taber L-18
Three Hills J-17
Valleyview D-13
Vegreville F-16
Vermilion F-19
Wainwright G-19
Westlock E-16
Wetaskiwin G-16
Whitecourt E-14

BRITISH COLUMBIA

Abbotsford M-8
Armstrong K-11
Burnaby M-8
Campbell River L-6
Castlegar M-13
Cedar M-7
Chetwynd C-9
Chilliwack M-9
Coldstream L-11
Comox L-6
Coquitlam M-8
Courtenay L-6
Cranbrook M-14
Creston M-14
Dawson Cr. C-10
Delta M-7
Duncan N-7
Elkford L-15
Fernie M-15
Ft. St. John C-10
Gibsons M-7
Golden J-13
Grand Forks M-12
Hope M-9
Houston E-5
Kamloops K-10
Kelowna L-11
Kent M-9
Kimberley L-14
Kitimat E-3
Ladysmith M-7
Langley M-8
Mackenzie D-8
Merritt L-10
Mission M-8
Nanaimo M-7
Nelson M-13
Oak Bay N-7
Oliver M-11
Osoyoos M-11
Parksville M-6
Peachland L-11
Penticton M-11
Port Alberni M-6
Port Hardy K-4
Powell River L-6
Prince George F-8
Prince Rupert E-2
Qualicum Beach M-6
Quesnel G-8
Revelstoke K-12
Richmond M-7
Rossland M-13
Saanich N-7
Salmon Arm K-11
Sechelt M-7
Sidney N-7
Smithers D-4
Sooke N-7
Spallumcheen L-11
Sparwood L-15
Summerland M-11
Surrey M-8
Terrace D-3
Trail M-13
Tumbler Ridge D-10
Vancouver M-7
Vanderhoof E-7
Vernon L-11
Victoria N-7
Westbank L-11
Whistler L-8
Williams Lake H-8
Winfield L-11

Selected Attractions

Banff National Park J-15
Elk Island National Park............................F-17
Glacier National Park K-13
Jasper National Park................................G-12
Kootenay National Park K-14
Mt. Terry Fox Provincial Park.......................G-12
Notikewin Provincial Park...........................A-13
Pacific Rim National Park N-6
Waterton Lakes National Park M-16
Yoho National Park J-14

Adjacent States and Provinces

Alaska 6
Idaho 33
Montana 66
Saskatchewan 124
Washington 114

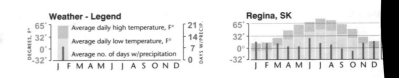

Weather - Legend

1 Segment Represents 20 Miles

1 Segment Represents 20 Kilometers

The Pas, MB

Winnipeg, MB

1 Segment Represents 20 Miles

1 Segment Represents 20 Kilometers

NORTHERN ONTARIO

WINNIPEG

Quick Reference Index
For index to places see page 142.

MANITOBA

Altona	N-16
Ashern	J-15
Beausejour	L-17
Birtle	L-12
Boissevain	N-13
Brandon	M-13
Camperville	H-13
Carberry	M-14
Carman	M-15
Cranberry Portage	D-12
Dauphin	J-13
Deloraine	N-12
East Selkirk	L-17
Emerson	N-16
Erickson	L-13
Flin Flon	C-11
Gilbert Plains	J-12
Gimli	K-16
Gladstone	L-14
Glenboro	M-14
Grandview	J-12
Gretna	N-16
Grunthal	M-17
Hamiota	L-12
Killarney	N-13
La Salle	M-16
Landmark	M-17
Lorette	M-17
MacGregor	M-14
Manitou	N-15
McCreary	K-14
Melita	N-12
Minnedosa	L-13
Mitchell	M-17
Morden	N-15
Morris	M-16
Neepawa	L-14
Niverville	M-16
Notre Dame de Lourdes	M-15
Pilot Mound	N-14
Pinawa	L-18
Pine Falls	K-17
Plum Coulee	N-16
Portage la Prairie	L-15
Powerview	K-17
Reston	M-12
Rivers	L-13
Riverton	K-16
Roblin	J-12
Rossburn	K-12
Russell	K-12
Selkirk	L-17
Shoal Lake	L-12
Souris	M-13
Southport	L-15
St-Pierre-Jolys	M-16
St. Claude	M-15
St. Malo	M-17
Ste. Anne	M-17
Ste. Rose du Lac	K-14
Steinbach	M-17
Stonewall	L-16
Stony Mountain	L-16
Swan River	H-12
Teulon	L-16
The Pas	E-12
Treherne	M-14
Virden	M-12
Winkler	N-15
Winnipeg	M-16
Winnipeg Beach	K-16
Winnipegosis	J-13

SASKATCHEWAN

Assiniboia	M-6
Balgonie	K-8
Battleford	F-4
Biggar	H-4
Birch Hills	F-7
Buffalo Narrows	A-4
Canora	J-10
Carlyle	M-10
Carnduff	N-11
Carrot River	F-9
Coronach	N-6
Creighton	C-11
Dalmeny	G-5
Davidson	J-6
Île-à-la-Crosse	B-4
Esterhazy	K-11
Estevan	N-9
Eston	J-3
Foam Lake	J-9
Ft. Qu'appelle	K-8
Gravelbourg	L-5
Grenfell	L-9
Gull Lake	L-3
Herbert	K-5
Hudson Bay	F-10
Humboldt	H-7
Indian Head	K-9
Kamsack	J-11
Kelvington	H-9
Kerrobert	H-3
Kindersley	H-3
Kipling	L-10
La Ronge	C-7
Langenburg	K-11
Langham	G-5
Lanigan	H-7
Leader	J-2
Lloydminster	E-2
Lumsden	K-7
Macklin	G-2
Maidstone	F-3
Maple Creek	L-2
Martensville	G-5
Meadow Lake	D-4
Melfort	F-8
Melville	K-10
Moose Jaw	L-6
Moosomin	L-11
Nipawin	F-8
North Battleford	F-4
Outlook	J-5
Oxbow	N-10
Pilot Butte	K-8
Preeceville	H-10
Prince Albert	F-7
Regina	K-8
Rosetown	H-4
Rosthern	G-6
Saskatoon	H-5
Shaunavon	M-3
Shellbrook	F-6
Spiritwood	E-5
Swift Current	K-4
Tisdale	F-8
Unity	G-3
Wadena	H-9
Wakaw	G-7
Waran	G-6
Watrous	H-7
Weyburn	M-8
Whitewood	L-10
Wilkie	G-3
Wynyard	H-8
Yorkton	J-10

Selected Attractions

Chopping Museum	L-10
Duck Mountain Provincial Park	H-12
Grasslands National Park	M-4
International Peace Garden	N-13
Mennonite Heritage Center	M-17
Prince Albert National Park	D-6
Riding Mountain National Park	K-12
Rusty Relic Museum	M-10
Soo Line Historical Museum	M-14
Spruce Woods Provincial Park	M-14

Adjacent States and Provinces

Alberta	123
Minnesota	60
Montana	66
North Dakota	85
Ontario	126

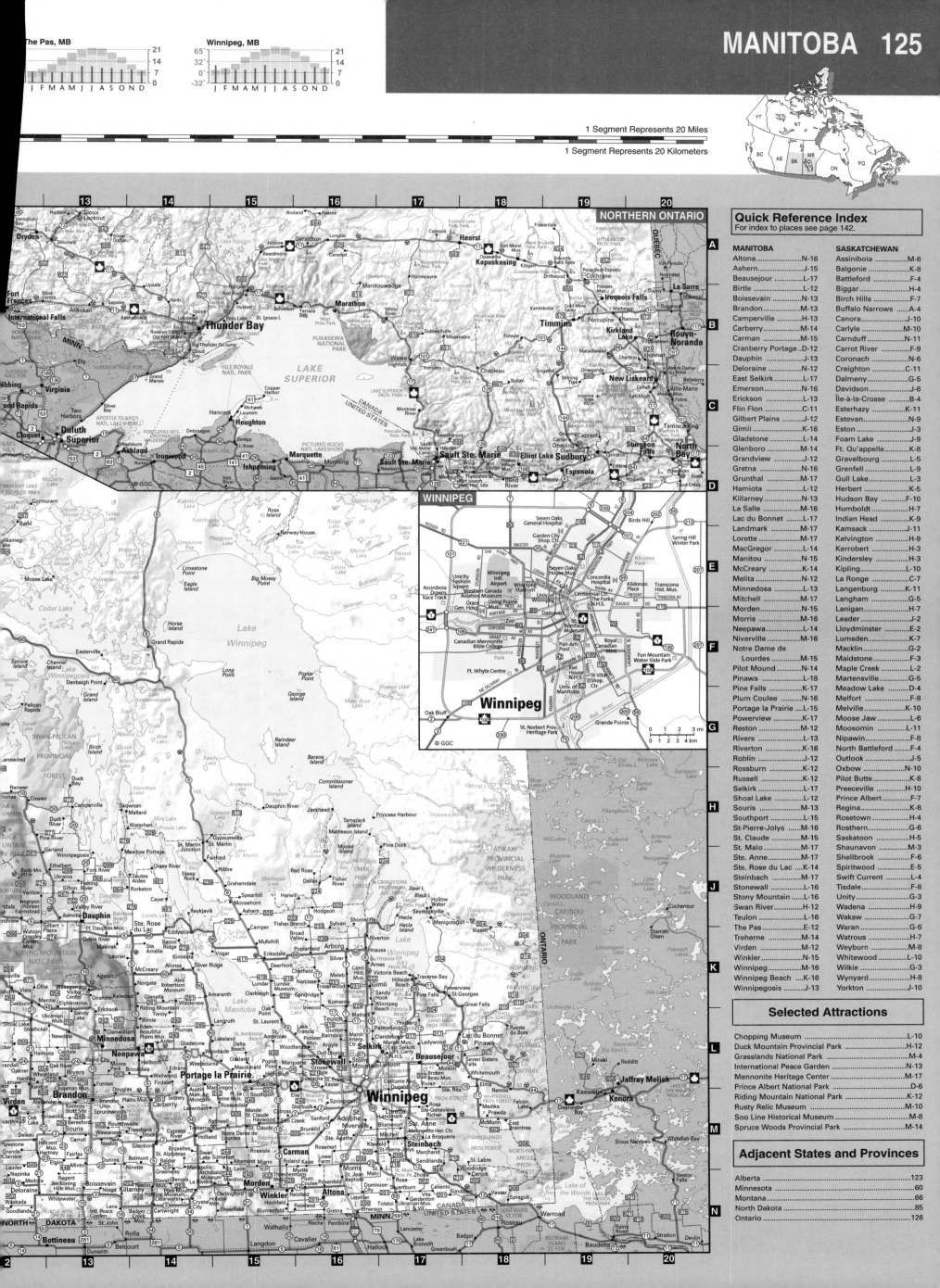

*"Loyal She Began,
Loyal She Remains"*

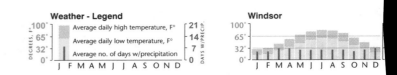

1 Segment Represents 20 Miles

1 Segment Represents 20 Kilometers

For continuation see page 125

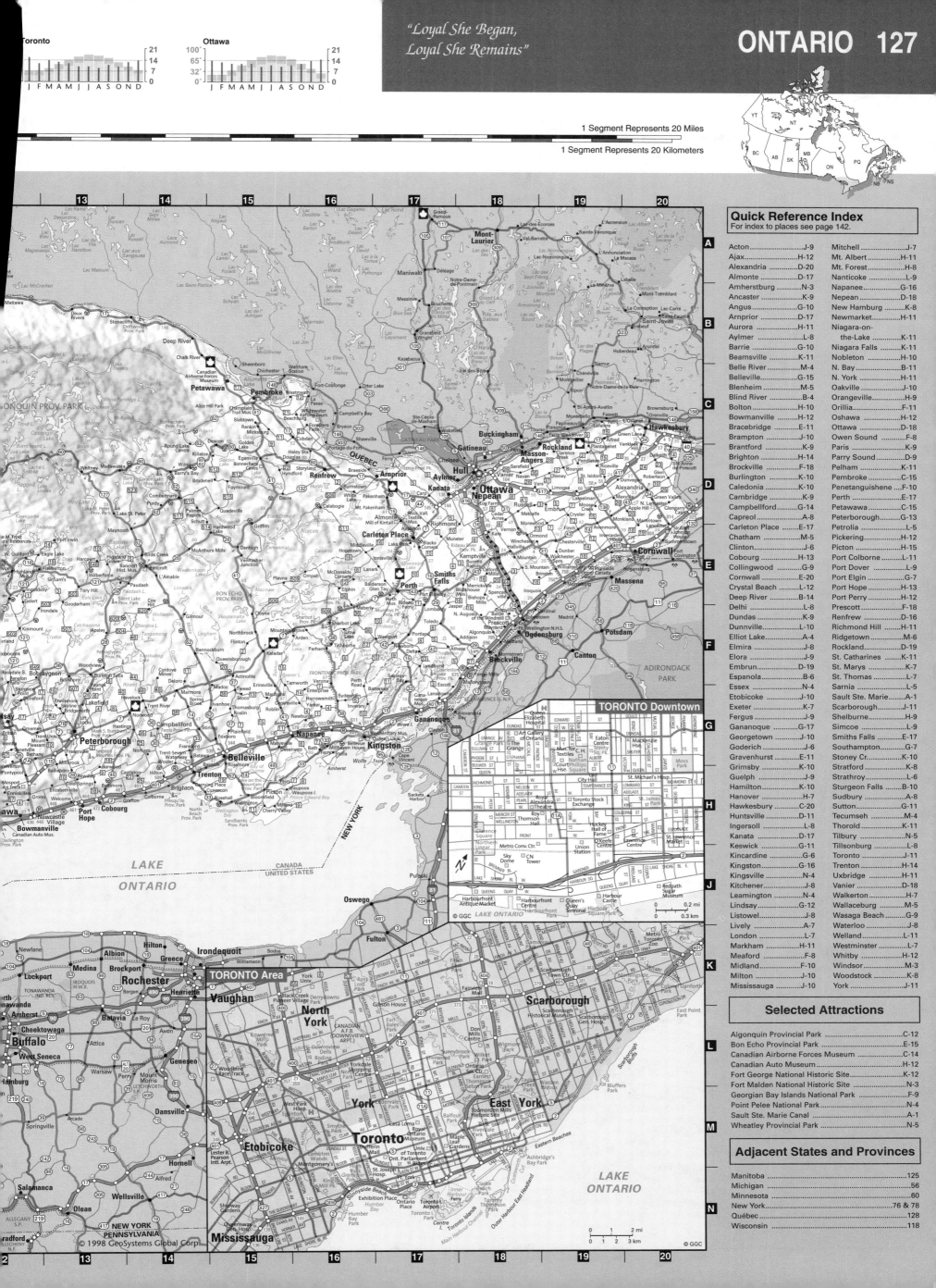

"Loyal She Began, Loyal She Remains"

Toronto

Ottawa

1 Segment Represents 20 Miles

1 Segment Represents 20 Kilometers

Quick Reference Index
For index to places see page 142.

Acton	J-9
Ajax	H-12
Alexandria	D-20
Almonte	D-17
Amherstburg	N-3
Ancaster	K-9
Angus	G-10
Arnprior	D-17
Aurora	H-11
Aylmer	L-8
Barrie	G-10
Beamsville	K-11
Belle River	M-4
Belleville	G-15
Blenheim	M-5
Blind River	B-4
Bolton	H-10
Bowmanville	H-12
Bracebridge	E-11
Brampton	J-10
Brantford	K-9
Brighton	H-14
Brockville	F-18
Burlington	K-10
Caledonia	K-10
Cambridge	K-9
Campbellford	G-14
Capreol	A-8
Carleton Place	E-17
Chatham	M-5
Clinton	J-6
Cobourg	H-13
Collingwood	G-9
Cornwall	E-20
Crystal Beach	L-12
Deep River	B-14
Delhi	L-8
Dundas	K-9
Dunnville	L-10
Elliot Lake	A-4
Elmira	J-8
Elora	J-9
Embrun	D-19
Espanola	B-6
Essex	N-4
Etobicoke	J-10
Exeter	K-7
Fergus	J-9
Gananoque	G-17
Georgetown	J-10
Goderich	J-6
Gravenhurst	E-11
Grimsby	K-10
Guelph	J-9
Hamilton	K-10
Hanover	H-7
Hawkesbury	C-20
Huntsville	D-11
Ingersoll	L-8
Kanata	D-17
Keswick	G-11
Kincardine	G-6
Kingston	G-16
Kingsville	N-4
Kitchener	J-8
Leamington	N-4
Lindsay	G-12
Listowel	J-8
Lively	A-7
London	L-7
Markham	H-11
Meaford	F-8
Midland	F-10
Milton	J-10
Mississauga	J-10
Mitchell	J-7
Mt. Albert	H-11
Mt. Forest	H-8
Nanticoke	L-9
Napanee	G-16
Nepean	D-18
New Hamburg	K-8
Newmarket	H-11
Niagara-on-the-Lake	K-11
Niagara Falls	K-11
Nobleton	H-10
N. Bay	B-11
N. York	H-11
Oakville	J-10
Orangeville	H-9
Orillia	F-11
Oshawa	H-12
Ottawa	D-18
Owen Sound	F-8
Paris	K-9
Parry Sound	D-9
Pelham	K-11
Pembroke	C-15
Penetanguishene	F-10
Perth	E-17
Petawawa	C-15
Peterborough	G-13
Petrolia	L-5
Pickering	H-12
Picton	H-15
Port Colborne	L-11
Port Dover	L-9
Port Elgin	G-7
Port Hope	H-13
Port Perry	H-12
Prescott	F-18
Renfrew	D-16
Richmond Hill	H-11
Ridgetown	M-6
Rockland	D-19
St. Catharines	K-11
St. Marys	K-7
St. Thomas	L-7
Sarnia	L-5
Sault Ste. Marie	A-1
Scarborough	J-11
Shelburne	H-9
Simcoe	L-9
Smiths Falls	E-17
Southampton	G-7
Stoney Cr.	K-10
Stratford	K-8
Strathroy	L-6
Sturgeon Falls	B-10
Sudbury	A-8
Sutton	G-11
Tecumseh	M-4
Thorold	K-11
Tilbury	N-5
Tillsonburg	L-8
Toronto	J-11
Trenton	H-14
Uxbridge	H-11
Vanier	D-18
Walkerton	H-7
Wallaceburg	M-5
Wasaga Beach	G-9
Waterloo	J-8
Welland	L-11
Westminster	L-7
Whitby	H-12
Windsor	M-3
Woodstock	K-8
York	J-11

Selected Attractions

Algonquin Provincial Park	C-12
Bon Echo Provincial Park	E-15
Canadian Airborne Forces Museum	C-14
Canadian Auto Museum	H-12
Fort George National Historic Site	K-12
Fort Malden National Historic Site	N-3
Georgian Bay Islands National Park	F-9
Point Pelee National Park	N-4
Sault Ste. Marie Canal	A-1
Wheatley Provincial Park	N-5

Adjacent States and Provinces

Manitoba	125
Michigan	56
Minnesota	60
New York	76 & 78
Québec	128
Wisconsin	118

TORONTO Downtown

TORONTO Area

LAKE ONTARIO

NEW YORK

PENNSYLVANIA

© 1998 GeoSystems Global Corp.

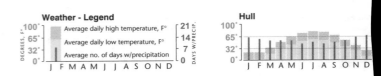

Weather - Legend

Average daily high temperature, F°
Average daily low temperature, F°
Average no. of days w/precipitation

Hull

1 Segment Represents 20 Miles

1 Segment Represents 20 Kilometers

MONTRÉAL

QUÉBEC

DISTANCES IN CANADA SHOWN IN KILOMETERS

OTTAWA–HULL

© GGC

The Fur Trade at Lachine National Historic Site

Bassin de Laprairie

KAHNAWAKE INDIAN RESERVATION

Montréal

Sept-Îles

1 Segment Represents 20 Miles
1 Segment Represents 20 Kilometers

EASTERN QUÉBEC

SHERBROOKE

Quick Reference Index

For index to places see page 142.

Acton Vale L-14
Alma C-16
Amos C-4
Anger L-8
Asbestos L-15
Aylmer M-8
Baie-St-Paul F-18
Bécancour J-14
Beauceville J-18
Beaupré G-17
Bedford M-13
Bernières-
  St-Nicolas H-16
Berthierville K-13
Black Lake K-16
Blainville L-12
Bromont M-14
Bromptonville L-15
Brownsburg L-11
Buckingham L-8
Cap-de-
  la-Madeleine J-14
Châteauguay M-12
Charlesbourg H-17
Charny H-17
Chicoutimi C-17
Coaticook M-16
Contrecoeur K-13
Cowansville M-14
Dolbeau B-15
Donnacona H-16
Drummondville K-14
Dunham M-14
E. Angus L-15
E. Broughton J-17
Farnham M-13
Gatineau L-8
Gentilly J-15
Granby M-14
Grand-Mère H-14
Hudson M-11
Hull M-8
Huntingdon N-11
Iberville M-13
Joliette L-12
Jonquière C-17
La Baie D-17
La Pocatière F-19
La Prairie M-12
La Sarre B-2
La Tuque F-14
Lac-Mégantic L-17
Lachine L-12
Lachute L-11
Laterrière D-17
Laurentides K-12
Laurier-Sta. J-16
Laval L-12
Lavaltrie L-12
Lebel-Sur-Quévillon ...B-6
Lennoxville L-15
L'Annonciation J-9
L'Assomption L-13
Longueuil L-12
Loretteville H-16
Louiseville J-13
Léry M-12
Lévis H-17
Malartic D-3
Marieville M-13
Melocheville M-12
Mirabel K-11
Mistassini B-15
Mont-Laurier J-8
Mont-Rolland K-11

Montmagny G-18
Montréal L-12
Métabetchouan C-15
Napierville M-13
Normandin B-14
Plessisville J-16
Pont-Rouge H-16
Princeville K-15
Québec H-17
Rawdon K-12
Repentigny L-12
Richmond L-15
Rigaud L-11
Rivière-du-Loup E-20
Roberval C-15
Rock Forest M-15
Rouyn-Noranda D-2
Roxboro L-12
St-Antonin E-20
St-Boniface-de-
  Shawinigan J-14
St-Césaire M-13
St-Dominique L-14
St-Eustache L-12
St-Félicien C-14
St-Gabriel K-13
St-Georges K-18
St-Georges H-14
St-Hubert L-13
St-Hyacinthe L-13
St-Jacques K-12
St-Jean-de-Matha K-12
St-Jean-Port-Joli G-18
St-Jean-
  Sur-Richelieu M-13
St-Jovite K-10
St-Jérôme L-11
St-Louis-de-France J-14
St-Pamphile G-19
St-Pascal F-19
St-Pie L-14
St-Prime C-14
St-Rémi M-12
St-Sauveur-
  des-Monts K-11
Ste-Adèle K-11
Ste-Foy H-17
Ste-Julie L-13
Ste-Madeleine L-13
Ste-Marie J-17
Ste-Mélanie K-12
Ste-Thérèse L-12
Salaberry-
  de-Valleyfield M-11
Senneterre C-5
Shawinigan H-14
Shawinigan-Sud J-14
Sherbrooke M-15
Sorel K-13
Stoke L-16
Terrebonne L-12
Thetford Mines K-17
Thurso L-9
Témiscaming H-2
Tracy K-13
Trois-Pistoles D-20
Trois-Rivières J-14
Val-David K-11
Val-d'Or D-4
Valcourt L-15
Verdun M-12
Victoriaville K-15
Warwick K-15
Waterloo M-14
Windsor L-15

Selected Attractions

Accordion Economuseum G-18
Coaticook Gorge M-16
Forges du St-Maurice J-14
Fort Chambly National Historic Site M-13
Fort Lennox National Historic Site M-13
Maurice National Park H-13
Mont Tremblant Provincial Park H-11
Papineau Manor National Historic Site L-10
Parc de Cons. du Saguenay D-18
Parc de la Gatineau L-7

Adjacent States and Provinces

Maine 48
New Brunswick 130
New Hampshire 71
New York ....76 & 78
Ontario 126
Vermont 110

© 1998 GeoSystems Global Corp.

Weather - Legend

Average daily high temperature, F°
Average daily low temperature, F°
Average no. of days w/precipitation

Saint John, NB

1 Segment Represents 20 Miles

1 Segment Represents 20 Kilometers

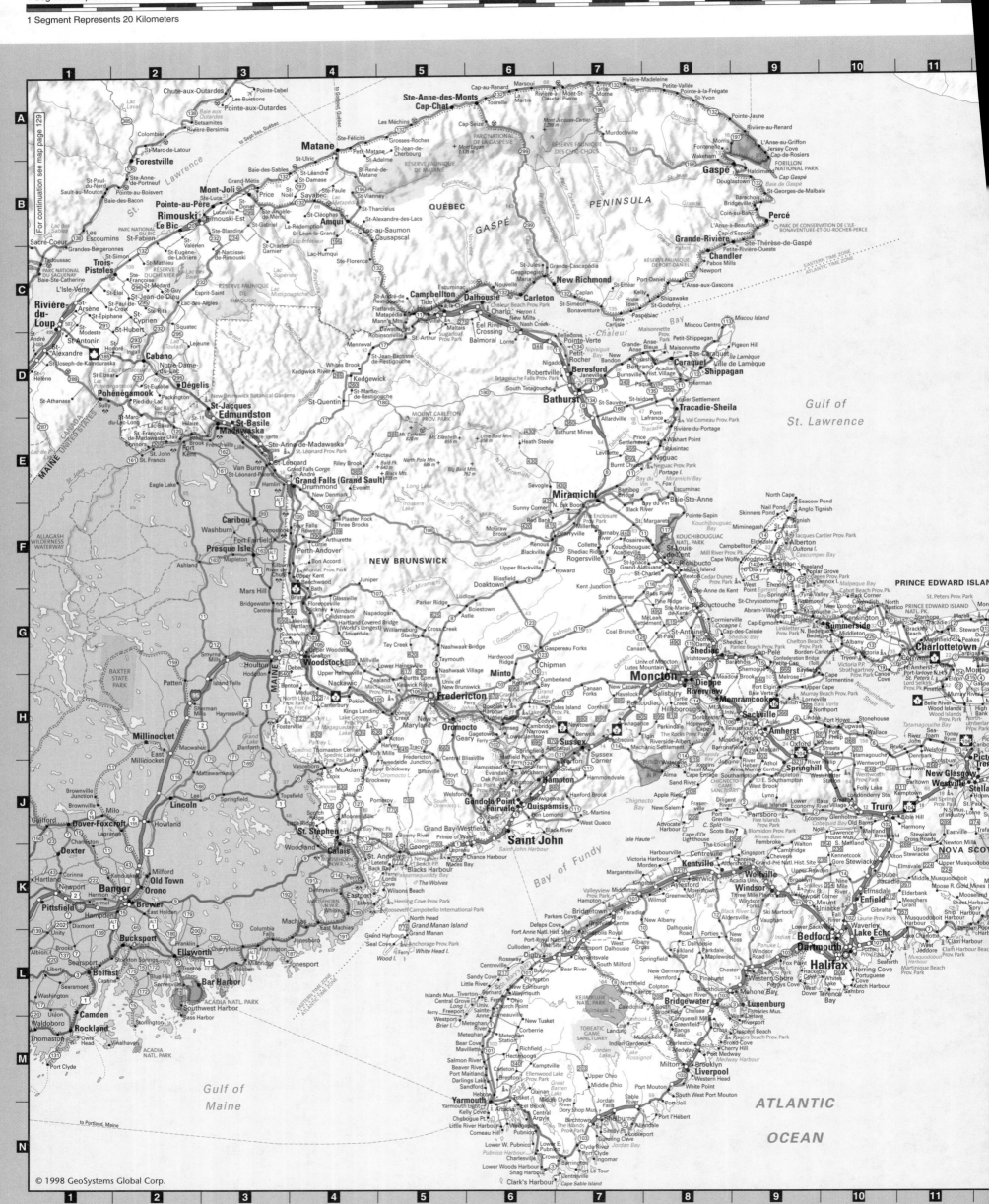

© 1998 GeoSystems Global Corp.

NF: "Seek Ye First the Kingdom of God"
PEI: "The Small under the Protection of the Great"

St. John's, NF

1 Segment Represents 20 Miles

1 Segment Represents 20 Kilometers

© 1998 GeoSystems Global Corp.

NEWFOUNDLAND

ATLANTIC OCEAN

QUÉBEC

Gulf of St. Lawrence

ATLANTIC OCEAN

HALIFAX

ATLANTIC OCEAN

Quick Reference Index
For index to counties and places see page 142.

Selected Attractions

Adjacent States and Provinces

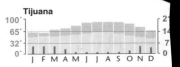

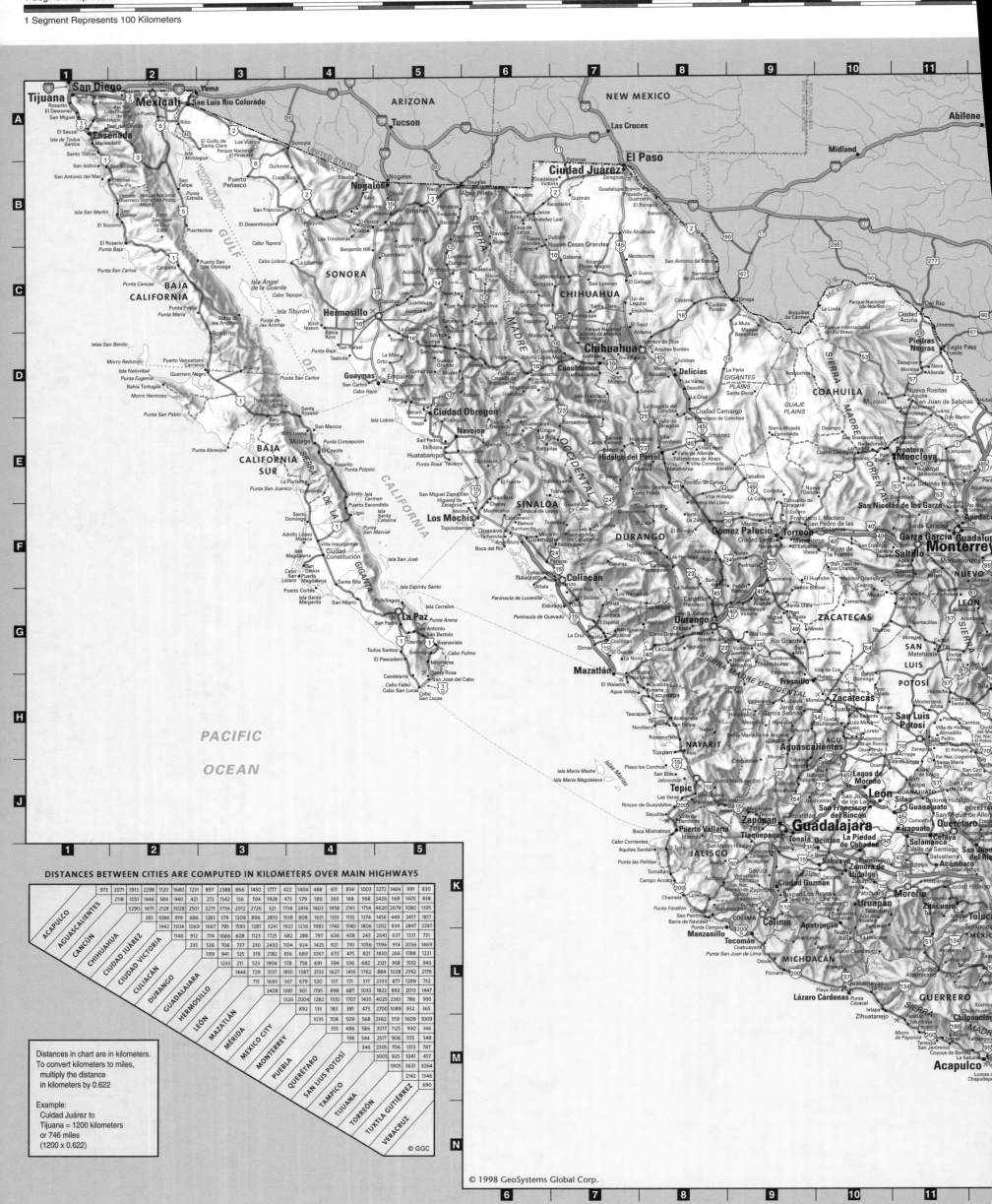

1 Segment Represents 100 Miles

1 Segment Represents 100 Kilometers

Quick Reference Index
For index to more places see page 142.

Acámbaro	K-11	Monclova	E-11
Acapulco	M-12	Monterrey	F-11
Acayucan	L-15	Morelia	K-11
Acuña	C-11	Moroleón	K-11
Aguascalientes	H-10	Navojoa	E-5
Apizaco	K-13	Nezahualcóyotl	K-12
Apodaca	F-11	Nogales	B-5
Atlixco	L-13	Nuevo Casas	
Caborca	B-4	Grandes	C-6
Campeche	K-18	Nuevo Laredo	E-12
Cancún	J-20	Oaxaca	M-14
Cárdenas	L-16	Ocotlán	K-10
Celaya	J-11	Orizaba	L-14
Chetumal	L-19	Papantla	J-13
Chihuahua	D-8	Pátzcuaro	K-11
Chilpancingo	M-12	Piedras Negras	D-11
Cholula	K-13	Puebla	K-13
Ciudad del Carmen	L-17	Puerto Vallarta	J-8
Ciudad Guzmán	K-9	Querétaro	J-11
Ciudad Hidalgo	K-11	Reynosa	F-13
Ciudad Juárez	B-7	Río Bravo	F-13
Ciudad Lerdo	F-9	Río Verde	H-12
Ciudad Madero	H-13	Sahuayo	K-10
Ciudad Mante	H-12	Salamanca	J-11
Ciudad Obregón	D-5	Salina Cruz	M-15
Ciudad Valles	H-12	Saltillo	F-11
Ciudad Victoria	G-12	San Andrés Tuxtla	L-15
Coatzacoalcos	L-15	San Cristóbal	
Colima	K-9	de las Casas	M-16
Comitán	M-17	San Francisco	
Córdoba	L-14	del Rincón	J-10
Cuauhtémoc	D-7	San Juan	
Cuautla	L-12	de Sabinas	D-11
Cuernavaca	L-12	San Juan del Río	K-12
Culiacán	F-7	San Luis Potosí	H-11
Delicias	D-8	San Luis Río	
Dolores Hidalgo	J-11	Colorado	A-2
Durango	G-8	San Miguel	
Ensenada	A-1	de Allende	J-11
Fresnillo	H-9	San Nicolás	
Frontera	E-11	de los Garza	F-11
Garza García	F-11	San Pedro	
Gómez Palacio	F-9	de los Colonias	F-11
Guadalajara	J-9	Santa Catarina	F-11
Guadalupe	F-11	Silao	J-11
Guadalupe	H-10	Tampico	H-13
Guamúchil	F-6	Tapachula	N-17
Guanajuato	J-11	Taxco	K-12
Guasave	F-6	Tecate	A-1
Guaymas	D-5	Tecomán	L-9
Huauchinango	K-13	Tehuacán	L-13
Hermosillo	C-5	Tepatitlán	J-9
Hidalgo	K-10	Tepic	J-9
Hidalgo del Parral	E-8	Teziutlán	K-13
Iguala	L-12	Tierra Blanca	L-14
Irapuato	J-11	Tijuana	A-1
Jiutepec	L-12	Tlalnepantla	K-12
Juchitán	M-15	Tlaquepaque	J-9
La Paz	G-5	Tlaxcala	K-13
La Piedad		Toluca	K-12
de Cabadas	K-10	Tonalá	J-9
Lagos de Moreno	J-10	Torreón	F-9
Las Choapas	L-15	Tulancingo	K-13
Lázaro Cárdenas	L-10	Tuxpan	J-13
León	J-10	Tuxtepec	L-14
Linares	F-12	Tuxtla Gutiérrez	M-16
Los Mochis	F-6	Uruapan	K-10
Manzanillo	L-8	Valle de Santiago	K-11
Matamoros	F-13	Veracruz	L-14
Matehuala	G-11	Villahermosa	L-16
Mazatlán	G-8	Xalapa	K-14
Mérida	J-18	Zacapu	K-10
Mexicali	A-2	Zacatecas	H-10
México City	K-12	Zapopan	J-9
Minatitlán	L-15	Zitácuaro	K-11

Selected Attractions

Chichén Itzá	J-19
Kohunlich Ruins	L-18
Mayapán	J-18
Parque Nacional Benito Juárez	M-14
Parque Nacional Cascada de Basaseachic	D-6
Parque Nacional Constitución de 1857	A-2
Parque Nacional Cumbres de Majalca	D-7
Parque Nacional Lagunas de Montebello	M-17
Parque Nacional Pico de Tancítaro	K-10
Parque Nacional Sierra San Pedro Mátir	B-2

Adjacent States

Arizona	8
California	12 & 14
New Mexico	74
Texas	104 & 106

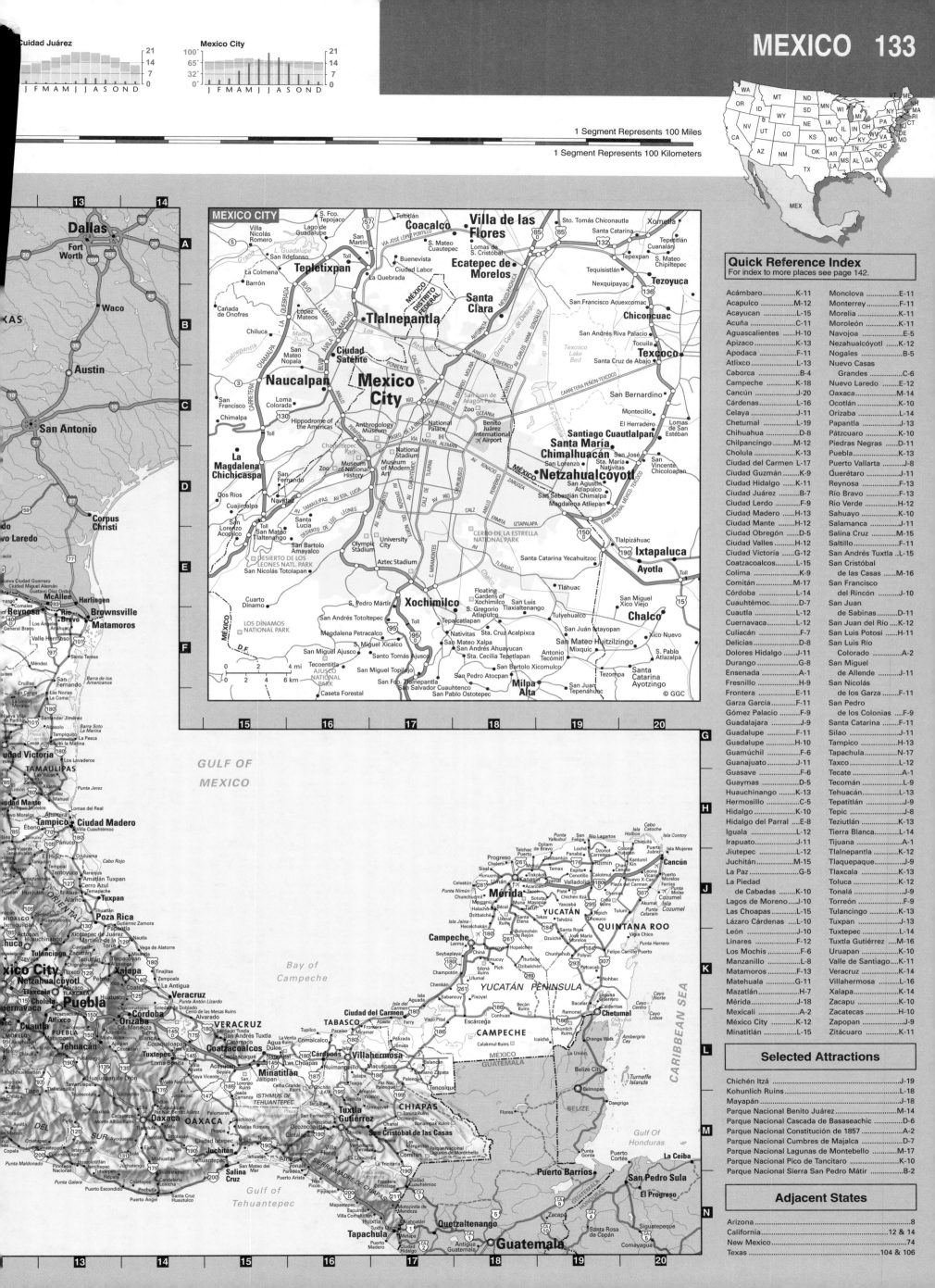

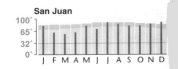

Weather - Legend

Average daily high temperature, F°	
Average daily low temperature, F°	
Average no. of days w/precipitation	

San Juan

1 Segment Represents 10 Miles

1 Segment Represents 10 Kilometers

1 Segment Represents 10 Miles

1 Segment Represents 10 Kilometers

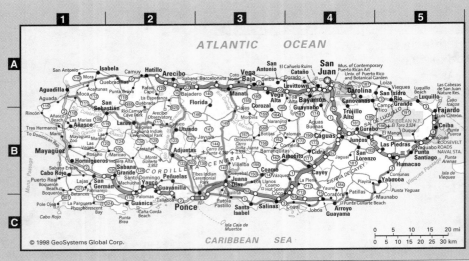

© 1998 GeoSystems Global Corp.

Quick Reference Index
For index to places see page 142.

Aguadilla	A-1	Hormigueros	B-1
Aibonito	B-4	Humacao	B-5
Arecibo	A-2	Isabela	A-1
Bayamón	A-4	Juana Díaz	B-3
Cabo Rojo	B-1	Levittown	A-4
Caguas	B-4	Manati	A-3
Carolina	A-4	Mayagüez	B-1
Cataño	A-4	Ponce	C-3
Cayey	B-4	Río Grande	B-5
Coamo	B-3	San Germán	B-1
Corozal	B-3	San Juan	A-4
Dorado	A-4	San Sebastián	B-1
Fajardo	B-5	Trujillo Alto	B-4
Guánica	C-2	Utuado	B-2
Guayama	C-4	Vega Alta	A-3
Guaynabo	B-4	Vega Baja	A-3
Gurabo	B-4	Yauco	B-2

Selected Attractions

Añasco Beach	B-1
Arecibo Observatory	B-2
Boquerón Beach	B-1
Caguana Indian Ceremonial Park	B-2
Caña Gorda Beach	C-2
Caribbean National Forest	B-5
Coamo Hot Springs	B-3
El Cañuelo Ruins	A-4
Las Cabezas de San Juan Nature Res.	A-5
Luquillo Beach	A-5
Mayagüez Zoo	B-1
Museum of Contemporary Puerto Rican Art	A-4
Phosphorescent Bay	C-1
Punta Guilarte Beach	C-4
Río Camuy Cave Park	B-2
Tibes Indian Ceremonial Park	B-3
University of Puerto Rico and Botanical Garden	A-4

Gallatin T-11
Greene M-5
Grundy E-10
Hamilton R-10
Hancock H-3
Hardin T-10
Henderson G-3
Henry E-5
Iroquois G-11
Jackson T-7
Jasper N-11
Jefferson Q-9
Jersey N-5
Jo Daviess A-6
Johnson U-9
Kane C-10
Kankakee F-11
Kendall D-10
Knox F-5
Lake A-11
La Salle E-9
Lawrence P-12
Lee C-8
Livingston G-9
Logan J-7
Macon K-9
Macoupin M-6
Madison P-6
Marion P-9
Marshall F-7
Mason J-6
Massac V-10
McDonough H-4
McHenry A-10
McLean G-9
Menard J-6
Mercer E-4
Monroe R-5
Montgomery M-7
Morgan L-6
Moultrie L-9
Ogle B-7
Peoria F-6
Perry R-8
Piatt J-9
Pike L-3
Pope U-10
Pulaski V-8
Putnam E-8
Randolph S-6
Richland P-11
Rock Island E-4
St. Clair Q-6
Saline T-10
Sangamon L-6
Schuyler J-4
Scott L-4
Shelby M-9
Stark F-6
Stephenson A-7
Tazewell H-7
Union T-8
Vermilion H-12
Wabash Q-12
Warren G-4
Washington R-7
Wayne Q-10
White R-11
Whiteside C-6
Will D-11
Williamson T-9
Winnebago A-8
Woodford G-8

Cities and Towns

Abingdon G-5
Albany C-5
Albion Q-11
Aledo E-4
Alexis F-4
Algonquin B-10
Alhambra P-7
Alpha E-5
Altamont N-9
Alton P-5
Altona F-5
Amboy D-8
Andalusia E-4
Andover E-5
Anna U-8
Annawan E-6
Antioch A-11
Arcola L-10
Argenta K-9
Arlington Heights B-11
Aroma Park F-12
Arthur L-10
Ashkum F-11
Ashland K-6
Ashley R-8
Ashmore L-11
Ashton C-8
Assumption L-8
Astoria J-5
Athens K-7
Atkinson E-6
Atlanta J-8
Atwood K-10
Auburn L-7
Augusta J-3
Aurora C-10
Ava S-7
Aviston Q-7
Avon G-5
Barry L-3
Bartonville G-7
Batavia C-10
Beardstown K-5
Beckemeyer Q-7
Beecher E-12
Belleville Q-6
Bellevue G-7
Belvidere B-9
Bement K-10
Benld N-6
Benton S-9
Berwyn C-12
Bethalto P-6
Bethany L-9
Bismarck J-12
Blandinsville H-4
Bloomington H-9
Blue Mound L-8
Bluffs L-4
Bluford R-9
Bolingbrook D-11
Bourbonnais E-11
Braceville E-10
Bradford E-7
Bradley E-11
Braidwood E-11
Breese Q-7
Bridgeport P-12
Brighton N-5
Brimfield G-6
Brookport V-10
Brownstown N-9
Buckley G-11
Buda E-7
Bull Valley A-10
Bunker Hill N-6
Bushnell H-5
Byron B-8
Cahokia Q-5
Cairo V-8
Calumet City D-12
Cambria T-8
Cambridge E-5
Camp Point J-3
Canton H-6
Capron A-9
Carbondale T-8
Carlinville M-6
Carlyle Q-8
Carmi R-11
Carpentersville B-10
Carrier Mills T-10
Carrollton M-5
Carterville T-8
Carthage H-3
Cary B-10
Casey M-11
Catlin J-12
Cedarville A-7
Central City Q-8
Centralia Q-8
Centreville Q-6
Cerro Gordo K-9
Chadwick B-6
Champaign J-11
Chandlerville J-5
Channahon D-10
Channel Lake A-11
Chapin L-5
Charleston M-11
Chatham L-7
Chatsworth G-10
Chebanse F-11
Chenoa G-9
Chester S-6
Chicago C-12
Chicago Heights D-12
Chillicothe F-7
Chrisman K-12
Christopher S-8
Cicero C-12
Cisne Q-10
Cissna Park G-11
Clay City P-10
Clayton J-3
Clifton F-11
Clinton J-9
Coal City E-10
Coal Valley E-5
Cobden T-8
Coffeen N-7
Colchester H-4
Colfax H-10
Collinsville Q-6
Colona D-5
Columbia Q-5
Cordova D-5
Cornell F-9
Cortland C-9
Coulterville R-7
Cowden M-9
Creal Sprs. T-9
Crescent City G-11
Crest Hill D-11
Crete D-12
Crossville R-11
Crystal Lake B-10
Cuba H-5
Cullom F-10
Dakota A-7
Dallas City G-3
Dalton City L-9
Danvers H-8
Danville J-12
Davis A-7
De Kalb C-9
De Soto S-8
Decatur K-9
Deer Creek G-8
Delavan H-7
Depue E-8
Des Plaines B-11
Diamond E-10
Dieterich N-10
Divernon L-7
Dixon C-7
Dongola U-8
Downers Grove C-11
Downs H-9
Du Quoin S-8
Dunlap G-7
Dupo Q-5
Durand A-8
Dwight F-10
Earlville D-9
E. Alton P-6
E. Carondelet Q-5
E. Dubuque A-4
E. Moline D-5
E. Peoria G-7
E. St. Louis Q-5
Edinburg L-7
Edwardsville P-6
Effingham N-10
El Paso G-8
Elburn C-10
Eldorado S-10
Elgin B-10
Elizabeth A-5
Elizabethtown U-10
Elkville S-8
Elmhurst C-11
Elmwood G-6
Elsah N-5
Elwood E-11
Enfield R-10
Equality T-10
Erie D-6
Eureka G-8
Evanston B-12
Evansville S-6
Fairbury G-10
Fairfield Q-10
Fairmount J-12
Fairview Heights Q-6
Farina P-9
Farmer City J-9
Farmersville M-7
Farmington G-6
Findlay L-9
Fisher H-10
Flanagan F-9
Flora P-10
Forrest G-10
Forreston B-7
Forsyth K-9
Fox Lake A-11
Fox River Grove B-10
Frankfort D-11
Franklin L-6
Franklin Grove C-8
Freeburg Q-6
Freeport B-7
Fulton C-5
Galatia S-10
Galena A-5
Galesburg F-5
Galva E-6
Gardner E-10
Geneseo D-5
Geneva C-10
Genoa B-9
Georgetown K-12
Germantown Q-7
Germantown Hills G-7
Gibson City H-10
Gifford H-11
Gillespie N-6
Gilman G-11
Girard M-6
Glasford H-6
Glen Carbon P-6
Glencoe B-12
Godfrey P-5
Golconda U-10
Golden J-3
Goreville T-9
Grafton N-5
Grand Ridge E-9
Grand Tower T-7
Granite City P-6
Grant Park E-12
Granville E-8
Grayslake A-11
Grayville R-11
Green Valley H-7
Greenfield M-5
Greenup N-11
Greenview J-7
Greenville P-7
Gridley G-9
Griggsville L-4
Hamilton H-2
Hampshire B-10
Hanna City G-6
Hanover B-5
Hardin N-4
Harrisburg T-10
Harristown K-8
Hartford P-6
Harvard A-9
Havana J-6
Hebron A-10
Hennepin E-8
Henry F-8
Herrin T-9
Herscher F-11
Heyworth H-9
Highland P-7
Highland Park B-12
Hillcrest C-8
Hillsboro N-7
Hinckley C-9
Homer J-11
Hoopeston H-12
Hopedale H-7
Hopkins Park F-12
Hudson G-9
Huntley B-10
Hurst S-8
Hutsonville N-12
Illiopolis K-8
Industry H-4
Irvington Q-8
Island Lake B-11
Jacksonville L-5
Jerseyville N-5
Johnston City S-9
Joliet D-11
Jonesboro U-8
Kankakee F-11
Kansas L-11
Karnak U-9
Keithsburg F-3
Kewanee E-6
Kincaid L-7
Kingston B-9
Kinmundy P-9
Kirkland B-9
Kirkwood G-4
Knoxville F-5
La Harpe G-3
La Moille D-8
La Salle E-8
Lacon F-7
Ladd E-8
Lake Bluff B-11
Lake Forest B-11
Lake Summerset A-7
Lake Villa A-11
Lake Zurich B-11
Lakewood B-10
Lanark B-6
Lawrenceville P-12
Le Roy H-9
Leaf River B-7
Leland D-9
Lemont D-11
Lena A-6
Lewistown H-5
Lexington G-9
Liberty K-3
Libertyville B-11
Lily Lake C-10
Lincoln J-8
Lindenhurst A-11
Litchfield N-7
Livingston N-6
Loami L-6
Lockport D-11
Long Creek K-9
Louisville P-10
Loves Park A-8
Lovington L-10
Lyndon D-6
Lynwood D-12
Machesney Park A-8
Mackinaw H-8
Macomb H-4
Macon L-9
Madison P-5
Mahomet J-10
Malta C-9
Manhattan E-11
Manito H-6
Mansfield J-10
Manteno E-12
Marengo B-9
Marine P-6
Marion T-9
Marissa R-7
Maroa J-9
Marseilles E-9
Marshall M-12
Martinsville M-12
Mascoutah Q-6
Mason City J-7
Matherville E-4
Matteson D-12
Mattoon M-10
Mazon E-10
McHenry A-10
McLean H-8
McLeansboro R-10
Mendon J-2
Mendota D-8
Meredosia K-4
Metamora G-8
Metropolis V-9
Milan D-4
Milford G-12
Milledgeville C-6
Millstadt Q-6
Minier H-8
Minonk F-8
Minooka D-10
Moline D-5
Momence E-12
Monee E-12
Monmouth F-4
Monticello J-10
Morris E-10
Morrison C-6
Morrisonville M-7
Morton G-7
Mossville G-7
Mound City V-8
Mounds V-8
Mt. Auburn L-8
Mt. Carmel Q-12
Mt. Carroll B-6
Mt. Morris B-7
Mt. Olive N-7
Mt. Pulaski K-8
Mt. Sterling K-4
Mt. Vernon R-9
Mt. Zion L-9
Moweaqua L-8
Mulberry Grove P-8
Mundelein B-11
Murphysboro T-8
Murrayville L-5
Naperville C-11
Nashville R-8
Nauvoo H-2
Neoga M-10
New Athens R-6
New Baden Q-7
New Berlin L-6
New Boston E-3
New Lenox D-11
Newark D-10
Newman K-11
Newton N-11
Niantic K-8
Noble P-11
Nokomis M-8
Normal H-9
Norris City S-10
N. Aurora C-10
N. Chicago A-11
Northbrook B-12
Oak Forest D-12
Oak Grove E-4
Oak Lawn C-12
Oak Park C-12
Oakland L-11
Oakwood J-12
Oblong N-11
Odell F-10
Odin Q-8
O'Fallon Q-6
Ogden J-11
Oglesby E-8
Okawville Q-7
Olney P-11
Onarga G-11
Oneida F-5
Oquawka F-3
Oreana K-9
Oregon B-8
Orion E-5
Orland Park D-11
Oswego D-10
Ottawa E-9
Palatine B-11
Palestine N-12
Palmyra M-6
Pana M-8
Paris L-12
Patoka P-8
Paw Paw D-9
Pawnee L-7
Paxton H-11
Payson K-3
Pearl City B-6
Pecatonica A-8
Pekin H-7
Peoria G-7
Peoria Heights G-7
Peotone E-12
Percy S-7
Peru E-8
Pesotum K-10
Petersburg K-6
Philo K-11
Pierron P-7
Pinckneyville S-8
Piper City G-11
Pittsburg T-9
Pittsfield L-4
Plainfield D-11
Plano D-10
Pleasant Hill M-4
Pleasant Plains K-6
Pocahontas P-7
Polo C-7
Pontiac F-9
Poplar Grove A-9
Port Byron D-5
Potomac H-12
Princeton E-7
Princeville F-7
Prophetstown D-6
Quincy K-2
Ramsey N-8
Rankin H-11
Rantoul H-11
Raymond M-7
Red Bud R-6
Reynolds E-4
Richmond A-10
Ridge Farm K-12
Ridgway S-11
Riverton K-7
Roanoke G-8
Robinson N-12
Rochelle C-8
Rochester L-7
Rock Falls C-7
Rock Island D-4
Rockford B-8
Rockton A-8
Rome F-7
Romeoville D-11
Roodhouse M-5
Roscoe A-8
Roseville G-4
Rosiclare U-10
Rossville H-12
Royalton S-8
Rushville J-4
St. Anne F-12
St. Charles C-10
St. David H-6
St. Elmo N-9
St. Francisville Q-12
St. Jacob P-6
St. Joseph J-11
Salem Q-9
Sandoval Q-8
Sandwich D-9
Savanna B-6
Savoy J-11
Saybrook H-10
Schram City N-7
Seneca E-9
Sesser S-8
Shabbona C-9
Shannon B-7
Shawneetown T-11
Sheffield E-7
Shelbyville M-9
Sheldon G-12
Sheridan D-9
Sherman K-7
Sherrard E-5
Shipman N-6
Shorewood D-11
Sidell K-12
Sidney J-11
Skokie B-12
Smithton Q-6
Somonauk D-9
Sorento N-7
S. Beloit A-8
S. Elgin C-10
S. Jacksonville L-5
S. Pekin H-7
Sparta R-7
Spr. Valley E-8
Springfield K-7
Stanford H-8
Staunton N-6
Steeleville S-7
Sterling C-7
Stewardson M-10
Stillman Valley B-8
Stockton A-6
Stonington L-8
Streator F-9
Stronghurst G-3
Sugar Grove C-10
Sullivan L-10
Sumner P-12
Swansea Q-6
Sycamore C-9
Tallula K-6
Tamaroa R-8
Tamms V-8
Tampico D-6
Taylor Sprs. N-7
Taylorville L-8
Teutopolis N-10
Thayer L-7
Thomasboro J-11
Thompsonville S-9
Tilden R-7
Tilton J-12
Tinley Park D-12
Tiskilwa E-7
Toledo M-11
Tolono K-10
Toluca F-8
Tonica E-8
Toulon F-6
Towanda H-9
Tower Hill M-9
Tremont H-7
Trenton Q-7
Troy P-6
Tuscola K-10
Union B-10
Urbana J-11
Valier S-8
Valmeyer R-5
Vandalia N-8
Vermont J-5
Vienna U-9
Villa Grove K-11
Viola E-4
Virden M-6
Virginia K-5
Walnut D-7
Wamac Q-8
Wapella J-9
Warren A-6
Warrensburg K-8
Warsaw H-2
Washburn F-8
Washington G-7
Wataga F-5
Waterloo R-5
Waterman C-9
Watseka G-12
Watson N-10
Waukegan A-11
Waverly L-6
Wayne City R-10
Wenona F-8
W. City S-9
W. Dundee B-10
W. Frankfort S-9
W. Peoria G-7
W. Salem Q-11
Westfield M-11
Westville J-12
Wheaton C-11
Wheeling B-11
White Hall M-5
Williamsfield F-6
Williamsville K-7
Willisville S-7
Wilmette B-12
Wilmington E-11
Wilsonville N-6
Winchester L-5
Windsor M-10
Winnebago B-8
Winthrop Harbor A-11
Witt M-8
Wood River P-6
Woodhull E-5
Woodlawn R-8
Woodstock A-10
Worden P-6
Wyanet E-7
Wyoming F-6
Yates City G-6
Yorkville D-10
Zeigler S-8
Zion A-11

INDIANA

see map pages 38-39

Counties

Adams F-12
Allen D-11
Bartholomew N-9
Benton F-4
Blackford G-11
Boone J-7
Brown N-8
Carroll G-7
Cass F-8
Clark R-10
Clay M-5
Clinton H-7
Crawford S-7
Daviess Q-5
Dearborn N-12
Decatur N-10
De Kalb C-12
Delaware H-11
Dubois S-6
Elkhart B-9
Fayette L-11
Floyd S-9
Fountain H-4
Franklin M-12
Fulton D-8
Gibson S-3
Grant G-9
Greene P-5
Hamilton J-8
Hancock K-9
Harrison T-9
Hendricks K-7
Henry K-11
Howard G-8
Huntington E-10
Jackson P-8
Jasper E-5
Jay G-12
Jefferson Q-10
Jennings Q-10
Johnson M-8
Knox Q-4
Kosciusko D-9
Lagrange B-11
Lake C-4
La Porte B-7
Lawrence P-7
Madison H-9
Marion L-9
Marshall C-8
Martin Q-6
Miami F-8
Monroe P-6
Montgomery H-6
Morgan M-7
Newton E-4
Noble C-11
Ohio P-12
Orange R-7
Owen N-5
Parke K-5
Perry T-6
Pike S-5
Porter C-5
Posey T-2
Pulaski D-6
Putnam L-5
Randolph H-12
Ripley N-11
Rush L-10
St. Joseph B-8
Scott R-9
Shelby L-10
Spencer T-5
Starke D-6
Steuben B-12
Sullivan P-4
Switzerland Q-12
Tippecanoe H-6
Tipton H-8
Union M-12
Vanderburgh T-3
Vermillion K-4
Vigo M-4
Wabash E-10
Warren G-4
Warrick T-4
Washington Q-8
Wayne J-12
Wells F-11
White F-6
Whitley D-11

Cities and Towns

Advance J-7
Akron D-9
Albany H-11
Albion C-11
Alexandria H-10
Amboy F-9
Amo L-7
Anderson J-10
Andrews E-10
Angola B-12
Arcadia H-9
Argos D-8
Ashley B-12
Atlanta H-9
Attica H-5
Auburn C-12
Aurora P-12
Austin Q-9
Avilla C-11
Avon K-7
Bainbridge K-6
Bargersville M-8
Batesville N-11
Battle Ground G-6
Bedford Q-7
Beech Grove L-8
Berne F-12
Beverly Shores B-5
Bicknell Q-4
Birdseye S-6
Blocher Q-10
Bloomfield P-6
Bloomingdale K-4
Bloomington N-7
Bluffton F-12
Boonville T-4
Boswell G-4
Bourbon C-8
Brazil M-5
Bremen C-8
Bright N-13
Bristol A-9
Brook E-4
Brooklyn M-7
Brookston F-6
Brookville M-12
Brownsburg K-7
Brownstown Q-9
Bruceville Q-4
Buffalo E-6
Bunker Hill F-8
Burlington G-7
Burnett M-4
Burnettsville F-7
Burns Harbor B-5
Butler C-13
Butlerville P-10
Cambridge City K-12
Camden F-7
Campbellsburg R-8
Cannelton U-6
Carbon L-5
Carlisle P-4
Carmel J-8
Carthage K-10
Cayuga J-4
Cedar Lake C-4
Centerville K-12
Chalmers F-6
Chandler T-4
Charlestown R-10
Chesterfield J-10
Chesterton B-5
Chrisney T-5
Churubusco D-11
Cicero J-9
Clarks Hill H-6
Clarksville S-10
Clay City N-5
Claypool D-9
Clayton L-7
Clear Creek N-7
Clermont K-8
Clinton L-4
Cloverdale M-6
Coalmont N-5
Coatesville L-6
Colfax H-6
Collegeville E-5
Columbia City D-10
Columbus N-9
Connersville L-12
Converse F-9
Corydon T-8
Corydon Jct. S-8
Covington H-4
Crawfordsville J-6
Cromwell C-10
Crothersville Q-9
Crown Point C-4
Culver D-7
Cumberland K-9
Cynthiana T-3
Dale T-5
Daleville J-10
Dana K-4
Danville K-7
Darlington J-6
Darmstadt T-3
Dayton G-6
Decatur E-12
Delong D-7
Delphi G-6
Demotte D-5
Denver E-8
Dillsboro P-12
Dublin K-11
Dubois S-6
Dugger P-4
Dunkirk G-11
Dunlap B-9
Dupont P-10
Dyer B-4
Earl Park F-4
E. Chicago B-4
E. Germantown K-12
Eaton H-11
Edgewood J-10
Edinburgh M-9
Edwardsport Q-4
Elberfeld T-4
Elizabethtown N-9
Elkhart B-9
Ellettsville N-7
Elnora Q-5
Elwood H-9
English S-7
Etna Green C-9
Evansville U-3
Fairland L-9
Fairmount G-10
Fairview Park L-4
Farmersburg N-4
Farmland H-12
Ferdinand S-6
Fillmore L-6
Fishers J-9
Flora G-7
Ft. Branch S-3
Ft. Wayne D-12
Fortville J-9
Fountain City J-12
Fowler F-4
Francesville E-6
Francisco S-4
Frankfort H-7
Franklin M-9
Frankton H-10
Freetown P-8
Fremont A-12
French Lick R-7
Fulton E-8
Galena S-9
Galveston F-8
Garrett C-12
Gary B-4
Gas City G-10
Gaston H-10
Geneva F-12
Georgetown S-9
Goodland F-4
Goshen B-9
Gosport M-6
Grabill D-12
Grandview U-5
Greencastle L-6
Greendale N-13
Greenfield K-10
Greens Fork K-12
Greensburg M-11
Greentown G-9
Greenville S-9
Greenwood L-8
Griffith B-4
Hagerstown J-12
Hamilton B-12
Hamlet C-7
Hammond B-4
Hanna C-6
Hanover Q-11
Hardinsburg R-8
Harmony M-5
Harrodsburg P-7
Hartford City G-11
Hartsville N-10
Hatfield U-4
Haubstadt T-3
Hayden P-10
Hazleton R-3
Hebron C-5
Henryville R-10
Highland B-4
Hillsboro J-5
Hoagland E-12
Hobart B-5
Holland S-5
Holton P-11
Homecroft L-8
Hope N-10
Howe A-11
Hudson B-12
Huntertown D-12
Huntingburg S-5
Huntington E-10
Hymera N-4
Indianapolis K-8
Ingalls J-9
Jamestown J-7
Jasonville N-5
Jasper S-5
Jeffersonville S-10
Jonesboro G-10
Kasson T-3
Kempton H-8
Kendallville C-11
Kennard K-10
Kentland F-4
Kewanna E-7
Kingman J-4
Kingsford Heights B-6
Kirklin H-8
Knightstown K-10
Knightsville M-5
Knox C-7
Kokomo G-8
Koontz Lake C-7
Kouts C-5
La Crosse C-6
La Fontaine F-10
La Paz C-8
La Porte B-6
Ladoga K-6
Lafayette G-6
Lagrange B-11
Lagro E-10
Lake Station B-5
Lake Vil. D-4
Lakes of the Four Seasons C-5
Laketon E-9
Lakeville B-8
Lanesville S-9
Laotto C-11
Lapel J-9
Laurel M-12
Lawrence K-9
Lawrenceburg N-13
Lebanon J-7
Leesburg C-9
Leo-Cedarville C-12
Lewisville K-11
Liberty L-12
Ligonier B-10
Linden H-6
Linton P-5
Linwood H-10
Lizton K-7
Logansport F-8
Long Beach A-6
Loogootee Q-6
Lowell C-4
Lydick B-7
Lynn J-12
Lynnville T-4
Lyons P-5
Madison Q-11
Manilla L-10
Marengo S-8
Marion G-10
Markle E-11
Markleville J-10
Marshall K-5
Martinsville M-7
Matthews G-10
Maxwell K-10
McCordsville K-9
Mecca L-4
Medaryville D-6
Medora Q-8
Mentone D-9
Meridian Hills K-8
Merrillville B-4
Mexico E-8
Michiana Shores A-6
Michigan City A-6
Michigantown H-7
Middlebury B-10
Middletown J-10
Milan N-12
Milford C-9
Millersburg B-10
Milltown S-8
Milroy M-11
Milton K-12
Mishawaka B-8
Mitchell Q-7
Monon E-6
Monroe F-12
Monroe City R-4
Monroeville E-13
Monrovia L-7
Montezuma K-4
Montgomery Q-5
Monticello F-6
Montpelier G-11
Mooreland J-11
Moores Hill N-12
Mooresville L-8
Morgantown M-8
Morocco E-4
Morristown L-10
Mt. Vernon U-2
Mulberry H-6
Muncie H-11
Munster B-4
Nappanee C-9
Nashville N-8
New Albany S-9
New Carlisle A-7
New Castle J-11
New Harmony T-2
New Haven D-12
New Market J-6
New Palestine L-9
New Paris B-9
New Pekin R-9
New Ross J-6
New Unionville N-7
New Whiteland L-8
Newburgh U-4
Newport K-4
Noblesville J-9
N. Judson D-6
N. Liberty B-7
N. Manchester E-10
N. Salem K-7
N. Terre Haute M-4
N. Vernon P-10
N. Webster C-10
Oakland City S-4
Oaktown Q-4
Odon Q-5
Ogden Dunes B-5
Oldenburg M-11
Oolitic P-7
Orestes H-10
Orland A-12
Orleans Q-7
Osceola B-8
Osgood N-11
Ossian E-12
Otterbein G-5
Owensville S-3
Oxford G-4
Palmyra S-8
Paoli R-7
Paragon M-7
Parker City H-11
Patoka S-3
Pendleton J-10
Pennville G-12
Perrysville J-4
Peru F-9
Petersburg R-4
Pierceton D-10
Pittsboro K-7
Plainfield L-7
Plainville Q-5
Pleasant Lake B-12
Pleasant View L-9
Plymouth C-8
Portage B-5
Porter B-5
Portland G-12
Poseyville T-2
Princes Lakes M-8
Princeton S-3
Redkey G-12
Remington F-5
Rensselaer E-5
Reynolds F-6
Richmond K-13
Ridgeville H-12
Rising Sun P-13
Roachdale K-6
Roann E-9
Roanoke E-11
Rochester D-8
Rockport U-5
Rockville K-5
Rolling Prairie B-7
Rome City B-11
Rosedale L-4
Rossville G-7
Royal Ctr. E-7
Rushville L-11
Russellville K-5
Russiaville G-8
St. Joe C-12
St. John C-4
St. Joseph S-9
St. Leon N-12
St. Meinrad T-6
St. Paul M-10
Salem R-8
San Pierre D-6
Sandborn P-5
Santa Claus T-6
Schererville B-4
Scottsburg Q-10
Seelyville M-4
Sellersburg S-10
Selma H-11
Seymour P-9
Shadeland G-6
Sharpsville G-8
Shelburn N-4
Shelby D-4
Shelbyville M-10
Sheridan J-8
Shipshewana B-10
Shirley K-10
Shoals R-6
Silver Lake D-9
Smithville P-7
S. Bend B-8
S. Whitley D-10
Southport L-8
Speedway K-8
Spencer N-6
Spiceland K-11
Star City E-7
Staunton M-5
Stockwell H-6
Stroh B-11
Sullivan P-4
Summitville H-10
Sunman N-12
Swayzee G-9
Sweetser F-9
Syracuse C-10
Taylorsville N-9
Tell City U-6
Terre Haute M-4
Thorntown J-7
Tipton H-9
Topeka B-10
Town of Pines B-6
Trafalgar M-8
Trail Creek A-6
Tri-Lakes C-11
Troy U-6
Underwood R-10
Union City H-13
Universal L-4
Upland G-10
Utica S-10
Valparaiso B-5
Van Buren F-10
Veedersburg J-4
Vernon P-10
Versailles P-11
Vevay Q-12
Vincennes Q-3
Wabash E-9
Wadesville T-3
Wakarusa B-9
Waldron M-10
Walkerton C-7
Walton F-8
Wanatah C-6
Warren F-11
Warren Park K-9
Warsaw D-9
Washington R-5
Waterford B-6
Waterloo C-12
Waveland K-5
Waynetown J-5
Webster J-12
Wellsboro B-6
W. Baden Sprs. R-7
W. College Corner L-13
W. Lafayette G-6
W. Lebanon H-4
W. Terre Haute M-4
Westfield J-8
Westpoint H-5
Westport N-10
Westville B-6
Wheatfield D-5
Wheatland R-4
Whiteland L-8
Whitestown J-8
Whiting B-4
Wilkinson K-10
Williamsport H-4
Winamac D-7
Winchester H-12
Windfall H-9
Winfield C-4
Winona Lake D-9
Winslow S-4
Wolcott F-5
Wolcottville B-11
Woodburn D-13
Worthington N-5
Yankeetown U-4
Yorktown H-10
Zanesville E-11
Zionsville J-8

IOWA

see map pages 40-41

Counties

Adair K-7
Adams L-6
Allamakee B-16
Appanoose M-12
Audubon H-6
Benton G-14
Black Hawk E-14
Boone G-8
Bremer D-14
Buchanan E-15
Buena Vista D-5
Butler D-12
Calhoun E-7
Carroll G-6
Cass K-6
Cedar H-17
Cerro Gordo C-11
Cherokee D-4
Chickasaw C-13
Clarke L-9
Clay C-5
Clayton D-16
Clinton G-19
Crawford G-5
Dallas H-8
Davis M-13
Decatur M-9
Delaware E-16
Des Moines L-17
Dickinson B-5
Dubuque F-17
Emmet B-6
Fayette C-14
Floyd C-12
Franklin D-11
Fremont L-4
Greene G-7
Grundy E-12
Guthrie J-7
Hamilton F-9
Hancock C-9
Hardin E-11
Harrison H-3
Henry L-16
Howard B-14
Humboldt D-8
Ida F-4
Iowa H-14
Jackson F-18
Jasper H-11
Jefferson L-14
Johnson H-15
Jones F-17
Keokuk J-13
Kossuth C-8
Lee M-16
Linn F-15
Louisa K-16
Lucas L-10
Lyon B-2
Madison K-8
Mahaska J-13
Marion J-11
Marshall G-11
Mills L-4
Mitchell B-12
Monona F-2
Monroe L-12
Montgomery L-5
Muscatine J-17
O'Brien C-4
Osceola B-4
Page M-5
Palo Alto C-7
Plymouth D-2
Pocahontas D-6
Polk H-10
Pottawattamie J-4
Poweshiek H-13
Ringgold M-8
Sac F-5
Scott H-19
Shelby J-5
Sioux C-3
Story G-10
Tama G-13
Taylor M-6
Union L-8
Van Buren M-14
Wapello L-13
Warren J-10
Washington J-15
Wayne M-11
Webster E-8
Winnebago B-9
Winneshiek B-15
Woodbury E-3
Worth B-11
Wright D-9

Cities and Towns

Ackley E-11
Adair J-7
Adel H-8
Afton L-8
Akron D-1
Albert City D-6
Albia L-12
Alden E-10
Algona C-8
Allison D-12
Alta D-5
Alton C-3
Altoona H-10
Ames G-10
Anamosa G-16
Anita J-6
Ankeny H-10
Aplington E-12
Armstrong B-7
Arnolds Park B-5
Asbury E-18
Atlantic J-6
Audubon H-6
Aurelia D-5
Avoca J-5
Bancroft B-8
Battle Creek F-4
Baxter H-11
Bedford M-6
Belle Plaine G-14
Bellevue F-19
Belmond D-10
Bettendorf J-19
Bloomfield M-13
Blue Grass J-18
Bondurant H-10
Boone G-9
Britt C-9
Brooklyn H-13
Buffalo J-18
Buffalo Ctr. B-9
Burlington M-17
Calmar C-15
Camanche H-19
Carlisle J-10
Carroll G-6
Cascade F-17
Cedar Falls E-13
Cedar Rapids G-15
Ctr. Point F-15
Centerville M-12
Central City F-16
Chariton L-11
Charles City C-12
Cherokee D-4
Clarence G-17
Clarinda M-5
Clarion D-9
Clarksville D-12
Clear Lake C-10
Clinton G-19
Colfax H-11
Colo G-11
Columbus Jct. K-16
Conrad F-12
Coon Rapids H-7
Coralville H-16
Corning L-6
Correctionville E-4
Corydon M-10
Council Bluffs K-3
Cresco B-14
Creston L-7
Dakota City D-8
Dallas Ctr. H-9
Danville L-16
Davenport J-18
Dayton F-8
De Soto J-8
De Witt H-19
Decorah B-15
Denison G-5
Denver D-13
Des Moines J-10
Dike E-13
Donnellson M-16
Dubuque E-18
Dunlap H-4
Durant H-17
Dyersville E-17
Dysart F-13
Eagle Grove D-9
Earlham J-8
Earlville E-16
Eddyville K-13
Edgewood E-16
Eldon L-14
Eldora F-11
Eldridge H-18
Elk Run Heights E-14
Elkader D-16
Emmetsburg C-7
Epworth E-17
Essex L-5
Estherville B-6
Evansdale E-14
Exira J-6
Fairbank E-14
Fairfax G-15
Fairfield L-15
Farley E-17
Fayette D-15
Forest City B-10
Ft. Dodge E-8
Ft. Madison M-16
Fredericksburg C-14
Garner C-10
George B-3
Gilbert G-9
Gladbrook F-12
Glenwood L-3
Glidden G-6
Gowrie F-8
Graettinger B-6
Grand Jct. G-8
Greene D-12
Greenfield K-7
Grimes H-9
Grinnell H-12
Griswold K-5
Grundy Ctr. F-12
Guthrie Ctr. H-7
Guttenberg D-17
Hamburg M-4
Hampton D-11
Harlan H-5
Hartford J-10
Hartley C-4
Hawarden C-2
Hedrick K-14
Hiawatha G-15
Holstein E-4
Hubbard F-11
Hudson E-13
Hull B-3
Humboldt D-8
Huxley G-10
Ida Grove F-4
Independence E-15
Indianola J-10
Inwood B-2
Iowa City H-16
Iowa Falls E-11
Janesville E-13
Jefferson G-7
Jesup E-14
Jewell F-9
Johnston H-9
Kalona J-15
Kanawha C-9
Keokuk N-16
Keosauqua M-15
Keota J-15
Kingsley E-3
Knoxville K-11
La Porte City F-14
Lake City F-6
Lake Mills B-10
Lake Park A-5
Lake View F-6
Lamoni M-9
Lansing B-16
Laurens D-6
Le Claire H-19
Le Grand G-12
Le Mars D-2
Lenox L-7
Leon M-9
Lisbon G-16
Logan H-3
Lone Tree J-16
Madrid G-9
Malvern L-4
Manchester E-16
Manilla G-5
Manly B-11
Manning G-6
Manson E-7
Mapleton F-3
Maquoketa G-18
Marcus D-4
Marengo H-14
Marion G-15
Marshalltown G-12
Mason City C-11
Maxwell G-10
McGregor C-17
Mechanicsville G-16
Mediapolis L-17
Melcher Dallas K-11
Milford B-5
Milo K-10
Missouri Valley J-3
Mitchellville H-10
Monona C-16
Monroe J-11
Montezuma J-13
Monticello F-17
Montrose N-16
Morning Sun K-17
Mt. Ayr M-8
Mt. Pleasant L-16
Mt. Vernon G-16
Moville E-3
Muscatine J-17
Nashua C-13
Neola J-4
Nevada G-10
New Hampton C-13
New London L-16
New Sharon J-13
Newell E-6
Newhall G-14
Newton H-11
Nora Sprs. C-12
N. English J-14
N. Liberty H-16
Northwood B-11
Norwalk J-9
Oakland K-5
Odebolt F-5
Oelwein D-15
Ogden G-8
Okoboji B-5
Onawa G-3
Orange City C-3
Osage B-12
Osceola L-9
Oskaloosa K-13
Ossian C-15
Ottumwa L-13
Panora H-7
Park View H-19
Parkersburg E-12
Paullina C-4
Pella J-12
Perry H-8
Pleasant Hill J-10
Pleasantville J-11
Pocahontas D-7
Polk City H-9
Postville C-15
Prairie City J-11
Preston G-19
Primghar C-4
Princeton H-19
Readlyn D-14
Red Oak L-5
Redfield J-8
Reinbeck F-13
Remsen D-3
Riceville B-13
Riverside J-16
Robins G-15
Rock Rapids A-3
Rock Valley B-2
Rockford C-12
Rockwell C-11
Rockwell City F-7
Roland F-10
Sac City E-6
St. Ansgar B-12
Sanborn B-4
Saylorville H-10
Schaller E-5
Schleswig F-4
Sergeant Bluff E-2
Seymour M-11
Sheffield D-11
Sheldon B-3
Shell Rock D-13
Shellsburg G-15
Shenandoah M-5
Sibley B-4
Sidney M-4
Sigourney K-14
Sioux Ctr. C-3
Sioux City E-2
Slater H-9
Sloan F-2
Solon H-16
Spencer C-5
Spirit Lake B-6
Springville G-16
State Ctr. G-11
Storm Lake E-5
Story City F-10
Strawberry Point D-16
Stuart J-8
Sully J-12
Sumner D-14
Tabor L-4
Tama G-13
Tipton H-17
Toledo G-13
Traer F-13
Treynor K-4
Tripoli D-14
Urbandale J-9
Victor H-14
Villisca L-6
Vinton F-14
Walcott H-18
Wall Lake F-5
Walnut J-5
Wapello K-17
Washburn E-14
Washington K-15
Waterloo E-13
Waukee J-9
Waukon B-16
Waverly D-13
Wayland K-15
Webster City E-9
Wellman J-15
W. Bend C-7
W. Branch H-16
W. Burlington L-17
W. Des Moines J-9
W. Liberty J-17
W. Point M-16
W. Union C-15
Williamsburg H-14
Wilton J-17
Winfield K-16
Winterset K-8
Woodbine H-4
Woodward H-9

KANSAS

see map pages 42-43

Counties

Allen H-17
Anderson F-17
Atchison C-17
Barber J-9
Barton F-9
Bourbon G-18
Brown B-16
Butler H-14
Chase F-14
Chautauqua K-15
Cherokee K-18
Cheyenne B-2
Clark J-6
Clay C-13
Cloud C-12
Coffey F-16
Comanche K-8
Cowley J-14
Crawford H-18
Decatur B-5
Dickinson E-13
Doniphan B-17
Douglas E-17
Edwards H-8
Elk J-15
Ellis D-7
Ellsworth E-10
Finney G-4
Ford H-6
Franklin F-17
Geary D-14
Gove E-5
Graham C-6
Grant H-3
Gray H-5
Greeley E-2
Greenwood G-15
Hamilton G-2
Harper K-11
Harvey G-12
Haskell H-4
Hodgeman G-6
Jackson C-16
Jefferson C-17
Jewell B-10
Johnson E-18
Kearny G-3
Kingman H-11
Kiowa J-8
Labette J-17
Lane F-5
Leavenworth D-17
Lincoln D-10
Linn F-18
Logan E-3
Lyon F-15
Marion G-13
Marshall B-14
McPherson F-11
Meade J-5
Miami E-18
Mitchell C-10
Montgomery J-16
Morris E-14
Morton J-2
Nemaha B-15
Neosho H-17
Ness F-7
Norton B-7
Osage F-16
Osborne C-9
Ottawa D-12
Pawnee F-8
Phillips B-8
Pottawatomie C-15
Pratt H-9
Rawlins B-4
Reno G-11
Republic B-12
Rice F-10
Riley C-13
Rooks C-8
Rush E-8
Russell D-9
Saline E-11
Scott F-4
Sedgwick H-12
Seward J-4
Shawnee D-16
Sheridan C-5
Sherman C-2
Smith B-9
Stafford G-9
Stanton H-2
Stevens J-3
Sumner K-12
Thomas C-4
Trego E-6
Wabaunsee D-15
Wallace D-2
Washington B-12
Wichita F-3
Wilson H-16
Woodson G-16
Wyandotte D-18

Cities and Towns

Axtell B-15
Baldwin City E-17
Basehor D-18
Baxter Sprs. K-18
Bazine F-7
Belle Plaine J-13
Belleville B-12
Beloit C-11
Bennington D-12
Bentley H-12
Bird City B-3
Blue Rapids B-14
Bonner Sprs. D-18
Bronson G-18
Bucklin J-7
Buhler G-11
Burden J-14
Burlingame E-16
Burlington G-16
Burrton G-12
Bushton F-10
Caldwell K-12
Caney K-16
Canton F-12
Carbondale E-16
Cawker City C-10
Cedar Vale K-14
Centralia B-15
Chanute H-17
Chapman D-13
Chase F-10
Cheney H-11
Cherokee J-18
Cherryvale J-17
Chetopa K-18
Cimarron H-5
Claflin F-9
Clay Ctr. C-13
Clearwater J-12
Clifton C-13
Clyde C-12
Coffeyville K-16
Colby C-4
Coldwater J-8
Colony G-17
Columbus K-18
Colwich H-12
Concordia C-12
Conway Sprs. J-12
Cottonwood Falls F-14
Council Grove E-14
Courtland B-11
Cunningham H-10
De Soto D-18
Dearing K-16
Deerfield G-4
Delphos C-11
Derby J-13
Dighton F-5
Dodge City H-6
Douglass J-13
Downs C-9
Dwight E-14
Easton C-17
Edgerton E-18
Edna K-17
Effingham C-17
El Dorado H-14
Elk City J-16
Elkhart K-2
Ellinwood F-9
Ellis D-7
Ellsworth E-10
Elmont D-16
Elwood B-18
Emporia F-15
Enterprise E-13
Erie H-17
Eskridge E-15
Eudora D-17
Eureka H-15
Florence G-13
Ft. Dodge H-6
Ft. Scott H-18
Fowler J-6
Frankfort B-14
Franklin H-18
Fredonia J-16
Frontenac J-19
Galena K-19
Galva F-12
Garden City G-4
Garden Plain H-12
Gardner E-18
Garnett F-17
Gas G-17
Geneseo F-10
Girard H-18
Glasco C-11
Glen Elder C-10
Goddard H-12
Goessel F-12
Goodland C-2
Gove D-5
Grainfield D-5
Grandview Plaza D-14
Great Bend F-9
Greeley F-17
Greenleaf B-13
Greensburg H-8
Gridley G-16
Grinnell D-5
Gypsum E-12
Halstead G-12
Hanover B-13
Harper J-11
Hartford F-16
Haven H-11
Haviland H-8
Hays E-8
Haysville H-12
Herington E-13
Hesston G-12
Hiawatha B-16
Highland B-17
Hill City C-7
Hillsboro F-13
Hoisington F-9
Holcomb G-4
Holton C-16
Holyrood E-10
Hope E-13
Horton B-16
Howard J-15
Hoxie C-5
Hoyt C-16
Hugoton J-3
Humboldt H-17
Hutchinson G-11
Independence J-16
Inman G-11
Iola G-17
Jetmore G-6
Jewell B-10
Johnson City H-2
Jct. City D-14
Kanopolis E-10
Kansas City D-18
Kechi H-13
Kensington B-8
Kingman H-11
Kinsley G-7
Kiowa K-10
Kismet K-5
La Crosse F-8
La Cygne F-18
La Harpe G-17
Lakin G-3
Lansing C-18
Larned G-8
Lawrence D-17
Le Roy G-16
Leavenworth C-18
Lebanon B-9
Lebo F-16
Lecompton D-17
Lenexa D-18
Leon H-14
Leonardville C-13
Leoti F-3
Lewis G-8
Liberal K-4
Lincoln D-10
Lindsborg F-12
Linn B-13
Linwood D-18
Little River F-11
Logan B-7
Longton J-15
Louisburg E-18
Lucas D-9
Lyndon E-16
Lyons F-10
Macksville G-8
Madison G-15
Maize H-12
Manhattan D-14
Mankato B-10
Maple Hill D-15
Marion F-13
Marquette F-11
Marysville B-14
McCune J-18
McLouth D-17
McPherson F-12
Meade J-5
Medicine Lodge J-9
Melvern F-16
Meriden D-16
Milford D-13
Miltonvale C-12
Minneapolis D-12
Minneola J-6
Moline J-15
Montezuma H-5
Moran G-17
Mound City G-18
Mound Valley J-17
Moundridge G-12
Mt. Hope H-12
Mulberry H-19
Mulvane J-13
Natoma D-8
Neodesha J-16
Ness City F-6
New Strawn F-16
Newton G-12
Nickerson G-11
N. Newton G-12
Norton B-6
Nortonville C-17
Norwich J-11
Oakley D-4
Oberlin B-5
Ogden D-14
Olathe D-18
Olpe F-15
Onaga C-15
Osage City E-16
Osawatomie F-18
Osborne C-9
Oskaloosa D-17
Oswego K-18
Otis F-8
Ottawa E-17
Overbrook E-16
Overland Park D-18
Oxford J-13
Ozawkie D-17
Paola E-18
Park City H-13
Parsons J-17
Pawnee Rock F-8
Peabody G-13
Perry D-17
Phillipsburg B-8
Pittsburg J-18
Plains J-5
Plainville D-8
Pleasanton G-18
Pomona E-17
Potwin G-13
Pratt H-9
Pretty Prairie H-11
Protection K-7
Quenemo E-17
Quinter D-6
Ransom E-6
Richmond F-17
Riley C-14
Riverton K-18
Rolla K-2
Rose Hill H-13
Rossville D-16
Russell E-9
Sabetha B-16
St. Francis B-2
St. George D-14
St. John G-9
St. Marys D-15
St. Paul J-17
Salina E-12
Satanta J-4
Scammon J-18
Scandia B-11
Scott City F-4
Scranton E-16
Sedan K-15
Sedgwick G-12
Seneca B-15
Severy H-15
Sharon Sprs. D-2
Shawnee D-18
Silver Lake D-16
Smith Ctr. B-9
Solomon E-12
S. Haven K-12
S. Hutchinson G-11
Spearville H-7
Spr. Hill E-18
Stafford G-9
Sterling G-10
Stockton C-8
Strong City F-14
Sublette J-4
Syracuse G-2
Thayer J-17
Tonganoxie D-17
Topeka D-16
Towanda H-13
Tribune F-2
Troy B-17
Turon H-10
Udall J-13
Ulysses H-3
Valley Ctr. H-12
Valley Falls C-17
Victoria E-8
WaKeeney D-6
Wakefield D-13
Wamego D-15
Washington B-13
Waterville B-14
Wathena B-18
Waverly F-16
Weir J-18
Wellington J-12
Wellsville E-17
Westmoreland C-14
White City E-14
Whitewater G-13
Wichita H-12
Wilson E-10
Winchester C-17
Winfield J-13
Yates Ctr. G-16

KENTUCKY

see map pages 44-45

Counties

Adair L-10
Allen M-7
Anderson G-11
Ballard D-3
Barren M-7
Bath G-14
Bell M-15
Boone D-12
Bourbon F-13
Boyd F-18
Boyle J-11
Bracken E-14
Breathitt J-16
Breckinridge H-6
Bullitt H-9
Butler L-6
Caldwell K-2
Calloway N-1
Campbell D-13
Carlisle E-3
Carroll E-11
Carter F-17
Casey K-11
Christian L-3
Clark H-14
Clay L-15
Clinton M-11
Crittenden K-1
Cumberland M-10
Daviess J-4
Edmonson K-7
Elliott G-17
Estill H-14
Fayette G-13
Fleming F-15
Floyd J-18
Franklin F-11
Fulton G-2
Gallatin E-11
Garrard J-12
Grant E-12
Graves F-4
Grayson K-6
Green K-9
Greenup E-17
Hancock H-5
Hardin H-8
Harlan M-17
Harrison F-13
Hart K-8
Henderson J-3
Henry F-11
Hickman F-3
Hopkins K-3
Jackson J-14
Jefferson G-9
Jessamine H-12
Johnson H-18
Kenton D-12
Knott K-17
Knox M-15
Larue J-9
Laurel L-13
Lawrence G-18
Lee J-15
Leslie L-16
Letcher L-17
Lewis E-16
Lincoln K-12
Livingston K-1
Logan M-5
Lyon L-1
Madison H-13
Magoffin H-17
Marion J-10
Marshall M-1
Martin H-19
Mason E-15
McCracken E-3
McCreary M-13
McLean K-4
Meade H-7
Menifee H-15
Mercer H-11
Metcalfe L-9
Monroe M-9
Montgomery G-14
Morgan H-17
Muhlenberg L-4
Nelson H-10
Nicholas F-14
Ohio J-5
Oldham F-9
Owen E-11
Owsley K-15
Pendleton E-13
Perry L-17
Pike J-19
Powell H-15
Pulaski L-13
Robertson E-14
Rockcastle K-13
Rowan F-16
Russell L-11
Scott F-12
Shelby F-10
Simpson M-6
Spencer H-10
Taylor K-10
Todd M-4
Trigg M-2
Trimble E-10
Union J-2
Warren L-6
Washington J-10
Wayne M-12
Webster J-3
Whitley M-13
Wolfe H-15
Woodford G-12

Cities and Towns

Aberdeen K-6
Adairville N-5
Albany N-11
Alexandria D-13
Allen J-18
Allensville M-4
Alton G-11
Alvaton M-7
Annville K-14
Anthoston H-3
Anton K-4
Arlington F-3
Ashland F-18
Auburn M-6
Audubon Park G-9
Augusta D-14
Avawam K-16
Baileys Switch M-14
Balltown J-9
Barbourville M-15
Bardstown H-9
Bardwell E-3
Barlow E-2
Baskett H-3
Beattyville J-15
Beaver Dam K-5
Beda J-5
Bedford E-10
Beech Grove J-3
Bellefonte E-18
Bellevue C-13
Belmont H-9
Belton L-5
Benham L-17
Benton E-5
Berea J-13
Bernstadt L-14
Berry E-13
Big Clifty J-7
Blackey L-17
Blaine G-18
Bloomfield H-10
Bonnieville K-8
Boone J-13
Booneville K-15
Boston H-9
Botto L-15
Bowling Green L-6
Bradfordsville J-11
Brandenburg G-7
Bremen K-4
Briensburg M-1
Brodhead K-13
Brooks G-9
Brooksville E-14
Brownsville L-7
Bryantsville J-12
Buckhorn K-16
Buckner F-9
Buechel G-
Buffalo J-
Burgin H-1
Burkesville M-1
Burlington C-1
Burning Sprs. K-1
Burnside L-12
Bush L-15
Butler D-13
Cadiz M-2
Cairo J-3
Calhoun J-4
California D-13
Calvert City E-5
Camargo G-14
Campbellsburg E-10
Campbellsville K-10
Campton J-16
Caneyville K-6
Cannel City H-16
Cannonsburg F-18
Carlisle F-14
Carrollton E-10
Catlettsburg F-18
Cave City L-8
Cawood M-17
Cecilia J-8
Centertown K-5
Central City K-4
Cerulean M-3
Chaplin H-10
Clarkson J-7
Claryville D-13
Clay K-2
Clay City H-14
Cleaton K-4
Clinton F-3
Cloverport H-6
Coal Run Vil. J-19
Columbia L-10
Columbus F-2
Corbin M-14
Corinth F-12
Corydon H-3
Covington C-12
Crab Orchard K-13
Crestwood F-9
Crittenden D-12
Crofton L-3
Cumberland L-17
Cynthiana F-13
Danville J-12
David J-18
Dawson Sprs. L-3
Dexter M-1
Dixon J-3
Dizney M-17
Dorton K-18
Dover D-14
Drakesboro L-5
Dry Ridge E-12
Dunmor L-5
Dwarf K-17
Earlington K-3
E. Bernstadt L-14
Eddyville L-1
Edmonton M-9
Ekron H-7
Elihu L-12
Elizabethtown J-8
Elkhorn City K-19
Elkton M-4
Eminence F-10
Ensor H-5
Epleys M-5
Erlanger C-12
Ermine L-18
Eubank K-12
Evarts M-17
Ewing F-14
Fairfield H-10
Falmouth E-13
Fancy Farm F-3
Ferguson L-12
Fern Creek G-9
Firebrick E-17
Flat Lick M-15
Flatwoods E-18
Fleming-Neon K-18
Flemingsburg F-15
Florence D-12
Fordsville J-6
Ft. Mitchell C-12
Fountain Run M-8
Fox Chase G-9
Frankfort G-11
Franklin M-6
Fredonia K-1
Fremont E-4
Frenchburg H-15
Fulton G-3
Galveston J-18
Gamaliel N-8
Garlin L-10
Garner K-17
Garrison E-17
Georgetown G-12
Germantown E-14
Ghent E-11
Glasgow L-8
Glencoe E-12
Glendale J-8
Goshen F-9
Graham K-4
Grand Rivers L-1
Gray M-14
Gray Hawk K-14
Grayson F-17
Greensburg K-9
Greenup E-18
Greenville L-4
Guston H-7
Guthrie N-4
Hagerhill H-18
Haldeman F-16
Halls Gap J-12
Hanson K-3
Hardin M-1
Hardinsburg H-6
Harlan M-16
Harold J-18
Harrodsburg H-12
Hartford K-5
Hawesville H-5
Hazard K-17
Hazel Green H-16
Hebron C-12
Hebron Estates G-9
Heidrick M-15
Henderson H-3
Hendron E-4
Hickman F-2
Hickory E-4
Hillsboro F-15
Hillview G-9
Hindman K-17
Hiseville L-8
Hitchins F-17
Hodgenville J-9
Hollyvilla G-9
Hopkinsville M-3
Horse Branch J-6
Horse Cave L-8
Huddy J-19
Hulen M-16
Hustonville K-12
Hyden L-16
Independence D-12
Inez H-19
Irvine J-14
Irvington H-7
Island K-4
Jackson J-16
Jamestown L-11
Jeffersontown G-9
Jeffersonville G-15
Jenkins L-18
Jonancy K-18
Jct. City J-12
Keavy L-14
Kenton D-13
Kevil D-3
Kingston J-13
Kuttawa L-1
La Ctr. E-3
La Fayette N-3
La Grange F-10
Lakeview Heights G-16
Lancaster J-12
Langley J-18
Laura H-19
Lawrenceburg G-11
Lebanon J-10
Lebanon Jct. H-9
Ledbetter E-4

Leesburg F-13
Leitchfield ...K-7
Letcher L-17
Lewisburg ...L-5
Lewisport ...H-5
Lexington ...G-13
Liberty K-11
Lily J-14
Limestone ...F-16
Livermore ...J-4
Livingston ...K-13
Livia D-14
Lone Oak ...E-4
Loretto J-10
Lost Creek ...J-16
Louisa G-18
Louisville ...G-12
Loyall M-16
Lynch L-18
Lyndon F-9
Maceo H-5
Mackville ...J-11
Madisonville ..K-3
Magnolia K-8
Majestic J-20
Manchester ...L-16
Marion K-1
Martin J-18
Masonville ...H-5
Massac E-3
Mayfield F-3
Mays Lick ...F-14
Maysville ...E-15
Mazie G-17
McHenry K-5
McKee K-14
McRoberts ...L-18
McVeigh J-19
Memphis Jct. ..L-7
Mentor D-13
Middlesboro ..N-15
Middletown ...G-9
Midway G-12
Millersburg ...F-14
Millstone L-18
Millville G-12
Milton F-10
Monterey F-11
Monticello ...M-11
Morehead G-16
Moreland J-11
Morganfield ..J-2
Morgantown ..K-6
Mortons Gap ..K-3
Mt. Olivet ...E-14
Mt. Sterling ..G-14
Mt. Vernon ...L-13
Mt. Washington G-9
Muldraugh ...H-8
Munfordville ..K-8
Murray N-1
Nazareth J-10
Nebo K-3
New Castle ...F-10
New Haven ...J-9
Newport C-13
Niagara H-12
Nicholasville .H-12
N. Corbin ...L-14
N. Middle-
town G-14
Nortonville ...L-3
Oak Grove ...N-3
Oakdale A-4
Oakland L-7
Okolona G-9
Olive Hill ...F-17
Oneida L-15
Owensboro ...H-5
Owenton E-12
Owingsville ...F-15
Oxford F-13
Paducah D-4
Paintsville ...H-18
Paris G-13
Park City L-8
Pathfork M-16
Peaks Mill ...F-12
Pembroke ...M-4
Perryville ...J-11
Petersburg ...C-11
Pewee Valley ..F-9
Phelps J-20
Philpot H-5
Pikeville J-19
Pine Knot ...N-13
Pineville M-15
Pioneer Vil. ..G-9
Pippa Passes .K-18
Pleasure Ridge
Park G-8
Pleasureville ..F-11
Plum Sprs. ...L-7
Poole J-3
Powderly K-4
Prestonsburg .H-18
Prestonville ..L-12
Princeton L-2
Prospect F-9
Providence ...K-2
Pryorsburg ...F-2
Pulaski M-12
Raceland E-18
Radcliff H-8
Ravenna J-14
Raywick J-10
Rectorville ...E-15
Reidland E-4
Rich Pond ...M-6
Richardsville ..L-6
Richmond ...H-13
Rineyville ...H-8
River Bluff ...F-9
Robards J-3
Rochester ...L-5
Rockholds ...M-14
Rockport K-5
Rome J-4
Royalton J-17
Russell H-18
Russell Sprs. .L-11
Ryland
Heights ...D-13
Sacramento ...K-4
Sadieville ...F-12
St. Charles ...L-3
St. Dennis ...G-8
Salem K-1
Salt Lick ...G-15
Salvisa H-11
Salyersville ...H-17
Samuels J-9
Sanders E-11
Sandgap L-14
Sandy Hook ..G-17
Sardis E-14
Saxton M-14
Science Hill ..L-12
Scottsville ...M-7
Sebree J-3
Shelbiana ...K-19
Shelbyville ...F-10
Shepherdsville .G-9
Shively G-8
Silver Grove ..C-13
Simpsonville ..G-10
Slaughters ...J-3
Slemp L-17
Smith Mills ...H-2
Smithfield ...F-11
Smithland ...D-4
Smiths Grove ..L-7
Somerset L-12
Sonora J-8
S. Carrollton ..K-4
S. Shore E-17
S. Wallins ...M-16
S. Williamson .J-19
Spottsville ...H-3
Springfield ...J-10
Stamping
Ground ...F-12
Stanford J-12
Stanley H-4
Stanton H-15
Stearns N-12
Stella F-4
Stephensburg .J-8
Stinnett L-16
Sturgis J-2
Sublett J-17
Summersville ..K-9
Summit J-8
Symsonia ...E-3
Taylorsville ...G-10

Tompkinsville .N-9
Topmost K-18
Totz L-17
Trenton N-4
Union D-12
Uniontown ...H-2
Upton K-9
Valley Station .G-8
Van Lear ...H-18
Vanceburg ...E-16
Vaughns Mill .H-14
Versailles ...G-12
Vicco K-17
Villa Hills ...C-12
Vine Grove ...H-8
Viper K-17
W. Liberty ...H-16
W. Point G-8
Wallins Creek .M-16
Walton F-12
Warfield H-19
Warsaw D-11
Water Valley ..F-3
Waverly H-2
Wayland J-18
Waynesburg ..J-12
Wheatcroft ...J-2
Wheelwright ..K-18
White Plains ..L-4
Whitesburg ...L-18
Whitesville ...H-4
Whitley City ..M-13
Wickliffe C-2
Williamsburg .M-14
Williamsport .E-12
Williamstown .E-12
Willisburg ...H-11
Wilmore H-12
Winchester ...G-14
Wingo F-2
Wofford M-14
Wonnie K-17
Woodburn ...M-14
Woodburn ...M-6
Woodbury ...L-6
Worthville ...E-11
Wurtland ...H-18
Yerkes K-16
Zebulon J-19
Zion H-3

LOUISIANA
see map pages
46-47

Parishes
Acadia K-8
Allen J-7
Ascension ...J-13
Assumption ..L-13
Avoyelles ...H-9
Beauregard ...K-7
Bienville C-7
Bossier B-5
Caddo C-5
Calcasieu ...K-5
Caldwell C-9
Cameron K-6
Catahoula ...E-10
Claiborne ...B-7
Concordia ...F-11
De Soto D-5
E. Baton
Rouge H-13
E. Carroll ...B-12
E. Feliciana ..H-13
Evangeline ...J-9
Franklin C-11
Grant E-8
Iberia L-11
Iberville J-11
Jackson C-8
Jefferson ...L-15
Jefferson
Davis K-7
Lafayette ...K-9
Lafourche ...M-14
La Salle E-9
Lincoln B-8
Livingston ...J-13
Madison C-12
Morehouse ...B-10
Natchitoches .D-6
Orleans K-15
Ouachita ...C-9
Plaquemines .M-15
Pointe Coupee H-11
Rapides G-8
Red River ...D-6
Richland C-10
Sabine E-6
St. Bernard ..L-16
St. Charles ..L-14
St. Helena ...H-13
St. James ...L-13
St. John The
Baptist ...K-14
St. Landry ...J-10
St. Martin ...K-11
St. Mary M-12
St. Tammany .K-15
Tangipahoa ..H-14
Tensas D-12
Terrebonne ..M-12
Union B-9
Vermilion ...L-10
Vernon H-7
Washington ..H-15
Webster B-6
W. Baton
Rouge J-12
W. Carroll ...B-11
W. Feliciana .G-11
Winn D-7

Cities and Towns
Abbeville ...K-9
Abita Sprs. ..J-15
Addis J-12
Albany J-14
Alexandria ...F-8
Alsen J-12
Amelia L-12
Amite H-14
Anacoco D-6
Arcadia C-7
Arnaudville ...J-10
Avondale ...L-15
Baker J-12
Baldwin L-11
Ball F-8
Baratania ...L-15
Basile J-8
Bastrop B-10
Baton Rouge ..J-12
Bawcomville ..C-9
Bayou Cane ..L-13
Bayou Goula ..K-12
Bayou Vista ..L-12
Belle Chasse ..L-15
Belle Rose ...L-13
Benton B-5
Bernice B-8
Berwick L-12
Blanchard ...B-5
Bogalusa ...H-16
Boothville ...M-17
Bossier City ..C-5
Boyce F-7
Breaux Bridge .K-10
Broussard ...K-9
Brusly J-12
Buras M-17
Cade K-10
Cameron L-6
Campti E-7
Carencro ...K-10
Carlyss K-6
Cecilia J-10
Centerville ...L-12
Chackbay ...L-13
Chalmette ...L-16
Charenton ...L-11
Chatham C-9
Chauvin M-14
Cheneyville ...G-8
Choudrant ...C-8
Church Point ..J-9
Clarence E-7
Clarks D-9
Clayton D-11
Clinton H-12
Columbia ...D-9
Convent K-13
Cotton Valley .B-6

Cottonport ...G-10
Coushatta ...D-6
Covington ...J-15
Crowley K-9
Cullen A-6
Cut Off M-14
De Quincy ...K-7
De Ridder ...J-6
Delcambre ...K-10
Delhi C-11
Des Allemands L-14
Destrehan ...K-14
Deville F-9
Donaldsonville K-13
Doyline C-5
Dubach B-8
Dulac M-13
Duson K-9
Eastwood ...B-6
Edgard K-14
Elton J-8
Empire M-16
Erath K-10
Erwinville ...J-11
Esterwood ...K-9
Eunice J-9
Farmerville ...B-9
Ferriday E-11
Florien F-6
Fordoche ...J-11
Franklin L-11
Franklinton ..H-15
French
Settlement ..J-13
Galliano M-14
Garyville K-14
Gibsland C-6
Gibson M-13
Glenmora ...G-8

Meadow M-15
Gonzales K-13
Grambling ...C-8
Gramercy ...K-13
Grand Coteau .J-10
Grand Isle ...N-15
Gray L-13
Greensburg ..H-13
Greenwood ...C-5
Gretna L-15
Gueydan K-9
Hackberry ...K-6
Hahnville ...K-14
Hammond ...J-14
Harrisonburg .E-10
Haughton ...C-6
Haynesville ..A-7
Henderson ...J-10
Hessmer G-9
Hodge C-8
Homer B-7
Houma M-13
Independence .H-14
Iota J-8
Iowa K-7
Jackson H-12
Jean Lafitte ..L-15
Jeanerette ...L-11
Jena E-9
Jennings K-8
Jonesboro ...C-8
Jonesville ...E-10
Junction City .A-8
Kaplan K-9
Kenner K-15
Killian J-14
Kinder J-7
Krotz Sprs. ..J-11
Labadieville ..L-13
Lacombe J-15
Lafayette ...K-9
Lafitte L-15
Lake Arthur ..K-8
Lake Charles ..K-6
Lake Providence A-12
Laplace K-14
Larose M-14
Lawtell J-9
Lecompte ...G-8
Leesville J-6
Leonville ...J-10
Livingston ...J-13
Livonia J-11
Lockport L-14
Logansport ...D-5
Loreauville ...K-10
Lydia L-11
Madisonville ..J-15
Mamou J-9
Mandeville ...J-15
Mangham ...C-10
Mansfield ...D-5
Mansura G-9
Many F-6
Maringouin ...J-11
Marion A-9
Marksville ...G-9
Marrero L-15
Mathews ...L-14
Melville H-10
Mer Rouge ...B-10
Meraux L-15
Merryville ...J-6
Metairie K-15
Minden B-6
Monroe C-9
Montegut ...M-14
Montgomery ..E-7
Mooringsport .A-5
Moreauville ...G-10
Morgan City ..L-12
Morganza ...H-11
Morse K-9
Moss Bluff ...K-7
Napoleonville .L-13
Natalbany ...J-14
Natchitoches ..E-7
New Iberia ...K-10
New Llano ...J-6
New Orleans ..K-15
New Roads ...H-11
Newellton ...D-12
Norco K-14
N. Shore H-14
Oak Grove ...B-12
Oakdale H-8
Oberlin J-7
Oil City A-5
Olla D-9
Opelousas ...J-10
Paincourtville .L-13
Patterson ...L-12
Pearl River ...J-16
Perry L-9
Pine Prairie ..H-9
Pineville F-8
Plain Dealing .A-5
Plaquemine ..J-12
Pointe a la
Hache M-16
Ponchatoula ..J-14
Port Allen ...J-12
Port Sulphur ..M-16
Port Vincent ..J-13
Prairieville ...J-13
Raceland L-14
Rayne K-9
Reserve K-14
Richwood ...C-9
Ridgecrest ...E-11
Ringgold C-6
Rosedale J-11
Roseland H-14
Rosepine ...J-6
Ruston C-8
St. Bernard ..L-16
St. Francis-
ville H-12
St. Gabriel ...J-12
St. Joseph ...D-12
St. Martinville .K-10
St. Rose K-14
Sarepta A-6
Schriever ...L-13
Scott K-9
Shreveport ...C-5
Sibley C-6
Simmesport ..G-10
Simsboro ...C-8
Slaughter ...H-12
Slidell K-16
Sorrento K-13
Springhill ...B-6
Sterlington ...B-9
Stonewall ...C-5
Sulphur K-6
Sunset J-9
Sun J-16
Swartz B-10
Tallulah C-12
Tangipahoa ..H-14
Terrytown ...L-15
Thibodaux ...L-13
Tickfaw J-14
Tioga F-8
Urania E-9
Varnado H-16
Vidalia F-11
Ville Platte ...H-9
Vinton K-6
Violet L-15
Vivian A-5
Walker K-6
Washington ..J-10
Waterproof ...E-12
Watson J-13
Welcome K-13
Welsh K-7
W. Monroe ...B-9
Westlake K-6
Westminster ..J-10
Westwego ...L-15
White Castle ..K-12
Wilson H-12
Winnfield ...D-8
Winnsboro ...D-11
Wisner D-11
Woodworth ...G-8
Youngsville ...K-10
Zachary H-12
Zwolle D-6

MAINE
see map pages
48-49

Counties
Androscoggin ..Q-3
Aroostook ...D-7
Cumberland ..P-2
Franklin N-2
Hancock M-8
Kennebec ...P-5
Knox Q-5
Lincoln Q-5
Oxford N-2
Penobscot ...J-7
Piscataquis ...G-6
Sagadahoc ...P-4
Somerset ...K-3
Waldo N-6
Washington ..L-11
York T-2

Cities and Towns
Alfred T-2
Anson M-4
Ashland D-7
Auburn Q-3
Augusta P-5
Bangor M-7
Bar Harbor ...P-9
Bar Mills S-2
Bass Harbor ..Q-8
Bath Q-4
Beals P-10
Belfast P-7
Benton N-5
Bernard Q-9
Berwick U-1
Bethel P-1
Biddeford ...T-3
Bingham L-4
Blaine E-8
Blue Hill P-8
Boothbay ...Q-4
Boothbay
Harbor R-5
Bowdoinham ..P-4
Brewer M-8
Bridgton P-2
Brooks N-7
Brownville Jct. .K-7
Brunswick ...P-4
Bucksport ...N-8
Calais M-12
Camden Q-7
Cape Cottage .S-3
Cape Elizabeth .T-3
Caribou D-8
Castine P-8
Chisholm ...P-3
Clinton N-5
Corinna M-6
Cumberland Ctr. S-3
Cumberland ..S-3
Damariscotta .R-5
Dexter L-6
Dixfield P-3
Dover-Foxcroft L-6
Dry Mills ...R-3
Dyer Cove ...S-4
Eagle Lake ...C-7
E. Harpswell ..R-4
E. Lebanon ..T-1
E. Millinocket .J-8
E. Wilton ...N-3
Easton M-13
Eastport ...N-13
Eddington ...M-8
Eliot U-1
Ellsworth ...N-8
Fairbanks ...N-4
Fairfield N-5
Falmouth ...S-3
Foreside ...S-3
Farmingdale ..Q-5
Farmington ..N-4
Ft. Fairfield ..D-10
Ft. Kent B-6
Freeport ...R-4
Friendship ...R-6
Fryeburg ...P-1
Gardiner Q-5
Glenburn ...M-7
Gorham S-3
Gray R-3
Greene Q-3
Greenville ...J-6
Guilford L-6
Hallowell ...Q-5
Hampden ...N-7
Hartland M-6
Hermon M-7
Higgins Beach .T-3
Houlton G-9
Howland K-8
Jackman J-3
Jonesboro ...M-10
Jonesport ...P-11
Kennebunk ..T-2
Kennebunk
Beach T-2
Kennebunkport .T-2
Kezar Falls ...S-1
Kingfield M-4
Kittery V-2
Kittery Point ..V-2
Lewiston ...Q-3
Limestone ...C-9
Lincoln K-8
Lisbon Q-4
Lisbon Falls ..R-4
Livermore Falls P-3
Lubec M-13
Machias M-10
Madawaska ...A-6
Madison M-4
Mapleton ...D-8
Mars Hill ...E-10
Mechanic Falls .Q-3
Medway J-8
Mexico P-3
Milbridge ...N-9
Millinocket ...J-7
Milo L-6
Monmouth ...Q-4
Moody Point ..U-2
Moody T-2
New Gloucester R-3
New Harbor ...R-6
Newport M-6
Norridgewock .N-5
N. Monmouth .Q-4
N. Scar-
borough ...S-3
N. Vassalboro .N-5

Slaughter ...H-12
N. Windham ..R-3
Northeast
Harbor Q-9
Norway Q-2
Oakfield G-9
Oakland N-5
Ogunquit ...U-1
Old Orchard
Beach T-3
Old Town ...M-8
Orland N-8
Orono M-8
Orrs Island ...S-4
Oxford Q-2
Patten G-8
Phillips N-3
Pine Point ...T-3
Pittsfield M-6
Pleasant
Point M-13
Portland S-3
Presque Isle ..D-8
Randolph ...Q-5
Richmond ...Q-5
Rockland ...Q-7
Rockport ...Q-7
Rumford P-3
Sabattus Q-4
Saco T-3
Sanford T-2
Sangerville ...L-6
Scarborough ..T-3
Searsport ...N-7
Sebago Lake ..S-2
Skowhegan ...N-5
Songo Lock ..R-2
S. Berwick ...U-2
S. Casco R-2
S. Eliot U-1
S. Harpswell ..S-4
S. Hiram ...S-1
S. Paris Q-2
S. Portland ...S-3
S. Sanford ...T-2
S. Windham ..S-3
Southwest
Harbor Q-9
Springvale ...T-2
Standish S-2
Stockton Sprs. .N-7
Stonington ...Q-8
Strong M-3
Tenants Harbor R-6
Thomaston ...R-6
Topsham ...P-4
Turner Q-3
Unity N-6
Van Buren ...B-10
Vinalhaven ...Q-6
Waldoboro ...Q-6
Warren Q-6
Washburn ...D-8
Waterboro ...T-2
Waterville ...N-5
Webster
Corner Q-4
Welchville ...Q-3
Wells U-2
Wells Beach ..U-2
W. Paris P-2
Westbrook ...S-3
Whiting M-11
Winslow N-5
Winterport ...N-7
Winthrop ...P-4
Wiscasset ...R-5
Woodland ...C-9
(Baileyville) ..L-12
Yarmouth ...S-3
York Harbor ..U-2
York Vil. U-2

MARYLAND
see map pages
50-51

Counties
Allegany B-5
Anne Arundel ..F-14
Baltimore ...C-14
Calvert H-14
Caroline G-17
Carroll B-11
Cecil C-16
Charles F-12
Dorchester ...J-16
Frederick ...C-9
Garrett C-2
Harford C-15
Howard E-12
Kent E-16
Montgomery ..E-11
Prince
George's ...E-13
Queen Anne's .G-17
St. Mary's ...K-14
Somerset ...L-18
Talbot G-16
Washington ..B-7
Wicomico ...J-18
Worcester ...K-19

Cities and Towns
Aberdeen ...D-15
Accident ...B-2
Accokeek ...F-12
Adamstown ...D-10
Annapolis ...F-14
Arnold E-14
Arundel on
the Bay F-14
Aspen Hill ...E-12
Baldwin D-14
Baltimore ...D-13
Barclay F-17
Barton C-3
Bartonsville ...D-10
Bay Ridge ...F-14
Bel Air C-15
Belcamp ...D-15
Beltsville ...F-12
Berlin K-20
Bethesda ...E-12
Bethlehem ...G-16
Betterton ...D-16
Boonsboro ...C-8
Boring C-13
Bowie F-13
Bowling Green .C-4
Boxhill North ..C-15
Braddock
Heights D-9
Brandywine ...H-13
Breezy Point ..H-14
Breton Bay ...J-13
Brock Hall ...F-13
Brunswick ...D-10
Bryans Road ..H-12
Bryantown ...G-13
Burkittsville ...D-9
Burtonsville ...F-12
California ...K-14
Calvert Beach .J-14
Calverton ...F-12
Cambridge ...H-16
Cape St. Claire F-14
Captains Hill ..K-20
Cardiff B-15
Cascade B-8
Catonsville ...D-13
Cavetown ...B-9
Cearfoss B-8
Cecilton E-17
Cedar Grove ..E-11
Centreville ...F-16
Chaptico H-13
Charlestown ..C-16
Charlotte Hall .H-13
Chesapeake
Beach H-14
Chesapeake
City D-17
Chesapeake
Ranch
Estates K-14
Chestertown ..E-16
Cheverly F-12
Church Hill ...F-16
Clarksburg ...E-11
Clear Spr. ...B-7
Clinton G-12
Cobb Island ..K-13

Cockeysville ..C-13
Colesville ...E-12
Columbia ...E-12
Corriganville ..B-4
Craigtown ...C-16
Cresaptown ...C-4
Crisfield M-17
Crofton F-13
Crownsville ...F-14
Cumberland ..B-4
Damascus ...D-11
Dares Beach ..H-14
Davidsonville .F-13
Dayton E-12
Deale G-14
Delmar J-18
Denton G-17
Dominion ...F-15
Doubs D-10
Dowell K-14
Drum Point ...K-14
Dublin C-15
Dundalk D-14
Dunkirk H-13
Easton G-16
Eden K-18
Edgemere ...E-14
Eldersburg ...D-12
Elkridge E-13
Elkton C-17
Ellerslie B-4
Elliott City ...E-13
Emmitsburg ..B-10
Essex D-14
Fairlead F-12
Fallston C-14
Feagaville ...D-10
Federalsburg ..H-17
Flohrville ...D-12
Fountain Head .B-9
Fowblesburg ..C-13
Frederick D-9
Friendly G-12
Friendsville ...B-1
Frostburg ...B-3
Fruitland K-18
Fulton E-12
Funkstown ...C-8
Gaithersburg ..E-11
Galena E-16
Galesville ...G-14
Gamber C-12
Gibson J-15
Glen Burnie ..E-13
Glenarden ...F-12
Glenn Dale ...F-13
Glenwood ...D-12
Glyndon C-13
Gold Beach ...J-13
Goldsboro ...F-17
Goshen E-11
Grantsville ...B-2
Grasonville ...F-15
Great Mills ...K-14
Green Haven ..E-14
Green Valley ..D-10
Greenbelt ...F-12
Greenmount ..C-12
Greensboro ..F-17
Hagerstown ..B-9
Halfway C-8
Hampstead ...C-12
Hancock B-7
Harewood
Park D-15
Harrisville ...B-16
Havre de
Grace C-16
Hebron J-17
Hereford ...C-13
Highland E-12
Hillcrest
Heights G-12
Hollywood ...K-14
Hopewell ...M-17
Hughesville ...H-13
Hurlock H-17
Hyattsville ...F-12
Indian Head ..H-11
Jacksonville ..C-14
Jarrettsville ...C-14
Jessup E-13
Joppatowne ..D-15
Keedysville ...C-9
Kent
Kingstown ...E-16
Kitzmiller ...C-2
Kenton F-16
La Plata H-12
La Vale B-4
Lake Shore ...E-14
Laurel F-12
Lawsonia ...M-17
Laytonsville ...E-11
Leitersburg ...B-9
Leonardtown ..J-14
Lewistown ...C-10
Lexington
Heights D-2
Linkwood ...H-16
Linthicum ...E-13
Lisbon D-11
Loch Lynn
Heights D-2
Lochearn ...D-13
Lonaconing ...C-3
Long Green ...C-14
Long Beach ..J-14
Longwoods ...G-16
Lothian G-14
Lunenburg ...C-10
Lutherville ...D-14
Manchester ...C-12
Mardela Sprs. .J-17
Marbury H-11
Marion L-18
Marriottsville .D-12
Maryland
Line C-13
Marydel F-17
Mayo F-14
McKeys Beach ..J-13
Mechanicsville H-13
Melrose B-12
Middle River ..D-14
Middletown ...D-9
Midland C-3
Millington ...E-17
Montgomery
Vil. E-11
Morningside ..F-12
Mountain Lake Park D-2
Myersville ...C-9
Nanticoke ...K-17
New Carrollton F-12
New Market ..D-10
New Windsor ..C-11
Newcomb ...G-15
Nikep C-3
Normans F-15
N. Beach ...H-14
N. East C-16
Oakland D-12
Ocean City ...K-20
Ocean Pines ..K-20
Odenton ...F-13
Oella D-13
Olney E-12
Overlea D-14
Owings Mills ..D-13
Oxford G-16
Oxon Hill ...G-12
Park Hall ...K-14
Parkville ...D-14
Parsonsburg ..J-19
Perry Hall ...D-14
Perryman ...D-15
Perryville ...C-16
Pikesville ...D-13
Piney Point ..L-13
Pittsville J-19
Plainville ...K-14
Pleasant Lake ..D-15
Pleasant Hills .D-14
Pocomoke
City L-18
Point of Rocks .D-9
Pomokey ...H-12
Poolesville ...E-11
Port Deposit ..C-16
Port Republic .J-14
Potomac
Heights H-11
Potomac Park ..C-3
Preston H-17
Prince
Frederick ...J-14
Princess Anne ..L-18
Queen Anne ..F-16
Queenstown ..F-15
Quince
Orchard E-11

Randallstown ..D-13
Randle Cliff
Beach H-14
Rawlings ...C-4
Redland E-11
Reisterstown ..D-12
Ridgely F-17
Rising Sun ...B-16
Riviera Beach ..E-14
Rock Hall ...E-15
Rock Point ...K-13
Rockdale D-13
Rockville ...E-11
Rosaryville ...G-13
Rose Haven ...H-14
Rosedale D-14
Rossville ...D-14
Royal Oak ...G-15
St. Charles ...H-12
St. Clement
Shores K-13
St. Inigoes ...L-14
St. Marys
City L-14
St. Michaels ..G-15
Salisbury ...K-18
Sandgates ...J-14
Sandyville ...C-12
Savage E-13
Secretary ...H-16
Severn E-13
Severna Park ..F-14
Shady Side ...G-14
Sharpsburg ...C-8
Sharptown ...J-17
Silver Spr. ...F-12
Simpsonville ..E-12
Smithsburg ...B-9
Snow Hill ...L-19
Solomons ...K-14
Sparks C-13
Spr. Garden ..C-10
Stevensville ...F-15
Suderville ...K-17
Suitland F-12
Sunderland ...H-14
Sunnybrook ..C-14
Swanton C-2
Sykesville ...D-12
Taneytown ...B-11
Taylorsville ...C-12
Thurmont ...C-10
Timonium ...D-14
Tonytank ...K-18
Town Point ...B-16
Towson D-11
Trappe H-16
Union Bridge ..C-11
Upper
Marlboro ...G-13
Vienna J-17
Waldorf H-12
Walkersville ...C-10
Waterloo ...E-13
Webster C-15
W. Friendship .D-12
Westernport ..C-3
Westminster ..C-12
Westover ...L-18
Wheaton ...E-12
White Plains ..H-12
Whiteford ...B-15
Willards J-19
Williamsport ..C-8
Willows H-14
Woodfield ...E-11
Woodlawn ...M-18
Woodsboro ..C-10
Yellow Spr. ...C-10

MASSACHUSETTS
see map pages
53-54

Counties
Barnstable ...K-17
Berkshire ...D-2
Bristol J-15
Dukes M-17
Essex M-13
Franklin C-5
Hampden ...F-4
Hampshire ...E-4
Middlesex ...H-13
Nantucket ...N-19
Norfolk H-13
Plymouth ...H-15
Suffolk E-14
Worcester ...F-8

Cities and Towns
Abington ...G-15
Accord H-15
Acton G-12
Acushnet ...K-15
Adams B-3
Agawam ...G-4
Amesbury ...A-15
Amherst E-6
Andover G-13
Arlington ...F-13
Ashburnham ..C-8
Ashland G-12
Assinippi ...G-15
Assonet K-14
Athol C-7
Attleboro ...H-13
Auburn F-10
Ayer D-11
Baldwinville ..C-8
Ballardvale ...G-13
Barnstable ...K-18
Barre E-8
Bedford G-13
Belchertown ..E-7
Bellingham ...G-12
Belmont ...E-13
Berkley J-14
Bernardston ..B-6
Beverly G-14
Billerica G-13
Blackstone ...G-11
Bondsville ...E-7
Boston H-14
Bourne J-17
Boxborough ..D-12
Boxford D-14
Boylston ...E-9
Braintree ...G-14
Brant Rock ...H-16
Brewster J-19
Bridgewater ..H-15
Brimfield ...F-7
Brockton ...G-14
Brookfield ...F-8
Brookline ...H-13
Bryantville ...H-15
Buckland ...C-5
Burlington ...G-13
Buzzards Bay ..J-17
Byfield C-14
Cambridge ...E-14
Canton G-14
Carlisle G-13
Carver H-16
Centerville ...K-18
Chaffinville ...E-9
Charlton F-9
Chatham K-20
Charlton City ..F-9
Charlton Depot .F-9
Chartley H-13
Chatham K-20
Chelmsford ...G-12
Chelsea E-14
Chester E-3
Chicopee ...F-5
Chiltonville ...J-17
Clinton E-10
Cochituate ...G-12
Cohasset ...H-15
Colrain B-5
Concord G-13
Conway C-5
Cordaville ...G-11
Cotuit K-18
Cummington ..D-4
Cuttyhunk ...M-16
Dalton D-3
Danvers G-14
Dartmouth ...K-14
Dedham ...G-13
Deerfield ...C-5
Dennis J-19
Dennis Port ..K-19
Dighton J-14
Dorchester ...H-14
Douglas G-10
Dover G-13
Dracut F-12
Dudley G-9
Duxbury ...H-16
E. Blackstone ..G-11
E. Bridgewater .H-15
E. Brookfield ..F-9
E. Dennis ...J-19
E. Douglas ...G-10
E. Falmouth ..K-17
E. Freetown ..J-15
E. Harwich ...K-20
E. Long-
meadow G-5
E. Orleans ...J-20

E. Pepperell ..C-11
E. Sandwich ..J-17
E. Wareham ..J-16
Eastham J-20
Easthampton ..E-5
Edgartown ...M-17
Essex C-16
Fairhaven ...K-15
Fall River ...K-14
Falls C-5
Feeding Hills ..G-5
Fiskdale G-8
Fitchburg ...C-9
Five Corners ..J-14
Forestdale ...J-17
Foxboro G-13
Framingham ..G-12
Franklin G-12
Gardner C-8
Georgetown ..B-14
Gilbertville ...E-7
Gloucester ...C-16
Grafton F-11
Granby E-6
Great
Barrington ...F-2
Green Harbor ..G-16
Greenfield ...C-5
Groton D-11
Groveland ...B-14
Hadley E-6
Halifax G-15
Hanover G-15
Hanson H-15
Hardwick ...E-8
Harvard D-11
Harwich K-19
Harwich Port ..K-19
Hatfield D-5
Haverhill ...B-14
Haydenville ...E-5
Hingham ...G-15
Hinsdale ...D-3
Holbrook ...G-14
Holden E-9
Holland G-8
Holliston ...F-12
Holyoke F-5
Hopedale ...F-11
Hopkinton ...F-12
Hortonville ...J-13
Housatonic ...E-2
Hudson E-11
Hull G-15
Humarock ...H-16
Huntington ...F-4
Hyannis K-18
Hyde Park ...H-14
Ipswich B-15
Jefferson ...E-9
Kingston ...G-16
Lakeville ...H-15
Lancaster ...D-10
Lanesborough .D-2
Lawrence ...B-14
Lee E-2
Leicester ...F-9
Lenox D-2
Lenox Dale ...E-2
Leominster ...D-10
Leverett ...D-6
Lexington ...G-13
Littleton ...G-12
Longmeadow ..G-5
Lowell F-12
Ludlow F-6
Lunenburg ...C-10
Lynn E-15
Lynnfield ...F-14
Malden E-14
Manchaug ...G-10
Manchester-
by-the-Sea ..C-16
Manomet ...J-17
Mansfield ...H-13
Marblehead ..E-15
Marion K-16
Marlborough ..E-12
Marshfield ...H-16
Marshfield
Hills H-16
Marstons
Mills K-18
Mashpee ...K-18
Mattapoisett ..K-16
Maynard ...E-11
Medfield G-13
Medford E-14
Medway F-12
Melrose E-14
Mendon G-11
Merrimac ...A-14
Methuen ...B-13
Middleboro ...H-15
Middleton ...G-14
Milford F-12
Millbury F-10
Millers Falls ..C-6
Millis F-12
Millville G-11
Milton H-14
Monponsett ..H-15
Monroe C-4
Montague ...D-6
Monterey ...F-2
Monument
Beach J-17
Nahant E-15
Nantucket ...N-19
Natick G-13
Needham ...H-13
New Bedford ..K-15
Newburyport ..A-15
Newton H-13
Norfolk G-12
N. Adams ...B-3
N. Amherst ...D-6
N. Attleboro ..H-13
N. Billerica ...G-12
N. Brookfield ..E-8
N. Chatham ...J-20
N. Cohasset ..G-15
N. Dartmouth .K-14
N. Eastham ...J-20
N. Easton ...H-14
N. Falmouth ..J-17
N. Grafton ...F-11
N. Middleboro .H-15
N. Oxford ...F-9
N. Pembroke ..G-15
N. Plymouth ..H-16
N. Reading ...G-14
N. Swansea ...J-14
N. Uxbridge ..G-11
Northampton ..E-5
Northborough .E-11
Northbridge ..F-11
Northfield ...B-6
Norton H-13
Norwell G-15
Norwood ...G-13
Oak Bluffs ...L-17
Ocean Bluff ..H-16
Ocean Grove ..J-14
Onset J-16
Orange C-7
Orleans J-20
Osterville ...K-18
Otter River ...C-8
Oxford G-9
Palmer F-7
Paxton E-9
Peabody ...G-15
Pembroke ...G-15
Pepperell ...C-11
Pigeon Cove ..B-16
Pinehurst ...G-13
Pittsfield D-2
Plainville ...H-13
Pleasant Lake ..J-19
Plymouth ...H-16
Plympton ...H-15
Pocasset ...J-17
Provincetown ..H-18
Quincy H-14
Randolph ...G-14
Raynham ...H-14
Raynham Ctr. ..H-14
Reading G-13
Rehoboth ...J-13
Revere E-14
Rochester ...J-15
Rock H-15
Rockland ...G-15
Rockport ...B-16
Rowley B-15
Royalston ...B-7
Rutland E-9
Sagamore ...J-17
Salem E-15
Salisbury ...A-15

Sand Hills ...F-16
Sandwich ...J-17
Saugus D-14
Scituate ...H-16
Scotland ...H-14
Seekonk ...J-13
Sharon G-14
Sheffield ...G-2
Shelburne
Falls C-5
Sherborn ...F-12
Shirley C-11
Shrewsbury ...F-10
Silver Lake ...H-16
Silver Oak ...E-13
Sippewisset ..K-17
Somerset ...J-14
Somerville ...E-14
S. Acton ...G-12
S. Ashburnham C-8
S. Berlin ...E-11
S. Bridgewater H-15
S. Dartmouth ..K-15
S. Deerfield ...D-5
S. Dennis ...K-19
S. Duxbury ...G-16
S. Easton ...G-14
S. Hadley ...E-5
S. Hadley Falls .F-6
S. Lancaster ..D-10
S. Middleboro .J-15
S. Orleans ...J-20
S. Walpole ...G-13
S. Yarmouth ..K-19
Southborough .E-12
Southbridge ..G-5
Southwick ...G-4
Spencer F-9
Springfield ...G-6
Sterling D-10
Stockbridge ..E-2
Stoneham ...E-14
Stoughton ...G-14
Stow E-11
Sturbridge ...G-8
Sudbury E-12
Sunderland ...D-5
Sutton F-10
Swampscott ..D-15
Swansea ...J-14
Taunton H-14
Teaticket ...K-17
Templeton ...C-8
Tewksbury ...G-13
Texas E-9
Three Rivers ..F-7
Topsfield ...C-15
Townsend ...C-10
Townsend
Harbor C-11
Truro H-19
Turners Falls ..C-6
Upton F-11
Uxbridge G-11
Vineyard
Haven L-17
Wakefield ...F-14
Wales G-8
Walpole G-13
Waltham ...E-13
Ware E-7
Wareham ...J-16
Warren F-8
Watertown ...E-13
Wayland ...E-13
Webster G-9
Wellesley ...H-13
Wellfleet ...H-20
Wenham ...C-15
W. Boxford ...B-14
W. Bridgewater G-14
W. Brookfield ..F-8
W. Chelmsford C-12
W. Concord ...G-12
W. Dennis ...K-19
W. Falmouth ..K-17
W. Groton ...C-11
W. Newton ...H-13
W. Springfield .G-4
W. Stockbridge .E-1
W. Townsend ..B-10
W. Upton F-11
W. Warren ...F-8
W. Wareham ..J-16
Westborough ..E-11
Westfield ...G-4
Westminster ..C-8
Westport ...K-14
Westwood ...G-13
Weymouth ...G-15
White Horse
Beach H-17
White Island
Shores J-16
Whitinsville ...F-11
Whitman ...G-15
Wilbraham ...F-6
Williamsburg ..D-5
Williamstown ..B-3
Wilmington ...G-13
Winchendon ..B-8
Winchester ...E-14
Winthrop ...E-15
Woburn E-14
Woods Hole ..L-17
Worcester ...F-10
Wrentham ...G-12
Yarmouth Port K-18

MICHIGAN
see map pages
56-57

Counties
Alcona K-10
Alger D-4
Allegan R-5
Alpena J-10
Antrim J-7
Arenac M-10
Baraga C-2
Barry R-6
Bay N-10
Benzie K-5
Berrien U-3
Branch U-7
Calhoun ...S-7
Cass U-4
Charlevoix ...H-7
Cheboygan ...G-8
Chippewa ...D-9
Clare M-8
Clinton Q-9
Crawford ...K-8
Delta E-5
Dickinson ...D-3
Eaton R-8
Emmet G-7
Genesee ...P-10
Gladwin M-9
Gogebic ...B-9
Grand Traverse K-6
Gratiot P-8
Hillsdale ...U-8
Houghton ...C-1
Huron N-12
Ingham R-9
Ionia Q-7
Iosco L-10
Iron C-1
Isabella N-8
Jackson S-9
Kalamazoo ...S-5
Kalkaska ...K-7
Kent Q-6
Keweenaw ...A-2
Lake M-5
Lapeer P-11
Leelanau ...J-5
Lenawee ...U-9
Livingston ...R-10
Luce D-7
Mackinac ...E-7
Macomb ...Q-12
Manistee ...L-5
Marquette ...D-4
Mason M-5
Mecosta ...N-6
Menominee ...E-3
Midland N-9
Missaukee ...L-7
Monroe U-11
Montcalm ...P-7
Montmorency .J-9
Muskegon ...Q-4
Newaygo ...P-5
Oakland Q-11
Oceana P-4
Ogemaw ...L-9
Ontonagon ..B-10
Osceola M-6
Oscoda J-9
Otsego H-8
Ottawa R-4
Presque Isle ..H-9
Roscommon ..L-8
Saginaw P-9
St. Clair R-12
St. Joseph ...U-6
Sanilac P-12
Schoolcraft ...E-6
Shiawassee ...Q-9
Tuscola P-10
Van Buren ...S-4
Washtenaw ...S-10
Wayne T-11
Wexford L-6

Cities and Towns
Acme J-6
Addison U-10
Adrian U-9
Alanson G-7
Algonac S-13
Allegan R-6
Allendale ...R-4
Alma P-8
Alpena J-11
Ann Arbor ...T-10
Argentine ...R-10
Armada Q-12
Ashley O-8
Athens U-6
Atlanta J-9
Au Gres M-10
Au Sable ...L-11
Auburn N-9
Augusta S-6
Bad Axe ...N-12
Baldwin M-5
Bancroft ...R-9
Bangor S-4
Baraga B-12
Baroda U-3
Bath R-9
Battle Creek ..T-7
Bay City ...N-10
Beaverton ...M-9
Bedford T-6
Belding P-7
Bellaire J-7
Bellevue ...S-7
Benton Harbor T-4
Berrien Sprs. ..U-4
Bertrand ...U-4
Bessemer ...B-9
Big Rapids ...N-6
Birch Run ...Q-10
Birmingham ..S-11
Bloomingdale ..S-5
Boyne City ...H-7
Breckenridge ..P-8
Bridgeport ...P-10
Bridgman ...U-3
Brighton ...S-10
Britton T-10
Bronson ...U-7
Brooklyn ...T-9
Brown City ...P-12
Buchanan ...U-4
Buena Vista ..P-10
Burr Oak ...U-6
Burt P-10
Byron R-9
Cadillac ...L-7
Caledonia ...R-6
Calumet ...A-2
Capac Q-12
Carleton ...U-11
Caro P-11
Carrollton ...P-9
Carson City ...P-7
Carsonville ...P-12
Caseville ...N-12
Caspian C-1
Cass City ...P-11
Cassopolis ...U-5
Cedar City ...T-9
Cedar Sprs. ..Q-6
Cement City ..T-9
Central Lake ..J-7
Centreville ...U-6
Charlevoix ...H-7
Charlotte ...R-8
Chassell ...B-12
Cheboygan ...G-8
Chelsea S-9
Clare M-8
Climax S-6
Clinton T-10
Clio Q-10
Coldwater ...U-7
Coleman ...N-9
Coloma T-4
Colon U-6
Columbiaville .Q-11
Comstock ...S-5
Comstock Park Q-5
Concord T-8
Constantine ..U-5
Coopersville ..Q-5
Corunna ...R-9
Covert T-4
Croswell ...P-13
Crystal Falls ..C-1
Cutlerville ...R-6
Davison Q-10
De Witt Q-9
Dearborn ...T-11
Decatur T-5
Deckerville ...P-12
Deerfield ...U-10
Detroit T-12
Detroit Beach .U-11
Dexter T-10
Dimondale ...R-8
Dollar Bay ...B-12
Dorr R-6
Douglas R-4
Dowagiac ...T-4
Dryden Q-11
Durand R-10
Eagle River ...A-12
E. Jordan ...H-7
E. Lansing ...R-8
E. Tawas ...L-11
Eastlake M-5
Eaton Rapids ..R-8
Eau Claire ...U-4
Eckerman ...D-7
Edmore P-7
Edwardsburg ..U-5
Elberta K-4
Elk Rapids ...J-6
Elkton N-12
Elsie P-8
Escanaba ...F-4
Essexville ...N-10
Evart M-7
Fair Plain ...T-4
Fairgrove ...P-11
Farmington ..S-11
Farwell M-8
Fennville ...R-4
Fenton R-10
Ferndale ...S-11
Ferrysburg ...Q-4
Flat Rock ...T-11
Flint Q-10
Flushing ...Q-10
Fostoria P-11
Fowler Q-8
Fowlerville ...R-9
Frankenmuth ..P-10
Frankfort ...K-4
Franklin S-11
Fraser S-12
Freeland ...P-9
Fremont ...P-5
Fruitport ...Q-4
Gaastra C-1
Gagetown ...N-11
Galesburg ...S-6
Galien U-3
Garden City ...T-11
Gaylord J-8
Gibraltar ...T-12
Gladstone ...F-4
Gladwin M-9
Gobles S-5
Goodrich ...Q-11

Grand Blanc ..R-10
Grand Haven ..R-4
Grand Ledge ..R-8
Grand Rapids ..Q-6
Grandville ...R-5
Grant P-5
Grass Lake ...T-9
Grawn K-5
Grayling K-8
Greenville ...Q-6
Greilickville ...J-5
Grosse Pointe
Woods S-12
Gwinn E-4
Hamilton ...R-5
Hamtramck ...S-12
Hancock ...A-12
Harbor Beach .N-13
Harbor Sprs. ..G-7
Harrison ...M-7
Harrisville ...K-11
Hart P-4
Hartford T-4
Harvey D-4
Haslett R-9
Hastings ...R-7
Hemlock ...P-9
Hersey M-7
Hesperia ...P-5
Hillman J-9
Hillsdale ...U-8
Holland R-4
Holly R-11
Holt R-8
Holton P-4
Homer T-8
Hopkins R-6
Houghton ...B-12
Houghton Lake L-8
Howard City ..P-6
Howell R-9
Hubbell A-12
Hudson U-9
Hudsonville ...R-5
Huntington
Woods S-11
Imlay City ...Q-12
Indian River ..G-8
Inkster T-11
Ionia Q-7
Iron Mountain .D-2
Iron River ...C-1
Ironwood ...B-8
Ishpeming ...D-4
Ithaca P-8
Jackson S-9
Jenison R-5
Jonesville ...U-8
Kalamazoo ...S-5
Kaleva L-5
Kalkaska ...K-7
Kawkawlin ...N-10
Kent City ...Q-5
Kentwood ...R-6
Kinde N-12
Kingsford ...D-2
Kingsley ...K-6
L'Anse B-12
Lake City ...L-7
Lake Linden ..A-12
Lake Michigan
Beach T-4
Lake Odessa ..R-7
Lake Orion ...R-11
Lakeview ...P-7
Lakewood Club P-4
Lambertville ..U-10
Lansing R-8
Lapeer Q-11
Laurium ...A-2
Lawrence ...T-5
Lawton T-5
Leland J-5
Lennon R-10
Leslie S-9
Lexington ...P-13
Lincoln Park ..T-11
Linden R-10
Litchfield ...T-8
Livonia S-11
Lowell Q-6
Ludington ...M-4
Luna Pier ...U-11
Lyons Q-7
Mackinac Island F-8
Mackinaw City .F-8
Madison
Heights S-11
Mancelona ...J-7
Manchester ...T-10
Manistee ...L-5
Manistique ...E-6
Manitou Beach .U-9
Manton L-6
Maple City ...J-5
Maple Rapids ..Q-8
Marcellus ...T-5
Marine City ...S-13
Marion L-7
Marlette ...P-12
Marquette ...D-4
Marshall ...S-7
Marysville ...R-13
Mason R-8
Mattawan ...S-5
Mayville ...P-11
McBain L-7
Melvindale ...T-11
Memphis ...R-12
Mendon U-6
Menominee ...F-2
Merrill P-9
Mesick L-6
Metamora ...Q-11
Michiana ...U-3
Middleville ...R-6
Midland N-9
Mikado K-11
Milan T-10
Milford S-11
Millington ...P-11
Mio K-9
Mohawk ...A-2
Monroe U-11
Montague ...Q-4
Montgomery ..U-7
Montrose ...Q-10
Morenci U-9
Morley N-6
Morrice R-9
Mt. Clemens ..S-12
Mt. Morris ...Q-10
Mt. Pleasant ..N-8
Muir Q-7
Mullet Lake ...G-8
Munising ...D-5
Muskegon ...Q-4
Muskegon
Heights Q-4
Napoleon ...T-9
Nashville ...R-7
Negaunee ...D-4
New
Baltimore ...R-12
New Buffalo ..U-3
New Era ...P-4
New Lothrop ..Q-9
Newaygo ...P-5
Newberry ...D-6
Niles U-4
N. Adams ...U-8
N. Branch ...Q-11
N. Muskegon ..Q-4
Northport ...J-5
Northville ...S-11
Norton Shores .Q-4
Norway D-2
Novi S-11
Oak Park ...S-11
Okemos R-9
Olivet R-7
Onaway H-9
Onekama ...L-5
Onsted T-9
Ontonagon ..B-11
Orchard Lake ..S-11
Ortonville ...R-11
Oscoda L-11
Ossineke ...J-10
Otisville ...Q-11
Otsego R-6
Ovid Q-8
Owosso R-9
Oxford R-11
Palmer D-1
Parma T-8
Paw Paw ...S-5
Paw Paw Lake T-4
Pearl Beach ...S-13
Peck Q-12
Pellston G-7
Pentwater ...P-4
Perry R-9
Petersburg ...U-10
Petoskey ...G-7
Pewamo Q-7
Pigeon N-11
Pinckney ...R-10
Pinconning ...N-10
Plainwell ...R-6
Plymouth ...S-11
Pontiac R-11
Port Austin ...M-12
Port Hope ...N-13
Port Sanilac ..P-13
Portage R-5
Portland ...Q-7
Potterville ...R-8
Prudenville ...L-8
Quincy U-7
Ramsay B-8
Rapid River ...E-5
Reading U-8
Reed City ...M-6
Reese P-10
Richland ...S-6
Richmond ...R-12
Rives Jct. ...S-8
Rochester ...R-11
Rockford ...Q-6
Rockwood ...T-12
Rogers City ...H-9
Romeo R-12
Romulus ...T-11
Roosevelt Park .Q-4
Roscommon ..K-8
Rose City ...L-9
Royal Oak ...S-11
Saginaw P-9
St. Charles ...P-9
St. Clair ...R-12
St. Clair
Shores S-12
St. Helen ...L-8
St. Ignace ...F-8
St. Johns ...Q-8
St. Joseph ...T-3
St. Louis ...P-8
Saline T-10
Sandusky ...P-12
Saranac ...Q-7
Saugatuck ...R-4
Sault Ste.
Marie D-8
Schoolcraft ...S-5
Scottville ...M-4
Sebewaing ...N-11
Shelby P-4
Shepherd ...N-8
Shields P-9
Shoreham ...T-3
Sister Lakes ..T-4
Skidway Lake .L-9
S. Haven ...S-4
S. Lyon S-10
S. Monroe ...U-11
S. Range ...B-12
Southfield ...S-11
Spr. Lake ...Q-4
Springport ...S-8
Stambaugh ...C-1
Standish ...M-10
Stanton P-7
Stephenson ..E-3
Sterling M-9
Stevensville ..T-3
Stockbridge ..S-8
Sturgis U-6
Swartz Creek ..R-10
Tawas City ...L-11
Taylor T-11
Tecumseh ...T-10
Tekonsha ...T-7
Temperance ..U-11
Three Oaks ...U-3
Three Rivers ..U-6
Traverse City ..K-6
Trenton T-12
Trout Lake ...D-8
Troy S-11
Twin Lake ...Q-4
Ubly N-12
Union City ...U-7
Unionville ...N-11
Utica S-12
Vanderbilt ...H-8
Vandercook Lake T-9
Vassar P-10
Vermontville ..R-7
Vicksburg ...S-5
Wakefield ...B-9
Waldron U-8
Walkerville ...P-5
Warren S-12
Waterford ...R-11
Watervliet ...T-4
Wayland R-6
Wayne T-11
Webberville ...R-9
West Branch ..L-9
Westland ...T-11
Westphalia ...Q-8
White Cloud ..P-5
White Pigeon ..U-6
Whitehall ...Q-4
Whittemore ...L-10
Williamston ...R-9
Wolf Lake ...Q-4
Woodland ...R-7
Wyandotte ...T-12
Wyoming ...R-5
Yale R-12
Ypsilanti ...T-10
Zeeland ...R-5
Zilwaukee ...P-10

MINNESOTA
see map pages
60-61

Counties
Aitkin L-8
Anoka Q-8
Becker K-4
Beltrami ...F-5
Benton O-7
Big Stone ...P-2
Blue Earth ...U-7
Brown S-6
Carlton L-10
Carver R-7
Cass J-6
Chippewa ...Q-4
Chisago ...P-9
Clay K-2
Clearwater ...F-5
Cook F-12
Cottonwood ..U-4
Crow Wing ...L-6
Dakota R-8
Dodge U-9
Douglas ...N-4
Faribault ...V-7
Fillmore ...V-10

Freeborn ...V-9
Goodhue ...S-10
Grant M-3
Hennepin ...Q-8
Houston ...V-12
Hubbard ...H-5
Isanti P-8
Itasca G-8
Jackson V-4
Kanabec ...N-9
Kandiyohi ...Q-5
Kittson B-1
Koochiching ..E-8
Lac Qui Parle ..Q-2
Lake H-11
Lake of The
Woods C-5
Le Sueur ...S-8
Lincoln S-2
Lyon S-3
Mahnomen ...J-3
Marshall ...D-2
Martin V-6
McLeod R-6
Meeker Q-6
Mille Lacs ...N-8
Morrison ...M-7
Mower V-9
Murray U-3
Nicollet ...S-7
Nobles U-3
Norman J-2
Olmsted ...U-10
Otter Tail ...L-3
Pennington ...D-2
Pine M-10
Pipestone ...T-2
Polk E-2
Pope P-4
Ramsey Q-8
Red Lake ...E-3
Redwood ...S-4
Renville R-5
Rice S-8
Rock U-2
Roseau B-3
St. Louis ...G-10
Scott S-8
Sherburne ...P-7
Sibley S-6
Stearns O-5
Steele U-8
Stevens N-3
Swift O-3
Todd M-5
Traverse ...M-2
Wabasha ...T-11
Wadena ...L-4
Waseca U-8
Washington ..Q-9
Watonwan ...U-5
Wilkin L-2
Winona U-11
Wright P-7
Yellow Med. ...R-3

Cities and Towns
Ada J-2
Adams V-9
Adrian V-3
Aitkin L-8
Akeley H-5
Albany P-6
Albert Lea ...V-8
Albertville ...Q-7
Alden V-8
Alexandria ...N-4
Amboy U-7
Andover ...Q-8
Annandale ...Q-7
Anoka Q-8
Apple Valley ..R-8
Appleton ...P-3
Arden Hills ...Q-8
Argyle C-2
Arlington ...S-7
Ashby M-3
Atwater Q-5
Aurora H-11
Austin V-9
Avon P-6
Babbitt G-11
Bagley G-4
Balaton ...T-3
Barnesville ...L-2
Barrett N-3
Battle Lake ...M-3
Baudette ...C-6
Baxter L-6
Bayport ...Q-9
Belgrade ...P-5
Belle Plaine ...S-7
Bemidji G-5
Bena G-7
Benson P-4
Bertha L-4
Big Falls ...E-8
Big Lake ...Q-7
Bird Island ...R-5
Biwabik ...G-11
Blackduck ...F-6
Blaine Q-8
Blooming
Prairie U-9
Bloomington ..R-8
Blue Earth ...V-7
Borup J-2
Bovey H-9
Braham P-9
Brainerd ...L-7
Breckenridge ..L-2
Brewster ...U-4
Brooklyn
Center Q-8
Brooklyn Park .Q-8
Browerville ...M-5
Browns Valley ..M-2
Brownsdale ...V-9
Brownsville ...V-12
Brownton ...R-6
Buffalo Q-7
Buffalo Lake ..R-5
Buhl G-10
Burnsville ...R-8
Butterfield ...U-5
Byron U-10
Caledonia ...V-12
Cambridge ...P-8
Canby R-2
Cannon Falls ..S-9
Carlton L-10
Carver R-7
Cass Lake ...G-6
Center City ...P-9
Ceylon V-6
Champlin ...Q-8
Chanhassen ..R-7
Chaska R-7
Chatfield ...U-10
Chisago City ..P-9
Chisholm ...G-10
Chokio N-3
Circle Pines ...Q-8
Clara City ...R-4
Claremont ...U-9
Clarissa ...M-5
Clarkfield ...R-3
Clearbrook ...F-4
Clearwater ...P-7
Climax F-1
Cloquet L-10
Cokato Q-6
Cold Spr. ...P-6
Coleraine ...H-9
Cologne ...R-7
Columbia
Heights Q-8
Comfrey ...T-5
Cook F-10
Coon Rapids ..Q-8
Corcoran ...Q-7
Cosmos R-5
Cottage Grove Q-9
Cottonwood ..R-3
Crookston ...E-2
Crosby L-7
Crosslake ...K-7
Crystal Q-8
Currie U-3
Dassel Q-6
Dawson R-2
Deer River ...G-7
Deerwood ...L-7
Delano Q-7
Dennison ...T-9
Detroit Lakes ..K-3
Dilworth ...K-2
Dodge Ctr. ...U-9
Duluth K-11
Eagle Bend ...M-5
E. Bethel ...P-8
E. Grand Forks F-1
E. Gull Lake ..L-6

Eden Valley ...Q-6
Edgerton ...U-2
Edina R-8
Elbow Lake ...N-3
Elgin T-11
Elk River ...Q-8
Ellendale ...U-8
Ellsworth ...V-3
Elmore V-7
Ely G-11
Emily K-7
Esko K-10
Evansville ...N-4
Eveleth G-11
Eyota U-11
Fairfax S-6
Fairfax S-6
Fairmont ...V-6
Faribault ...T-9
Farmington ..S-8
Fergus Falls ...M-3
Fertile F-3
Floodwood ...J-10
Foley O-7
Forest Lake ...Q-9
Fosston ...F-3
Frazee K-4
Freeport ...P-6
Fridley Q-8
Fulda U-4
Gaylord S-7
Gibbon S-6
Gilbert G-11
Glencoe ...R-6
Glenville ...V-8
Glenwood ...P-4
Glyndon ...K-2
Good Thunder .U-7
Goodhue ...S-10
Goodview ...U-11
Graceville ...N-2
Grand Marais .F-12
Grand
Meadow ...V-10
Grand Rapids ..H-8
Granite Falls ..R-4
Greenbush ...B-3
Grove City ...Q-6
Hallock ...B-1
Halstad ...H-1
Ham Lake ...Q-8
Hamburg ...R-6
Hancock ...P-3
Hanska U-6
Harmony ...V-11
Hastings ...R-9
Hawley K-3
Hayfield ...U-10
Hayward ...V-9
Hector R-5
Henderson ...S-7
Hendricks ...S-2
Henning ...M-4
Herman N-3
Heron Lake ...U-4
Hibbing ...G-10
Hills V-2
Hinckley ...N-9
Hoffman ...N-3
Hokah V-12
Holdingford ...O-6
Houston V-12
Howard Lake ..Q-7
Hoyt Lakes ...G-11
Hugo Q-9
Hutchinson ...R-6
International
Falls C-8
Ironton L-7
Isanti P-8
Isle N-8
Ivanhoe ...S-2
Jackson U-5
Janesville ...U-8
Jasper U-2
Jordan S-7
Kandiyohi ...Q-5
Karlstad ...C-2
Kasota T-7
Kasson U-10
Keewatin ...G-10
Kenyon T-9
Kerkhoven ...Q-4
Kiester V-8
Kimball Q-6
La Crescent ...V-12
Lake Benton ..T-2
Lake City ...T-11
Lake Crystal ..U-6
Lake Park ...K-3
Lake Shore ...L-6
Lakefield ...U-5
Lakeville ...R-8
Lamberton ...T-4
Lanesboro ...V-11
Le Center ...T-8
Le Roy V-10
Le Sueur ...S-7
Le Ctr. T-8
Lester Prairie ..R-6
Lewiston ...U-11
Lindstrom ...P-9
Lino Lakes ...Q-8
Litchfield ...Q-6
Little Falls ...N-6
Little Fork ...D-8
Long Prairie ..M-5
Lonsdale ...S-8
Luverne ...U-2
Lyle V-9
Mabel V-11
Madelia ...U-6
Madison ...Q-2
Madison Lake ..U-7
Mahnomen ...J-3
Mahtomedi ...Q-9
Mankato ...U-7
Mantorville ...U-10
Maple Grove ..Q-8
Maple Lake ...Q-7
Mapleton ...U-7
Marine on St. Croix Q-9
Marshall ...S-3
Mazeppa ...T-10
McIntosh ...F-3
McGregor ...L-9
Melrose ...P-5
Menahga ...K-4
Mendota
Heights Q-8
Milaca O-8
Minneapolis ..Q-8
Minnesota Lake U-7
Minnetonka ...Q-8
Montevideo ...Q-3
Monticello ...Q-7
Montgomery ..S-8
Moorhead ...K-2
Moose Lake ..L-10
Mora O-9
Morgan S-5
Morris N-3
Morristown ...T-8
Motley L-5
Mountain Iron .G-10
Mtn. Lake ...U-5
Nashwauk ...G-10
New Brighton ..Q-8
New Prague ...S-8
New Richland ..U-8
New Ulm ...T-6
New York Mills L-4
Nicollet ...T-7
Nisswa L-6
Norwood ...R-7
Northfield ...S-8
Norwood ...R-7
Oak Park
Heights Q-9
Oakdale ...Q-9
Odin U-5
Ogilvie O-8
Oklee E-3
Olivia R-5
Onamia ...N-8
Ordway ...R-5
Orono Q-8
Orr E-10
Ortonville ...P-2
Osakis N-5
Oslo D-1
Osseo Q-8
Owatonna ...U-8
Park Rapids ..J-5
Parkers Prairie .M-4
Paynesville ...P-5
Pelican Rapids .L-3
Pequot Lakes ..K-7

Canaseraga P-8
Canastota L-15
Candor Q-13
Canisteo Q-9
Canton C-17
Cape Vincent E-13
Carmel U-23
Carthage F-16
Cassadaga P-2
Castile N-7
Castleton-on-Hudson N-23
Cato K-12
Catskill Q-22
Cattaraugus P-4
Cayuga L-12
Cayuga Heights P-13
Cazenovia L-15
Celoron Q-2
Ctr. Brunswick M-23
Ctr. Moriches X-27
Centereach W-26
Centerport W-25
Central Bridge M-21
Central Islip X-25
Central Square J-14
Central Valley U-22
Centre Island W-24
Champlain A-23
Chappaqua V-23
Charlton L-22
Chateaugay A-21
Chatham P-23
Chaumont F-14
Chazy A-23
Cheektowaga L-4
Chelsea T-22
Chenango Bridge Q-15
Cherry Creek P-3
Cherry Valley M-19
Chester U-21
Chestnut Ridge V-22
Chittenango L-15
Churchville K-8
Cincinnatus N-15
Circleville T-21
Clarence Ctr. L-5
Clarksville N-22
Claverack Q-23
Clayton E-14
Clayville L-17
Cleveland K-15
Clifton Park L-23
Clifton Sprs. L-10
Clinton L-17
Clintondale S-22
Clyde K-11
Cobleskill M-20
Cohocton N-9
Cohoes M-23
Cold Spr. U-22
Colden N-5
Colonie M-22
Columbiaville P-23
Commack X-25
Comstock H-24
Congers V-22
Conklin R-15
Constantia K-14
Cooperstown M-18
Copake Q-23
Copenhagen F-16
Copiague X-24
Coram W-26
Corfu L-6
Corinth K-22
Corning Q-11
Cornwall-on-Hudson U-22
Cortland N-14
Country Knolls L-22
Coxsackie P-22
Croghan F-17
Crompond U-22
Croton-on-Hudson V-22
Croton Falls U-23
Crown Heights T-22
Crown Point F-24
Cuba Q-6
Cuddebackville U-20
Cutchogue W-28
Dannemora B-22
Dansville N-8
De Ruyter M-15
De Witt L-14
Deer Park X-25
Delevan N-5
Delhi Q-18
Delmar N-22
Denton U-21
Depew L-5
Deposit R-17
Derby M-4
Dexter F-14
Dobbs Ferry W-23
Dolgeville K-19
Dover Plains S-24
Dryden P-13
Dundee N-11
Dunkirk N-2
Dwaar Kill T-21
Earlville M-16
E. Aurora M-5
E. Glenville L-22
E. Hampton W-29
E. Islip X-25
E. Ithaca P-13
E. Marion V-28
E. Meadow X-24
E. Middletown U-21
E. Moriches X-27
E. Northport W-25
E. Patchogue X-26
E. Quogue X-27
E. Randolph Q-4
E. Rochester K-9
E. Rockaway Y-23
E. Setauket W-25
E. Shoreham W-26
Eastchester W-23
Eastport X-27
Eatons Neck W-24
Eden N-4
Edenville V-21
Edwards D-17
Elba L-7
Elbridge L-13
Elizabethtown E-23
Ellenville S-21
Ellicott M-4
Ellicottville Q-5
Elma M-5
Elmira R-11
Elmira Heights Q-11
Elmont X-23
Elnora L-22
Endicott Q-14
Endwell Q-14
Evans Mills E-15
Fair Haven J-12
Fairmount L-14
Fairport K-9
Fairview S-22
Falconer Q-3
Fallsburg S-20
Farmers Mills T-23
Farmingville X-26
Fayetteville L-14
Firthcliffe U-22
Fishkill T-22
Fishkill Plains T-23
Flanders W-27
Florida U-21
Fonda L-20
Forestville N-3
Ft. Covington A-20
Ft. Edward J-23
Ft. Johnson L-21
Ft. Montgomery U-22
Ft. Plain L-19
Ft. Salonga W-25
Frankfort L-18
Franklinville P-5
Fredonia P-2
Freeport Y-24
Freeville N-13
Frewsburg R-3
Friendship Q-7
Fulton J-13
Fultonville L-20
Gang Mills Q-10
Gansevoort K-23
Gardnertown T-22
Gasport K-5
Gates K-8
Geneseo M-8
Geneva M-11
Ghent P-23
Glasco R-22
Glen Cove X-24
Glen Park F-15
Glenham T-22
Glens Falls J-23
Gloversville L-20
Godeffroy U-20
Golden Bridge U-23
Gorham M-10
Goshen U-21
Gouverneur D-16
Gowanda P-4
Granite Sprs. U-23
Granville J-24
Great Neck X-23
Greece K-8
Green Haven T-23
Greene P-15
Greenfield Ctr. K-22
Greenport V-28
Greenwich K-24
Greenwood Lake V-21
Groton N-13
Gurn Spr. K-23
Hadley J-22
Hagaman L-21
Hamburg M-4
Hamilton M-16
Hammondsport P-10
Hampton Bays W-28
Hancock R-17
Hannibal J-12
Harriman U-21
Harrison W-23
Harrisville E-17
Hauppauge X-25
Haverstraw V-22
Hawthorne V-23
Head of the Harbor W-25
Hempstead X-24
Henrietta L-9
Herkimer L-18
Heuvelton C-16
Hicksville X-24
High Falls S-21
Highland S-22
Highland Falls U-22
Highland Mills U-22
Hillburn V-21
Hillcrest V-22
Hillside Lake T-23
Hilton J-8
Holbrook X-26
Holland N-5
Holley K-7
Homer N-14
Honeoye M-9
Honeoye Falls L-9
Hoosick Falls L-24
Hopewell Jct. T-23
Hornell P-8
Horseheads Q-11
Houghton P-6
Howells U-20
Hudson Q-23
Hudson Falls J-23
Huguenot U-20
Huntington W-24
Huntington Bay W-24
Huntington Station X-24
Hurley R-22
Hyde Park S-22
Ilion L-18
Interlaken N-12
Inwood Y-23
Irondequoit K-8
Irvington W-23
Island Park Y-23
Ithaca P-13
Jamesport W-27
Jamestown Q-2
Jefferson Heights Q-22
Jeffersonville S-18
Jericho X-24
Johnson U-20
Johnson City Q-15
Johnstown L-20
Jordan L-13
Katonah U-23
Keeseville C-23
Kendall J-7
Kenmore L-4
Kerhonkson S-21
Kiamesha Lake S-20
Kinderhook P-23
Kings Park W-25
Kings Point X-23
Kingston R-22
Kiryas Joel U-21
Lackawanna M-4
Lacona H-14
Lagrangeville T-23
Lake Carmel T-23
Lake Erie Beach N-3
Lake George J-23
Lake Luzerne J-22
Lake Peekskill U-23
Lake Placid D-22
Lake Pleasant H-20
Lake View M-4
Lakewood Q-2
Lansing N-13
Lattingtown W-24
Laurel W-27
Lawrence Y-23
Le Roy L-7
Leeds P-22
Levittown X-24
Lewiston K-3
Liberty S-19
Lido Beach Y-24
Lima L-9
Lime Lake P-5
Limestone R-5
Lincolndale U-23
Lindenhurst X-24
Little Falls L-19
Little Valley Q-4
Livingston Manor R-19
Livonia M-8
Lloyd S-22
Lloyd Harbor W-24
Loch Sheldrake S-20
Lockport K-5
Locust Valley W-24
Long Beach Y-23
Loudonville M-23
Lowville G-16
Ludingtonville T-23
Ludlowville N-12
Lynbrook Y-23
Lyndonville J-6
Lyons L-11
Lyons Falls H-17
Macedon L-10
Machias P-5
Madrid B-17
Mahopac U-23
Maine Q-14
Malone B-20
Malta L-22
Mamaroneck W-23
Manchester L-10
Manhasset X-23
Manlius L-15
Mannsville G-14
Manorville W-27
Marathon P-14
Marcellus L-13
Margaretville Q-19
Marion K-10
Marlboro T-22
Massapequa Y-24
Massapequa Park Y-24
Massena A-18
Mastic X-26
Mastic Beach X-26
Mattituck W-28
Mattydale K-14
Maybrook T-21
Mayfield K-21
Mayville Q-1
McGraw N-14
Mechanicville L-23
Medford X-26
Medina K-6
Melrose M-23
Melrose Park L-12
Merrick Y-24
Mexico J-14
Middle Falls K-23
Middle Island W-26
Middleburgh N-21
Middleport K-5
Middletown U-20
Middleville K-18
Milford N-18
Millbrook S-23
Miller Place W-26
Millerton R-24
Millwood V-23
Milton T-22
Mineola X-23
Minetto J-13
Mineville E-23
Minoa L-14
Modena T-22
Mohawk L-18
Mohegan Lake U-23
Monroe U-21
Monsey V-22
Montauk V-30
Montgomery T-21
Monticello T-19
Montour Falls P-11
Montrose V-22
Mooers A-23
Moravia M-13
Morris N-17
Morrisonville B-23
Morristown C-16
Morrisville L-16
Mt. Ivy V-22
Mt. Kisco V-23
Mt. Morris M-8
Mt. Sinai W-26
Mt. Vernon M-4
Mt. Vernon W-23
Mumford L-8
Munnsville L-16
Munsons Corners N-14
Muttontown X-24
Myers Corner T-22
Nanuet V-22
Napanoch S-21
Naples N-9
Nassau N-23
Nedrow L-14
Nelliston L-19
Nelsonville U-22
Nesconset X-25
New Baltimore P-23
New Berlin N-17
New City V-22
New Hamburg T-22
New Hampton U-21
New Milford V-21
New Paltz S-22
New Rochelle W-23
New Windsor U-22
New York X-22
Newark L-10
Newark Valley Q-14
Newburgh T-22
Newfane J-5
Newfield P-12
Newport K-18
Niagara Falls K-3
Nichols R-13
Nissequogue W-25
Norfolk B-18
N. Bellport X-26
N. Boston M-4
N. Chili K-8
N. Collins N-4
N. Haven W-28
N. Hornell P-8
N. Rose K-11
N. Salem U-24
N. Sea W-28
N. Syracuse K-14
N. Tonawanda L-4
Northport W-25
Northville K-21
Norwich N-16
Norwood B-18
Noyack W-28
Nunda N-7
Nyack V-22
Oakdale X-25
Oakfield L-6
Oceanside Y-24
Odessa P-12
Ogdensburg B-16
Olcott J-5
Old Field W-25
Old Forge G-18
Olean Q-5
Oneida K-16
Oneonta P-18
Orange Lake T-22
Orangeburg W-22
Orchard Park M-4
Oriskany K-17
Oriskany Falls L-16
Oscawana Corners U-23
Ossining V-23
Oswego J-13
Otego P-17
Otisville U-20
Ovid N-11
Owego Q-14
Oxford P-16
Oyster Bay W-24
Painted Post Q-10
Palatine Bridge L-20
Palenville Q-22
Palmyra L-10
Panama Q-2
Parish J-14
Parishville C-19
Patchogue X-26
Patterson T-23
Pawling T-23
Peach Lake U-24
Pearl River W-22
Pecksville T-23
Peconic V-28
Peekskill U-22
Pelham W-23
Pelham Manor W-23
Penn Yan N-11
Perry M-7
Peru C-23
Phelps L-11
Philadelphia E-15
Philmont Q-23
Phoenix K-13
Pine Bush T-21
Pine Island U-20
Pine Plains R-23
Pine Valley Q-11
Pittsford L-9
Pittstown M-24
Plainview X-24
Plandome X-23
Plattekill T-22
Plattsburgh B-23
Pleasant Valley S-23
Pleasantdale M-23
Pleasantville V-23
Poestenkill M-23
Poland K-18
Pomona V-22
Port Byron L-12
Port Chester W-23
Port Ewen R-22
Port Henry E-23
Port Jefferson W-26
Port Jefferson Station W-26
Port Jervis U-19
Port Leyden H-17
Port Washington X-23
Porter Corners K-22
Portville R-6
Potsdam B-18
Pottersville G-22
Poughkeepsie S-22
Poughquag T-23
Pound Ridge V-24
Prattsburg N-10
Pulaski H-14
Purdys U-23
Putnam Lake T-24
Quogue X-27
Randolph Q-3
Ransomville K-4
Rapids K-5
Ravena N-22
Red Creek K-12
Red Hook R-22
Red Oaks Mill T-22
Remsen J-17
Rensselaer N-23
Rhinebeck R-22
Richburg R-7
Richfield Sprs. M-18
Richmondville N-20
Ridge W-26
Ridgebury U-20
Ripley Q-1
Riverhead W-27
Riverside W-27
Rochdale S-23
Rochester K-9
Rockland R-19
Rocky Point W-26
Rome K-16
Ronkonkoma X-25
Roscoe R-19
Rosendale S-22
Rotterdam M-22
Round Lake L-22
Rouses Point A-24
Rushville M-10
Rye W-23
Sackets Harbor F-14
Sag Harbor W-28
St. Andrew T-21
St. James W-25
St. Johnsville L-19
St. Regis Falls B-20
Salamanca Q-4
Salem K-24
Sand Ridge K-14
Sandy Creek H-14
Saranac Lake D-21
Saratoga Sprs. K-22
Saugerties Q-22
Sauquoit L-17
Savona P-10
Sayville X-26
Scarsdale W-23
Schaghticoke L-23
Schenectady M-22
Schoharie N-21
Schroon Lake G-22
Schuyler Falls C-23
Schuylerville K-23
Scotchtown T-21
Scotia M-22
Scottsville L-8
Sea Cliff X-23
Selden W-26
Selkirk N-23
Seneca Falls L-12
Sharon Sprs. M-19
Shelter Island V-28
Shelter Island Heights V-28
Sherburne N-16
Sherman Q-1
Sherrill L-16
Shinnecock Hills W-28
Shirley X-26
Shoreham W-26
Shortsville L-10
Shrub Oak U-23
Sidney P-17
Silters N-23
Silver Creek N-3
Silver Sprs. N-7
Sinclairville Q-2
Skaneateles L-13
Sleepy Hollow V-23
Sloatsburg V-21
Smithtown X-25
Sodus K-11
Sodus Point K-11
Somers U-23
Sound Beach W-26
S. Bethlehem N-22
S. Cairo P-22
S. Corning Q-11
S. Dayton P-3
S. Dover S-24
S. Fallsburg S-20
S. Hill P-13
S. Lockport K-5
Southampton W-28
Southold V-28
Southport R-11
Sparrow Bush U-19
Spencer Q-13
Spencerport K-8
Speonk X-27
Spr. Valley V-22
Sprs. W-29
Springville N-5
Springwater N-9
Staatsburg S-22
Stamford P-19
Stannards Q-7
Star Lake E-18
Sterling Forest V-21
Stillwater L-23
Stone Ridge S-21
Stony Brook W-25
Stony Point V-22
Stottville P-23
Suffern V-22
Sugar Loaf U-21
Summitville T-20
Sylvan Beach K-15
Sylvan Lake T-23
Syosset X-24
Syracuse L-14
Tannersville Q-21
Tappan W-22
Tarrytown V-23
Terryville W-26
Theresa E-15
Thiells V-22
Thornwood V-23
Ticonderoga F-24
Tillson S-22
Tivoli R-22
Tompkins Cove V-22
Tonawanda L-4
Town Line L-5
Tribes Hill L-21
Troy M-23
Trumansburg N-12
Tuckahoe W-28
Tully M-14
Tupper Lake E-20
Tuxedo Park V-21
Unadilla P-17
Union Sprs. M-12
Utica K-17
Vails Gate U-22
Valatie P-23
Valhalla V-23
Valley Cottage V-22
Valley Stream X-23
Van Etten Q-12
Vernon L-16
Verplanck V-22
Vestal R-14
Vestal Ctr. R-14
Victor L-9
Victory Mills K-23
Vil. Green K-13
Voorheesville N-22
Waddington B-17
Walden T-21
Wallkill T-21
Walton Q-18
Wampsville L-15
Wanakah M-4
Wappingers Falls T-22
Warrensburg H-22
Warsaw M-7
Warwick V-21
Washington Heights U-20
Washingtonville U-21
Water Mill W-28
Waterloo L-11
Watertown F-15
Waterville L-17
Watkins Glen P-11
Waverly R-12
Wayland N-9
Webster K-9
Weedsport L-12
Wellsburg R-12
Wellsville Q-7
Wesley Hills V-22
W. Babylon X-24
W. Carthage F-16
W. Chazy B-23
W. Elmira R-11
W. Glens Falls J-23
W. Hurley R-21
W. Islip X-25
W. Mahopac U-23
W. Sand Lake N-23
W. Sayville X-26
W. Seneca M-4
W. Winfield L-17
Westbrookville T-20
Westbury X-24
Westfield P-1
Westhampton X-27
Westhampton Beach X-27
Westmere M-22
Westons Mills R-6
Westport E-24
Westtown U-20
White Plains W-23
Whitehall H-24
Whitesboro K-17
Whitney Point P-15
Williamson K-10
Willsboro D-24
Wilson J-4
Wilton K-23
Windsor Q-16
Wingdale T-24
Witherbee E-23
Wolcott K-11
Woodbourne S-20
Woodinville T-23
Woodridge S-20
Woodstock R-21
Worcester N-19
Wurtsboro T-20
Wyoming M-7
Yaphank X-26
Yonkers W-22
Yorkshire N-5
Yorktown U-23
Yorktown Hts. V-23
Youngstown K-3
Zena R-22

NORTH CAROLINA

see map pages 82-83

Counties

Alamance D-9
Alexander D-4
Alleghany B-4
Anson H-6
Ashe B-3
Avery D-1
Beaufort F-16
Bertie C-16
Bladen J-11
Brunswick K-12
Buncombe L-6
Burke D-2
Cabarrus F-5
Caldwell C-2
Camden B-18
Carteret H-17
Caswell B-9
Catawba E-3
Chatham E-9
Cherokee M-2
Chowan C-17
Clay M-2
Cleveland F-2
Columbus K-12
Craven F-15
Cumberland H-11
Currituck B-18
Dare D-19
Davidson E-6
Davie D-5
Duplin H-13
Durham C-10
Edgecombe D-14
Forsyth C-6
Franklin D-12
Gaston F-3
Gates B-16
Graham M-2
Granville B-11
Greene E-14
Guilford C-8
Halifax C-14
Harnett F-10
Haywood L-4
Henderson M-6
Hertford B-15
Hoke G-9
Hyde E-18
Iredell D-4
Jackson M-4
Johnston F-12
Jones G-15
Lee F-9
Lenoir G-14
Lincoln F-4
Macon M-3
Madison K-6
Martin D-16
McDowell D-1
Mecklenburg G-5
Mitchell D-1
Montgomery F-7
Moore F-8
Nash D-13
New Hanover K-13
Northampton B-15
Onslow H-15
Orange D-9
Pamlico G-16
Pasquotank B-17
Pender J-13
Perquimans C-18
Person C-10
Pitt E-14
Polk F-1
Randolph E-7
Richmond G-8
Robeson H-10
Rockingham B-7
Rowan E-5
Rutherford E-1
Sampson G-12
Scotland H-8
Stanly F-6
Stokes B-6
Surry B-5
Swain L-3
Transylvania M-5
Tyrrell D-18
Union G-6
Vance C-11
Wake E-11
Warren B-13
Washington D-17
Watauga C-2
Wayne F-13
Wilkes C-4
Wilson E-13
Yadkin C-5
Yancey J-7

Cities and Towns

Aberdeen G-8
Ahoskie C-16
Albemarle F-6
Andrews M-2
Angier F-11
Apex E-10
Archdale D-7
Arlington C-4
Asheboro E-7
Asheville L-6
Atlantic Beach H-17
Aulander C-15
Avery Creek L-6
Ayden F-15
Badin F-6
Bakersville D-1
Balfour M-6
Banner Elk C-1
Bayboro G-16
Beaufort H-17
Belhaven E-17
Belmont F-4
Benson F-11
Bent Creek L-6
Bessemer City F-3
Bethel D-15
Bethlehem D-3
Beulaville H-14
Biltmore Forest L-6
Biscoe F-7
Black Mtn. L-6
Bladenboro J-11
Blowing Rock C-2
Boger City F-3
Boiling Spr. Lakes L-13
Boiling Sprs. F-2
Bolivia L-13
Bonnie Doone G-10
Boone C-2
Boonville C-5
Brevard M-5
Broadway F-10
Brogden F-13
Bryson City L-3
Buies Creek F-11
Burgaw J-13
Burlington C-8
Burnsville K-7
Butner C-11
Cajah Mtn. D-2
Calabash L-11
Camden B-18
Candor F-8
Canton L-5
Cape Carteret H-16
Carolina Beach L-13
Carrboro D-9
Carthage F-8
Cary D-10
Castle Hayne K-13
Chadbourn K-10
Chapel Hill D-10
Charlotte G-4
Cherryville F-3
China Grove E-5
Claremont E-3
Clarkton J-11
Clayton E-12
Clemmons D-6
Clinton G-12
Clyde L-5
Coats F-11
Columbia D-18
Columbus M-7
Concord F-5
Conover E-3
Conway B-15
Cooleemee D-5
Cornelius F-4
Creedmoor C-11
Cricket C-3
Cullowhee M-5
Currituck B-19
Dallas F-3
Danbury B-6
Davidson E-4
Denton E-7
Dobbins Heights H-8
Dobson B-5
Dortches D-13
Drexel E-2
Dunn F-11
Durham D-10
E. Flat Rock M-6
E. Rockingham H-8
E. Spencer E-6
Eastover G-10
Eden B-7
Edenton C-17
Elizabeth City B-18
Elizabethtown J-11
Elkin C-4
Ellerbe G-7
Elm City D-13
Emerald Isle H-16
Enfield C-14
Enochville E-5
Erwin F-11
Etowah M-6
Fair Bluff K-10
Fairmont J-9
Fairplains C-4
Fairview L-6
Farmville E-14
Fayetteville G-10
Flat Rock B-5
Fletcher L-6
Forest City F-1
Four Oaks F-12
Franklin M-4
Franklinton C-12
Fremont E-13
Fuquay-Varina E-10
Gamewell D-2
Garland H-12
Garner E-11
Garysburg B-14
Gaston B-14
Gastonia F-3
Gatesville B-16
Gibsonville C-8
Glen Raven C-8
Goldsboro F-13
Gorman D-10
Graham C-9
Granite Falls D-3
Granite Quarry E-6
Greensboro C-7
Greenville E-15
Grifton F-15
Half Moon H-14
Halifax B-14
Hamlet H-8
Harkers Island H-17
Harrisburg F-5
Havelock H-16
Haw River C-9
Hayesville N-2
Hays C-4
Hazelwood L-5
Henderson B-12
Hendersonville M-6
Hertford C-17
Hickory E-3
High Point D-7
Highlands N-4
Hillsborough C-9
Holly Sprs. E-10
Hope Mills G-10
Hudson D-3
Huntersville F-4
Icard E-3
Indian Trail G-5
Jackson B-14
Jacksonville H-15
James City G-16
Jamestown D-7
Jefferson B-3
Jonesville C-4
Kannapolis F-5
Kenansville G-13
Kenly E-13
Kernersville C-7
Kill Devil Hills C-20
King C-6
Kings Mtn. F-3
Kingstown F-2
Kinston F-14
Kitty Hawk C-19
Knightdale D-12
La Grange F-14
Lake Junaluska L-5
Lake Waccamaw K-11
Landis E-5
Laurel Park M-6
Laurinburg H-8
Leland K-13
Lenoir D-2
Lewiston Woodville C-15
Lewisville C-6
Lexington D-6
Liberty D-8
Lillington F-10
Lincolnton F-3
Locust F-6
Long Beach L-13
Long View E-3
Louisburg C-12
Lowell F-4
Lowesville F-4
Lucama E-13
Lumberton J-10
Madison B-7
Magnolia H-13
Maiden E-3
Manteo D-20
Mar-Mac F-13
Marion E-1
Mars Hill K-6
Marshall K-6
Marshville G-6
Masonboro K-13
Matthews G-5
Maxton H-9
Mayodan B-7
Maysville H-15
Mebane C-9
Middlesex D-12
Millers Creek C-3
Mint Hill G-5
Mocksville D-5
Monroe G-5
Mooresville E-4
Moravian Falls C-3
Morehead City H-17
Morganton E-2
Morrisville D-10
Mt. Airy B-5
Mt. Gilead G-7
Mt. Holly F-4
Mt. Olive G-13
Mt. Pleasant F-6
Mtn. Home M-6
Mulberry C-3
Murfreesboro B-15
Murphy M-2
Myrtle Grove K-13
Nags Head D-20
Nashville D-13
New Bern G-16
New Hope D-11
New Hope F-13
Newland C-1
Newport H-16
Newton E-3
Norlina B-12
N. Hickory D-3
N. Topsail Beach J-15
N. Wilkesboro C-4
Norwood G-6
Ogden K-14
Oriental G-17
Oxford C-11
Parkwood D-10
Pembroke H-9
Pilot Mtn. B-6
Pine Knoll Shores H-16
Pine Level E-12
Pinebluff G-8
Pinehurst G-8
Pinetops D-14
Pineville G-4
Piney Green H-15
Pittsboro E-9
Pleasant Garden D-8
Plymouth D-17
Polkville F-2
Princeton F-12
Princeville D-14
Pumpkin Ctr. H-15
Raeford G-9
Raleigh E-11
Ramseur E-8
Randleman D-7
Red Sprs. H-9
Reidsville B-8
Rich Square C-15
Richlands H-14
River Bend G-15
Roanoke Rapids B-14
Robbins F-8
Robbinsville M-2
Robersonville D-15
Rockingham H-7
Rockwell E-6
Rocky Mt. D-14
Rose Hill H-13
Roseboro G-11
Rowland J-9
Roxboro B-10
Royal Pines L-6
Rural Hall C-6
Rutherfordton F-1
St. Pauls H-10
St. Stephens E-3
Salem E-2
Salisbury E-5
Sanford F-9
Sawmills D-3
Saxapahaw D-9
Scotland Neck C-14
Seaboard B-14
Seagate K-13
Selma E-12
Seven Lakes F-8
Shallotte L-12
Sharpsburg D-13
Shelby F-2
Sherrills Ford E-4
Siler City E-8
Silver City G-9
Silver Lake K-13
Smithfield E-12
Sneads Ferry J-15
Snow Hill F-14
S. Gastonia G-3
S. Weldon B-14
Southern Pines G-9
Southern Shores C-19
Southport L-13
Sparta B-4
Spencer E-6
Spindale F-1
Spr. Hope D-12
Spr. Lake G-10
Spruce Pine D-1
Stallings G-5
Stanley F-4
Stantonsburg E-13
Star F-7
Statesville E-4
Stokesdale C-7
Stoneville B-7
Stony Point D-4
Summerfield C-7
Surf City J-14
Swannanoa L-6
Swanquarter F-18
Swansboro H-16
Swepsonville D-9
Sylva M-4
Tabor City K-10
Tarboro D-14
Taylorsville D-3
Thomasville D-7
Toast B-5
Tobaccoville C-6
Trent Woods G-15
Trenton G-15
Trinity D-7
Troutman E-4
Troy F-7
Tryon M-7
Valdese E-2
Vanceboro F-15
Vander G-10
Wadesboro G-7
Wake Forest D-11
Walkertown C-6
Wallace H-13
Walnut Cove C-6
Wanchese D-20
Warrenton B-12
Warsaw G-13
Washington E-16
Waxhaw H-5
Waynesville L-5
Weaverville K-6
Weddington G-5
Welcome D-6
Weldon B-14
Wendell E-12
Wentworth B-7
W. Jefferson B-3
Whispering Pines F-9
Whitakers C-14
White Plains B-5
Whiteville K-11
Wilkesboro C-4
Williamston D-16
Wilmington K-13
Wilson E-13
Windemere K-13
Windsor D-16
Wingate G-6
Winston-Salem C-6
Winterville E-15
Winton B-16
Woodfin L-6
Woodland B-15
Wrightsboro K-13
Wrightsville Beach K-14
Yadkinville C-5
Yanceyville B-9
Zebulon D-12

NORTH DAKOTA

see map page 85

Counties

Adams H-3
Barnes E-11
Benson C-8
Billings F-2
Bottineau B-6
Bowman H-1
Burke A-4
Burleigh E-7
Cass E-12
Cavalier A-9
Dickey G-10
Divide A-2
Dunn E-3
Eddy D-9
Emmons G-7
Foster D-9
Golden Valley E-1
Grand Forks D-11
Grant G-5
Griggs D-10
Hettinger G-3
Kidder E-8
La Moure G-10
Logan G-8
McHenry B-6
McIntosh H-8
McKenzie C-2
McLean D-5
Mercer E-4
Morton F-5
Mountrail C-4
Nelson C-10
Oliver E-5
Pembina B-11
Pierce C-7
Ramsey C-10
Ransom F-11
Renville A-5
Richland G-12
Rolette B-8
Sargent G-11
Sheridan D-7
Sioux G-6
Slope G-2
Stark F-3
Steele D-11
Stutsman E-9
Towner B-9
Traill E-12
Walsh B-11
Ward C-5
Wells D-8
Williams B-2

Cities and Towns

Abercrombie G-13
Adams B-10
Amidon G-2
Anamoose D-7
Aneta D-11
Arthur E-12
Ashley H-9
Beach F-1
Belcourt A-8
Belfield F-2
Berthold C-5
Beulah E-5
Bismarck F-6
Bottineau A-7
Bowbells A-4
Bowman G-2
Burlington C-5
Buxton D-12
Cando B-9
Cannon Ball G-7
Carrington E-9
Carson G-5
Casselton F-12
Cavalier A-11
Center E-5
Cooperstown D-10
Crosby A-2
Devils Lake C-9
Dickinson F-3
Drake C-7
Drayton B-12
Dunseith A-7
Edgeley G-10
Edinburg B-11
Edmore B-10
Elgin G-5
Ellendale H-10
Emerado C-12
Enderlin F-12
Fairmount H-13
Fargo F-13
Fessenden D-8
Finley D-11
Flasher G-6
Fordville C-11
Forman G-11
Fort Totten C-9
Fort Yates H-6
Gackle F-9
Garrison D-5
Gilby C-11
Glen Ullin F-5
Glenburn B-6
Golden Valley E-4
Grafton B-11
Grand Forks C-12
Granville C-6
Grenora B-1
Gwinner G-11
Halliday E-4
Hankinson H-12
Harvey D-8
Harwood E-12
Hatton D-11
Hazelton G-7
Hazen E-5
Hebron F-4
Hettinger H-3
Hillsboro E-12
Hoople B-11
Hope E-11
Horace F-12
Hunter E-12
Jamestown F-10
Kenmare B-4
Killdeer E-3
Kindred F-12
Kulm G-9
La Moure G-10
Lakewood Park C-9
Lakota C-10
Langdon B-10
Lansford B-5
Larimore C-11
Leeds C-8
Leonard F-12
Lidgerwood H-12
Lignite A-4
Lincoln F-6
Linton G-7
Lisbon G-11
Maddock C-8
Mandan F-6
Mandaree D-3
Manning E-3
Manvel C-12
Mapleton F-12
Max D-5
Mayville D-12
McClusky D-7
McVille D-10
Medina F-9
Medora F-2
Michigan C-10
Milnor G-12
Minnewaukan C-9
Minot C-5
Minto C-12
Mohall B-5
Mott G-4
Munich B-9
Napoleon G-8
Neche A-11
New England G-3
New Leipzig G-4
New Rockford D-9
New Salem F-5
New Town C-4
Northwood D-11
Oakes G-11
Page E-11
Park River B-11
Parshall C-4
Pembina A-12
Portland D-12
Powers Lake B-3
Ray B-3
Reeder H-3
Regent G-3
Reynolds D-12
Richardton F-4
Riverdale D-5
Rolette B-8
Rolla A-8
Rugby B-8
South Heart F-3
Sawyer C-6
Scranton G-3
Selfridge H-6
Sherwood A-5
Sheyenne D-9
Saint John A-8
Saint Thomas B-11
Stanley B-4
Stanton E-5
Steele F-8
Strasburg G-7
Surrey C-6
Tappen F-8
Thompson D-12
Tioga B-3
Towner B-7
Turtle Lake D-6
Underwood D-6
Valley City F-11
Velva C-6
West Fargo F-12
Wahpeton G-13
Walhalla A-11
Washburn E-6
Watford City D-2
Westhope A-6
White Shield D-5
Williston C-2
Willow City B-7
Wilton E-6
Wimbledon E-10
Wishek G-8
Wyndmere G-12
Zap E-4

OHIO

see map pages 86-89

Counties

Adams T-7
Allen H-4
Ashland H-12
Ashtabula D-18
Athens R-13
Auglaize K-4
Belmont M-17
Brown S-6
Butler Q-2
Carroll J-17
Champaign L-6
Clark N-6
Clermont R-4
Clinton Q-6
Columbiana J-18
Coshocton K-13
Crawford H-9
Cuyahoga F-14
Darke L-2
Defiance F-3
Delaware K-9
Erie F-11
Fairfield N-10
Fayette P-8
Franklin N-9
Fulton D-5
Gallia T-12
Geauga E-16
Greene P-6
Guernsey L-15
Hamilton R-2
Hancock H-6
Hardin J-6
Harrison L-17
Henry F-5
Highland S-7
Hocking Q-11
Holmes J-13
Huron G-11
Jackson S-11
Jefferson K-19
Knox K-11
Lake D-17
Lawrence U-11
Licking M-11
Logan K-6
Lorain F-13
Lucas D-6
Madison N-7
Mahoning G-18
Marion J-8
Medina G-13
Meigs S-13
Mercer J-2
Miami M-4
Monroe P-17
Montgomery P-3
Morgan P-14
Morrow J-10
Muskingum M-14
Noble N-16
Ottawa D-8
Paulding G-2
Perry N-12
Pickaway P-9
Pike S-9
Portage F-17
Preble P-2
Putnam G-5
Richland H-11
Ross R-8
Sandusky F-8
Scioto T-10
Seneca G-9
Shelby L-4
Stark H-16
Summit G-15
Trumbull E-18
Tuscarawas K-15
Union L-7
Van Wert H-3
Vinton R-11
Warren Q-4
Washington Q-15
Wayne H-14
Williams E-2
Wood F-7
Wyandot H-8

Cities and Towns

Aberdeen U-6
Ada H-6
Addyston R-2
Adelphi Q-10
Adena L-18
Akron G-15
Albany R-13
Alexandria M-11
Alger J-6
Alliance H-17
Amanda P-10
Amelia S-4
Amherst E-12
Amsterdam K-18
Andersonville Q-9
Andover D-19
Anna K-4
Ansonia L-2
Antwerp F-2
Apple Creek J-14
Aquilla E-17
Arcadia G-7
Arcanum M-3
Archbold E-4
Arlington H-7
Ashland H-12
Ashley K-9
Ashtabula C-18
Ashville P-9
Athens R-13
Attica G-10
Atwater G-17
Aurora F-16
Austintown G-19
Avon E-13
Avon Lake E-13
Bailey Lakes H-12
Bainbridge E-16
Bainbridge R-8
Ballville F-9
Baltic K-15
Baltimore N-11
Barberton G-15
Barnesville M-17
Barton M-18
Batavia S-4
Bay View E-10
Bay Vil. E-14
Beach City J-15
Beallsville N-17
Beavercreek P-5
Beaverdam H-5
Bedford E-15
Bellaire M-19
Bellbrook P-5
Belle Ctr. K-6
Bellefontaine L-6
Bellevue F-10
Bellville J-11
Belmont M-17
Beloit H-17
Belpre R-15
Berea F-14
Bergholz K-18
Berlin K-14
Berlin Heights F-11
Bethel S-5
Bethesda M-17
Bettsville F-8
Beverly Q-15
Bevis R-3
Blanchester R-5
Bloomdale G-7
Bloomingburg P-8
Bloomville G-9
Blue Ash R-3
Bluffton H-6
Boardman G-19
Bolivar J-16
Boston Heights F-15
Botkins K-4
Bowling Green E-7
Bradford M-3
Bradner F-7
Bremen P-12
Brewster J-15
Briarwood Beach G-14
Bridgetown R-2
Brilliant L-19
Brimfield G-16
Brookfield F-19
Brookside M-18
Brookville N-3
Brunswick F-14
Bryan E-3
Buchtel Q-13
Buckeye Lake N-11
Bucyrus H-9
Buffalo N-15
Burlington V-11
Burton E-17
Butler J-12
Byesville M-15
Cadiz L-18
Cairo H-5
Calcutta J-19
Caldwell P-15
Caledonia J-9
Cambridge M-15
Camden P-2
Campbell G-19
Canal Fulton H-15
Canal Winchester N-10
Canfield G-18
Canton H-16
Cardington K-10
Carey H-8
Carlisle P-4
Carroll N-11
Carrollton J-17
Castalia E-10
Catawba Island D-10
Cedarville P-6
Celina J-3
Centerburg L-10
Centerville P-4
Chagrin Falls E-16
Champion F-18
Chardon D-17
Chauncey Q-13
Cherry Grove S-4
Chesapeake V-12
Chesterland E-16
Cheviot R-2
Chickasaw K-3
Chillicothe R-9
Christiansburg M-5
Cincinnati S-3
Circleville P-9
Clarington N-18
Clarksburg Q-9
Clarksville Q-5
Clayton N-4
Cleveland E-15
Cleveland Heights E-15
Cleves R-2
Clinton H-15
Clyde F-9
Coal Grove V-11
Coalton S-11
Coldwater K-3
College Corner P-2
Columbiana H-19
Columbus M-9
Columbus Grove H-5
Commercial Point N-9
Conesville L-14
Conneaut C-19
Continental G-4
Convoy H-2
Coolville R-14
Copley G-15
Corning P-13
Cortland F-19
Coshocton L-14
Covington M-4
Craig Beach G-17
Crestline H-10
Creston G-14
Cridersville J-5
Crooksville N-13
Crown City U-12
Crystal Lakes N-5
Cuyahoga Falls G-15
Cygnet F-7
Dalton H-15
Danville K-12
Dayton N-4
De Graff L-5
Defiance F-4
DeForest F-18
Delaware L-9
Delphos H-4
Delta D-5
Dennison K-16
Deshler F-6
Devola Q-16
Dillonvale L-18
Dover K-16
Doylestown G-15
Dresden M-13
Drexel P-4
Dublin M-9
Duncan Falls N-14
Dunkirk H-7
E. Canton H-16
E. Cleveland E-15
E. Fultonham N-13
E. Liverpool J-19
E. Palestine H-19
E. Rochester J-17
E. Sparta J-16
Eastlake D-16
Eaton N-2
Eaton Estates F-13
Edgerton E-2
Edgewood C-18
Edison K-10
Edon E-2
Eldorado N-2
Elida H-4
Elmore E-8
Elyria F-13
Empire K-19
Englewood N-4
Enon N-5
Euclid D-15
Excello Q-3
Fairborn N-5
Fairfield Q-3
Fairlawn G-15
Fairport Harbor D-16
Farmersville P-3
Fayette D-4
Fayetteville R-5
Felicity T-5
Findlay G-7
Five Points P-4
Fletcher M-5
Flushing M-17
Forest H-7
Forest Park R-3
Forestville S-4
Ft. Jennings H-4
Ft. Loramie L-4
Ft. McKinley N-4
Ft. Recovery K-2
Ft. Shawnee J-5
Fostoria G-8
Frankfort Q-8
Franklin P-4
Franklin Furnace U-10
Frazeysburg M-13
Fredericksburg J-14
Fredericktown K-11
Freeport L-16
Fremont F-9
Gahanna M-10
Galena L-10
Galion J-10
Gallipolis T-13
Gambier K-12
Garfield Heights E-15
Geneva C-18
Geneva-on-the-Lake C-18
Genoa E-8
Georgetown T-5
Germantown P-4
Gettysburg M-3
Ghent G-15
Gibsonburg E-8
Girard G-19
Glandorf G-5
Glenmoor J-19
Gloria Glens Park G-14
Glouster Q-13
Gnadenhutten L-16
Grafton F-13
Grand Rapids E-6
Granville M-11
Gratis P-3
Green H-16
Green Camp K-8
Green Sprs. F-9
Greenfield R-8
Greenford H-18
Greentown H-16
Greenville M-2
Greenwich G-11
Grove City N-9
Groveport N-10
Grover Hill G-3
Hamden R-11
Hamersville T-5
Hamilton Q-3
Hamler F-5
Hanover M-12
Hanoverton J-18
Harbor Hills N-12
Harrison R-2
Harrod J-6
Hartford L-10
Hartville H-16
Harveysburg Q-5
Haskins E-6
Hayesville H-12
Heath M-12
Hebron M-11
Hicksville F-2
Hilliard M-9
Hillsboro R-7
Hiram F-17
Holgate F-5
Holland D-6
Holmesville J-14
Homeworth H-17
Hopedale L-18
Howard K-12
Hubbard G-19
Huber Heights N-5
Huber Ridge M-10
Hudson Vil. F-16
Huron E-11
Irondale J-19
Ironton V-11
Jackson S-11
Jackson Ctr. K-5
Jacksonville Q-13
Jamestown P-6
Jefferson D-18
Jeffersonville P-7
Jeromesville H-13
Jerry City F-7
Jewett K-17
Johnstown M-10
Jct. City P-12
Kalida G-4
Kent G-16
Kenton J-7
Kettering P-4
Killbuck K-13
Kingston Q-10
Kinsman E-19
Kirkersville M-11
Kirtland D-16
Kitts Hill U-11
La Croft J-19
La Rue J-8
Lafayette J-5
Lagrange F-13
Lakemore G-16
Lakeside E-10
Lakeview K-5
Lakewood E-14
Lancaster P-11
Laporte F-13
Laura M-3
Laurelville Q-10
Leavittsburg F-18
Lebanon Q-4
Leesburg R-7
Leetonia H-18
Leipsic G-5
Lewis Ctr. L-9
Lewisburg N-3
Lexington J-11
Liberty Ctr. E-5
Lima J-5
Lincoln Vil. N-9
Lindsey E-8
Lisbon H-18
Litchfield G-13
Lithopolis N-10
Lodi G-13
Logan Q-12
London N-7
Lorain E-13
Lordstown F-18
Lore City M-16
Loudonville J-12
Louisville H-16
Loveland R-4
Lowell Q-15
Lowellville G-19
Lucas J-12
Lucasville T-9
Luckey E-7
Lynchburg R-6
Lyons D-5
Macedonia F-15
Madison D-17
Madison-on-the-Lake C-17
Magnetic Sprs. L-8
Magnolia J-16
Malta P-14
Malvern J-17
Manchester U-7
Mansfield J-11
Mantua F-17
Maple Heights E-15
Marblehead E-10
Marengo K-10
Marietta Q-16
Marion J-9
Marshallville H-14
Martins Ferry M-19
Martinsville R-6
Marysville L-8
Mason Q-4
Massieville R-9
Massillon H-15
Maud Q-4
Maumee E-7
Mayfield Heights E-16
McArthur R-11
McClure F-5
McComb G-6
McConnelsville P-14
McDermott T-9
McDonald G-19
McGuffey J-6
Mechanicsburg M-7
Medina G-14
Mendon J-3
Mentor D-16
Mentor-on-the-Lake D-16
Metamora D-6
Miamisburg P-4
Middle Point H-3
Middlefield E-17
Middleport S-13
Middletown Q-3
Midvale K-16
Milan F-11
Milford R-4
Milford Ctr. L-7
Millbury E-8
Millersburg K-14
Millersport N-11
Millville Q-2
Mineral City J-16
Mineral Ridge G-18
Minerva J-17
Minerva Park M-9
Minford T-10
Mingo Jct. L-19
Minster K-4
Mogadore G-16
Monroe Q-4
Monroeville F-10
Montgomery R-4
Montpelier D-3
Moraine P-4
Morral J-8
Morrow Q-5
Mt. Blanchard H-7
Mt. Carmel S-4
Mt. Gilead K-10
Mt. Orab S-5
Mt. Pleasant L-18
Mt. Repose R-4
Mt. Sterling P-8
Mt. Vernon K-11
Mt. Victory K-7
Mowrystown S-6
Mulberry R-4
Munroe Falls G-16
Murray City Q-13
Nankin H-12
Napoleon E-5
Navarre J-15
Neapolis E-6
Neffs M-18
Nelsonville Q-12
Nevada H-9
New Albany M-10
New Athens L-17
New Boston T-9
New Bremen K-4
New Carlisle M-5
New Concord M-14
New Holland Q-8
New Knoxville K-4
New Lebanon N-3
New Lexington P-13
New London G-12
New Miami Q-3
New Middletown G-19
New Paris N-2
New Philadelphia K-16
New Richmond S-4
New Straitsville P-12
New Vienna R-6
New Washington H-10
New Waterford H-19
Newark M-12
Newcomerstown L-15
Newport Q-16
Newton Falls F-18
Newtonsville R-5
Niles F-18
N. Baltimore F-7
N. Bend R-2
N. Canton H-16
N. College Hill R-3
N. Fairfield G-11
N. Fork Vil. R-9
N. Hampton M-5
N. Industry J-16
N. Kingsville C-19
N. Lewisburg L-7
N. Lima H-19
N. Olmsted E-14
N. Perry C-17
N. Ridgeville E-13
N. Royalton F-14
Northfield F-15
Northridge M-6
Northridge N-4
Northwood D-7
Norton G-15
Norwalk F-11
Norwood R-3
Oak Harbor E-9
Oak Hill T-11
Oakwood G-4
Oakwood P-4
Oberlin F-12
Obetz N-9
Ohio City H-3
Oregon D-8
Orrville H-14
Orwell E-18
Ostrander L-8
Ottawa G-5
Ottawa Hills D-7
Ottoville H-4
Owensville S-4
Oxford Q-2
Painesville D-16
Pandora H-5
Parkman E-17
Parma E-14
Parma Heights F-15
Pataskala M-11
Paulding G-3
Payne G-2
Peebles S-7
Pemberville E-7
Peninsula F-15
Perry D-17
Perry Heights H-16
Perrysburg E-7
Perrysville J-12
Petersburg H-19
Phillipsburg N-3
Philo N-14
Pickerington N-10
Piketon S-9
Pioneer D-3
Piqua M-4
Pitsburg M-3
Plain City M-8
Pleasant City N-15
Pleasant Grove N-14
Pleasant Hill M-4
Pleasantville N-11
Plymouth G-11
Poland G-19
Pomeroy S-13
Port Clinton E-10
Port Jefferson L-5
Port Washington L-15
Portage F-7
Portsmouth U-9
Powell M-9
Powhatan Point N-18
Proctorville V-12
Prospect K-8
Quaker City M-16
Quincy L-5
Racine S-14
Ravenna G-16
Rawson H-6
Rayland L-19
Reading R-3
Red Lion Q-4
Reminderville F-16
Republic G-9
Reynoldsburg N-10
Richfield F-15
Richmond K-18
Richmond Dale R-10
Richmond Heights E-15
Richwood K-8
Ridgeway K-7
Rio Grande T-12
Ripley U-6
Risingsun F-8
Rittman G-14
Roaming Shores D-18
Rock Creek D-18
Rockbridge P-11
Rockford J-2
Rocky Ridge E-8
Rocky River E-14
Rosemount T-9
Roseville N-13
Ross R-2
Rossford D-7
Rudolph F-7
Rushsylvania K-7
Russells Point K-6
Russellville T-6
Russia L-3
Rutland S-13
Sabina Q-7
St. Clairsville M-18
St. Henry K-2
St. Louisville L-12
St. Marys K-4
St. Paris M-5
Salem H-18
Salineville J-18
Sandusky E-10
Sardinia S-6
Sardis P-18
Savannah H-12
Saybrook C-18
Scio K-17
Sciotodale T-10
Seaman T-7
Sebring H-17
Senecaville N-16
Seven Mile Q-3
Seville G-14
Shadyside M-19
Shaker Heights E-15
Sharonville R-3
Shawnee P-13
Shawnee Hills M-9
Sheffield E-13
Sheffield Lake E-13
Shelby H-11
Sherwood F-3
Shiloh N-4
Shiloh H-11
Shreve J-13
Sidney L-4
Silica D-6
Silver Lake G-16
Smithfield L-18
Smithville H-14
Solon E-16
Somerset N-12
S. Amherst F-12
S. Bloomfield P-9
S. Charleston N-7
S. Lebanon Q-4
S. Point V-11
S. Russell E-16
S. Solon P-7
S. Vienna N-7
S. Webster T-10
S. Zanesville N-13
Spencer G-13
Spencerville J-4
Spr. Valley P-5
Springboro P-4
Springdale R-3
Springfield N-6
Sterling H-14
Steubenville K-19
Stockport Q-14
Stony Ridge E-7
Stoutsville P-10
Stow G-16
Strasburg J-15
Streetsboro F-16
Strongsville F-14
Struthers G-19
Stryker E-4
Sugar Grove P-11
Sugarcreek K-15
Summit Station M-10
Sunbury L-10
Swanton D-6
Sycamore H-9
Sylvania D-6
Syracuse S-14
Tallmadge G-16
The Plains Q-13
Thornville N-12
Thurston N-11
Tiffin G-9
Tiltonsville L-19
Timberlake D-16
Tipp City M-4
Toledo D-7
Tontogany E-6
Toronto K-19
Tremont City M-6
Trenton Q-3
Trimble Q-13
Trotwood N-4
Troy M-4
Tuscarawas K-16
Twinsburg F-15
Tylersville Q-3
Uhrichsville K-16
Union N-4
Union City L-2
Uniontown H-16
Upper Arlington M-9
Upper Sandusky H-8
Urbana M-6
Utica L-12
Valley City F-14
Van Wert H-3
Vandalia N-4
Vanlue G-7
Vermilion E-12
Verona N-3
Versailles L-3
Vienna F-19
Wadsworth G-15
Wakeman F-12
Walbridge D-7
Wapakoneta J-4
Warren F-18
Warrensville Heights E-15
Warsaw L-13
Washington Court House Q-7
Washingtonville H-18
Waterford Q-15
Waterville E-6
Wauseon E-5
Waverly S-9
Wayne F-7
Wayne Lakes M-2
Waynesburg J-16
Waynesfield J-5
Waynesville Q-5
Wellington G-12
Wellston S-11
Wellsville J-19
W. Alexandria N-3
W. Carrollton City P-4
W. Farmington E-18
W. Jefferson N-8
W. Lafayette L-14
W. Liberty L-6
W. Manchester N-3
W. Mansfield K-7
W. Milton M-4
W. Portsmouth T-9
W. Salem G-13
W. Union T-7
W. Unity D-4
Westerville M-10
Westfield Ctr. G-14
Westlake E-14
Weston F-6
Wharton H-7
Wheelersburg U-10
White Oak R-3
Whitehouse E-6
Wickliffe D-15
Wilberforce P-6
Willard G-10
Williamsburg S-5
Williamsport P-9
Williston D-8
Willoughby D-16
Willoughby Hills D-16
Willowick D-15
Willshire J-2
Wilmington Q-6
Winchester T-6
Windham F-17
Winona H-18
Wintersville K-19
Woodbourne P-4
Woodsfield N-17
Woodville E-8
Wooster H-14
Worthington M-9
Wyoming R-3
Xenia P-5
Yellow Sprs. N-6
Yorkville M-19
Youngstown G-19
Zanesville N-13

OKLAHOMA

see map pages 90-91

Counties

Adair D-19
Alfalfa B-11
Atoka J-16
Beaver B-6
Beckham G-8
Blaine E-11
Bryan K-16
Caddo G-11
Canadian F-12
Carter J-13
Cherokee D-18
Choctaw K-17
Cimarron B-2
Cleveland G-13
Coal H-16
Comanche H-10
Cotton J-11
Craig B-18
Creek E-16
Custer E-9
Delaware C-19
Dewey E-10
Ellis D-8
Garfield C-12
Garvin H-13
Grady G-12
Grant B-12
Greer G-8
Harmon H-7
Harper B-8
Haskell F-18
Hughes G-16
Jackson H-8
Jefferson K-12
Johnston J-15
Kay B-14
Kingfisher E-12
Kiowa G-9
Latimer G-18
Le Flore H-19
Lincoln E-14
Logan E-14
Love K-14
Major D-10
Marshall K-14
Mayes C-18
McClain G-13
McCurtain J-19
McIntosh F-17
Murray H-14
Muskogee E-17
Noble C-14
Nowata B-17
Okfuskee F-15
Oklahoma E-13
Okmulgee E-17
Osage C-15
Ottawa B-19
Pawnee D-15
Payne D-14
Pittsburg H-17
Pontotoc H-15
Pottawatomie G-14
Pushmataha J-18
Roger Mills E-8
Rogers C-17
Seminole F-15
Sequoyah E-19
Stephens H-12
Texas B-4
Tillman J-10
Tulsa E-16
Wagoner D-17
Washington B-16
Washita F-10
Woods B-10
Woodward C-9

Cities and Towns

Achille K-16
Ada H-15
Adair C-18
Afton B-19
Alex G-12
Allen G-15
Altus H-9
Alva B-10
Anadarko G-11
Antlers J-17
Apache G-11
Arapaho F-10
Ardmore J-14
Arkoma F-20
Arnett D-8
Atoka J-16
Barnsdall C-16
Bartlesville B-16
Beaver B-6
Beggs E-16
Bethany F-13
Bethel Acres F-14
Billings C-13
Binger F-11
Bixby D-17
Blackwell B-13
Blair H-9
Blanchard G-13
Boise City B-2
Bokchito K-16
Boley F-15
Boswell K-17
Bray H-12
Bristow E-16
Broken Arrow D-17
Broken Bow K-19
Buffalo B-8
Burns Flat F-9
Byng H-15
Cache H-10
Caddo K-16
Calera K-16
Calumet F-12
Canton D-10
Canute F-9
Carnegie G-10
Carney E-14
Cement G-12
Central High H-12
Chandler E-14
Checotah F-18
Chelsea C-18
Cherokee B-11
Cheyenne E-8
Chickasha G-12
Choctaw F-14
Chouteau D-18
Claremore C-17
Clayton H-18
Cleveland D-15
Clinton F-10
Coalgate H-16
Colbert K-15
Colcord D-19
Collinsville C-17
Comanche J-12
Commerce B-19
Copan B-16
Cordell F-9
Corn F-10
Covington D-13
Coweta D-17
Cowlington F-19
Crescent E-13
Cushing D-15
Cyril G-11
Davenport E-15
Davis H-14
Depew E-15
Dewar F-17
Dewey B-16
Dickson J-14
Dill City F-9
Drumright D-15
Duncan J-12
Durant K-16
Earlsboro F-15
Edmond E-13
El Reno F-12

Eldorado J-8
Elgin H-11
Elk City F-8
Elmore City H-13
Enid C-12
Erick G-8
Eufaula F-17
Fair Oaks D-17
Fairfax C-15
Fairland B-19
Fairview D-11
Fletcher H-11
Forgan B-6
Ft. Cobb G-11
Ft. Gibson E-18
Ft. Towson K-18
Frederick J-9
Garber C-13
Geary E-11
Geronimo J-11
Glenpool D-16
Goldsby G-13
Goodwell C-4
Gore F-18
Grandfield J-10
Granite G-9
Grove C-19
Guthrie E-13
Guymon B-4
Haileyville G-17
Hall Park F-13
Hammon E-9
Harrah F-14
Hartshorne G-17
Haskell E-17
Healdton J-13
Heavener G-20
Helena C-11
Hennessey D-12
Henryetta F-16
Hinton F-11
Hobart G-9
Holdenville G-16
Hollis H-7
Hominy C-15
Hooker B-5
Howe G-19
Hugo K-18
Hulbert D-18
Hydro F-10
Idabel K-19
Inola D-17
Jay C-19
Jenks D-16
Jones F-14
Kansas D-19
Kellyville E-16
Keota F-19
Kiefer D-16
Kingfisher E-12
Kingston K-15
Kiowa H-17
Konawa G-15
Krebs G-17
Lahoma C-12
Langley C-18
Langston E-14
Latta H-15
Laverne B-7
Lawton H-11
Lexington G-13
Lindsay H-13
Locust Grove D-18
Lone Grove J-14
Lone Wolf G-9
Luther E-14
Madill K-15
Mangum G-8
Mannford D-16
Marietta K-14
Marlow H-12
Maud G-15
Maysville H-13
McAlester G-17
McLoud F-14
Medford B-12
Meeker F-14
Miami B-19
Midwest City F-13
Minco F-12
Moore F-13
Mooreland C-9
Morris E-17
Morrison D-14
Mounds E-16
Mtn. View G-10
Muldrow F-20
Muskogee E-18
Mustang F-13
Newcastle F-13
Newkirk B-14
Ninnekah G-12
Noble G-13
Norman G-13
N. Enid C-12
Nowata B-17
Oakhurst D-16
Oakland K-15
Oilton D-15
Okarche E-12
Okay E-18
Okeene D-11
Okemah F-16
Oklahoma City F-13
Okmulgee E-16
Olustee H-8
Oologah C-17
Owasso D-17
Panama G-19
Paoli H-14
Park Hill E-19
Pauls Valley H-14
Pawhuska B-16
Pawnee C-15
Perkins D-14
Perry D-13
Picher A-19
Piedmont E-12
Pink F-14
Pocola F-20
Ponca City B-14
Pond Creek C-12
Porter E-17
Porum F-18
Poteau G-19
Prague F-15
Pryor C-18
Purcell G-13
Quapaw B-19
Quinton G-18
Ramona C-16
Red Oak G-18
Ringling J-13
Roff H-15
Roland F-20
Rush Sprs. H-12
Ryan K-12
Salina C-18
Sallisaw F-19
Sand Sprs. D-16
Sapulpa D-16
Savanna H-17
Sayre F-8
Seiling D-10
Seminole F-15
Sentinel G-9
Shady Point G-19
Shattuck D-8
Shawnee F-14
Shidler B-15
Skiatook C-16
Slaughterville G-13
Snyder H-10
S. Coffeyville B-17
Spencer F-13
Sperry C-16
Spiro F-19
Sterling H-12
Stigler F-18
Stillwater D-14
Stilwell E-19
Stonewall H-15
Stratford H-14
Stroud E-15
Sulphur H-14
Tahlequah D-19
Talihina H-19
Taloga D-10
Tecumseh F-14
Temple J-11
Texhoma C-3
The Village F-13
Thomas E-10
Tipton J-9
Tishomingo J-15
Tonkawa C-13
Tryon E-14
Tulsa D-16
Turley D-16
Tuttle F-12
Tyrone B-5
Union City F-12
Valliant K-19
Velma J-13
Verden G-12
Vian F-19
Vici D-9
Vinita B-18
Wagoner D-18
Walters J-11
Warner F-18
Watonga E-11
Waukomis D-12
Waurika J-12
Wayne G-13
Waynoka C-10
Weatherford F-10
Webbers Falls F-18
Welch B-18
Weleetka F-16
Wellston E-14
W. Siloam Sprs. D-19
Westville D-20
Wetumka F-16
Wewoka G-15
Wilburton G-18
Wilson J-13
Wister G-19
Woodward C-9
Wright City K-19
Wynnewood H-14
Wynona C-16
Yale D-15
Yukon F-12

OREGON
see map pages 92-93

Counties
Baker E-15
Benton F-3
Clackamas D-5
Clatsop A-3
Columbia B-4
Coos J-2
Crook G-9
Curry L-1
Deschutes H-8
Douglas K-4
Gilliam C-9
Grant F-12
Harney K-12
Hood River C-7
Jackson M-4
Jefferson E-8
Josephine L-2
Klamath M-6
Lake K-9
Lane G-5
Lincoln E-2
Linn F-5
Malheur J-15
Marion D-4
Morrow C-11
Multnomah C-5
Polk E-3
Sherman C-9
Tillamook C-3
Umatilla C-12
Union D-14
Wallowa C-15
Wasco E-7
Washington C-3
Wheeler E-10
Yamhill D-3

Cities and Towns
Albany E-4
Aloha C-4
Altamont M-6
Amity D-4
Ashland M-4
Astoria A-3
Athena B-13
Aumsville E-4
Aurora D-4
Baker City E-14
Bandon K-1
Barview J-1
Bay City C-2
Beaverton C-4
Bend G-7
Boardman B-11
Boring C-5
Brookings N-1
Brownsville F-4
Bunker Hill J-1
Burns H-12
Canby D-5
Cannon Beach B-2
Canyon City F-12
Canyonville K-3
Carlton D-4
Cascade Locks C-6
Cave Jct. M-2
Central Point M-4
Chenoweth C-7
Chiloquin L-6
Clatskanie A-4
Coburg G-4
Columbia City B-4
Condon D-9
Coos Bay J-1
Coquille J-2
Cornelius C-4
Corvallis F-3
Cottage Grove H-4
Creswell G-4
Culver F-7
Dallas E-3
Dayton D-4
Depoe Bay E-2
Dexter G-4
Drain H-3
Dundee D-4
Dunes City G-2
Eagle Point L-4
Elgin C-14
Enterprise C-15
Estacada D-5
Eugene G-4
Fairview C-5
Falls City E-3
Florence G-2
Forest Grove C-4
Fossil E-9
Four Corners E-4
Garibaldi C-2
Gearhart B-2
Gervais D-4
Glendale L-3
Gold Beach M-1
Gold Hill M-4
Goshen G-4
Grants Pass M-3
Green K-3
Gresham C-5
Halsey F-4
Harbor N-1
Harrisburg F-4
Hayesville D-4
Heppner D-11
Hermiston B-11
Hillsboro C-4
Hines H-12
Hood River C-7
Hubbard D-4
Independence E-4
Irrigon B-11
Island City D-14
Jacksonville M-4
Jasper G-4
Jefferson E-4
John Day F-12
Joseph C-15
Jct. City G-4
Keizer D-4
Keno M-6
Klamath Falls M-6
La Grande D-14
Lafayette D-4
Lake Oswego C-5
Lakeside H-2
Lakeview M-9
Lebanon F-4
Lincoln Beach E-2
Lincoln City E-2
Lowell G-4
Lyons E-5
Madras F-8
Malin N-7
McMinnville D-4
Medford M-4
Merlin L-3
Merrill N-7
Mill City E-5
Millersburg E-4
Milton-Freewater B-13
Mission C-13
Molalla D-5
Monmouth E-4
Moro C-8
Mt. Angel D-4
Myrtle Creek K-3
Myrtle Point K-2
Neotsu D-2
Newberg D-4
Newport E-2
N. Albany E-4
N. Bend J-1
N. Plains C-4
Nyssa G-16
Oakland J-3
Oakridge H-5
Odell C-7
Ontario G-16
Oregon City D-5
Pacific City D-2
Pendleton C-12
Philomath F-3
Phoenix M-4
Pilot Rock C-12
Port Orford L-1
Portland C-5
Powers K-2
Prairie City F-13
Prineville F-8
Rainier B-4
Redmond G-8
Reedsport H-2
Riddle K-3
Rockaway Beach C-2
Rogue River L-3
Rose Lodge D-2
Roseburg J-3
Ruch M-4
St. Helens B-4
Salem E-4
Sandy C-5
Santa Clara G-4
Scappoose B-4
Scio E-4
Seaside B-2
Shady Cove L-4
Sheridan D-3
Sherwood C-4
Siletz E-2
Silverton D-4
Sisters F-7
Springfield G-4
Stanfield B-12
Stayton E-4
Sublimity E-4
Sutherlin J-3
Sweet Home F-4
Talent M-4
Terrebonne F-8
The Dalles C-8
Tigard C-4
Tillamook C-2
Toledo E-2
Tri City K-3
Troutdale C-5
Tualatin C-4
Turner E-4
Umatilla B-11
Union D-14
Vale G-16
Veneta G-3
Vernonia B-4
Waldport F-2
Wallowa C-15
Warm Sprs. E-7
Warrenton A-2
W. Linn C-5
Weston B-13
White City M-4
Willamina D-3
Wilsonville D-4
Winston K-3
Woodburn D-4
Yamhill D-4
Yoncalla H-3

PENNSYLVANIA
see map pages 94-97

Counties
Adams R-15
Allegheny M-4
Armstrong M-5
Beaver M-1
Bedford Q-9
Berks N-19
Blair N-10
Bradford F-17
Bucks N-23
Butler L-4
Cambria M-8
Cameron H-10
Carbon K-21
Centre L-11
Chester R-22
Clarion H-5
Clearfield J-10
Clinton H-12
Columbia J-18
Crawford F-4
Cumberland Q-14
Dauphin N-16
Delaware R-22
Elk H-9
Erie D-3
Fayette R-5
Forest G-6
Franklin R-12
Fulton R-11
Greene S-2
Huntingdon M-11
Indiana L-7
Jefferson H-7
Juniata P-13
Lackawanna H-21
Lancaster R-19
Lawrence K-2
Lebanon N-18
Lehigh M-21
Luzerne J-19
Lycoming H-16
Mercer H-2
Mifflin N-12
Monroe J-22
Montgomery P-22
Montour K-17
McKean F-9
Northampton L-22
Northumberland L-16
Perry N-14
Philadelphia Q-23
Pike H-24
Potter F-12
Schuylkill M-18
Snyder L-15
Somerset R-7
Sullivan H-18
Susquehanna E-20
Tioga E-14
Union K-15
Venango H-4
Warren F-6
Washington P-2
Wayne F-22
Westmoreland P-6
Wyoming G-19
York R-16

Cities and Towns
Abbottstown R-16
Adamstown P-19
Akron Q-19
Albion E-2
Alburtis N-21
Alexandria N-11
Aliquippa M-2
Allensville N-12
Allentown M-22
Almedia K-18
Altoona N-10
Ambler Q-23
Ambridge M-2
Anita K-7
Annville P-17
Apollo M-5
Applewold L-5
Archbald G-21
Ardmore R-23
Arendtsville R-14
Arnold M-4
Arona P-5
Ashland L-18
Ashley J-20
Aspers R-15
Atglen R-20
Athens E-17
Auburn M-19
Austin F-11
Avalon N-3
Avella P-1
Avis J-14
Avon P-18
Avondale S-21
Avonia D-2
Avonmore N-5
Baden M-2
Bally N-21
Bangor L-23
Bareville Q-19
Barnesboro M-8
Bath L-22
Beach Lake F-23
Beallsville Q-3
Beaver M-2
Beaver Falls L-2
Beaver Meadows K-20
Beaverdale P-9
Beavertown L-15
Bechtelsville N-21
Bedford R-9
Beech Creek K-13
Belfast L-23
Belle Vernon Q-4
Bellefonte L-12
Belleville M-12
Bellevue N-3
Bellwood M-10
Bendersville R-14
Bentleyville Q-3
Benton J-18
Berlin R-7
Bernville N-19
Berrysburg M-16
Berwick K-19
Berwyn Q-22
Bessemer K-1
Bethel N-18
Bethel Park P-3
Bethlehem M-22
Big Beaver L-2
Big Run K-8
Biglerville R-14
Birdsboro P-20
Black Lick N-6
Blairsville N-6
Blakely G-21
Blakeslee J-21
Blanchard K-13
Blooming Valley F-3
Bloomsburg K-18
Blossburg F-15
Blue Ridge Summit S-14
Boalsburg L-12
Bobtown S-3
Boiling Sprs. Q-15
Bolivar N-7
Bonneauville S-15
Boswell Q-7
Bowmanstown L-21
Boyertown P-21
Brackenridge M-4
Bradford E-9
Bradford Woods M-3
Briar Creek K-18
Brickerville P-18
Bridgeville P-3
Bristol Q-24
Brittany Farms P-23
Brockport J-8
Brockway J-8
Brodheadsville K-22
Brookside H-14
Brookville J-7
Brownstown Q-19
Brownsville Q-3
Bruin K-4
Bryn Mawr Q-23
Buckingham P-24
Burgettstown N-1
Burlington E-17
Burnham M-13
Butler L-4
California Q-4
Callery L-3
Cambridge Sprs. E-3
Camp Hill P-16
Campbelltown P-17
Canadensis J-23
Canonsburg P-2
Canton F-16
Carbondale G-22
Carlisle P-15
Carmichaels R-3
Carroll Valley S-14
Carrolltown M-8
Castanea J-14
Catasauqua M-22
Catawissa K-18
Cecil P-2
Centerville Q-3
Central City Q-8
Centre Hall L-13
Chalfont P-23
Chambersburg R-13
Charleroi Q-3
Chatwood R-21
Cherry Tree M-8
Chester R-22
Chester Heights R-22
Chester Hill L-10
Chicora K-4
Christiana R-20
Clairton P-4
Clarendon F-7
Clarion J-6
Clark H-1
Clarks Summit G-21
Claysburg P-9
Claysville Q-1
Clearfield K-10
Cleona P-18
Clintonville J-4
Clymer M-7
Coaldale L-20
Coalport L-9
Coatesville R-20
Cochranton G-3
Cokeburg Q-3
Collegeville Q-22
Columbia R-18
Columbus E-5
Colver N-8
Confluence S-6
Conneaut Lake F-2
Conneaut Lake Park F-2
Conneautville F-2
Connellsville R-5
Connoquenessing L-3
Conway M-2
Conyngham K-19
Coopersburg N-22
Cooperstown G-4
Coraopolis N-2
Cornwall P-18
Corry E-5
Coudersport F-11
Cranesville E-2
Cresson N-9
Cressona M-19
Curtisville M-4
Curwensville K-9
Dale N-21
Dallas H-20
Dallastown R-17
Dalton G-21
Danville K-17
Darby R-23
Dauphin P-16
Davidsville P-7
Dawson Q-4
Dayton L-6
Deemston Q-3
Deer Lake M-19
Delaware Water Gap K-23
Delmont N-5
Delta S-18
Denver P-19
Derry P-6
Dickson City G-21
Dillsburg Q-15
Donora Q-4
Dover R-16
Downingtown R-21
Doylestown P-23
Drifton K-20
Dublin N-23
DuBois J-8
Duboistown J-15
Dunbar R-5
Duncannon N-15
Duncansville N-10
Dunmore H-21
Dunnstown J-14
Duryea H-20
Dushore G-18
Eagleville Q-22
E. Bangor L-23
E. Berlin R-16
E. Brady K-5
E. Butler L-4
E. Greenville N-22
E. Petersburg Q-18
E. Prospect R-18
E. Stroudsburg K-23
E. Uniontown R-4
E. Vandergrift M-5
Easton M-23
Ebensburg N-8
Economy M-2
Edgewood L-17
Edgeworth M-2
Edinboro E-3
Elco Q-4
Eldred E-10
Elizabethtown Q-17
Elizabethville N-16
Elkland D-14
Ellport L-2
Ellsworth Q-3
Ellwood City L-2
Elverson Q-20
Elysburg L-17
Emigsville R-17
Emlenton J-4
Emmaus N-22
Emporium G-11
Enola P-16
Ephrata Q-19
Erie C-3
Ernest M-7
Espy K-18
Etna N-3
Evans City L-3
Everett R-10
Everson Q-5
Export N-5
Exton Q-21
Factoryville G-20
Fairbrook M-12
Fairchance S-4
Fairdale R-3
Fairfield S-14
Fairless Hills Q-24
Fairview L-17
Fairview D-2
Falls G-20
Falls Creek J-8
Farmington S-5
Farrell J-1
Fawn Grove S-18
Fayette City Q-4
Fayetteville R-13
Felton R-17
Ferndale U-1
Finleyville P-3
Fisher H-6
Fleetwood N-20
Flemington J-14
Flying Hills P-20
Fogelsville M-21
Ford City L-5
Ford Cliff L-5
Forest City F-22
Forest Grove N-3
Ft. Loudon R-12
Fountain Hill M-22
Frackville L-19
Franklin T-2
Franklin Park M-3
Franklintown Q-15
Fredericksburg F-3
Fredericksburg N-18
Fredonia H-2
Fredricktown R-3
Freeburg L-16
Freedom M-2
Freeland K-20
Freemansburg M-22
Freeport M-4
Friedens Q-7
Galeton F-13
Gallitzin N-9
Gap R-20
Garden View H-15
Garrett R-7
Geistown P-8
Genesee D-12
Gettysburg S-15
Gilberton L-19
Gilbertsville P-21
Girard D-2
Girardville L-18
Glassport P-4
Glen Lyon J-19
Glen Rock S-17
Glenburn G-21
Glendon M-23
Glenolden R-23
Glenside Q-23
Goldsboro Q-17
Gordon L-18
Grampian K-9
Grantville P-17
Grassflat K-11
Gratz M-17
Great Bend D-20
Green Lane P-22
Greencastle S-12
Greensburg P-5
Greenville H-2
Grove City J-3
Halifax N-16
Hallam R-17
Hallstead D-20
Hamburg M-20
Hanover S-16
Harleysville P-22
Harmony L-3
Harrisburg P-16
Harrisville J-3
Harveys Lake H-19
Hastings M-8
Hatfield P-22
Hawley G-23
Hawthorn K-6
Hazleton K-20
Hellertown M-22
Hermitage J-1
Herndon M-16
Hershey P-17
Hiller R-3
Hollidaysburg N-10
Homer City N-7
Hometown L-20
Honesdale G-23
Honey Brook Q-20
Hooversville Q-8
Hopwood R-4
Horsham P-23
Houston P-2
Houtzdale L-10
Howard K-13
Hughesville J-17
Hulmeville Q-24
Hummels Wharf L-16
Hummelstown P-17
Huntingdon N-11
Hyde K-9
Hydetown F-4
Hyndman S-8
Imperial N-2
Indian Lake R-8
Indiana M-7
Industry M-1
Irvona L-9
Irwin P-4
Jacobus R-17
Jamestown G-2
Jeannette P-5
Jefferson S-16
Jefferson P-3
Jenkintown Q-23
Jenners Q-7
Jennerstown Q-7
Jermyn G-21
Jerome Q-7
Jersey Shore J-14
Jim Thorpe L-21
Johnsonburg G-9
Johnstown P-8
Jonestown N-18
Juniata Terrace M-13
Kane F-8
Kenilworth P-21
Kennett Square R-21
Kersey H-9
King of Prussia Q-22
Kingston H-20
Kittanning L-5
Knox J-5
Knoxville E-14
Koppel L-2
Kulpmont L-18
Kulpsville P-22
Kunkletown L-22
Kutztown N-21
Laceyville F-19
Lake Ariel G-22
Lake City D-2
Lakemont N-10
Lamar K-13
Lancaster Q-18
Landisville Q-18
Lanesboro E-21
Langhorne P-24
Lansdale P-23
Lansdowne R-23
Lansford L-20
Laporte H-17
Latrobe P-6
Laurel Run J-20
Laureldale N-20
Laurelton L-15
Lawrenceville D-15
Leacock Q-19
Lebanon P-18
Leechburg M-5
Leesport N-20
Lehighton L-21
Leola Q-19
Levittown Q-24
Lewis Run E-9
Lewisburg K-16
Lewistown M-13
Library P-3
Ligonier P-6
Lilly N-9
Lime Ridge K-18
Linesville F-2
Linglestown P-16
Linntown K-16
Lionville Q-21
Lititz Q-18
Littlestown S-15
Liverpool M-15
Lloydell P-9
Lock Haven J-14
Loganton K-14
Loganville S-17
Lorane P-20
Loretto N-9
Loyalhanna P-6
Loysville P-14
Lucernemines M-7
Lucinda H-6
Lykens M-17
Lyndora L-3
Lynnwood Q-4
Lyons N-21
Macungie N-21
Madera L-10
Madison P-4
Mahanoy City L-19
Malvern Q-22
Manchester Q-17
Manheim Q-18
Manorville L-5
Mansfield E-15
Mapleton N-12
Marcus Hook S-22
Marianna Q-3
Marietta Q-17
Marion S-13
Marion Ctr. L-7
Marion Heights L-18
Mars M-3
Marshallton L-17
Martins Creek L-23
Martinsburg P-10
Marysville P-16
Masontown R-3
Matamoras H-25
Mather R-3
Mausdale K-17
Mayfield G-21
Maytown Q-17
McAdoo K-20
McAlisterville M-14
McCandless M-3
McClure M-14
McConnellsburg R-11
McDonald N-2
McKean D-3
McKees Rocks N-3
McKeesport P-4
McMurray P-3
McSherrystown S-15
McVeytown N-12
Meadville F-3
Mechanicsburg P-15
Mechanicsville K-17
Mechanicsville M-19
Media R-22
Mercer J-2
Mercersburg S-12
Meridian L-3
Meshoppen F-19
Meyersdale S-7
Middleburg L-15
Middleport L-19
Middletown Q-17
Midland M-1
Midway N-2
Mifflin M-14
Mifflinburg K-15
Mifflintown M-14
Mifflinville K-18
Mildred G-18
Milesburg K-12
Milford H-24
Mill Creek N-12
Mill Hall J-13
Mill Vil. E-3
Millersburg N-16
Millerstown N-15
Millersville R-18
Millsboro R-3
Millville J-17
Milroy M-13
Milton K-16
Minersville M-18
Mocanaqua J-19
Modena R-21
Mohnton P-20
Monaca M-2
Monessen Q-3
Monongahela P-3
Monroeton F-18
Monroeville N-4
Mont Alto S-13
Montgomery J-16
Montgomeryville P-23
Montoursville J-16
Montrose E-20
Moon N-2
Morrisville P-25
Morrisville R-2
Moscow H-21
Moshannon K-11
Mt. Carmel L-18
Mt. Cobb H-22
Mt. Holly Sprs. Q-15
Mt. Jewett F-9
Mt. Joy Q-18
Mt. Lebanon N-3
Mt. Pleasant Q-5
Mt. Pocono J-22
Mt. Union P-12
Mt. Wolf Q-17
Mountainhome J-23
Mountville Q-18
Muncy J-16
Murrysville N-4
Myerstown N-18
Nanticoke J-20
Nanty Glo N-8
Natrona Heights M-4
Nazareth L-22
Nemacolin R-3
Nescopeck K-19
Nesquehoning L-20
New Alexandria N-6
New Beaver L-2
New Berlin L-16
New Bethlehem K-6
New Bloomfield N-15
New Brighton L-2
New Britain P-23
New Castle K-2
New Eagle P-3
New Florence P-7
New Freedom S-17
New Galilee L-1
New Holland Q-19
New Hope N-24
New Kensington M-4
New Milford E-21
New Oxford R-15
New Philadelphia M-19
New Salem R-4
New Salem R-16
New Stanton P-5
New Tripoli M-21
New Wilmington J-2
Newell Q-4
Newmanstown P-19
Newport N-15
Newtown P-24
Newville Q-14
Nicholson F-20
Noblestown N-2
Norristown Q-22
N. Apollo M-5
N. East C-4
N. Vandergrift M-5
N. Wales P-23
Northampton M-22
Northumberland L-16
Norvelt P-5
Noxen H-19
Nuangola J-20
Nuremberg K-19
Oakdale N-2
Oakland K-2
Oakland D-21
Oakmont N-4
Oakwood K-2
Ohioville M-1
Oil City G-4
Old Forge H-21
Oliver R-4
Olyphant G-21
Orangeville K-18
Orbisonia P-12
Orwigsburg M-19
Osceola Mills L-10
Oxford S-20
Paintersville M-14
Palmerton L-21
Palmyra P-17
Palo Alto M-19
Paoli Q-22
Paradise R-19
Parker J-4
Parkesburg R-20
Parryville L-21
Patton M-9
Paxtonia P-16
Pen Argyl L-23
Penn P-5
Penn Hills N-4
Penndel Q-24
Pennsburg N-22
Perkasie N-23
Perryopolis Q-4
Petersburg M-11
Philadelphia R-23
Philipsburg L-11
Phoenixville Q-22
Picture Rocks H-17
Pine Grove N-18
Pine Grove Mills M-12
Pittsburgh N-3
Pittston H-20
Plains H-20
Platea D-2
Pleasant Gap L-12
Pleasant Hill P-18
Pleasantville G-5
Plum N-4
Plumville L-7
Plymouth J-20
Plymptonville K-10
Pocono Pines J-22
Point Marion S-3
Polk H-4
Port Allegany E-10
Port Carbon M-19
Port Matilda L-11
Port Royal N-14
Portage P-9
Portland K-23
Pottstown P-21
Pottsville M-19
Prospect K-3
Punxsutawney K-7
Quakertown N-22
Quarryville R-19
Ramey L-10
Reading P-20
Reamstown P-19
Red Hill N-22
Red Lion R-17
Reedsville M-13
Reinerton M-17
Renovo H-12
Republic R-4
Reynoldsville J-8
Rheems Q-17
Rices Landing R-3
Richboro P-24
Richfield M-15
Richland P-19
Richlandtown N-22
Ridgway H-8
Riegelsville M-23
Rimersburg K-5
Ringtown L-19
Roaring Spr. P-10
Robesonia P-19
Rochester M-2
Rockhill Furnace P-12
Rockwood R-7
Rome E-18
Roseto L-23
Rossiter L-8
Rothsville Q-19
Roulette F-11
Rouseville G-4
Royalton Q-17
Royersford Q-22
Rural Valley L-6
Russell E-7
Russellton M-4
Saegertown F-3
St. Clair M-19
St. Lawrence P-20
St. Marys H-9
Salisbury S-7
Salix P-8
Saltsburg N-5
Salunga Q-18
Sanatoga P-21
Sand Hill P-18
Sandy J-8
Sandy Lake H-3
Sankertown N-9
Saxonburg L-4
Saxton P-10
Saylorsburg K-22
Sayre D-17
Schnecksville M-21
Schuylkill Haven M-19
Schwenksville P-22
Scotland R-13
Scottdale Q-5
Scranton H-21
Selinsgrove L-16
Sellersville P-23
Seneca H-4
Seven Fields M-3
Seven Valleys S-16
Seward N-7
Shamokin L-17
Shamokin Dam L-16
Sharon H-1
Sharpsville H-1
Sheffield F-7
Shenandoah L-19
Shickshinny J-19
Shillington P-20
Shinglehouse E-11
Shippensburg Q-13
Shippenville H-5
Shoemakersville N-20
Shrewsbury S-17
Sidman P-8
Silverdale P-23
Sinking Spr. P-20
Skippack P-22
Skyline View P-17
Slatington L-21
Slickville N-5
Sligo J-5
Slippery Rock K-3
Smethport E-10
Smithfield S-4
Smithton Q-4
Snow Shoe K-12
Snydertown L-17
Somerset R-7
Souderton P-22
S. Bethlehem K-6
S. Coatesville R-20
S. Connellsville R-5
S. Fork P-8
S. Greensburg P-5
S. Heights M-2
S. New Castle K-2
S. Philipsburg L-11
S. Pottstown P-21
S. Renovo H-12
S. Waverly D-17
S. Williamsport J-16
Spangler M-8
Spartansburg E-5
Spr. City Q-21
Spr. Grove R-16
Spr. Hill P-9
Springboro E-2
Springdale N-4
Spry R-17
State College L-12
Steelton P-16
Stewartstown S-17
Stockdale Q-4
Stockertown L-23
Stoneboro H-3
Stonybrook R-17
Stowe P-21
Stoystown Q-7
Strasburg R-19
Strattanville J-6
Stroudsburg K-23
Sugar Grove D-6
Sugar Notch J-20
Sugarcreek H-4
Summerhill P-8
Summerville J-7
Summit Hill L-20
Sunbury L-16
Susquehanna E-21
Sutersville P-4
Sweet Valley H-19
Swiftwater J-22
Swoyersville H-20
Sykesville K-8
Tamaqua L-20
Tannersville K-22
Tarentum M-4
Tatamy L-23
Telford P-22
Temple N-20
Terre Hill Q-19
Thompsontown M-15
Thorndale R-21
Three Sprs. Q-11
Throop G-21
Tidioute F-6
Tioga E-15
Tionesta G-5
Tipton M-10
Titusville F-5
Topton N-21
Toughkenamon S-21
Towanda F-18
Tower City M-17
Trainer S-22
Trappe P-22
Tremont M-18
Tresckow K-20
Trevorton L-17
Troy F-16
Trumbauersville N-22
Tullytown Q-25
Tunkhannock G-20
Turbotville J-16
Tuscarora L-19
Tyrone M-10
Ulysses E-12
Union City E-4
Uniontown R-4
Valley View M-17
Vanderbilt R-4
Vandergrift M-5
Vandling F-22
Verona N-4
Vinco N-8
Vintondale N-8
Walnut Bottom Q-14
Walnutport L-21
Wampum L-2
Warminster P-23
Warren E-7
Warrensville H-16
Washington Q-2
Waterford E-3
Watsontown J-16
Wattsburg D-4
Waymart G-22
Wayne Q-22
Wayne Heights S-13
Waynesboro S-13
Waynesburg R-2
Weatherly K-20
Weigelstown R-16
Weissport L-21
Wellsboro F-14
Wernersville P-19
Wesleyville C-3
W. Brownsville Q-3
W. Chester R-21
W. Decatur K-10
W. Grove S-20
W. Hazleton K-20
W. Kittanning L-5
W. Lawn P-20
W. Mayfield L-2
W. Middlesex J-1
W. View N-3
W. York R-16
Westfield E-13
Westmont P-7
Westover L-9
Wheatland J-1
White Haven K-20
White Oak P-4
Whitehall M-22
Wilcox G-9
Wilkes-Barre J-20
Williamsburg N-11
Williamsport J-15
Williamstown M-17
Willow Grove Q-23
Willow Street R-18
Wilson M-23
Wind Gap L-22
Windber P-8
Windsor R-17
Winterstown S-17
Wolfdale P-2
Womelsdorf P-19
Woodland K-10
Worthington L-5
Wrightsville Q-17
Wyalusing F-18
Wyomissing P-20
Yardley P-25
Yeagertown M-13
Yocumtown Q-16
Yoe R-17
York R-17
York Haven Q-17
York Sprs. R-15
Youngsville E-6
Youngwood P-5
Yukon P-4
Zelienople L-3
Zion K-13

RHODE ISLAND
see map page 99

Counties
Bristol G-6
Kent G-3
Newport H-7
Providence E-3
Washington (S. County) J-3

Cities and Towns
Adamsville J-8
Allenton J-5
Alton K-2
Ashaway K-2
Ashton D-5
Avondale L-1
Barrington F-6
Berkeley D-5
Bonnet Shores J-5
Bradford K-2
Bristol G-6
Carolina K-3
Central Falls E-5
Charlestown L-3
Chepachet D-3
Clayville F-3
Coventry Ctr. G-3
Cranston F-5
Cumberland Hill D-5
Diamond Hill C-5
E. Greenwich G-5
E. Providence E-5
Exeter H-4
Foster Ctr. F-2
Galilee L-4
Glendale D-3
Green Hill L-4
Greenville E-4
Hamilton J-5
Harmony E-4
Harrisville D-3
Hope F-4
Hope Valley J-3
Jamestown J-6
Jerusalem L-4
Kingston J-4
Little Compton J-7
Manville D-5
Matunuck L-4
Middletown J-6
Mt. View H-5
Narragansett Pier K-5
Newport J-6
N. Foster E-2
N. Providence E-5
N. Scituate E-4
Pascoag D-3
Pawtucket E-5
Perryville K-4
Plum Point J-5
Point Judith L-5
Portsmouth H-7
Providence E-5
Quidnessett H-5
Quidnick G-4
Quonochontaug L-3
Rice City G-2
Rockville J-2
Saunderstown J-5
Shannock K-3
Slatersville C-4
Slocum J-4
S. Foster E-3
Spragueville E-4
Tarkiln D-3
Tiverton H-7
Usquepaug J-3
Valley Falls D-5
Wakefield K-4
Wallum Lake C-2
Warren F-6
Warwick G-5
Watch Hill L-1
Weekapaug L-2
W. Kingston J-4
W. Warwick G-4
Westerly L-2
Wickford H-5
Woonsocket C-4

SOUTH CAROLINA
see map page 100

Counties
Abbeville D-3
Aiken E-5
Allendale H-6
Anderson C-3
Bamberg G-7
Barnwell G-5
Beaufort J-7
Berkeley G-10
Calhoun E-7
Charleston H-9
Cherokee A-5
Chester C-6
Chesterfield C-9
Clarendon E-9
Colleton H-7
Darlington C-9
Dillon C-11
Dorchester G-8
Edgefield E-5
Fairfield C-6
Florence E-10
Georgetown F-11
Greenville B-3
Greenwood D-4
Hampton H-7
Horry D-12
Jasper J-7
Kershaw C-8
Lancaster C-7
Laurens C-4
Lee D-9
Lexington E-6
Marion D-11
Marlboro C-10
Mccormick E-4
Newberry C-5
Oconee B-2
Orangeburg F-7
Pickens B-3
Richland E-7
Saluda D-5
Spartanburg B-4
Sumter E-8
Union B-5
Williamsburg F-10
York B-7

Cities and Towns
Abbeville D-4
Aiken F-5
Allendale G-6
Anderson C-3
Andrews F-10
Ballentine D-6
Bamberg F-7
Barnwell G-6
Batesburg-Leesville E-6
Beaufort J-8
Belton C-3
Belvedere F-5
Bennettsville C-10
Bishopville D-9
Blacksburg A-6
Blackville F-6
Bluffton K-7
Boiling Sprs. A-5
Bowman F-8
Branchville G-7
Briarcliffe Acres E-12
Brookdale F-7
Brunson H-6
Bucksport E-11
Buffalo B-5
Burnettown F-5
Burton J-7
Calhoun Falls D-3
Camden D-8
Cameron F-8
Catawba B-7
Cayce D-7
Centerville C-3
Central B-3
Charleston H-9
Cheraw B-10
Cherryvale E-8
Chesnee A-5
Chester B-6
Chesterfield B-9
Clearwater F-5
Clemson B-3
Clinton C-5
Clio C-10
Clover A-6
Columbia D-7
Conway E-12
Cottageville H-8
Coward D-10
Cowpens A-5
Dalzell D-8
Darlington C-10
Denmark F-7
Dentsville D-7
Dillon C-11
Due West C-4
Easley B-3
E. Gaffney A-5
Eastover E-8
Edgefield E-5
Elgin B-8
Elgin D-7
Elloree F-8
Enoree B-5
Estill H-6
Eureka Mill B-6
Fairfax G-6
Florence D-10
Folly Beach H-9
Forestbrook E-12
Ft. Lawn B-7
Ft. Mill A-7
Fountain Inn B-4
Gaffney A-5
Garden City F-12
Gaston E-7
Gayle Mill B-6
Georgetown F-11
Gloverville F-5
Golden Grove B-3
Goose Creek G-9
Graniteville F-5
Gray Court C-4
Great Falls C-7
Greenville B-4
Greenwood D-4
Greer B-4
Hampton H-7
Hanahan H-9
Hardeeville J-7
Harleyville G-8
Hartsville C-9
Heath Sprs. C-8
Hemingway E-11
Hilton Head Island K-7
Holly Hill F-8
Hollywood H-9
Homeland Park C-3
Honea Path C-4
Inman A-4
Irmo D-6
Irwin B-7
Isle of Palms H-10
Iva C-3
Jackson F-5
Jefferson C-8
Joanna C-5
Johns Island H-9
Johnsonville E-11
Johnston E-5
Jonesville B-5
Kershaw C-8
Kiawah Island J-9
Kingstree E-10
Ladson G-9
Lake City E-10
Lake View C-11
Lake Wylie A-7
Lamar D-9
Lancaster B-7
Landrum A-4
Lane F-10
Latta C-11
Laurel Bay J-7
Laurens C-4
Lesslie B-7
Lexington D-6
Liberty B-3
Lincolnville G-9
Little River E-13
Loris D-12
Lugoff D-8
Manning E-9
Marietta A-3
Marion D-11
Mauldin B-4
Mayesville D-9
Mayo A-5
McBee C-9
McColl B-10
McCormick E-4
Meggett H-9
Monarch Mills B-5
Moncks Corner G-9
Mt. Pleasant H-10
Mullins D-11
Murrells Inlet F-12
Myrtle Beach E-12
New Ellenton F-5
Newberry D-5
Nichols D-11
Ninety Six D-4
Norris B-3
North F-7
N. Augusta F-5
N. Charleston H-9
N. Hartsville C-9
N. Myrtle Beach E-13
Oak Grove D-7
Olanta E-9
Orangeburg F-7
Pacolet B-5
Pacolet Mills B-5
Pageland B-8
Pamplico D-10
Pendleton B-3
Pickens B-3
Piedmont B-3
Pinewood E-8
Port Royal J-8
Prosperity D-6
Quinby D-10
Rains D-11
Ravenel H-9
Red Bank E-6
Red Hill E-12
Ridge Spr. E-5
Ridgeland J-7
Ridgeville G-9
Rock Hill B-7
Roebuck B-5
St. George G-8
St. Matthews E-7
St. Stephen F-9
Saluda D-5
Sampit F-11
Sandy Sprs. C-3
Santee F-8
Scranton E-10
Seabrook Island J-9
Seneca B-2
Shannontown E-8
Shell Point J-7
Simpsonville B-4
Six Mile B-3
Slater A-3
Socastee E-12
Society Hill C-10
S. Congaree E-7
Spartanburg B-5
Springfield F-6
Sullivans Island H-10
Summerton F-8
Summerville G-9
Sumter E-8
Surfside Beach F-12
Swansea E-7
Taylors B-4
Tega Cay A-7
Timmonsville D-9
Travelers Rest A-3
Turbeville E-9
Union B-5
Utica B-2
Varnville H-7
Wagener E-6
Walhalla B-2
Walterboro H-8
Ware Shoals C-4
W. Pelzer B-3
Westminster B-2
Whitmire C-5
Williamston C-3
Williston F-6
Winnsboro C-7
Winnsboro Mills C-7
Woodruff B-4
Yemassee H-7
York A-6

SOUTH DAKOTA
see map page 101

Counties
Aurora E-9
Beadle D-10
Bennett F-5
Bon Homme G-10
Brookings D-12
Brown B-9
Brule F-9
Buffalo E-8
Butte C-2
Campbell A-7
Charles Mix G-9
Clark C-10
Clay G-12
Codington C-11
Corson A-5
Custer F-1
Davison F-10
Day B-11
Deuel D-12
Dewey C-6
Douglas F-9
Edmunds B-8
Fall River G-2
Faulk C-8
Grant B-12
Gregory G-9
Haakon D-5
Hamlin D-11
Hand D-9
Hanson E-10
Harding B-2
Hughes D-7
Hutchinson F-10
Hyde D-8
Jackson F-5
Jerauld E-9
Jones E-6
Kingsbury D-11
Lake E-12
Lawrence D-2
Lincoln F-12
Lyman E-7
Marshall B-10
McCook E-11
McPherson A-9
Meade D-3
Mellette F-6
Miner E-11
Minnehaha F-12
Moody E-12
Pennington E-3
Perkins B-4
Potter C-8
Roberts B-12
Sanborn E-10
Shannon F-3
Spink C-10
Stanley D-6
Sully C-7
Todd G-6
Tripp F-7
Turner F-11
Union G-12
Walworth B-7
Yankton G-11
Ziebach C-5

Cities and Towns
Aberdeen B-9
Alcester G-12
Alexandria F-11
Allen F-4
Alpena E-10
Antelope F-6
Arlington D-11
Armour F-10
Aurora D-12
Avon G-10
Baltic E-12
Belle Fourche D-2
Beresford G-12
Big Stone City B-12
Bison B-4
Black Hawk E-2
Blunt D-7
Bonesteel G-9
Bowdle B-8
Box Elder E-3
Brandon F-12
Bridgewater F-11
Bristol B-10
Britton A-10
Brookings D-12
Bruce D-12
Bryant D-11
Buffalo B-2
Burke G-8
Canistota F-11
Canton F-12
Castlewood D-12
Centerville G-12
Chamberlain E-8
Chancellor F-12
Cherry Creek D-5
Chester E-12
Clark C-11
Clear Lake C-12
Colman E-12
Colome G-8
Colton E-12
Corsica F-10
Crooks F-12
Custer E-2
De Smet D-11
Deadwood D-2
Dell Rapids E-12
Delmont G-10
Doland C-10
Dupree C-5
Eagle Butte C-5
Edgemont F-2
Elk Point H-12
Elkton D-12
Emery F-11
Estelline D-12
Ethan F-10
Eureka A-8
Faith C-4
Faulkton C-8
Flandreau E-12
Ft. Pierre D-7
Ft. Thompson E-8
Frederick A-9
Freeman F-11
Gannvalley E-9
Garretson F-12
Gary C-12
Gayville G-11
Geddes G-9
Gettysburg C-7
Gregory G-8
Groton B-10
Harrisburg F-12
Hartford F-12
Hayti D-11
Hecla A-10
Hermosa E-3
Herreid A-7
Highmore D-8
Hill City E-2
Hosmer B-8
Hot Sprs. F-2
Hoven C-8
Howard E-11
Hudson G-12
Humboldt F-11
Hurley F-12
Huron D-10
Ipswich B-9
Irene G-11
Iroquois D-10
Isabel B-5
Jefferson H-12
Kadoka E-5
Kennebec E-7
Keystone E-2
Kimball F-9
Kyle F-4
Lake Andes G-9
Lake Norden D-11
Lake Preston D-11
Langford B-10
Lead D-2
Lemmon A-4
Lennox F-12
Leola B-9
Little Eagle B-6
Lower Brule E-8
Madison E-11
Manderson G-4
Marion F-11
Martin G-5
Marty G-10
McIntosh A-5
McLaughlin A-6
Menno G-11
Midland E-6
Milbank B-12
Miller D-9
Mission G-6
Mitchell F-10
Mobridge B-7
Montrose F-11
Mound City B-7
Mt. Vernon F-10
Murdo E-6
New Underwood E-3
Newell D-2
N. Sioux City H-12
Oacoma E-8
Oglala G-3
Olivet G-11
Onida D-7
Parker F-11
Parkston F-10
Parmelee F-6
Philip E-5
Piedmont E-2
Pierre D-7
Pine Ridge G-3
Plankinton F-9
Platte F-9
Pollock A-7
Porcupine G-4
Presho E-7
Pukwana E-8
Rapid City E-2
Redfield C-9
Roscoe B-8
Rosebud G-6
Rosholt A-12
Roslyn B-11
St. Francis G-6
Salem F-11
Scotland G-11
Selby B-7
Sioux Falls F-12
Sisseton B-11
S. Shore C-12
Spearfish D-2
Spencer F-11
Spr. Creek G-6
Springfield G-10
Stickney F-10
Sturgis D-2
Summit B-11
Tabor G-11
Tea F-12
Timber Lake B-6
Tripp G-10
Tulare D-9
Tyndall G-10
Valley Sprs. F-12
Veblen A-11
Vermillion G-12
Viborg G-12
Volga D-12
Wagner G-10
Wakonda G-11
Wall E-4
Wanblee F-5
Warner B-9
Watertown C-11
Waubay B-11
Webster B-11
Wessington D-9
Wessington Sprs. E-9
White D-12
White Lake F-9
White River F-6
Whitewood D-2
Willow Lake D-11
Wilmot B-12
Winner F-7
Wolsey D-9
Woonsocket E-10
Worthing F-12
Yankton G-11

TENNESSEE
see map pages 102-103

Counties
Anderson C-18
Bedford E-12
Benton C-7
Bledsoe E-15
Blount D-19
Bradley F-17
Campbell B-18
Cannon D-13
Carroll C-6
Carter K-15
Cheatham B-10
Chester E-6
Claiborne A-19
Clay A-14
Cocke M-12
Coffee E-13
Crockett D-4
Cumberland C-17
Davidson C-12
Decatur E-7
Dekalb C-13
Dickson C-9
Dyer C-3
Fayette F-3
Fentress B-17
Franklin G-13
Gibson D-4
Giles F-10
Grainger C-20
Greene L-13
Grundy F-14
Hamblen L-12
Hamilton F-16
Hancock K-12
Hardeman F-4
Hardin F-7
Hawkins K-13
Haywood D-3
Henderson E-6
Henry B-7
Hickman D-9
Houston B-8
Humphreys C-8
Jackson B-14
Jefferson M-11
Johnson K-16
Knox C-20
Lake B-3
Lauderdale D-3
Lawrence G-9
Lewis E-9
Lincoln G-12
Loudon D-18
Macon A-13
Madison E-4
Marion F-14
Marshall F-11
Maury E-9
McMinn F-17
McNairy F-6
Meigs E-17
Monroe E-19
Montgomery B-9
Moore F-12
Morgan C-17
Obion B-4
Overton B-15
Perry E-8
Pickett A-16
Polk G-18
Putnam C-14
Rhea E-16
Roane D-18
Robertson B-11
Rutherford D-12
Scott B-18
Sequatchie E-15
Sevier D-20
Shelby F-2
Smith B-14
Stewart B-8
Sullivan K-15
Sumner B-12
Tipton E-2
Trousdale B-13
Unicoi L-14
Union B-20
Van Buren D-15
Warren D-14
Washington L-14
Wayne F-8
Weakley B-5
White D-15
Williamson D-11
Wilson B-12

Cities and Towns
Adams A-10
Adamsville F-6
Alamo D-4
Alcoa D-19
Alexandria C-13
Algood C-15
Allardt B-17
Altamont E-14
Ardmore G-11
Arlington F-2
Arthur A-20
Ashland City B-10
Athens E-17
Atoka E-2
Atwood C-5
Bakewell F-16
Banner Hill L-14
Bartlett F-2
Baxter C-14
Bean Station K-12
Beersheba Sprs. E-14
Belinda City C-12
Bells D-4
Benton F-17
Bethel Sprs. F-6
Big Sandy B-7
Blaine C-20
Bloomingdale K-14
Blountville K-15
Bluff City K-15
Bolivar F-4
Braden E-3
Bradford C-5
Brentwood C-11
Briceville C-19
Brighton E-2
Bristol J-15
Brownsville E-4
Bruceton C-7
Bulls Gap L-12
Burlison E-2
Burns C-9
Byrdstown A-16
Calhoun F-17
Camden C-7
Campaign D-14
Carthage B-14
Caryville B-18
Cedar Hill A-10
Celina A-15
Centertown D-14
Centerville D-9
Central K-15
Chapel Hill E-11
Charleston F-17
Charlotte C-9
Chattanooga G-15
Church Hill K-13
Clarksville A-9
Cleveland F-17
Clifton F-7
Clinton C-19
Coalmont F-14
Collegedale G-16
Collierville G-2
Collinwood F-8
Colonial Heights K-14
Columbia E-10
Concord D-19
Cookeville C-15
Copperhill G-18
Cordova F-2
Cornersville F-11
Corryton C-20
Covington E-3
Cowan F-13
Crab Orchard D-17
Cross Plains A-11
Crossville D-16
Crump F-6
Culleoka E-10
Dandridge M-11
Dayton E-16
Decatur E-17
Decaturville E-7
Decherd F-13
Dickson C-9
Dover B-8
Doyle D-15
Dresden B-5
Ducktown G-18
Dunlap F-15
Dyer C-5
Dyersburg C-3
Eagleton Vil. D-19
Eagleville D-12
E. Ridge G-16
Eastview G-6
Elizabethton K-15
Elkton G-11
Elora G-12
Englewood E-18
Erin B-8
Erwin L-14
Estill Sprs. F-13
Ethridge F-9
Etowah F-18
Fairfield Glade C-17
Fairmount F-15
Fairview C-10
Fall Branch K-14
Farragut D-19
Fayetteville F-12
Ft. Pillow D-2
Fowlkes C-3
Franklin D-11
Friendship D-4
Friendsville D-19
Gadsden D-5
Gainesboro B-14
Gallatin B-12
Gallaway F-3
Gates D-3
Gatlinburg N-11
Germantown F-2
Gilt Edge E-2
Gleason B-6
Goodlettsville B-11
Gordonsville C-14
Grand Jct. G-4
Gray K-14
Graysville E-16
Green Hill C-12
Greenback E-19
Greenbrier B-11
Greeneville L-13
Greenfield C-5
Gruetli-Laager F-14
Guys G-6
Halls D-3
Halls Crossroads C-19
Hampton L-15
Harriman D-18
Harrison G-16
Harrogate A-20
Hartsville B-13
Helenwood B-18
Henderson E-5
Hendersonville B-12
Henning D-3
Hohenwald E-9
Hollow Rock C-7
Hopewell F-17
Hornbeak B-4
Humboldt D-5
Hunter K-15
Huntingdon C-6
Huntland G-13
Huntsville B-18
Iron City G-9
Jacksboro B-19
Jackson E-5
Jamestown B-16
Jasper G-14
Jefferson City L-11
Jellico A-19
Johnson City K-14
Jonesborough L-14
Karns C-19
Kenton B-4
Kimball G-14
Kingsport K-14
Kingston D-18
Kingston Sprs. C-10
Knoxville C-19
La Follette B-19
La Vergne C-12
Lafayette B-13
Lake City C-19
Lakeland F-2
Lakesite F-16
Lakewood B-12
Lawrenceburg F-9
Lebanon C-13
Lenoir City D-19
Lewisburg E-11
Lexington E-6
Liberty C-13
Limestone L-14
Linden E-8
Livingston B-15
Lobelville D-8
Loretto G-9
Loudon D-18
Louisville D-19
Luttrell C-20
Lyles D-9
Lynchburg F-12
Lynnville F-10
Madisonville E-18
Manchester E-13
Marbledale C-20
Martin B-5
Maryville D-19
Mascot C-20
Mason E-3
Maury City D-4
Maynardville B-20
McEwen C-8
McKenzie C-6
McMinnville E-14
Medina D-5
Memphis F-1
Mentor D-19
Michie G-6
Middle Valley F-16
Middleton G-5
Milan D-5
Millersville B-11
Millington E-2
Minor Hill G-10
Monteagle F-14
Monterey C-16
Morrison E-14
Morristown L-12
Moscow G-3
Mosheim L-13
Mt. Carmel K-14
Mt. Juliet C-12
Mt. Pleasant E-10
Mtn. City K-16
Munford E-2
Murfreesboro D-12
Nashville C-11
New Hope G-14
New Johnsonville C-7
New Market L-11
New Tazewell B-20
Newbern C-4
Newport M-12
Niota E-18
Nolensville D-11
Norris C-19
Oak Grove K-14
Oak Ridge C-18
Oakland F-3
Obion B-4
Oliver Sprs. C-18
Oneida B-18
Ooltewah G-16
Orlinda A-12
Overall D-12
Palmer F-15
Paris B-6
Parsons E-7
Pegram C-10
Petersburg F-12
Petros C-18
Philadelphia E-18
Pigeon Forge M-11
Pikeville E-16
Pinson E-5
Piperton G-3
Pittman Ctr. N-12
Pleasant Hill C-16
Portland A-12
Powell C-19
Powells Crossroads F-15
Pulaski F-10
Puryear B-6
Ramer G-5
Red Bank G-16
Red Boiling Sprs. A-14
Riceville F-17
Rickman B-15
Ridgely B-3
Ridgetop B-11
Ripley D-3
Rives B-4
Roan Mtn. L-15
Robbins B-17
Rockford D-19
Rockwood D-17
Rogersville K-13
Russellville L-12
Rutherford C-5
Rutledge L-11
Ryall Sprs. G-16
St. Joseph G-9
Sale Creek F-16
Saltillo F-7
Samburg B-4
Savannah F-7
Scotts Hill E-7
Selmer F-6
Sevierville D-20
Sewanee F-14
Seymour D-20
Sharon B-5
Shawanee A-20
Shelbyville E-12
Signal Mtn. G-15
Smithville D-14
Smyrna D-12
Sneedville K-12
Soddy-Daisy F-16
Solway C-19
Somerville F-3
S. Carthage B-14
S. Fulton A-5
S. Pittsburg G-14
Sparta D-15
Spencer D-15
Spr. City E-17
Spr. Hill D-11
Springfield B-11
Stanton E-3
Strawberry Plains C-20
Summertown E-9
Sunbright B-17
Surgoinsville K-13
Sweetwater E-18
Talbott L-11
Tasso F-17
Tazewell B-20
Tellico Plains F-18
Tennessee Ridge B-8
Thompsons Station D-11
Tiptonville B-3
Townsend D-20
Tracy City F-14
Trenton C-5
Trezevant C-6
Trimble B-4
Troy B-4
Tullahoma F-13
Tusculum L-13
Unicoi L-15
Union City B-4
Vanleer B-9
Vonore E-18
Walden F-15
Walnut Hill K-15
Walterhill D-12
Wartburg C-17
Wartrace E-12
Watauga K-15
Watertown C-13
Waverly C-8
Waynesboro F-8
Westmoreland A-13
Westover E-5
White Bluff C-10
White House B-12
White Pine L-12
Whiteville F-4
Whitwell F-15
Williston F-3
Winchester F-13
Winfield A-18
Witt L-12
Woodbury D-13
Woodland Mills A-4

Wrigley D-9
Yorkville C-4

TEXAS
see map pages 104-107

Counties
Anderson L-20
Andrews K-8
Angelina L-22
Aransas J-18
Archer E-15
Armstrong ...E-10
Atascosa P-19
Austin F-8
Bailey F-9
Bandera P-14
Bastrop P-17
Baylor G-14
Bee M-17
Bexar N-15
Blanco D-10
Bonan J-10
Bosque G-22
Bowie A-20
Brazoria M-19
Brazos M-19
Brewster P-7
Briscoe E-11
Brooks U-16
Brown K-17
Burleson N-19
Burnet M-16
Caldwell M-17
Calhoun R-19
Callahan H-17
Cameron ...W-18
Camp H-21
Carson C-10
Cass H-22
Castro P-22
Chambers ...P-22
Cherokee ...K-21
Childress ...E-12
Clay G-16
Cochran D-9
Coke K-12
Coleman J-15
Collin E-12
Collingsworth ...E-12
Colorado P-16
Comal P-16
Comanche ...K-15
Concho K-15
Cooke G-17
Coryell H-16
Cottle F-12
Crane L-8
Crockett M-10
Crosby D-10
Culberson ...B-8
Dallam B-8
Dallas H-19
Dawson J-9
Deaf Smith ...D-8
Delta G-20
Denton H-18
Dewitt Q-17
Dickens G-11
Dimmit S-13
Donley E-11
Duval T-15
Eastland J-16
Ector K-8
Edwards P-12
Ellis J-18
El Paso K-16
Erath K-16
Falls L-18
Fannin G-19
Fayette P-18
Fisher F-12
Floyd G-13
Foard G-13
Ft. Bend Q-19
Franklin K-19
Freestone ...K-19
Frio J-8

Cities and Towns
Abernathy G-10
Abilene J-15
Agua Dulce ...W-16
Alamo W-16
Alba J-20
Albany J-14
Aledo G-17
Algoa Q-21
Alice T-16
Allen G-18
Alpine N-6
Alto L-21
Alvarado H-18
Alvin Q-21
Alvord D-10
Amarillo D-10
Ames N-22
Amherst P-22
Anahuac P-22
Anderson N-20
Andrews J-8
Angleton Q-21
Anna H-18
Annetta J-7
Anson J-13
Anthony A-1
Aransas Pass ...V-16
Archer City ...G-15
Arcola Q-21
Argyle G-21
Arlington H-18
Arp K-21
Asherton S-13
Aspermont ...H-12
Athens K-20
Atlanta H-22
Aubrey H-17
Aurora H-17
Austin N-17
Avinger G-22
Azle H-17
Bailey's Q-21
Prairie Q-21
Baird J-14
Balch Springs ...H-19
Ballinger K-14
Balmorhea M-6
Bandera P-14
Bangs J-15
Banquete T-17
Barrett P-21
Barstow L-7
Bartlett L-17
Bastrop N-17
Batesville S-13
Bay City R-20
Baytown P-22
Beasley Q-20
Beaumont N-23
Beckville J-22
Beeville U-16
Bellaire P-21
Bellmead L-18
Bells G-19
Bellville Q-20
Belton M-17
Benavides T-15
Benjamin G-13
Berryville K-20
Bertram M-16
Bevil Oaks ...N-23
Big Lake M-10
Big Sandy J-21
Big Spring K-10
Big Wells R-13
Bishop T-16
Blanco P-15
Blanket K-15
Blessing R-19
Blooming
Grove K-18
Bloomington ...S-18
Blossom G-20
Blue Ridge ...G-18
Boerne P-15
Bogata G-20
Boling Q-20
Bonham G-19
Booker B-12
Borger C-10
Bovina E-8
Bowie G-16
Boyd H-17
Brackettville ...Q-12
Brady K-15
Brazoria R-20
Breckenridge ...J-15
Bremond M-18
Brenham N-19
Briar H-17
Midland M-18
Milam M-18
Mills K-16
Mitchell K-11
Montague G-16
Montgomery ...N-20
Moore C-9
Morris H-22
Motley F-11
Nacogdoches ...L-22
Navarro M-24
Newton M-24
Nolan K-11
Nueces T-17
Ochiltree B-11
Oldham D-8
Orange N-23
Palo Pinto J-16
Panola K-23
Parker J-17

Gilmer J-21
Gladewater ...J-21
Glen Rose ...K-16
Godley J-17
Goldthwaite ...L-15
Goliad R-18
Gonzales Q-17
Gorman K-15
Graford H-16
Graham H-15
Granbury J-16
Grand Saline ...J-20
Grandfalls L-8
Grandview ...K-17
Granger M-17
Granite Shoals ...M-15
Grapeland L-20
Grapevine H-18
Greenville ...H-19
Gregory S-17
Groesbeck ...L-19
Groom D-11
Groves P-23
Groveton M-21
Gruver B-10
Gun Barrel
City J-20
Gunter G-18
Guthrie G-12
Hale Ctr. E-9
Hallettsville ...Q-18
Hallsville J-22
Hamilton L-16
Hamlin H-12
Happy E-10
Hardin N-22
Hargill V-16
Harker
Heights M-17
Harlingen W-17
Hart E-9
Haskell H-13
Hawkins J-21
Hawley J-13
Hearne M-18
Hebbronville ...U-15
Helotes Q-15
Hemphill L-23
Hempstead ...N-19
Henderson ...K-22
Henrietta G-15
Hereford E-9
Hewitt L-18
Hico K-16
Hidalgo W-16
Highlands P-21
Hillsboro K-18
Hillsdale G-15
Holland M-17
Holliday G-15
Hollywood
Park P-15
Hondo Q-14
Honey Grove ...G-20
Hooks G-22
Horizon City ...K-2
Horseshoe
Bay T-18
Houston P-20
Howe G-18
Hubbard K-18
Hudson L-21
Hughes Spgs. ...H-22
Humble P-21
Hungerford ...Q-20
Huntington ...L-22
Huntsville ...N-20
Hutto N-17
Idalou G-10
Inez R-18
Ingleside T-18
Ingleside on
the Bay T-18
Ingram P-14
Iowa Colony ...Q-21
Iowa Park F-15
Iraan M-9
Irving H-18
Italy K-18
Itasca K-18
Jacksboro H-16
Jacksonville ...K-21
Jamaica
Beach Q-22
Jasper M-23
Jayton H-12
Jefferson H-22
Jewett L-19
Joaquin K-23
Johnson City ...N-15
Jollyville N-16
Jones Creek ...R-20
Jonestown ...N-16
Josephine H-19
Joshua J-17
Jourdanton ...R-15
Junction N-13
Justin H-17
Karnes City ...S-16
Katy P-20
Kaufman J-19
Keene K-17
Keller H-17
Kemah Q-21
Kemp J-19
Kendleton ...Q-20
Kenedy S-16
Kerens K-19
Kermit K-7
Kerrville P-14
Kilgore J-21
Killeen M-17
Kingsland ...M-16
Kingsville T-16
Kirby P-15
Kirbyville M-23
Knox City G-13
Kosse L-18
Kountze N-22
Kress F-10
Krum H-17
Kyle P-16
La Coste Q-15
La Feria W-17
La Grange P-18
La Grulla W-15
La Marque ...Q-22
La Paloma X-16
La Porte P-21
La Pryor R-13
La Vernia Q-16
La Villa W-16
Ladonia G-19
Lago Vista ...N-16
Laguna
Heights W-18
Laguna Vista ...W-18
Lake Dallas ...H-18
Lake Jackson ...R-20
Lake
Tanglewood ...D-10
Lakehills P-14
Lakeport J-22
Lakeside City ...G-15
Lakeway N-16
Lamesa J-9
Lampasas ...M-16
Lancaster H-18
Laredo T-14
League City ...Q-21
Leakey P-13
Leander N-16
Lefors D-11
Leon Valley ...Q-15
Leonard G-19
Levelland E-9
Lewisville H-18
Lexington ...N-18
Liberty N-22
Liberty Hill ...N-16
Lindale J-20
Linden H-22
Lindsay G-17
Lipscomb B-12
Little Cypress ...N-24
Little River- ...
Live Oak Q-16
Livingston ...N-21
Llano M-15
Lockhart P-17
Lockney F-10
Log Cabin J-19
Lometa L-16
Lone Oak H-20
Lone Star H-22
Longview J-21
Loraine K-11
Lorena L-18
Lorenzo G-10
Los Fresnos ...W-17

Lott L-18
Louise Q-19
Lovelady M-21
Lubbock G-9
Lufkin L-22
Luling Q-17
Lumberton ...N-23
Lyford V-17
Lytle Q-15
Mabank J-19
Macdona Q-15
Madisonville ...M-20
Magnolia N-20
Malakoff K-19
Manchaca ...N-16
Mansfield H-17
Manvel Q-21
Marble Falls ...N-16
Marfa N-5
Markham R-20
Marlin L-18
Marshall J-22
Mart L-18
Martindale ...P-16
Mason M-15
Matador F-11
Mathis S-17
Maud G-22
Mauriceville ...N-23
Maypearl J-18
McAllen W-16
McCamey M-9
McGregor L-17
McKinney H-18
McLean D-12
McQueeney ...P-16
Melissa H-18
Memphis E-12
Menard L-14
Mentone K-6
Mercedes W-16
Meridian K-17
Merkel J-13
Mertzon K-11
Mesquite H-18
Mexia L-19
Miami C-12
Midland L-8
Midlothian ...J-18
Miles K-12
Milford K-18
Millsap J-16
Mineola J-20
Mineral Wells ...J-16
Mission W-16
Missouri City ...P-21
Monahans L-7
Monte Alto ...W-16
Monte Alto ...W-16
Moody L-17
Morton D-8
Moulton P-18
Mt. Enterprise ...K-22
Mt. Houston ...P-21
Mt. Pleasant ...H-21
Mt. Vernon ...H-21
Muenster G-17
Muleshoe E-8
Murchison ...J-20
Nacogdoches ...L-22
Naples H-21
Natalia Q-15
Navasota N-20
Nederland ...N-23
Needville Q-20
New Boston ...G-22
New Braunfels ...P-16
New Deal G-10
New London
Ctr. K-21
New
Summerfield K-22
New Waverly ...N-21
Newcastle G-15
Newton M-23
Nixon Q-17
Nocona G-16
Nolanville M-17
Noonday J-21
Nordheim S-17
North
Houston P-20
Oak Ridge
North N-21
Oak Trail
Shores J-16
Oakwood L-20
Odem S-17
O'Donnell H-10
Olmos H-15
Olney H-15
Olton F-9
Omaha H-21
Onalaska N-21
Orange N-24
Orange Grove ...S-16
Ore City J-22
Overton K-21
Ovilla H-18
Oyster Creek ...Q-21
Ozona M-11
Paducah F-12
Paint Rock ...L-13
Palacios R-19
Palestine K-20
Palmer H-18
Palmview W-16
Palo Pinto J-16
Pampa D-11
Panhandle ...D-10
Panorama
Village N-20
Paris G-20
Pasadena P-21
Patton Vil. N-21
Payne Sprs. ...J-19
Pearland Q-21
Pearsall R-14
Pecos L-7
Perryton B-11
Petersburg ...G-10
Petrolia F-16
Pflugerville ...N-16
Pharr W-16
Pilot Point ...G-18
Pine Forest ...N-23
Pine Island ...N-20
Pinehurst N-20
Pinehurst N-24
Pinehurst N-24
Pittsburg H-21
Plains G-8
Plainview F-10
Plano H-18
Pleak Q-20
Pleasanton ...R-15
Plum Grove ...N-21
Point H-20
Point Comfort ...R-19
Ponder H-17
Port Aransas ...T-18
Port Arthur ...P-23
Port Isabel ...W-18
Port Lavaca ...R-19
Port Neches ...N-23
Porter Heights N-21
Portland T-17
Post H-10
Poteet R-15
Poth Q-16
Pottsboro G-18
Prairie View ...N-20
Premont U-16
Presidio P-7
Princeton H-18
Progreso W-16
Prosper H-18
Quanah F-13
Queen City ...H-23
Quinlan H-19
Quintana R-20
Quitman H-20
Ralls G-10
Ranger J-16
Rankin M-9
Ransom
Canyon G-10
Raymondville ...V-17
Red Oak H-18
Redwater G-22
Refugio S-18
Reno H-17
Reno H-21
Rhome H-17
Rice K-19
Richardson ...H-18
Richland K-19
Richland Spgs. ...L-15
Richmond Q-20
Richwood Q-21
Riesel L-18
Rio Grande
City V-15
Rio Hondo W-17
Rio Vista K-17
Rising Star ...K-14

Robert Lee ...K-12
Robinson L-18
Robstown T-17
Roby H-12
Rockdale M-18
Rockport S-18
Rocksprings ...P-12
Rockwall H-19
Rogers M-17
Roma V-14
Roman Forest N-21
Ropesville ...G-9
Roscoe J-12
Rosebud L-18
Rosenberg ...P-20
Rotan H-12
Round Rock ...N-16
Rowena K-13
Roxton G-20
Royse City ...H-19
Rule H-13
Runaway Bay ...H-17
Runge R-17
Rusk K-21
Sabinal Q-14
Sachse H-19
Sadler G-18
Salado M-17
San Angelo ...L-12
San Antonio ...Q-15
San Benito ...W-17
San Diego T-16
San Elizario ...L-2
San Felipe P-20
San Juan W-16
San Marcos ...P-16
San Saba L-15
Sanderson ...N-7
Sanger G-17
Santa Anna ...L-14
Santa Fe Q-21
Santa Maria ...W-17
Santa Rosa ...V-17
Sarita U-16
Savoy G-19
Schertz P-15
Schulenburg ...P-18
Scotland G-15
Seabrook P-21
Seadrift S-18
Seagoville H-18
Seagraves H-9
Sealy P-19
Seguin Q-16
Seminole H-8
Seven Points ...J-19
Seymour G-14
Shallowater ...G-9
Shamrock D-12
Shepherd N-21
Sherman G-18
Shiner Q-18
Sierra Blanca ...L-3
Silsbee N-23
Silverton E-11
Simonton P-20
Sinton S-17
Skellytown ...C-11
Slaton G-10
Smithville P-18
Snook N-19
Snyder J-11
Socorro K-2
Somerset Q-15
Somerville ...N-19
Sonora N-11
Sour Lake N-22
Spearman B-11
Splendora N-21
Spr. K-4
Springtown ...H-17
Spur G-11
Stafford P-20
Stamford H-13
Stanton L-9
Stephenville ...K-16
Sterling City ...K-11
Stinnett C-10
Stockdale Q-16
Stowell P-23
Stratford B-9
Strawn J-16
Sudan F-9
Sugar Land ...P-20
Sullivan City ...V-15
Sulphur Sprs. ...H-20
Sundown H-9
Sunray C-10
Sunrise
Beach N-10
Surfside
Beach R-21
Sweeny Q-20
Sweetwater ...J-12
Taft S-17
Tahoka H-10
Tatum K-22
Taylor N-17
Teague L-19
Temple M-17
Tenaha K-23
Terrell J-19
Texarkana G-23
Texas City ...Q-22
The Colony ...H-18
The
Woodlands ...N-21
Thorndale N-18
Thornton L-19
Thorntonville ...L-8
Thrall N-17
Three Rivers ...T-16
Throckmorton ...H-14
Tiki Island Q-22
Tilden T-15
Timpson K-22
Tioga G-18
Tolar J-16
Tom Bean G-19
Tomball N-20
Tool J-19
Trent J-13
Trenton G-19
Trinidad K-19
Trinity M-21
Troup K-21
Troy M-17
Tulia E-10
Turkey F-4
Tuscola K-13
Tye J-13
Tyler K-21
Universal City ...Q-16
Uvalde Q-13
Valley Mills ...L-17
Valley View ...G-17
Van J-20
Van Alstyne ...G-18
Van Horn M-4
Van Vleck R-20
Vega D-9
Venus H-18
Vernon F-14
Victoria R-18
Vidor N-23
Vinton K-1
Waco L-18
Waelder Q-17
Wake Vil. G-23
Waller N-20
Wallis P-20
Walnut Sprs. ...K-17
Waples P-20
Waskom J-23
Waxahachie ...J-18
Weatherford ...J-16
Weimar P-18
Wellington ...E-12
Wells L-21
Weslaco W-16
West K-18
West Columbia ...Q-20
W. Lake Hills ...N-16
W. Odessa ...L-8
W. Tawakoni ...J-19
Westfield N-21
Westway K-2
Wharton Q-20
Wheeler D-12
White Deer ...D-11
White Oak J-21
White Settlement ...H-17
Whitehouse ...K-21
Whitesboro ...G-18
Whitewright ...G-19
Whitney K-17

Wichita Falls ...G-15
Wickett L-7
Willis N-21
Willow Park ...H-17
Wills Point ...J-19
Wilson M-17
Wimberley ...P-16
Windcrest ...Q-16
Wink K-7
Winnie P-23
Winnsboro ...H-21
Winters K-13
Wolfe City ...G-19
Wolfforth G-9
Woodbranch ...N-21
Woodcreek ...P-16
Woodsboro ...S-17
Woodville ...M-22
Woodway L-17
Wortham K-19
Wylie H-18
Yoakum Q-18
Yorktown R-17
Zapata U-14
Zavalla L-22

VERMONT
see map page 110

Counties
Addison F-4
Bennington ...K-3
Caledonia D-6
Chittenden ...E-4
Essex C-8
Franklin B-4
Grand Isle B-3
Lamoille C-5
Orange E-6
Orleans B-6
Rutland H-3
Washington ...D-5
Windham L-5
Windsor H-5

Cities and Towns
Alburg A-3
Arlington K-3
Ascutney J-6
Barre E-5
Bartons- ....
Bellows Falls ...L-6
Bennington ...L-3
Berlin Corners ...E-5
Bethel G-5
Bolton D-4
Bradford F-7
Brandon G-3
Brattleboro ...M-5
Bristol E-3
Burlington D-3
Cambridge ...C-4
Canaan A-9
Castleton H-2
Chelsea F-6
Chester K-5
Chittenden ...G-4
Clarendon H-4
Colchester D-3
Danville D-7
Derby Ctr. A-7
Derby Line A-7
Dorset K-3
Duxbury D-5
E. Barre E-6
E. Calais D-6
E. Hardwick ...C-6
E. Middlebury ...F-3
E. Montpelier ...D-5
E. Putney L-5
East River City ...D-4
Elmore C-5
Enosburg Falls ...A-4
Essex Ctr. C-3
Essex Jct. D-3
Fair Haven H-2
Fairfax C-4
Forest Dale ...G-3
Georgia Ctr. ...C-3
Glover C-6
Grand Isle B-3
Graniteville ...E-5
Greensboro ...C-6
Groton E-6
Guildhall D-8
Guilford M-5
Hardwick C-6
Harmonville ...L-5
Hartford H-6
Hartland H-6
Highgate Ctr. ...A-4
Hinesburg D-3
Hyde Park C-5
Island Pond ...B-8
Isle LaMotte ...B-3
Jacksonville ...M-4
Jeffersonville ...C-4
Jericho D-4
Jericho Ctr. ...D-4
Johnson C-5
Jonesville D-4
Londonderry ...K-5
Ludlow J-5
Lunenburg ...D-8
Lyndon C-7
Lyndonville ...C-7
Manchester ...K-3
Manchester Ctr. ...K-3
Marshfield D-6
Mechanicsville ...D-3
Middlebury ...F-3
Middletown
Spgs. H-3
Milton C-3
Montgomery ...B-5
Montpelier D-5
Morrisville C-5
Morrisville C-5
Newbury F-7
Newfane L-6
Newport A-7
N. Bennington ...L-3
N. Ferrisburg ...E-3
N. Hartland ...H-6
N. Hero B-3
N. Pownal M-3
N. Springfield ...J-6
N. Troy A-6
N. Westminster ...K-6
Northfield E-5
Northfield Falls ...E-5
Norwich H-6
Old Bennington L-3
Orleans B-6
Pittsford G-4
Plainfield E-6
Post Mills G-6
Poultney H-3
Pownal M-3
Pownal Ctr. ...M-3
Proctor H-4
Putney L-5
Quechee H-6
Randolph F-5
Randolph Ctr. ...F-5
Readsboro ...M-4
Richford A-5
Richmond D-4
Riverton D-5
Roosevelt D-5
Rutland H-4
S. Barre E-5
S. Burlington ...D-3
S. Royalton ...G-5
S. Shaftsbury ...L-3
St. Albans B-3
St. Albans Bay ...B-3
St. Johnsbury ...D-7
Saxtons River ...K-6
Shaftsbury L-3
Sharon G-6
Shelburne D-3
Shelburne Falls D-3
S. Burlington ...D-3
S. Londonderry ...K-5
Springfield J-6
Stowe D-4
Swanton B-3
Troy A-6
Underhill D-4
Vergennes E-3
Vershire F-6
Waitsfield D-4
Wallingford ...J-4
Wardsboro L-5
Waterbury D-5
Waterbury Ctr. ...D-5
Wells J-3
Wells River ...E-7
W. Brattleboro M-5
W. Burke C-7
W. Fairlee F-6
W. Glover C-6
W. Milton C-3
W. Rutland H-3
Westminster ...K-6
White River Jct. ...H-6
Whiting G-3
Williamstown ...E-5
Williston D-3
Windsor H-6
Winooski D-3
Woodstock H-5

VIRGINIA
see map pages 112-113

Counties
Accomack H-20
Albemarle G-10
Alleghany H-6
Amelia J-12
Amherst G-8
Appomattox ...H-9
Arlington D-14
Augusta G-8

Bath G-7
Bedford H-7
Bland L-2
Botetourt J-7
Brunswick N-13
Buchanan B-6
Buckingham ...H-10
Campbell H-8
Caroline G-14
Carroll N-4
Charles City ...K-15
Charlotte L-10
Chesterfield ...K-13
Clarke D-13
Craig J-5
Culpeper F-12
Cumberland ...J-11
Dickenson C-6
Dinwiddie L-13
Essex H-15
Fairfax D-14
Fauquier E-13
Floyd L-5
Fluvanna H-11
Franklin L-7
Frederick C-11
Giles L-5
Gloucester ...J-17
Goochland ...J-12
Grayson N-4
Greene F-11
Greensville ...N-14
Halifax M-9
Hanover H-13
Henrico K-14
Henry N-7
Highland G-7
Isle of Wight ...L-15
James City ...K-16
King And
Queen H-16
King George ...F-13
King William ...H-14
Lancaster H-17
Lee D-2
Loudoun C-13
Louisa H-11
Lunenburg ...L-11
Madison F-11
Mathews K-17
Mecklenburg ...N-11
Middlesex J-16
Montgomery ...K-5
Nelson H-9
New Kent J-15
Northampton ...L-18
Northumber- ...
Nottoway L-12
Orange F-12
Page E-11
Patrick N-5
Pittsylvania ...M-8
Powhatan J-12
Prince Edward ...L-10
Prince George ...L-13
Prince William ...E-14
Pulaski L-3
Rappahannock E-12
Richmond H-16
Roanoke K-6
Rockbridge ...H-7
Rockingham ...E-9
Russell C-5
Scott D-4
Shenandoah ...E-11
Smyth M-2
Southampton ...N-14
Spotsylvania ...F-13
Stafford F-13
Surry L-15
Sussex M-14
Tazewell K-2
Warren E-12
Washington ...D-6
Westmoreland ...G-16
Wise C-4
Wythe M-3
York K-16

Cities and Towns
Abingdon D-6
Accomac H-19
Accotink C-12
Achilles K-17
Adwolf D-7
Alberta M-13
Albin C-12
Alexandria D-14
Allison Gap ...M-1
Altavista J-8
Amelia Court
House K-13
Amherst H-9
Amonate L-1
Annandale D-16
Appalachia D-5
Appomattox ...H-9
Arlington D-15
Ashburn D-14
Ashland J-14
Atkins M-2
Avon D-16
Bailey's ....
Barboursville ...G-10
Bassett N-6
Bastian L-3
Bealeton E-13
Bedford J-8
Bee Haven ...L-1
Bensley K-14
Berryville D-13
Big Island J-8
Big Stone Gap ...C-4
Blacksburg ...K-5
Blackstone L-12
Bland L-3
Blakes K-17
Bland L-3
Blue Ridge ...K-7
Blue Field A-9
Bon Air J-14
Bowling
Green G-14
Boyce C-13
Boydton N-11
Boykins N-15
Bracey N-12
Bridgewater ...F-10
Brightwood ...F-12
Bristol D-6
Broadway E-10
Brodnax M-12
Brooke F-14
Brookneal J-9
Buchanan J-7
Buckingham ...H-10
Buena Vista ...H-8
Burke C-12
Burkeville ...L-12
Callaghan H-6
Callao H-17
Cape Charles ...K-18
Castlewood ...C-6
Cedar Bluff ...L-1
Centreville D-14
Chantilly D-14
Charlottesville G-11
Charlotte Court
House L-10
Chase City ...N-11
Chatham M-8
Chesapeake ...M-18
Chester K-14
Chesterfield ...K-13
Chilhowie M-2
Chincoteague ..H-20
Chincoteague
Christiansburg ...L-5
Church Rd. ...L-13
Clarksburg D-13
Clarksville N-11
Clifton Forge ...H-7
Clinchco C-5
Clintwood C-5
Cloverdale K-6
Coeburn C-5
Colonial
Beach G-15
Colonial
Heights K-14
Columbia
Furnace D-10
Concord H-8
Courtland N-14
Covington H-6
Craigsville G-7
Crewe L-12

Crimora G-10
Crozet G-10
Culpeper F-12
Cumberland ...J-11
Dahlgren F-14
Dale City E-14
Daleville K-7
Damascus N-1
Dante C-5
Danville N-8
Dayton F-10
Deltaville J-17
Dendron L-14
Dillwyn J-11
Disputanta ...L-14
Dryden D-3
Dublin L-4
Dumfries E-14
Dungannon ...C-5
Eagle Rock ...J-7
Eastville K-18
Edinburg E-11
Elkton F-10
Elliston K-5
Emory M-1
Emporia N-14
Evington J-8
Ewing D-2
Exmore J-19
Fairfax D-14
Fairlawn L-4
Falls Church ...D-14
Falmouth F-14
Farmville H-11
Fieldale N-6
Fincastle K-6
Fishersville ...G-8
Floyd L-5
Forest H-8
Fort Royal E-12
Franklin N-15
Fredericksburg ...F-14
Fries M-3
Front Royal ...E-12
Galax N-4
Gate City D-4
Glade Spr. M-1
Glasgow H-7
Gloucester ...K-17
Gloucester
Point K-17
Goochland ...J-13
Gordonsville ...G-12
Gore C-11
Goshen G-8
Grantsville .....
Gretna M-8
Groseclose ...L-2
Grottoes G-8
Grundy B-6
Gwynn K-17
Halifax M-9
Hamilton C-13
Hampden
Sydney K-11
Hanover H-14
Harrisonburg ...F-9
Haymarket ...E-13
Haysi C-5
Heathsville ...H-17
Helen L-1
Helper H-3
Henefer E-3
Hildale N-1
Hinckley J-5
Holden D-7
Honeyville A-4
Hurricane N-6
Hyrum E-3
Independent ...
Inez D-1
Iron Gate H-7
Irvington H-17
Ivanhoe M-3
Jarratt M-14
Jefferson D-16
Jewell Ridge ...L-1
Jonesville D-3
Kenbridge M-12
Keokee C-4
Keysville L-10
Kilmarnock ...H-17
King and Queen
Courthouse ...H-16
King George ...G-15
King William ...H-14
Kinsale H-17
Lacey Spr. E-10
Lacrosse N-12
Ladysmith ...G-14
Lake Ridge ...E-14
Lakeside K-14
Lancaster H-17
Laurel K-14
Lawrenceville ...M-13
Lebanon C-6
Leesburg C-13
Lexington H-8
Lincolnia C-12
Loa D-5
Lorton D-15
Louisa H-12
Lovettsville ...C-13
Lovingston ...H-9
Lunenburg ...M-11
Luray E-11
Lynch Station ...J-8
Lynchburg H-8
Lyndhurst G-8
Madison F-12
Madison
Heights K-9
Manassas E-13
Manassas Park E-14
Mappsville ...H-19
Marion M-1
Marshall E-13
Martinsville ...N-7
Mathews K-17
Mavisdale D-11
Maxwelton ...D-5
McClure B-5
McGaheysville ...F-10
McKenney ...L-13
McLean D-15
Meadowview ...D-6
Mechanicsville ...H-14
Melfa J-19
Middleburg ...D-13
Middletown ...D-12
Midlothian K-13
Milford G-14
Mineral H-12
Monroe H-9
Monterey G-7
Montross H-16
Montvale K-7
Moorefield B-10
Moseley K-13
Mt. Jackson ...E-10
Mt. Sidney F-9
Mt. Solon F-9
Nain D-12
Narrows L-4
Nassawadox ...J-18
Naxera K-17
New
Baltimore E-13
New Castle ...J-6
New Hope G-8
New Market ...E-10
Newport News L-17
Newsoms N-15
Nickelsville ...C-6
Nokesville E-14
Norfolk M-18
North K-17
Norton C-4
Oakton D-14
Occoquan E-14
Onancock J-19
Onley J-19
Opal E-13
Orange G-12
Palmyra H-11
Parksley J-19
Patrick Sprs. ...N-5
Pearisburg ...K-4
Pembroke K-4
Penhook L-7
Penn Laird F-10

Pennington Gap D-3
Petersburg ...L-14
Pocahontas ...K-2
Poquoson L-17
Portsmouth ...M-17
Pound B-4
Powhatan J-12
Prince George ...L-15
Pulaski L-4
Purcellville C-13
Quantico F-14
Quinque G-11
Radford L-4
Raven B-6
Reedville H-18
Remington E-13
Reston D-14
Rhoadesville ...G-13
Rich Creek K-4
Richlands L-1
Richmond K-14
Ridgeway N-7
Roanoke K-6
Rochelle F-12
Rockville J-13
Rocky Mt. L-7
Rose Hill D-2
Round Hill C-3
Rural Retreat ...M-2
Rushmere L-15
Rustburg J-9
St. Paul C-5
Salem K-6
Saltville M-1
Saluda J-16
Sandston K-14
Saxis H-19
Seaford L-17
Sedley N-15
Shawsville L-5
Shenandoah ...F-10
Sherando H-8
Shipman H-10
Short Pump ...J-13
Smithfield L-16
S. Boston N-9
S. Hill N-12
Speedwell M-3
Spotsylvania ...F-13
Springfield D-15
Stafford F-14
Stanardsville ...G-11
Stanley E-11
Stanleytown ...N-6
Staunton G-8
Stephens City ...C-12
Stephenson ...C-12
Stevens Creek ...M-3
Stonega C-4
Stony Creek ...M-14
Strasburg D-11
Stuart N-5
Stuarts Draft ...G-8
Suffolk M-17
Surry L-16
Sussex M-14
Sutherland ...L-13
Tangier J-18
Tappahannock H-16
Tazewell L-2
Thornburg G-14
Timberlake J-8
Timberville ...E-10
Toano K-16
Triangle E-14
Troutville K-7
Urbanna J-17
Vansant B-6
Verona G-8
Victoria L-11
Vienna D-14
Vienna D-14
Vinton K-6
Virginia
Beach M-18
Wachapreague J-19
Wallace D-6
Warrenton E-13
Warsaw H-16
Waverly M-14
Waynesboro ...G-8
Weber City D-4
Weems H-17
W. Point J-15
White Marsh ...K-17
White Plains ...L-13
White Stone ...H-17
Williamsburg ...K-16
Winchester ...C-12
Windsor M-16
Wise C-4
Woodbridge ...E-14
Woodlawn N-4
Woodstock E-11
Wytheville ...M-3
Yorktown K-17
Zion
Crossroads ...H-12

WEST VIRGINIA
see map page 117

Counties
Barbour D-7
Berkeley C-12
Boone G-3
Braxton E-5
Brooke B-2
Cabell F-2
Calhoun E-5
Clay F-5
Doddridge C-6
Fayette G-5
Gilmer E-5
Grant D-10
Greenbrier H-6
Hampshire ...D-11
Hancock A-2
Hardy D-11
Harrison C-6
Jackson E-3
Jefferson C-13
Kanawha F-4
Lewis D-6
Lincoln F-3
Logan H-3
McDowell J-3
Marion C-6
Marshall B-7
Mason D-2
Mercer J-4
Mineral C-10
Mingo H-2
Monongalia ...B-7
Monroe J-6
Morgan B-12
Nicholas G-5
Ohio A-6
Pendleton E-9
Pleasants C-5
Pocahontas ...G-7
Preston C-8
Putnam F-3
Raleigh H-4
Randolph E-8
Ritchie C-5
Roane E-4
Summers J-5
Taylor C-7
Tucker D-8
Tyler B-6
Upshur E-7
Wayne G-2
Webster E-7
Wetzel B-6
Wirt D-4
Wood D-3
Wyoming J-3

Cities and Towns
Alderson H-6
Alum Creek ...F-3
Ansted G-5
Arthurdale C-8
Athens J-4
Auburn D-5
Aurora C-8
Bancroft E-3
Barboursville ...F-2
Barrackville ...C-7
Bayard D-9
Beckley H-4
Beech Bottom ...B-2
Belington D-8
Belle F-4
Belmont C-4
Belva F-5
Benwood B-7
Berkeley Spgs. B-12
Bethany B-2
Beverly D-8
Big Chimney ...F-4
Big Sandy G-4
Birch River ...F-6
Blacksville B-7
Blaine C-9
Bluefield J-4
Bolivar C-13
Boomer G-4
Bradley H-4
Bradshaw J-3
Bramwell J-4
Bridgeport C-7
Brownton C-7
Bruceton Mills ...B-8
Buckhannon ...D-7
Buffalo E-3
Bunker Hill ...C-12
Burnsville E-6
Cabins E-9
Cairo C-5
Camden-on- ...
Gauley F-6
Cameron B-6
Capon Bridge ...C-11
Cass F-7
Cassville B-7
Cedar Grove ...F-4
Ceredo F-1
Chapmanville ...G-3
Charles Town ...C-13
Charleston F-4
Chattaroy H-2
Cheat Neck ...B-8
Chelyan F-4
Chesapeake ...F-4
Chester A-2
Clarksburg C-7
Clay F-5
Clearview B-1
Clendenin F-4
Coal City H-4
Coal Fork F-4
Cool Ridge ...H-4
Corinne J-3
Cottageville ...E-3
Covel J-3
Crab Orchard ...H-4
Craigsville F-6
Cross Lanes ...F-3
Crum H-1
Culloden F-2
Danese H-5
Daniels H-4
Davis D-9
Davy J-3
Delbarton H-2
Despard C-7
Dunbar F-3
Dunlow G-2
Eccles H-4
Eleanor E-3
Elizabeth D-4
Elk Garden ...C-10
Elkins D-8
Elkview F-4
Ellenboro C-5
Enterprise C-7
Fairdale H-4
Fairlea H-6
Fairmont C-7
Fairview B-7
Falling Waters B-13
Fayetteville ...G-5
Fenwick F-6
Ferrellsburg ...G-2
Flemington ...C-7
Follansbee B-2
Ft. Ashby C-11
Ft. Gay G-1
Franklin F-9
Friendly B-5
Gary J-3

Gassaway E-6
Gauley Bridge ...G-4
Gerrardstown ...C-12
Gilbert J-3
Glen Dale A-6
Glen Rogers ...J-3
Grafton C-7
Grantsville E-5
Granville B-7
Hamlin G-2
Harman E-8
Harpers
Ferry C-13
Harrisville C-5
Harts G-2
Hedgesville ...C-12
Helen H-4
Henderson E-2
Hico G-5
Hillsboro G-6
Hinton H-5
Holden H-2
Hooverson
Heights B-2
Hundred B-6
Huntersville ...F-7
Huntington ...F-1
Hurricane F-3
Iaeger J-3
Inwood C-12
Jane Lew D-6
Junior D-8
Kanawha D-4
Kearneysville ...C-13
Kenova F-1
Kermit H-1
Keyser C-10
Keystone J-4
Kimball J-4
Kincaid G-4
Kingwood C-8
Kopperston ...J-3
Lavalette F-1
Lester H-4
Lewisburg H-6
Lindside J-5
Logan H-3
Lost Creek D-6
Lubeck C-3
Lumberport ...C-7
Mabscott H-4
Madison G-3
Malden F-4
Man H-3
Mannington ...C-7
Marlinton G-7
Marlowe B-13
Martinsburg ...C-13
Mason D-2
Masontown ...C-8
Matewan J-2
Matoaka J-4
Maybeury J-4
Maysel E-5
McMechenB...B-7
Mcdowell J-3
Meadow Bridge H-5
Middlebourne ...C-5
Mill Creek D-8
Milton F-2
Mineral Wells ...C-4
Mineralwells ...C-4
Monongah C-7
Montcalm J-4
Montgomery ...G-4
Moorefield ...D-10
Morgantown ...B-8
Moundsville ...A-6
Mt. Gay H-2
Mt. Hope H-5
Mullens J-4
New
Cumberland ...A-2
New Haven D-3
New
Martinsville ...B-5
Newburg C-8
Newell A-2
Nitro F-3
Northfork J-4
Nutter Fort C-7
Oak Hill H-4
Oceana J-3
Paden City B-6
Parkersburg ...C-4
Parsons D-8
Paw Paw C-11
Pennsboro C-5
Petersburg ...D-10
Peterstown ...K-5
Philippi D-7
Piedmont C-10
Pinch F-4
Pine Grove ...B-6
Pineville J-3
Poca F-3
Point Pleasant ...E-2
Powellton G-4
Pratt G-4
Prichard G-1
Princeton J-4
Pruntytown ...C-7
Quinwood G-6
Racine G-3
Rainelle G-5
Rand F-4
Ranson C-13
Ravenswood ...D-3
Red Jacket ...H-2
Reedsville C-8
Reedy E-4
Ridgeway C-12
Ripley E-3
Rivesville C-7
Roderfield J-3
Romney C-11
Ronceverte ...H-6
Rowlesburg ...C-8
Rupert G-5
St. Albans F-3
St. Marys C-4
Salem C-6
Terra Alta C-8
Thomas D-9
Tornado F-3
Tunnelton C-8
Union J-6
Valley Grove ...A-6
Vienna C-3
War K-3
Wayne G-1
Webster Sprs. ...F-6
Weirton B-2
Welch J-3
Wellsburg B-2
W. Liberty A-6
W. Milford D-6
W. Union C-5
Weston D-6
Wheeling A-6
White Sulphur
Sprs. H-7
Whitesville ...H-3
Williamson ...H-2
Williamstown ...C-3
Winfield E-3

WISCONSIN
see map pages 118-119

Counties
Adams M-7
Ashland E-5
Barron F-3
Bayfield D-4
Brown H-9
Buffalo K-3
Burnett E-2
Calumet H-8
Chippewa G-4
Clark H-5
Columbia M-7
Crawford N-5
Dane N-6

Distances in chart are in miles.
To convert miles to kilometers,
multiply the distance
in miles by 1.609.

Example:
New York, NY to
Boston, MA = 215 miles
or 346 kilometers
(215 x 1.609)

ALBANY, NY
ALBUQUERQUE, NM
AMARILLO, TX
ATLANTA, GA
BALTIMORE, MD
BILLINGS, MT
BIRMINGHAM, AL
BISMARCK, ND
BOISE, ID
BOSTON, MA
BUFFALO, NY
CHARLESTON, SC
CHARLESTON, WV
CHARLOTTE, NC
CHEYENNE, WY
CHICAGO, IL
CINCINNATI, OH
CLEVELAND, OH
COLUMBUS, OH
DALLAS, TX
DENVER, CO
DES MOINES, IA
DETROIT, MI
EL PASO, TX
HARTFORD, CT
HOUSTON, TX
INDIANAPOLIS, IN
JACKSON, MS
JACKSONVILLE, FL
KANSAS CITY, MO
LAS VEGAS, NV
LITTLE ROCK, AR
LOS ANGELES, CA
LOUISVILLE, KY
MEMPHIS, TN
MIAMI, FL
MILWAUKEE, WI
MINNEAPOLIS, MN
MOBILE, AL
MONTPELIER, VT
MONTREAL, PQ
NASHVILLE, TN
NEW ORLEANS, LA
NEW YORK, NY
NORFOLK, VA
OKLAHOMA CITY, OK
OMAHA, NE
ORLANDO, FL
PHILADELPHIA, PA
PHOENIX, AZ
PITTSBURGH, PA
PORTLAND, ME
PORTLAND, OR
RALEIGH, NC
RAPID CITY, SD
RENO, NV
RICHMOND, VA
ST. LOUIS, MO
SALT LAKE CITY, UT
SAN ANTONIO, TX
SAN DIEGO, CA
SAN FRANCISCO, CA
SEATTLE, WA
TAMPA, FL
TORONTO, ON
VANCOUVER, BC
WASHINGTON, DC
WICHITA, KS

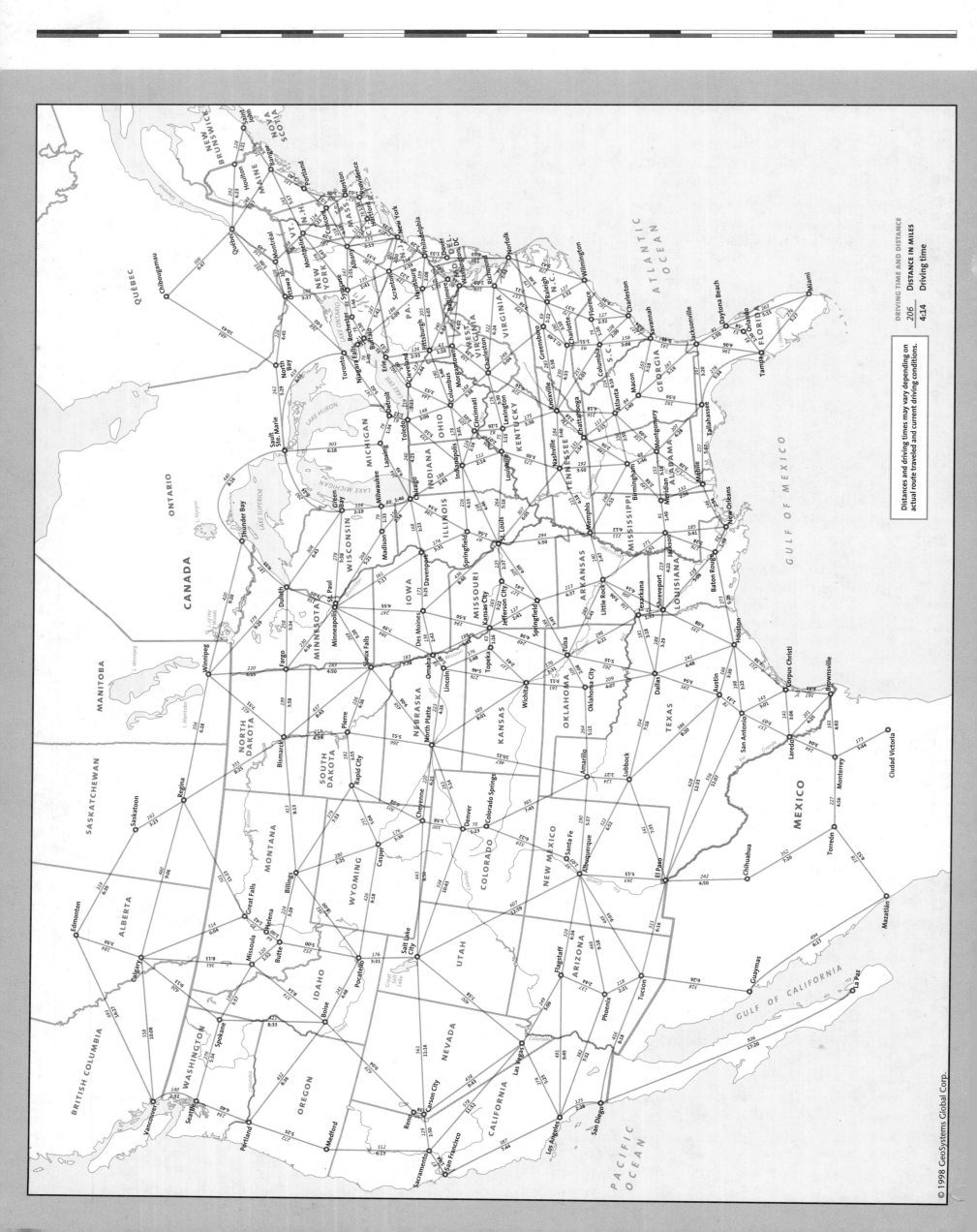

DRIVING TIME AND DISTANCE
206   DISTANCE IN MILES
4:14   Driving time

Distances and driving times may vary depending on actual route traveled and current driving conditions.

© 1998 GeoSystems Global Corp.